DELIUS: A LIFE IN LETTERS
1862–1908

DELIUS

A Life in Letters

I

1862–1908

Lionel Carley

Harvard University Press

Cambridge, Massachusetts

1983

Published in Great Britain by Scolar Press
in association with The Delius Trust

Library of Congress Cataloging in Publication Data
Delius, Frederick, 1862-1934.
　Delius, a life in letters, 1862-1908.

　Bibliography: p.
　Includes index.
　　1. Delius, Frederick, 1862-1934. 2. Composers –
England – Correspondence. I. Carley, Lionel.
II. Title.
ML410.D35A4 1984　780'.92'4 [B]　83-16626
ISBN 0-674-19570-1

Front endpaper: St John's River scene, Florida, in the 1880s.
Rear endpaper: Hardanger.

Contents

List of Letters

List of Illustrations

The illustrations in this book are largely drawn from the collection of the author or from the archive of The Delius Trust. Other sources are given in the captions. Where known, the name of the artist or photographer is recorded in the captions.

Introduction

There are in the Delius Trust Archive in London several thousand letters. Most of the originals are those addressed to the composer, whereas much the larger proportion of Delius's own letters in the Archive have gradually been acquired in copy form from collections, public and private, in Europe, the United States and Australia. The letters are in English, German, French, Norwegian and Danish.

My own association with the Delius Trust (and therefore with the composer's correspondence) dates from 1966, when I was invited to become the Trust's honorary archivist – serving the composer's literary and musical estate as curator of its constituent letters, musical manuscripts and other documents. Prior to this, Rachel Lowe had acted as archivist, and in the brief two or three years which she was able to give to her task, Delius's legacy of music and correspondence was physically ordered and catalogued with a thoroughness and care which had not been devoted to it before, nor has it enjoyed since. The fruits of her scholarship were ultimately to become the *Catalogue of the Music Archive* and her comparatively recently published *Delius Collection of the Grainger Museum* catalogue, as well as a corpus of informed essays based primarily on the Trust's holdings.

When I came to the Archive, comparative order had, therefore, been created out of a measure of chaos. Delius's scores had been microfilmed and bound into volumes; and the letters had been sorted into files and a basic card index of correspondents compiled. Thanks to Rachel Lowe's quite exceptional work, I was able to concentrate on that aspect of the Archive which most interested me – the enormous correspondence – and to consider in what form it might best be prepared for publication.

Again, some work had been done by various hands over the years. Sir Thomas Beecham had enlisted the services of Dr Berta Geissmar, formerly Furtwängler's secretary, when he was preparing his own biography of Delius. She had transcribed and typed, for his working purposes, a considerable number of the German letters in the Archive, and some of her transcripts had served as the basis for translations commissioned from various sources. Sir Thomas was a demanding taskmaster, and Dr Geissmar's transcripts bear many marks of having been made hurriedly at his behest. But at least they formed a foundation for reference for a number of years. Not quite so reliable were many of the subsequent translations, which have sometimes thrown up unforeseen problems for scholars of Delius and have in part been the cause of an irritatingly wide area of factual error in Beecham's otherwise informative and entertaining biography, and, indeed, occasionally in other essays and monographs on Delius.

My task has been gradually to transcribe the whole correspondence in order to present it in easily legible form, and then at least to begin retranslating the foreign letters, using only the best of the existing translations as a basis for fresh versions, and discarding those that are inferior. Before any of this could be done, all the letters at the time in the Archive were systematically photocopied, and duplicate files were opened. There were many letters which had not been transcribed. The French and Scandinavian correspondences I undertook myself, but the far larger bulk of English and German letters I could never have embarked upon without help, although a considerable number of those files which interested me particularly I put aside to transcribe personally. Whether commissioned, or volunteered by two or three enthusiastic helpers, each transcribed batch of Delius's correspondence, as it was completed over the years, was checked word for word against the originals before being placed in a further set of covers. This work is still continuing.

The work of translation or retranslation has been a still slower process, and a fairly careful code of practice has been followed. As far as possible, translations have had, of course, to be both literal and literate. It was felt that there could be little scope for free versions of material which grammatically or stylistically in its original form was awkward and angular, obscure or oblique: original characteristics ought, if possible, somehow to be mirrored in the translation.

A major difficulty with the correspondence conducted by Delius and his wife throughout their lives is its exceptionally polyglot character. The one redeeming factor is that at least the languages involved derive exclusively from the western perimeters of Europe (although this is not necessarily true of the correspondents). Many letters are in 'second' languages: Delius's Norwegian friends usually wrote to him in German or, occasionally, in English or French, rather than in Norwegian. His German friends sometimes felt the need to write in French or English. Delius himself wrote in German, French and Norwegian, as well as in English. A great many letters in the Delius Trust Archive reflect the intensely cosmopolitan background of their writers, with words, sentences, sometimes paragraphs changing, for a while, the main language in mid-stream.

I recently received your letter in French. Bravo Fritz, you are making progress, the whole letter from beginning to end in *one* language is something that's against your principles (Halfdan Jebe to Frederick Delius, January 1905).

How far, then, can one go in accurately reflecting an original letter which itself may have been rather erratically written in a second language – a language

with which the correspondent was not entirely conversant? Not too far, one
feels, since in translation the writer's first errors may be compounded. Nor is
what he or she obviously meant to write properly conveyed. If, therefore, some
of the translations in this book appear at least superficially to be rather more
stilted than others, what I hope will be borne in mind is how the original letter
may have read to its recipient. Add to this another factor – the inability of some
of the writers to express themselves clearly and concisely in their own languages
(Rodin's French, for example, could be notably cryptic) – and a further insight
may be gained into some of the more unexpected difficulties of rendering a great
deal of this material into a fully intelligible English.

Delius's parents were German, and theirs was the language, together with
English, which he grew up with and indeed used during his many visits to
Germany. And yet Jelka Delius was to write to Rodin in February 1904 that it
was *she* who was translating and adapting the libretto of *Koanga* for performance
in Elberfeld: 'my husband does not know German well enough'. To many people
even Delius's English speech sounded unusual. Percy Grainger and Eric Fenby
discussed his 'lack of ear for English', Grainger pointing out that his German
and Scandinavian were 'as moth-eaten as his English. I think he grew up in a
home where no language was mastered'. Grainger also mentioned what he
discerned as '½-Yorkshire, ½-German peculiarities of speech'.

It would, of course, have been a great help to have been able to reprint
Delius's correspondence as it stands, each letter reproduced in its original
language only, as in Torsten Eklund's exemplary edition of the correspondence
of Strindberg. But it would be idle to suggest either that Delius is a figure quite
comparable with Strindberg on the world stage or that his correspondence could
yet be presented other than in English to reach those who would most wish to
read it.

If, then, my intention has been to present unambiguous translations where
translations have been necessary, it has also been my intention to preserve most
of the original features of all the letters now printed for the first time. The
editorial hand has, by design, been light. The writers' original punctuation, or
lack of it, has been reproduced as closely as possible; spelling and grammatical
errors have not been corrected but have been recorded faithfully (and occasionally with pleasure); inconsistent usage of accents in foreign words has been
allowed to stay; paragraphing remains as far as possible just as in the originals.
Editorial intervention in punctuation has only in rare cases been permitted
where without it the sense of a passage might be particularly obscure or somehow
impaired. Where mistakes occur in the spelling of proper names, the correct or
most commonly accepted form is given, together with variants, in the index.

I have preferred to retain certain forms of address as written: letters translated
from the German or Norwegian, for example, do not offer 'Mr' or 'Mrs' for *Herr*,
Frau or *fru*. And where I have sensed the faintly ridiculous, as in rendering into
English Jelka Rosen's *Mon maître* to Rodin, I have preferred to leave the form of

address in its original language. I cannot claim complete consistency in the rendering of the usual valedictions that bring the non-English letters to a close; such expressions as 'Best wishes', 'Kind regards', 'Yours sincerely' and their many variations clothe a still greater variety of expressions in the original language. It should also be noted that if apparent archaisms like 'Fare well' appear (for *Lebe wohl* and its Norwegian equivalent), this is because Delius sometimes used such forms in his English correspondence.

Where words were underlined in the original letter, they are italicized in this text. Similarly, capital letters or italics have been used to distinguish the printed or embossed elements of letter-headings.

Dates are printed exactly as in the original letters. No attempt has been made to systematize them. Where a date was not given by the writer, square brackets enclose my own dating, with any necessary evidence of place, whether deduced from postmarks or from internal or other evidence. Where the information a postmark contains may be of particular interest or significance, the postmark, whether originating or receiving, is quoted in the footnotes in its basic form.

In preparing this edition, I have utilized in the main primary sources for the purpose of any connecting narrative and for my annotations to the letters. Wide reference is made to other unpublished letters written to, by or about Delius, and I have been prepared to quote extensively from such letters when they can enlarge usefully on points already made or when they can fill significant gaps in Delius's documented life. The gathering of such supportive material has progressed over the course of some years, and visits to France, Germany, Switzerland, Norway, Sweden, Denmark and the United States have yielded much more material, both from public and private collections. Occasionally, however, I have had to turn to printed sources for letters whose originals have not been to hand.

The form of this book grew naturally. I have long admired Torsten Eklund's edition of the letters of Strindberg, the first volume of which was published in 1948. At the time of writing, Volume 15 was the latest to have been published, ending with Letter 5530, written in April 1907. Eklund has been an excellent model, and I have aimed to emulate the succinct critical apparatus following each letter. However, where Strindberg never stopped writing letters (how he ever found the time to put together such an enormous corpus of plays, novels and essays into the bargain, one can never know), Delius was a considerably less prolific correspondent, and far fewer of his own letters have survived. A different approach was therefore called for, and a measure of coherence has been aimed at by printing letters both to and from Delius. Gradually, a life began to unfold, and the addition of short passages of interlocking narrative, year by year, is intended to help set the scene and fill a number of gaps. Furthermore, it is clearly appropriate to include a list of the principal compositions Delius worked on in any one year. The fact that, for the present, the first letter in the Archive dates from 1886 has meant summarizing the first twenty-five years or so of

Delius's life. And the existence of a modest, but important amount of mostly unpublished autobiographical material has made desirable the addition of a number of short appendices. Finally, the recent discovery and acquisition of further pictorial material has meant that this work could usefully be illustrated, often by Delius's own artist friends.

A word on the appendices: they take in Delius's own memories of his early life in Bradford, the diaries he kept during his summer holidays from 1887 to 1891 and his later recollections of Grieg and Strindberg. Also included are Jelka Delius's own memoir of her first meeting with the composer and of his life at the time, together with a note on C. F. Keary's novel *The Journalist*, published in 1898, in which one of the principal characters is very clearly — although not wholly — based on Delius.

What material, then, has *not* been available? For a start, we have it on record that letters, photographs and mementoes of Delius that remained with friends in Jacksonville, Florida, during the later 1880s and 1890s, were lost in the conflagration that destroyed the greater part of the town in 1901. And although there is a reference or two to letters written to Danville friends some time after Delius's stay in Virginia in 1885 and 1886, none apart from those to the Rueckert sisters has yet been discovered.

Then there were the letters written to people who were known to destroy their incoming correspondence. Christian Sinding, for example, did so, with the result that a body of valuable documentary evidence from an early period of Delius's life and compositional activity can be said, with certainty, no longer to exist. Delius, however, did preserve Sinding's letters, written largely between the later 1880s and the mid-1890s, and through these it is possible to adduce a great deal about his own life at this time.

Again, we can be fairly certain that the letters written by Delius to Georges-Daniel de Monfreid, artist and friend of Gauguin, although fewer in number than those to Sinding, are also no longer extant, since de Monfreid, at least during youth and into middle age, almost always destroyed his correspondence. Fortunately, he had the foresight to preserve the letters, including those referring to Delius, sent to him by Gauguin, whose work he admired above all others.

There is, too, the extensive range of correspondence which Delius devoted to various figures in the German musical world, a proportion of which is unlikely to have survived the depredations of two world wars. Delius's first conductor protagonist, Hans Haym, exchanged a considerable correspondence with the Deliuses, probably beginning in 1897 and certainly ending only a year or two before his death in 1921. All trace, however, of Delius's letters to Haym was lost many years ago, the conductor's son and daughter (both of whom only recently died) confirming to me that the family no longer possessed them and believing them to have been destroyed. Again, the result is that a large part of our knowledge of this key relationship and, indeed, of some of the earliest

Delius performances in Germany is based largely on those letters written by Haym to Delius between 1901 and 1910 which remain in the Delius Trust Archive. Similarly, discussion with members of the Cassirer family has led me to the conclusion that Delius's letters to the conductor Fritz Cassirer are gone. But, once again, at least there are the forty letters and postcards that Cassirer himself sent to Delius which remain to help us document the course of another important collaboration.

We can forget, too, the sequence of letters sent by Delius to one of the most intimate of his friends, the Norwegian violinist and composer Halfdan Jebe. Jebe's roaming, Bohemian life cannot remotely be characterized as that of a man who carefully preserves the letters of his friends for posterity. Had they somehow survived, we should have had an extraordinarily intimate glimpse of Delius the man, as is amply demonstrated by the dozen letters from Jebe which have survived, somehow narrowly escaping the fate which we may well have assumed that Jelka Delius had in store for them after her husband's death. Later, in 1907 and 1908, there was a short but lively correspondence between Havergal Brian and Delius. Brian's letters are in the Delius Trust Archive, but when I asked him some years ago if I might see the letters Delius wrote to him, he confessed that he had not kept them. Very much later, and beyond the scope of this first of two volumes of letters, the extensive and important correspondence between the Deliuses and Eric Fenby, from 1928 to 1935, is represented by only the Deliuses' side; Eric Fenby and I are drawn to the conclusion that his own letters were destroyed, along with many others, by Jelka Delius, probably at some point during that short period of less than a year which separated her husband's death from her own.

Of all the people represented by their letters in this volume, it is Edvard Munch who in curious fashion slightly redresses the balance, since I have been able to include draft letters written to Delius that the composer never received – and that the writer indeed never posted. The files of the Munch Museum are bulging with letters written by the artist to various of his friends but never actually dispatched. Often these letters contain much that is of interest – the sole reason for their appearance here.

This book falls naturally into three divisions. One third of the letters were written between 1886 and 1899, when the Delius Orchestral Concert of 30 May clearly signalled the end of the years of apprenticeship and the arrival of the first works of maturity. Another third takes us through the breakthrough years in Germany and documents the composer's establishment on the continent of Europe, at least, as a major figure (if not a cult figure) on the contemporary musical scene. The final third comprises the two years 1907 and 1908, when Delius, now at his creative peak, at last found acceptance in the country of his birth, and found himself lionized, too, by the brighter stars of a younger musical generation in England.

As for the content of these letters, it must at the outset be acknowledged that if we seek to find serious descriptions of the process of composition, we have to look to other composers. Delius very seldom wrote anything approaching a description of his own compositional techniques. He wrote about the difficulties encountered in getting his music published and performed, about the problems of his friends, about his views on art, literature, the music of other composers, about his travels, his meetings. We are able to discern his relatively privileged position, for although he never seemed to have very much money to spare (and there is no evidence to suggest that he spent casually or prodigally), he did not have to teach or to work in other fields to maintain himself as a composer – whereas contemporaries like Elgar, Bantock, Brian, Holst all had to 'work' in greater or smaller measure in order to earn a living. On the surface, Delius had time to write letters, but this book makes it very clear that he took composition entirely seriously and indeed dedicated his life to it. The evidence is in the legacy of his works.

We know something of his asperity in later years. What illuminates many of these pages, however, is a lot of good humour and a warm pleasure in friendships that were cherished on both sides. When Delius had a friend, he had a friend indeed. The letters written to him by Grieg, Sinding, Bantock, Grainger – to name just a few – are from people who loved the man. The letters Jelka wrote to him are those of a woman who loved him above all others. And the letters he wrote in return to Jelka can often seem unexpectedly affectionate and sponta-neous to those of us who are only acquainted with the conventional public image of a cool, aloof and cynical Delius.

Not that the latter qualities are never in evidence. Delius kept a beady eye on Jelka's relatives when a family squabble developed after Serena Rosen's death. It was in his own interest that Jelka should be one of the principal beneficiaries of her mother's estate, and his letters cannot hide his active interest in the outcome. He soon set about severing the links between themselves and Jelka's greatest friend, Ida Gerhardi, for motives that are not entirely clear but that do not seem touched with nobility or generosity. On holiday with Jelka in Norway, his concern over his wife's health did not prevent him from slipping the leash and leaving her, miserably depressed and lonely, while he went on a long walking tour. And if he liked his friends well, his enemies fared ill under his tongue, as the occasional more caustic letter can show.

We have, too, the picture of the great wanderer, the walker, the traveller, with its implications of a continual seeking out of new impressions, a quest for new sensations and a constant returning, when he had fixed them sufficiently, to those places which gave him the greatest contentment – above all, the huge Norwegian fellscapes, in whose silent grandeurs he found himself most com-pletely fulfilled.

Perhaps one of the most surprising revelations that a study of Delius's letters affords is the demolition of the pervasive myth that he rarely, if ever, lifted a hand towards procuring the publication or the performance of his music. Delius, it is perfectly clear, was a doer by nature – a *bejahende Natur* by his own admission – and it should perhaps have been apparent to us much earlier that a Nietzschean yea-sayer is, by definition, not going to sit quietly in a corner hoping piously that some day his musical offerings may just interest someone. Delius spent years actively promoting his music. He wrote letter after letter to publishing houses in various countries, as well as calling on publishers personally to try to persuade them to take up his work. He did the same thing with promoters, and, naturally enough, he cultivated artists who were interested in his work, encouraging them to perform it whenever and wherever possible. When money came his way, he did a great deal of promotional work himself. We see this clearly at the time of the 1899 concert, when he was seriously considering founding, with his London promoter, an organization whose primary aim would be the production and performance of English operas. And a few years later he was to be an active co-founder of the ill-fated Musical League – an enormously ambitious undertaking for its time. He became the League's vice-president (Elgar was president), but gradually began to lose interest after the first impetus, growing impatient once more with what he condemned as English apathy towards newer music, and impatient too with internal bickerings among the League's activists. He was keen on conducting his own works (another promotional activity, after all), but was poor at the job – a fact which he grew reluctantly to recognize.

So these pages depict Delius as a doer, an active promoter of his own music at a time when his protagonists were few and rarely of sufficient influence to help establish his works in the repertoire. With the advent of Beecham, all that changed, and the legend probably dates from this time – from the composer's mid-forties – when Beecham came to see it as a personal mission in life to perform Delius's music as often as possible. Only now could the composer afford to sit back and let others take up the reins.

Delius's life was undeniably a fascinating one. His music partly mirrors that life, and is partly its antithesis – yet further cause for fascination. The idyllic, sovereign beauty of *In a Summer Garden* from out of the cynic: coolly disdainful of his peasant neighbours in Grez, calculatingly exploitative of his wife, contemptuously dismissive of so many of his contemporaries. Towards the end, the visionary magnificence of *Songs of Farewell*, a flower from out of physical decay. His body at times tortured with pain, Delius was yet convulsed by the urge to create the sublime, to fashion beauty, where beauty had no future, out of the memory of things past. The key to Delius lies in his *Ich bin eine bejahende Natur*. In just these words the contradictions are resolved.

Acknowledgements

I am grateful to the Delius Trustees for their permission to quote from among
the letters written by Delius and others which are now in the Trust's Archive in
London. And I am especially indebted to the Trust and to the late Frau Marie-
Luise Baum, of Wuppertal, for their joint grant, which enabled me to devote
in 1977 the best part of a sabbatical year to preparatory work for this edition.
To the owners of copyright material, apart from the Delius Trust itself, I am
grateful for permission to reproduce such material in this volume. My apologies
go to any copyright owners whom I have been unable to trace or may inadver-
tently have overlooked.

John Boulton Smith and Andrew Boyle willingly shared with me some of
their expert knowledge of Norwegian art and music, and I am grateful to them
for answering many of my questions and for placing some of their valuable time
at my disposal. I am equally indebted to Lewis Foreman and Stephen Lloyd;
their wide knowledge of English music in the nineteenth and twentieth centuries I have shamelessly exploited for my own ends. For following up some
metaphorically overgrown paths in the United States, I owe my thanks to
Professor William Randel and his wife, Janet. And for similarly helping me to
solve some Scandinavian problems, I owe my thanks to Dr John Bergsagel.
Pierre Bance and Fräulein Evelin Gerhardi kindly read through and checked
my French and German translations respectively, and I am glad to record my
thanks for their help.

For help, advice or co-operation in other forms, I would like warmly to thank
Shirley, Lady Beecham, Nigel Bicknell, John Bird, Christopher Brunel, Uta
von Delius, Hans Peter Dieterling, Dr Eric Fenby, Mrs Dorothy Gordon, Mme
Annie Joly-Segalen, Dr Philip Jones, Rachel Lowe, Mme Anna Merle d'Au-
bigné, Ola Mølmen, Dr Arbie Orenstein, Albi Rosenthal, Dr Gunnar Rugstad,
Frau Malve Steinweg, Torbjørn Støverud, Lena Svanberg and Malcolm Walker.
While they lived, Louise Courmes and Rudolf and Eva Haym talked with me
and wrote to me about Delius; I remain indebted to them, as I am to the late
Havergal Brian, for having allowed me to reproduce much material.

I am indebted, indeed, to Frau Malve Steinweg and Fräulein Evelin Gerhardi,
of Lüdenscheid, for their very kind hospitality and for working with me through

many of the letters, paintings and drawings of Ida Gerhardi, their aunt. Yet a further debt to Evelin Gerhardi, as to my sister, Joan Pallister, I willingly and particularly gratefully acknowledge for the hard work they so readily gave in assisting me in the transcription or typing of some of these letters. While working on Delius's letters, I also enjoyed the hospitality of the Munch Museum in Oslo and the Grainger house in White Plains, New York, and wish to record my thanks to Director Alf Bøe of Oslo Kommunes Kunstsamlinger and to Stewart Manville and the late Ella Grainger.

A number of institutions were especially helpful to me, and I enjoyed a wide range of their services. My thanks therefore to: the senior staff of the Munch Museum (Curators Arne Eggum, Marit Lande Pedersen and Gerd Woll, and Librarian Sissel Biørnstad); the Grainger Museum, University of Melbourne (Professor George Loughlin and Curator Kay Dreyfus); the Bergen Public Library (Karen Falch Johannessen and Lise McKinnon); the Central Library, Bradford (Derek Bell); the Library of the Royal Academy of Music (Jane Harington and Joan Slater); the Bibliothèque Nationale, Paris (Jean-Michel Nectoux); the Musée Rodin, Paris (Director Cécile Goldscheider); the Library of Congress, Washington, D.C. (Wayne Shirley); Jacksonville University, Jacksonville, Florida (Dr Frances Kinne); the Jacksonville Public Library (Jeff Driggers); the Delius Association of Florida (in particular Jeanne Donahoo); the Delius Society, London (Estelle Palmley, Rodney Meadows, Christopher Redwood and members of the Committee); the Percy Grainger Library Society, White Plains, New York (Stewart Manville and the late Ella Grainger); the Danville Historical Society, Danville, Virginia (Mary C. Fugate); the British Council (Barrie Iliffe, Avril Wood and James Edmondston); the Balfour Gardiner Estate (John Eliot Gardiner); the Grieg House at Troldhaugen (Sigmund Torsteinson); the British Library; the Central Music Library, Westminster; the Oslo University Library; the Royal Library, Stockholm; the Royal Norwegian Embassy, London.

Work on this edition was made easier for me by the continuing encouragement of individual members of the Delius Trust, and I wish to record my deep thanks to Major Norman Millar, Sir Thomas Armstrong, Felix Aprahamian, Robert Threlfall, Martin Williams and the late Philip Emanuel, as well as to David Nott, until recently co-Trustee. To Rachel Lowe, who preceded me as honorary archivist to the Trust, goes my gratitude for laying the first firm foundations on which I have been able to build. My debt to Robert Threlfall is incalculable, and I shall ever be grateful for his constant readiness to share with me the expertise he has brought to Delius scholarship. His pioneering *Catalogue of the Compositions of Frederick Delius* (hereafter 'RT'), at last available, is a quite indispensable work of reference.

One happy result of undertaking a study of the life and background of Frederick Delius has been that I have come to know – and to count as treasured friends – Eric Fenby and his wife, Rowena. I therefore dedicate this work to them, as a small token of that friendship and at the same time of my unqualified admiration and regard for Dr Fenby's unique contribution to music.

Lionel Carley, 1983

Chronology

1862   Born in Bradford, Yorkshire (29 January).

1868/9   Already plays the piano, now begins violin lessons.

1874–78   Pupil at Bradford Grammar School.

1878–80   Pupil at International College, Isleworth, Middlesex.

1880–83   Apprenticeship in the family wool business takes him to Gloucestershire, Germany, France, Sweden, and on to Norway.

1884–85   Orange farming in Florida.

1885–86   Teaches music in Virginia.

1886–88   Student at Leipzig Conservatorium. Friendship with Grieg begins.

1888   Moves to Paris. Now concentrates on composition.

1891   First public performance of an orchestral work (in Norway).

1894   First public performance in France of an orchestral work.

1896   Meets Jelka Rosen, German painter.

1897   Revisits Florida and Virginia, then settles in Grez-sur-Loing. First public performance in Germany of an orchestral work.

1899   Delius Orchestral Concert in London (30 May).

1903   Marries Jelka Rosen in Grez-sur-Loing (23 September).

1904   Major performances in Germany, including the opera *Koanga*.

1907   First performance of the opera *A Village Romeo and Juliet* (in Berlin). Breakthrough in London, with the Piano Concerto and *Appalachia*. First meeting with Beecham.

1908   *A Mass of Life* in Munich. *Sea Drift* in Sheffield. Becomes Vice-President of The Musical League.

1910   *A Village Romeo and Juliet* in London.

1914–18   A series of moves during the war years. Heightened creative activity in spite of signs of ill health.

1919   First performance of the opera *Fennimore and Gerda* (in Frankfurt).

1920   Some financial problems.

1921   Has chalet built at Lesjaskog in Norway.

1923   *Hassan* a financial and artistic success in London.

1925   Onset of blindness and paralysis.

1928   Eric Fenby comes to Grez as Delius's amanuensis.

1929   Delius Festival in London.

1934   Dies in Grez-sur-Loing (10 June).

1935   Jelka Delius dies in London (28 May).

FOR ERIC AND ROWENA FENBY

Ich bin eine bejahende Natur

1862–1888
From Bradford to Leipzig

Fritz Delius was born on 29 January 1862 in Bradford, Yorkshire. His family background was German, his parents having emigrated to England in mid-century from Bielefeld, an important textile town in Westphalia. They had left Germany in order to settle in the North Country where the flourishing wool trade offered rich rewards to those merchants and entrepreneurs who were prepared to invest both money and hard work in establishing new business concerns. The Bradford Germans were part of a wider influx of settlers from central Europe who founded commercial dynasties in the industrial heartlands of Yorkshire and Lancashire, and for a long time Germans formed a strong ethnic minority in that centre of the English wool trade.

The Westphalian Deliuses were in the early nineteenth century a widespread and highly respected family whose members were engaged over a broad range of the professions. Ernst Friedrich Delius (1790–1831), *Stadtdirektor* and *Bürgermeister* of Bielefeld and grandfather of the composer, had served as an officer under Blücher during the later Napoleonic Wars. The three of his sons who survived into manhood decided, as did so many other Deliuses, to emigrate in pursuit of greater fortunes. Ernst, the eldest, made his way to Manchester and established himself as a dealer in wool. Both of his younger brothers, Julius and Theodor, in due course followed him. Julius, born in 1822, was the only one of the three to marry. He moved after a while to Bradford, establishing a branch of the recently founded Manchester business there, and took out naturalization papers, returning briefly to Germany in 1856 to marry Elise Krönig, who was fifteen years his junior. Together they returned to Bradford, where Julius Delius, Yorkshire businessman, was now to found a Yorkshire family.

Elise Delius was destined to have fourteen children, two of whom died in infancy; Fritz (his baptismal name, which he abandoned for the Anglicized Frederick only at the age of forty) was her fourth child. He grew up in the company of an older and a younger brother and nine sisters, enjoying a normal, robust childhood that compensated for an infancy which had been marked by delicate health. Home for the Deliuses was Claremont, a street of pleasant and quite substantial houses favoured by the newer generation of Bradford merchants. On rising upland it was just a few minutes' walk from the centre of the town. It was in walking distance too from the warehouse of Delius and Company, as well as from Mr Frankland's little preparatory school, to which Fritz was sent at the age of nine, and from Bradford Grammar School, where he was first registered at the age of twelve.

Music had been a substantial feature of his life from an early age:

My father loved music intensely and used to tinker on the piano when he knew he was alone. He was a great concert-goer and he often had chamber-music in his house. My mother was not musical at all, but she had great imagination, and was rather fantastically inclined. . . .

I cannot remember the first time when I began to play the piano: it must have been very early in my life. I played by ear, and I used to be brought down in a little velvet suit after dinner to play for the company. My mother would say: 'Now make up something', and then I improvised. When I was six or seven, I began taking violin lessons from Mr. Bauerkeller, of the Hallé orchestra, who came over from Manchester especially to teach me. Later on, I had another teacher, Mr. Haddock from Leeds. My first great musical impression was hearing the posthumous Valse of Chopin which a friend of my father's played for me when I was ten years old. It made a most extraordinary impression on me. Until then, I had heard only Haydn, Mozart and Beethoven, and it was as if an entirely new world had been opened up to me. I remember that after hearing it twice I could play the whole piece through from memory. *

During the 1870s, Delius's widening musical experiences included a first acquaintance, registered with wonder and excitement, with the works of Wagner and Grieg. And from all the kaleidoscopic impressions of those years, a visit to Covent Garden for a performance of *Lohengrin* was to remain etched in his memory long into adulthood.

In 1878 his studies at Bradford Grammar School came to an end, and he was dispatched, now aged sixteen, to the International College, at Spring Grove, Isleworth, a leafy outer suburb of London. He was to remain at this progressive establishment for two years, with further opportunities to indulge his love of music by attending concert and opera performances in the capital, and indeed by making his first hesitant attempts at composition. Another passion developed in his Yorkshire childhood and continued at Isleworth was for cricket, a sport for which he was never to lose his early enthusiasm.

With his departure from Spring Grove, Fritz Delius's schoolboy days were over. It was 1880, and he was eighteen. In accordance with his father's wishes, he was taken into the family business, thus finding himself in the office of Delius and Company in Bradford and facing what was, for him, the unpleasant

---

* Philip Heseltine, *Frederick Delius* (London: John Lane, The Bodley Head, 1923), pp. 3, 5.

prospect of a lifetime in the wool trade. It was not a prospect, however, that he was at any time to take really seriously. The idea of somehow making a musical career was already predominant in his mind.

During the next three years, Delius embarked on a series of travels, somewhat loosely dedicated to business, which considerably widened his horizons. His first excursion, in 1880, was to Stroud, in Gloucestershire, which had been for centuries a centre of the English wool trade, but was now in decline, as the trade's axis shifted north towards the plentiful labour and rapid mechanization of the new mills of Yorkshire. In Stroud, agent Fritz Delius enjoyed for a while his first commercial successes in promoting the company's interests, and the result was that some time after his return to Bradford his father agreed to his attachment to the large manufacturing firm of Wilhelm Vogel, at Chemnitz in Saxony. While at Stroud, Delius had been able to travel by train to London to renew his earlier acquaintance with the musical life of the capital, and at Chemnitz later in 1880 he was, in a similar vein, to make forays to Berlin, Leipzig and Dresden. At Chemnitz he took violin lessons with Hans Sitt, a distinguished teacher. Business matters, however, were largely neglected, and, in consequence, in the spring of 1881 he was recalled by his father to Bradford. It was not long, though, before he was again sent abroad on business, this time to Scandinavia. He sailed from Hull to Gothenburg at the beginning of June 1881, and then made his way to Norrköping, the centre of the Swedish wool trade. For a time he concentrated, with some success, on business matters, and then he travelled on to Stockholm, a city whose sparkling summer beauty could hardly have failed to captivate him. From Stockholm he made his way across Sweden to Norway, beginning the long love affair with that country and its great natural beauty that was to have a marked effect on his adult life. Returning to England from Bergen in the autumn, with business having been virtually forgotten since the first weeks in Norrköping, the errant son found himself in further trouble with his father.

Still undaunted, Julius Delius decided to try again. Fritz was once more dispatched abroad, this time to Saint-Etienne, in central France, probably towards the end of 1881. His violin accompanied him, but good music was in rather shorter supply in Saint-Etienne than in most of his previous haunts. For a while, Fritz endured the tedium of applying himself to the wool business in that undistinguished town, but the eternal truant in him led him in February 1882 to a fresh bolt-hole – the Riviera. Developing a taste for the gaming-table, he surprised himself by winning sufficient money to stay on there for several weeks, taking every available opportunity to hear good music in the locality. Julius Delius's agent in Saint-Etienne sent back a report on this latest transgression, and once more Fritz was ordered home – but not without first paying a visit to his urbane uncle Theodor, now resident in Paris, in whom Fritz probably discerned a future ally and patron.

For the next year or two a state of subdued revolt, punctuated by heated arguments, existed on the part of son towards father. Outwardly at least Fritz still had to make a show of interest in a business career. A part of his father's wealth, suitably diverted, could yet help him to make music the mainstay of his life. So it was that he was allowed to make a second trip to Scandinavia, around the middle of 1882. It was probably conceded to him on the basis of the relative success of his efforts in Norrköping the previous summer. It seems, however, that even that success was this time not to be repeated: Fritz spent the two months away from home further exploring the northern landscapes that had made such an impression on him during his first visit.

Julius, whose older brother in Manchester had recently died, tried once again to find a place for his recalcitrant son, this time in the Manchester company. The experiment was short-lived, and Fritz, now apparently monumentally indifferent to business life, was soon back in Bradford.

His last major excursion on behalf of Delius and Company appears to have been to Paris in 1883. Once again it was to prove abortive, reflecting a continual decline in the young Delius's business acumen. However, another factor had now entered the son's calculations for the future. His older brother, Ernst, had slipped the family leash and with typically Delian wanderlust had left England altogether to try his hand at sheep-farming in New Zealand. It seemed that it *was* possible to escape without actually being cut off by Julius. His father, however, remained implacably opposed to a musical career: a gentleman was at liberty to enjoy listening to music, indeed to enjoy making music as a perfectly acceptable pastime, but it was not to be expected that a Delius boy, destined for a share of the family business, should become a professional musician.

Looking at the matter from the viewpoint of Delius *père* – a music lover, after all, who had had many fine artists play in his own home – it must be said that he may have quite rightly discerned that Fritz, who was a tolerable pianist and a quite talented violinist, was simply not a good enough player to achieve perhaps more than second or third rank as an orchestral performer. And in England, at least at that time, this would have furnished at best a precarious existence, the alternative being a fairly penurious living as a teacher. As for becoming a composer and living comfortably on the proceeds of composition, Julius Delius may perhaps largely be forgiven for failing to perceive or appreciate such a faint possibility. He had a thriving business to which Fritz, following the departure of Ernst, was the natural successor, and Julius saw it as his clear duty to make his son aware not only of his responsibility to the family, but also of the necessity to ensure his own future livelihood and security.

The answer to Fritz's problems at last offered itself around the end of 1883. Commercial opportunities in orange-growing in Florida were being quite widely advertised in England, and it occurred to Fritz that that exotic part of the world, far from Bradford, might well furnish him with the line of escape he needed. His father agreed to the proposed venture, in which Fritz was joined by Charles Douglas, son of another prosperous Bradford businessman, and on 2 March 1884 the two young Yorkshiremen sailed from Liverpool for New York. Their destination was Solana Grove, an orange plantation on which Julius Delius had taken an option, situated on the right bank of the St Johns River in Florida. Once there, Douglas did not stay long, but Delius settled in, soon procuring a piano and making musical friends and acquaintances in Jacksonville, some 50 kilometres downriver to the north. One of these, Thomas Ward, an organist from Brooklyn, was invited for a time to Solana Grove, and under his expert and sympathetic tutoring, Delius gained a thorough grounding in musical technique. Already obviously endowed with a natural feeling for harmony, but until now lacking the technical apparatus to rationalize and commit harmonic ideas to paper, Delius found Ward's instruction of lasting benefit. Overlaid on Ward's tuition was a further, uncommon musical influence: the singing of the Negroes on Delius's plantation.

The cultivation of oranges was almost inevitably left to the Negro workers, overseen conscientiously enough by Delius's foreman, Albert Anderson, while the aspiring composer himself soaked up the elements of the Florida atmosphere, Ward's teaching and the Negroes' songs, all to find their first flower in his orchestral suite *Florida*, composed in 1886–87. Something of the flavour of Delius's Solana Grove days is conveyed in a brief reminiscence by Anderson's sister-in-law, Julia Sanks:

Time an' time I tell Mister Delius he ought to go to the church, I don' care which, because the Lord He don't know denomination. Just like He don't know color. But Mister Delius, he pay no mind. He tinkered with that piano. . . . I was nothin' but a child, hardly, when we sing to him first – Albert and Eliza and me. Oh, we loved to go there. It was a happy place.

She reported that Delius was not hard to work for and cooked for himself most of the time:

Maybe he don't care what he eat if he can be at his piano or his fiddle. Long as he make his music, he just don't mind what else. He didn't have no conveniences. He didn't care about the fruits, neither. He didn't do yard work to speak of. It was a trouble to Albert, and a worry. He weren't much for hard work, Mister Delius, and that's a fact. Just that music. I ain't heard nothing like it since. I disremember what I sang to him except the hymns. . . . It was Albert mostly he wanted to hear.*

Delius deserted Solana Grove in the summer of 1885, in spite of his father's having exercised as early as August 1884 his option to purchase the plantation outright, in a vain attempt to encourage Fritz to settle there. Young Delius left

---

* Gloria Jahoda, *The Other Florida* (New York: Charles Scribner's Sons, 1967), pp. 266–7.

behind him, whether by accident or design, a number of unpaid bills. After spending a few weeks in Jacksonville, he struck north for Virginia, attracted by a newspaper advertisement for a music teacher, and by the beginning of October he had established himself in Danville, a town largely dedicated to the tobacco industry. He soon became busily involved in Danville's musical life, and by taking up further teaching appointments, he found that for the first time music could earn him a tolerable living. His initial employer there, John Frederick Rueckert, was Leipzig-trained, and it may have been as a result of his encouragement, following that of Ward, that Delius decided that the Leipzig Conservatorium – then the most prestigious musical establishment in Europe – might well hold the key to his future. Following his disappearance from Florida, his parents had become genuinely anxious about him, and Julius Delius finally gave his grudging consent and financial support to a course of studies at Leipzig. Fritz first made his way from Danville to New York, and then sailed for Liverpool in June 1886. At Bradford he wasted little time in preparing for his move to Leipzig, finally settling into lodgings in the Harkort-strasse at the beginning of August.

Delius's two years in the United States have left us his first tentative compositional essays: the little piano piece 'Zum Carnival' (RT IX/1), presumed to date from 1885; and two songs, 'Over the mountains high' (Bjørnson) (RT V/2) and 'Zwei bräune Augen' (H. C. Andersen) (RT V/3), both dated in manuscript 1885. A further short piano piece, 'Pensées Mélodieuses' (RT IX/2), is also dated 1885.

If, formally, Delius was in Leipzig to earn himself a diploma and to benefit from the teachings of such men as Reinecke, Jadassohn and Sitt (under the latter he had, of course, already studied briefly at Chemnitz), there is no doubt that for him the greater profit was simply to be in a city where good music could be heard at almost every waking hour, and moreover to be among other students whose friendship, once made, would have a bearing on his subsequent musical career. Percy Pitt, a young fellow-student during that first year at Leipzig, left for his own biographer material which provides a useful picture of life and activities in and around the Conservatorium at that period:

At Leipzig could be heard practically everything there was to hear. On Thursday evenings, except in the summer, there were orchestral concerts in the Great Hall of the New Gewandhaus which were world-famous; the conductor, Reinecke, was not indeed as inspiring as the orchestra was accomplished, but the soloists were the pick of the Continent; and to the full rehearsals on Wednesday mornings the students were admitted on presentation of their identity cards. There they heard some of the greatest artists of the time: Sarasate, Joachim, Sophie Menter, Saint-Säens, Anton Rubinstein, Hans von Bülow, Davidov, d'Albert, Essipov. . . . On Saturdays there were chamber concerts in the Small Hall of the Gewandhaus – the Gewandhaus, Cloth Hall, once a mart for textiles. There were string quartets elsewhere; there were the choral Euterpe concerts; there was the Liszt Society; . . . there were two churches, St. Thomas and St. Nicolas. . . . Their choirs were celebrated.

And as for opera, municipal of course, it flowed in one rich and constant stream; everything by everybody, except *Parsifal*, which was still copyright and confined to Bayreuth. The conductors were Arthur Nikisch and Gustav Mahler, founts of joy and inspiration. . . . And all this was to be enjoyed in the company of kindred spirits, young and hopeful and wild with enthusiasm. *'Kneipen'*, it was called – to go and hear the opera, and then on to supper at Helbig's with a dozen fellows who had been there too, to talk and argue and laugh and drink the light German beer. . . .

The musical education at the Conservatorium was not at the time all it might have been. The school was living on its reputation. It was quite as happy-go-lucky as its students; nor did the professors appear to mind very much whether one worked or not as long as fees were paid. They might no doubt have argued that they provided the opportunity of learning, and that if a lad . . . had anything in him there was no need to do more. But this was to take too proud a view of the individual; we are not so glacial and remote in our personal development as not to be the better for inspiring example, stirring sympathy, and the exchange of ideas. Great schools are not the fruit of such *laissez-faire* theories. The place, nevertheless, was not only built like a rabbit-warren, but crowded like one, with students of all nationalities. The English were fairly well represented, both in numbers and talent; one was named Delius. . . .

Every Friday evening there was a students' concert. The young vocalists and instrumentalists there sang and played, with a richly mixed effect, whatever they chose: concertos and vocal arias, chamber music, instrumental soli, *Lieder*. There was a string orchestra, with a piano to represent the wind parts. The ordeal was much fiercer than appearance before the general public, and the comments more candid and unsparing. . . . Composers had their chance at the bi-weekly orchestral practices. There was a possibility of having one's works tried out before a 'real' audience, at Bonorand's restaurant in the Rosenthal Park outside the city. The music with which Bonorand, if he it still was, used to entertain his patrons generally took the form of an orchestral concert; and students could get their works included in the programme. They did not have to pay Bonorand anything; but as they had to supply the orchestral material, and put down a hundred marks for the bandmaster's tip and the musicians' beer, it could only be done when money was plentiful.*

Most of Delius's more important friendships at Leipzig were formed with Norwegians. It is likely that the first of these was with Christian Sinding, who, like Delius, had arrived in the city for the autumn semester of 1886. He was studying with the same teachers. Two young violinists, Arve Arvesen and Johan Halvorsen, friends of Sinding, were also in Leipzig. They too became Delius's friends. Delius spent the summer vacation of 1887 largely in Norway, and in July and August he sketched a series of *Norske Wiser* (RT X(ii)3) on his travels there. In the autumn semester of 1887 his own circle widened significantly to take in Grieg, who had come to winter in the city and to study orchestration: it was Sinding who was responsible for effecting this precious introduction.

---

* J. Daniel Chamier, *Percy Pitt of Covent Garden and the B.B.C.* (London: Edward Arnold, 1938), pp. 30–33.

Norwegians, of course, were not his only friends. There were useful links with Adolph Brodsky, leader of the celebrated Brodsky Quartet and now teaching in Leipzig, and in the second winter with Ferruccio Busoni, to whom he was introduced by Grieg. On one memorable occasion Delius and the Griegs sat together with Busoni at a performance of Busoni's second quartet in the old Gewandhaus.

At Leipzig, Delius's attempts at composition gradually became more assured: a number of part-songs (RT IV/1) were composed to German texts which were themselves sometimes translations of Norwegian poems. If both pleasing and singable, they reveal only little of the really mature composer whom we recognize from compositions dating from the first years of the twentieth century. This is not true, however, of the *Florida* suite (RT VI/1) of 1886–7, with its harmonic pointers to the future, first played for the price of that barrel of beer in the Rosenthal Park, presumably at Bonorand's restaurant, early in 1888. Hans Sitt conducted, while Delius, Sinding and the Griegs sat and listened. There were other works, too, dating from the Leipzig days: a piano piece from 1887, 'Norwegian Sleigh Ride' (RT IX/3), later to be orchestrated; and a tone-poem, *Hiawatha*, after Longfellow (RT VI/2), begun in 1887 and completed in January 1888. The original score of this latter work has not survived complete.

No letters that Delius wrote before his arrival at Leipzig have yet been traced. One letter he wrote in 1886 has recently been found. None, apparently, survives from 1887. Not until 1888 does the present documentary legacy represented by the composer's correspondence begin to be preserved.

(1)
Fritz Delius to Gertrude Rueckert

Leipzig, Dec 11/86
Royal Conservatory of music

My dear Miss Gertrude,

After all this time has elapsed since I left Danville I dont suppose you will expect this letter, however I always liked to surprise people & I hope it is not unpleasantly. For the last 5 months I have been studying here at the Conservatory where I expect to remain 3 years. Leipzig is a very nice town with a very fine Opera house & concerts almost every night; All the greatest Artist[s] come here so we have fine opportunities to hear good music. Ask Miss Blanch how she would like to study 6 hours a day Composition & Bach? What are you playing now? Have you got that run in "Whispering winds" down fine yet? I shall be glad to receive news from you & learn how you are all getting on. Mr Hoppe[1] wrote me that poor Mr Crowder died a short time ago. I felt very much grieved to hear of the poor boy's death, so very young. It seems only yesterday that I went with him down to the Warehouses to watch the sales.[2] Is Mr Maggee[3] still living with you, please give my kindest regards if he is still there. There are a great many soldiers here. A few weeks ago I saw 25,000 marching to the autumn manoevres near Leipzig. They looked very fine marching past. People think there is going to be war with France & Russia. If Germany gets beaten I suppose we shall have 2 or 3 battles around Leipzig, which would scarcely be pleasant, & difficult to study with the bullets flying around ones ears. Tell your father I have a quartett at my lodgings every sunday morning. A fine violinist, cellist & viola, I play the piano. It is indeed very enjoyable. We play Schumann, Beethoven Mozart, Haydn etc. Ask him also if he cannot drop over for a week or so & have a little music. The other night I played in a concert here for the benefit, Well! of what do you think? Of the *English Church*. The church *wanted money* for some fund or other, & it was a great success. The climate is very cold & strikes me rather unpleasantly but I suppose I shall get used to it. Now, write soon & let me know how you all are. I wish you all a Merry Christmas & many happy new years. Give my kindest regards to Your father Miss Blanche, your mother, Mr Dodson[3] & wishing you every happiness.

I remain,
sincerely yours,
Fritz Delius

Has Mr Rishton got a set of new *teeth* yet? remember me also to Viner she certainly makes good batter bread

Autograph letter, signed and dated, written in English.

The original is in the Delius Trust Archive, London. It is the earliest letter written by Delius that is preserved in the Archive. Three further communications from Delius to Gertrude Rueckert are dated 1889 and 1890.

Marie Gertrude (1871–1957) and Blanche Loraine Rueckert (1869–1901): daughters of John Frederick Rueckert (1840–1905), a grandson of the German poet, Friedrich Rückert, and a leading musician in Danville, Virginia, at this period. Having left Florida, Delius had established himself in Danville towards the end of the summer of 1885 as tutor to the Rueckert sisters. He was also to teach music at the Roanoke Female College.

1   'Delius, and another musical man named Hoppe, believed to be German, boarded with a family named Richardson in North Danville, where they had two bedrooms, their meals being sent up to their joint sitting room.' This rare reference to Hoppe was made by Gerard Tetley in an article based largely on the recollections of Mrs Willamina Phifer Giles, daughter of Robert Phifer, published in the *Richmond Times-Dispatch* on 16 May 1948. The letter Delius referred to has not been preserved, although there appears to have been some slight correspondence between the two men for a time. Writing to Gertrude Rueckert Dodson on 7 March 1890, Delius noted, 'Mr Hoppe wrote to me the other day.' And the two letters from Robert Phifer to Delius that have been preserved also contain references to Hoppe (see Letter 53).

2   Tobacco was Danville's main industry; where Delius had earlier listened to the Negro workers on his plantation in Florida, in Danville he heard the Negro hands singing in chorus in the tobacco stemmeries.

3   Presumably a relative of Mrs Isabelle (Belle) McGehee Phifer. Robert Phifer, her musician husband, had become a good friend of Delius during the latter's stay in Danville (see Letter 53, note).

4   Gertrude was to marry Dodson in February 1890.

1888

Delius's studies at the Leipzig Conservatorium came to an end in the spring, and on 11 April he returned to Bradford, staying there only briefly before making his way to Paris. Probably the most important legacy of the two Leipzig years was the forging of Delius's friendships with his Norwegian fellow-students and with Grieg. Delius was never to acknowledge any special debt to his Conservatorium teachers or to his formal course of studies, but he was always to remain grateful to people like Grieg, Sinding and Arvesen for giving him such ready entry to Norwegian artistic and social circles. Certainly, the greater part of our knowledge of Delius's life and work during the next few years derives from the correspondence of Grieg and of Sinding and from the letters that Delius himself wrote to Grieg.

Delius left England on 6 May to settle in France, with little idea, it may be assumed, that that country was to be home for him for the rest of his life. He had dined with the Griegs, who were in London for a time, two days earlier, and now an allowance from his father was to enable him to live in Paris and to devote himself to composition. Initially he stayed at the home of his uncle Theodor and explored Paris with great thoroughness before finally getting down for some weeks to serious and uninterrupted work. Much of the summer he then spent in Brittany, where he found the atmosphere congenial and well-suited to further compositional activity.

Returning to Paris late in October, Delius made another short stay with his uncle, before moving in November to a small rented cottage at Ville d'Avray. From there he made occasional excursions to Paris to savour the autumn season's musical delights and, perhaps, some of the capital's more worldly pleasures.

Hiawatha, tone-poem after Longfellow (RT VI/2). Completed January.

Paa Vidderne, melodrama (Ibsen) (RT III/1). Begun June; completed October.

Five Songs from the Norwegian (RT V/5).

Swedish folk-song arrangement (RT X(i)1).

'Hochgebirgsleben', song (Ibsen) (RT V/6).

'O schneller, mein Ross!', song (von Geibel) (RT V/7).

Zanoni, incidental music (Bulwer Lytton) (RT I/1). Summer. Unfinished.

Suite for violin and orchestra (RT VII/1). Summer?

Rhapsodic Variations, for large orchestra (RT VI/3). September. Unfinished.

Three pieces for string orchestra (RT VI/4). *c*. September.

String Quartet (RT VIII/1). Finished October/November, but MS has survived incomplete.

(2)
Fritz Delius to Edvard Grieg

Harkort Str 5.^{IV} [Leipzig]
Saturday [18 February 1888]

Dear Grieg.

I should like to let you know what pleasure your quartet[1] gave me & in what a strange mood it left me. It will be of little importance to you if I tell you how much I love & esteem you, but it is true & comes from my heart & so I thank you for all the pleasure that I feel in your works.

> With affectionate greetings
> I remain
> Yours
> Fritz Delius

Autograph letter, signed and undated, written in German.

The original is in the Bergen Public Library, Bergen, Norway, where thirty-seven letters and postcards written by Delius to Edvard and Nina Grieg are preserved; the last, to Nina Grieg, was written in 1920. This is the first extant letter from Delius to Grieg.

Edvard Hagerup Grieg (1843–1907): Norwegian composer, conductor and pianist. He first studied under his mother, who was a pianist, and then entered the Leipzig Conservatorium at the age of fifteen, studying there under Richter, Reinecke and Moscheles, among others. He subsequently studied with Gade in Copenhagen. With his contemporary Rikard Nordraak (1842–66), Grieg was the first to explore the possibilities of a Norwegian national style in music. He travelled and performed throughout Europe, but from now on lived chiefly at Troldhaugen, a house he recently had built near Bergen. He married Nina Hagerup (1845–1935), a singer, in 1867.

1   String Quartet in G minor, op. 27 (1877–8). It was performed in Leipzig by the Brodsky Quartet on 18 and 19 February 1888.

(3)

Edvard Grieg to Fritz Delius

Leipzig, 28/2/88

Dear Sir,

I was pleasantly surprised, indeed stimulated, by your manuscripts[1] and I detect in them signs of a most distinguished compositional talent in the grand style, which aspires to the highest goal. Whether you will reach this goal only depends upon what turn your affairs take. If you will permit me, in the interests of your future, to offer you a piece of advice, (it is as an older artist that I take the liberty of doing this) it would be this, that you devote yourself now, while you are still young, fully to the pursuit of your art, rather than accept a formal position, and that you follow both your own true nature and the inner voice of your ideals and your inclinations. However, in order to achieve this it is essential that you choose the national and artistic environment as dictated to you by your genius.

It is my most fervent wish that you will one day find in your own country the recognition which you deserve, as well as the material means towards the achievement of your splendid goal and I do not doubt for a moment that you will succeed.

With the assurance of my warm sympathy

Yours very truly
Edvard Grieg.

Autograph letter, signed and dated, written in German.

The original is in the Delius Trust Archive. It is the earliest dated item of seventy-one communications written by Edvard and Nina Grieg to Delius between 1888 and 1920.

Written in a notably formal style, quite different from that of other letters in the Grieg–Delius correspondence, this carefully phrased and fulsome piece of propaganda was evidently intended for Delius's father. The weighty recommendation from the older composer was to be followed by a meeting, arranged by Delius, between Grieg and Julius Delius in London later in the year. Two sentences in letters from Grieg to his friend Frants Beyer (see Letter 9), written at this period, convey rather more accurately the real tenor of the relationship: 'I am just back from a long afternoon walk in lovely spring weather together with Sinding and the "Hardangervidde-man" ' (Leipzig, 13 February 1888); and 'This English-American, deeply musical, splendid Hardanger-vidde-man. . . . You must get to know him. He is like us in nothing but feeling! But in the end that's everything!' (Leipzig, 20 February 1888) (cf. Marie Beyer, ed., *Breve fra Edvard Grieg til Frants Beyer: 1872–1907* [Kristiania: Steenske Forlag, 1923], pp. 91, 95).

See Delius's diary entries for 24 July 1887 *et seq*. (Appendix III) for a description of his walking tour over the Hardanger Vidde.

1   Apart from a few early songs and unaccompanied choruses, together with the piano pieces 'Zum Carnival', 'Pensées Mélodieuses' and 'Norwegian Sleigh Ride', little has survived of Delius's work prior to 1888. Two larger-scale works, the orchestral suite *Florida* and the tone-poem *Hiawatha*, could well have been the principal pieces of evidence available to Grieg in pronouncing his judgement.

(4)
Fritz Delius to Edvard Grieg

Claremont
Bradford.
12 April/ 88. England.

Dear Grieg

I arrived here yesterday after rather an unpleasant journey. I got to Düsseldorf at 9 in the morning & left at 4.24 p.m., via Flushing; the Rotterdam train left too early for me as I had first to visit my sister. I believe this route will suit you best, it is fast & comfortable. The ships are also very comfortably fitted out & only take 7 hours for the crossing. In Flushing I was so tired that I went to bed right away & noticed nothing until Queenboro', the crossing was very calm, too, just like on the Hardanger Fjord. We got to London at 8 o'clock in the morning. But the journey was very cold. Still, it is somewhat warmer in England than over there, even if you will not be able to pick roses in the streets. I do not think that I shall stick it out for very long here. I already miss you all very much & have suddenly arrived in so completely different an atmosphere that I feel rather depressed. If you should feel like spending a couple of days here in Bradford I should be very pleased to make you & your wife welcome, but if not I hope we will meet at least once in London before my departure for Paris.[1] Please give your wife my best wishes & write me a few lines when you have the time & inclination. Hoping you are well & happy

> I remain
> Yours
> Fritz Delius

Autograph letter, signed and dated, written in German.

The original is in the Bergen Public Library.

1   Grieg replied from Leipzig on 16 April: 'I am afraid that we shall not be able to accept your kind invitation to come to Bradford. And a meeting in London? Well, that is likely to be little more than a handshake. But in Norway! That's where it must be –' He also wrote, 'I must tell you that *very* seldom has getting to know someone given me so much pleasure.'

(5)

Christian Sinding to Fritz Delius

Leipzig 19 April 88.

Dear friend,

You cannot believe how much I miss you. I have hardly ever before met a person I could trust so completely, and at times an almost sentimental feeling comes over me when I think of you. But I hope you will not laugh too much at me on that account. Likewise, I hope it will not be too long before we see each other again. It is a good thing, however, that you left your friend Mr. Braun[1] behind for me. He is really a splendid fellow with a sound, ingenuous nature such as one seldom sees. In addition he has, as far as I can tell, a very great musical talent. He has shown me things which frankly staggered me. Another proof of how little this damned anaemic Conservatoire-erudition really signifies. Herr Sitt[2] has got him to go through the Theory of Harmony – Jadassohn's[2] of course; but he will soon know what it is all about. At the moment he is finding it damned hard, and daily says how "blessed much he has "geschafft"."[3] But that won't matter, he is too level-headed to get spoilt and Sitt is, it seems, a very good teacher.

– Last night I went with the Griegs to Mr. Braun's, where we drank champagne. I proposed a toast to you, which was responded to with great pleasure. You really are very much missed here, you old Joseph.

I am to send you many good wishes from the Brodskys.[4] I got a pretty rough moral thrashing from Frau Picard[5] yesterday, because I had not yet replied to your letter, and I hasten to put this right before I see her again today. I hope you will not judge me quite so harshly on account of my laziness. – I am greatly looking forward to the promised letter from Paris.

Greetings from the Griegs, who are leaving on Monday, and from Mr. Braun and myself.

Yours
Christian Sinding

Autograph letter, signed and dated, written in German. Envelope addressed: An / Herrn Fritz Delius, Tonkünstler. / Claremont / Bradford / England. Postmark: LEIPZIG 19–4 88. Receiving postmark: BRADFORD AP 21 88.

The original is in the Delius Trust Archive. It is the earliest item in a prolific correspondence of which only Sinding's letters are extant. The bulk of the correspondence that is preserved was written between 1888 and 1898, but two last letters are dated 1905. One late reference to Sinding is to occur in a letter from Johan Selmer (see Letter 25) to Delius, written on 23 August 1908: 'I know that Sinding has visited you in the idyllic setting of Grez.'

Christian Sinding (1856–1941): Norwegian composer. Despite clear Germanic influence, at home his music was considered to be generally Norwegian in character. He wrote four symphonies, a piano concerto and three violin concertos, and his wide range extended to piano pieces (of which 'Rustle of Spring' is best known) and around 250 songs. His brother Otto was a considerable painter and poet, and another brother, Stephan, was a leading sculptor.

1 Charles Braun (1868–?): musically gifted and financially well-situated young English fellow-student of Delius and Sinding at Leipzig (cf. Rugstad, p. 56), where he was a regular and welcome participant in the Griegs' whist sessions. A number of references to him occur in Sinding's letters of this period, and the fact that Sinding looked upon him as a possible financial benefactor is underlined in the Norwegian composer's letter from Leipzig to Delius, dated 22 May 1888: 'Braun has spoken about engaging me as a "travelling tutor" if I cannot stay here any longer because of the confounded money, and he will then go to Vienna or Paris. And I really think now that I can lead him as safely through the maze of the fugue as Sitt can.' Shortly afterwards, Sinding confirmed that Braun had completed 'a most voluminous work', the cantata *Ritter Olaf*. This was first performed under its English title, *Sir Olaf*, in Liverpool, Braun's native city, on 5 March 1889, at the Philharmonic Hall. A second cantata by Braun, *Sigurd*, was given there in December 1890.

2 Hans Sitt (1850–1922) and Salomon Jadassohn (1831–1902): two of Delius's teachers at Leipzig. Sitt was a member of the Brodsky Quartet, which was formed in Leipzig. Delius had already taken violin lessons from him while living and working for a time in Chemnitz. Sinding, in one of his letters to Delius, acknowledged Sitt to be 'certainly a good teacher', and Grieg, while finding his instrumentation 'occasionally coarse', recognized his personal kindness and wealth of knowledge.

3 *wie 'verflucht viel er "geschafft" hat.'*

4 Adolph Brodsky (1851–1929): Russian-born violinist. He became professor of violin at the Leipzig Conservatorium in 1880, and was founder of the celebrated quartet which bore his name. Delius, like Sinding, became a member of his circle at Leipzig. In 1895 Brodsky took up the post of professor of violin at the Royal Manchester College of Music, where shortly afterwards he was appointed principal.

5 Olga Picard: *née* Skadowsky in Russia, separated from her husband, Gabriel Picard, a university lecturer in Paris, in 1887. Towards the end of that year, she moved to her sister's home in Leipzig. Her sister Anna was Brodsky's wife, and Sinding, on meeting Olga in the Brodsky ménage, promptly fell in love with her (cf. Rugstad, pp. 56–7).

(6)
Fritz Delius to Edvard Grieg

Claremont
Bradford,
25 [April]/88.

Dear Grieg

Many thanks for your letter, which gave me much pleasure. At all events, you will now be in London & I hope after a pleasant journey. Our wonderful time in Leipzig has now melted away into the past. I have never lived through such a congenial time. It has been a cornerstone in my life, I hope there will be three more to come.

Next Saturday I am coming to London & go straight on to Reading where I shall stay with an acquaintance until Monday. On Monday I travel to London & will be staying at the Hotel Métropole where I shall be constantly at your disposal. I invite you & your dear wife herewith to supper with me at the Hotel Métropole on the 4th May & to spend yet another of our jolly evenings together.[1] If you can, it would be a pleasure for me to show you various things of interest during the day. In short to be your guide. If the 5th should suit you better it would also suit me. On the 6th I travel to Paris. The weather here is very cold, I am freezing miserably. My father has delighted me by giving me the score of Tristan & Isolde. Please write me a few lines when you can.

Give my best wishes to your wife

Your devoted
Fritz Delius

Autograph letter, signed and dated '25/88', written in German.

The original is in the Bergen Public Library.

The Griegs' visit to London had as its main purpose their attendance at the Philharmonic Society's concert on 3 May, with Grieg as soloist in his own Piano Concerto and as conductor of his *Two Elegiac Melodies*.

1   Nina Grieg replied from their Clapham address on 26 April: 'we . . . accept with pleasure your kind invitation for the 4*th* May. – Grieg hopes very much that you will come to the rehearsal.'

(7)
Fritz Delius to Edvard Grieg

43 Rue Cambon
Paris
[mid-May 1888]

Dear Grieg,

I have now settled down a bit & must confess that I feel very happy here. There is something in the atmosphere that is quite different from Germany or England. The hustle & bustle here is extraordinary, one is bound to think that every street-urchin enjoys life. The concerts are over. I heard the last Lamoureux Concert & must confess that as far as ensemble & finesse are concerned the orchestra is far superior to Leipzig. I heard Parsifal Prelude, Tannhäuser Overture, Lohengrin Prelude to 1st Act, Women's March & Prelude to 3rd Act, Dance Marcabre Saint Saens, L'Arlesienne, Bizet & something from Bizet's opera The Pearl Fishers, quite excellent. [1] I am meeting a lot of artists, musicians & writers. But I can't do much work. In a few weeks' time I am going to Spain, Seville or Granada, am already longing for it. [2] It is beautiful, very beautiful here but I will soon have to have some peace & quiet. I heard a new opera by Lalo at the Opera Comique, but found it utterly trivial. Also Aida at the big Opera, quite excellent. How did your concert come off, did it bring in pounds stirling en masse for you. I have not heard anything from Sinding nor from Mr Braun. The weather is quite marvellous, not a cloud. My kind regards to your wife. I hope that you are both keeping well & happy. Please excuse this superficial letter, as soon as I have some peace you shall receive a much more detailed one.

Farewell & write me a few lines.

Your devoted
Fritz Delius

———————————

Autograph letter, signed and undated, written in German.

The original is in the Bergen Public Library.

Delius was now established in his uncle Theodor's apartment, near the Paris Opera, and was already being introduced to some of Theodor's many artist friends.

1   On hearing of Delius's concert-going in Paris, Sinding wrote to him on 22 May commenting on the amount of German music in this particular programme and suggesting that 'German music sounds better in Germany than in France'.

2   This proposed visit to Spain was not to be realized. Perhaps the reason lay in an impecunious and overworked Sinding being unable to get away. 'How am I then

supposed to come to Spain,' he asked Delius rhetorically in a letter from Leipzig dated 27 June. 'Speak not to me of it.'

(8)
Fritz Delius to Edvard Grieg

43. Rue Cambon.
Paris. June 20/88.

My good, dear Grieg,

How are you, where are you? What are you doing? & how did you get on in London? You have no idea how much I miss you & have missed you since not seeing you any more. This evening I felt that I just wanted to say it to you. Yes! I think of you very often. I have been all alone here for the past 18 days. My uncle was in London & has only just come back today. I have been working the whole time & have written a lot, several songs, and Ibsen's *Paa Vidderne*,[1] for tenor voice, & an orchestral piece.[2] For you I have written two songs in remembrance which I should like to send as soon as I know your correct address. Next year I am certainly coming to Trollhaugen,[3] if I am alive. Give my greetings to the North, until I am able to do so myself. It is very beautiful in Paris, but I would not like to stay here for ever. The French are very artistic, but it is always merely art, the great vitality of Nature is missing, at least in music. It is all too refined & affected – But one can learn much, very much here. The people are very free & have power, & everyone lives & is free: a great contrast to Germany. Moral freedom is widespread here too. In a few weeks' time I travel to Spain, Seville first. I will write & tell you all about it. From time to time I go to the Morgue where people who have died are laid out, suicides, or murdered. Oh, it's saddening to go in there. There are always 4 or 5 pitiful corpses looking so eternally wretched. Yes, you can very soon come across the two extremes here. The people of luxury in their fine carriages in the Bois de Boulogne & the miserable suicides in the Morgue. If only I had *you* here I could show you so very much. Things you could weep over, but also other things which would amuse you a lot. Now & again I also go where the very poorest people live. I dress shabbily & then go everywhere undisturbed. You can see 5 different worlds here in Paris, it is immensely interesting. If you have time write me a few lines. I shall continue to give you news of myself from time to time, until I can eventually greet you in your own home in the *North*. Yes, one day I think I shall come & stay put up there. Give my best wishes to your dear wife, & remember

Your friend
Fritz Delius

Autograph letter, signed and dated, written in German.

The original is in the Bergen Public Library.

1   Henrik Ibsen (1828–1906): internationally celebrated Norwegian dramatist and poet. Delius was later to become acquainted with him (see Letters 74 and 76). Ibsen's poem in nine sections, *Paa Vidderne* (1859–60), was set by Delius to a German translation, *Auf dem Hochgebirge*, made by L. Passarge, and the composition was dedicated to Grieg. 'An original idea to make "Paa Vidderne" into a recitation', wrote Sinding on 6 October. 'How did you hit on that?'

2   Probably the tone-poem *Hiawatha*.

3   Troldhaugen: Grieg's home, near Bergen.

(9)
Edvard Grieg to Fritz Delius

Troldhaugen
Hop Station
near *Bergen*, Norway
9th August 88

Dear Delius, I ought really to have told you before that I am a bad correspondent, otherwise you might perhaps find yourself capable of doubting my feelings of friendship for you. I ought long ago to have written, even if I had not got your last kind letter. I received it the day before yesterday and, to my surprise, see now that it was despatched from Paris on 20 *June*, – a proof that the post, too, is a human institution! And you have set "på Vidderne" to music! I can't tell you how curious I am to see the piece, however on the other hand I would rather not see it yet, for I have long had the idea of setting the very same poem to music. But – my curiosity is too great and I solemnly undertake not to steal from you!! That is, no *notes*, for I hope to have stolen your friendship once and for all, so that you shall never have it back. As a result I only need to tell you that you will be received in our house with open arms, if and when you come. Don't let the beauty of Spain make you forget Nordic Nature and your Nordic friends! In a few days I am going to Birmingham with my friend Beyer,[1] but I am afraid must first visit London for orchestra rehearsals. I am going by steamer from here to Aberdeen and am not really looking forward to the whole business. As soon as possible I shall return home, and shall stay at home until January, when I shall probably go to Berlin and London and perhaps also to Paris. But I have not yet learnt where to hide myself away, in order to work quietly on my own. Every day I receive visits from all possible nationalities – well, that too has its interesting points – and indeed from all sorts of townsfolk seeking the refreshment of an excursion to the countryside and making poor, unfortunate

Troldhaugen their destination.—You have probably read that my last concert in London was a resounding success. The Music Festival in Copenhagen was also very successful.[2] However, with the news of the death of my friend Edmund Neupert[3] in New York I have aged 10 years over the past fortnight. He was only 46 years old! One of the most genuine and most selfless artists who ever lived! How long am *I* to be spared? *Do* come next year. Sinding must join us too. (I dare say you know that he was in Copenhagen as well, and that next winter he is going to live at Brodsky's?)[4]

My wife sends you her kind regards.

As does your friend

Edvard Grieg.

Write soon!
I am looking forward to the songs!

Autograph letter, signed and dated, written in German. Envelope addressed: Fritz Delius *Esq.* / Claremont / *Bradford* / *England*. Postmark: BERGEN 9 VIII 88. Receiving postmark: BRADFORD AU 13 88. A musical phrase was pencilled by Delius on the back of the envelope.

The original is in the Delius Trust Archive.

Delius's whereabouts are imprecise. This letter from Grieg was 'sent on' (see Letter 10) from Bradford to St Malo, but no evidence has yet been discovered to suggest that Delius had visited England in the meantime. Probably he had neglected to give Grieg a forwarding address on leaving Paris, and Grieg therefore had prudently chosen to write to Bradford.

1 Frants Beyer: Grieg's neighbour at Troldhaugen and a close friend. He often accompanied the composer on his mountain walking tours. It was at the Birmingham Festival of 1888 that Grieg's overture *In Autumn* was performed.

2 A Nordic Music Festival had been held in Copenhagen in June 1888. It had helped to establish Sinding's reputation. 'My quintet had an excellent performance,' he wrote to Delius on 27 June, 'and I was suddenly something of a genius. And people who formerly rejected me with scorn now licked my arse with the best of appetites.'

3 Edmund Neupert (1842–88): Norwegian composer, pianist and teacher. His brilliant technique had in his time brought about comparisons with Liszt and Rubinstein. Of his compositions, the Studies were particularly admired. He had long been a friend of Grieg and was soloist in the first performance of the Concerto in A minor, which was dedicated to him.

4 In his letter of 27 June to Delius, Sinding had written, 'Brodsky has offered "in the interests of Art" to let me spend the coming winter at his home, in such a way that I should consider it as a loan to be paid back later when I fall on better times.'

(10)
Fritz Delius to Edvard Grieg

chez Madam Chapalan
Sillon (Maison Insley)
St Malo.
(Ille & Vilaine)
[mid-August 1888]

My dear Grieg

Your letter was sent on here from Bradford, it came the day before yesterday &
I cannot tell you how happy I was to hear something from you again. The same
morning I got up thinking of you, as you had been wandering about with me
the whole night. I also began to write a few things for string orchestra[1] & as I
was at work your letter came. Now I should explain myself a little. I have
decided not to go to Spain for the time being. I might not then be able to come
to Norway next year, & that I am absolutely determined to do. Instead of going
to Spain I calmly went to Brittany & I settled down at the seaside where I do a
lot of bathing & a lot of work. It almost reminds me of Norway, there are so
many cliffs, some places are very wild. I shall stay here until the middle or end
of October & then go to Paris again, to my uncle's. Where I shall stay this
winter I haven't yet decided. I hoped that you would want to come to Leipzig
again & I would have come too, maybe I shall go there yet again. Perhaps I shall
stay 2—3 months in Paris as there are the concerts to take in, & when I was last
there they were over & I should like to hear the 9th Symphony at the Conservatoire, as they are supposed to do it tremendously well. I have also found a poet
in Paris[2] who will write an opera for me, & I still have a lot to discuss with you.
I shall write to you about this when everything is more definite. During the
time I have been here I have dramatized *Zanoni*, the novel by Bulwer Lytton (I
talked to you about it once) & am writing incidental music for it, as an opera it
doesn't go well.[3] *Paa Vidderne* I will send to you as soon as I have finished some
revisions. You say you will steal no notes from me. I believe that, Grieg. I really
believe that you are incapable of stealing, notes at least. My friendship &
sympathy you have already taken long since & I tell you frankly, never in my
life have I met a nature which has won all my love as yours has. In my life I have
been left so much to my own resources that I have become egotistic without
realizing it & have really only cared about myself & worked for myself. You are
the only man who has ever changed that & drawn my whole attention to you
yourself & awakened the feelings which I now have for you. Now, take care of
yourself, Grieg, & for a long time too, so that we may get to know each other
still better. We must have many more splendid times together. Whenever you
think of dying you must think that there is someone who holds you to this earth
through the [strength][4] of his feelings. Poor Neupert, he must have been a real

artist, now he too has joined the great host. I believe, however, that he would have lived much, much longer if he had only taken a little care of himself, I didn't know him, but heard a lot about him in America. How glad I shall be to set foot on Norwegian moorland again & to look over the wide distances. Are we going to the Jotunheim?[5] next summer? Yes! Sinding must come with us too – that will be splendid. You will receive the manuscripts as soon as possible. In the meantime farewell, & give my regards to your good wife & also to your friend [Beyer?][4] whom indeed I do not know & write to me when you have the time & inclination. Good luck & a very pleasant stay in Birmingham is the wish of your friend

Fritz Delius

Autograph letter, signed and undated, written in German.

The original is in the Bergen Public Library.

1 These works appear not to have survived.

2 The poet remains unidentified, this being the only reference made to him in the letters of this period.

3 An autograph draft piano score of incidental music for this projected dramatized version of Bulwer Lytton's romance *Zanoni* (1842) is in the Delius Trust Archive. On 1 June Sinding had enquired, 'Have you got a text for an opera?'

4 A number of words are obliterated in the original letter.

5 Mountain range in central southern Norway that includes the country's highest peak, Galdhøppigen.

(11)

Edvard Grieg to Fritz Delius

Troldhaugen
Hop Station
near Bergen, Norway
23 September 88

My dear Delius,

Voilà! At last I sit in my distant corner of the world and have to thank you warmly for letter, for telegram, for songs and for all your expressions of friendly sentiments.[1] Andersen says somewhere that man has talent or rather originality where an animal has instinct. But that is wrong. For man has both at the same time. My *instinct* told me from our first meeting that our sympathies were mutual. Very well then: next year! Yes indeed! I will do *all* I can to ensure that I have the pleasure of being able to receive you. No Music Festivals next summer! And Sinding must join us as well. Have you had any news of him? I have heard nothing from him for a long time. You have probably heard that he is supposed to be living at Brodsky's this winter. I think that is marvellous. – We are really delighted with your songs and my wife is most grateful to you for the dedication.[2] (Her name is *Nina*, not *Lina*.) How strange that I have set nearly all the texts too. I find it very difficult to write and tell you all that I would like to say to you about the songs. But you will understand me better when we can meet and talk. There are so many beautiful and deeply felt things in them, – the passage

I just cannot forget, and will certainly show you one day that I can steal after all. And then again there are other things which I find difficult to accept, not where ideas are concerned, for you never lack inventiveness, but in the form and in the treatment of the voice. A Norwegian melody and a Wagnerian treatment of the voice are dangerous things indeed to try to reconcile. But we can discuss this. Perhaps I am too narrow-minded. I am very much looking forward to the melodrama.[4] There is much that is suitable for it, much that isn't. But the poem exerts such a strong appeal that one just cannot get it out of one's mind.

The overture "In Autumn" sounded quite superb and its performance gave me great pleasure. After Christmas my wife and I will probably go to England again for a couple of months. I have been invited to conduct the suite from "Peer Gynt" at the Philharmonic Society and to perform some of my chamber music at the Monday Popular Concerts. I shall try it once but I hope never again. I would much rather stay at home, but "Troldhaugen" implores me most urgently to provide a few £ sterling!

Farewell, dear friend, and let us hear from you soon.

With our best wishes
Yours
Edvard Grieg

Autograph letter, signed and dated, written in German. Both envelope and notepaper bear the monogram EG. Envelope addressed: Monsieur Fritz Delius./ chez Madame Chapalan/ Sillon (Maison Insley)/ *St. Malo./ France.* Postmark: BERGEN 24 IX 88. Receiving postmarks: PARIS and ST MALO (dates obscured).

The original is in the Delius Trust Archive.

1   Part of an undated letter from Delius written earlier in the month runs: 'Today I am sending you two more songs. . . . Did you receive my telegram to Birmingham? along with letter?'

2   The album of *Five Songs from the Norwegian* bears the inscription 'Frau Nina Grieg gewidmet', although a little earlier Delius had written to tell Grieg, 'I have taken the liberty of dedicating 6 songs to your dear wife.' First published in 1890, the songs and their dates are discussed in Threlfall, pp. 91–3.

3   From 'Sehnsucht' ('Longing'), translated into German by Edmund Lobedanz from the original Norwegian of Theodor Kjerulf.

4   *Paa Vidderne.*

(12)
Fritz Delius to Edvard Grieg

St Malo, Oct 19 / 88

My dear Grieg,

Hearty thanks for your kind letter which gave me much pleasure. I definitely believe that mankind has instinct. My instinct has seldom led me astray, my reason often. When I first met you it was no longer instinct for I had already been acquainted with you so long through your music. I believe nothing reveals a human being so openly as music. A poet can (probably) dissemble but a composer must show himself or nothing at all. You have absolutely no idea how I look forward to next summer, when we will talk of all this. In the meantime I have written [. . .]¹ songs which I would like to add to the others as an album, since they are nearly all written in one mood. The poems appealed so much to me, & I was so much at home with them that I composed, without any hesitation, in the way which seemed most natural to me. All this we will discuss, so much do I attach to your criticism. Paa Vidderne was finished some time ago, next week I travel back to Paris & from there I will send you the score with some songs. I have a feeling that we will meet in Paris this winter. You must certainly see Paris one day: it is ten times more beautiful than London. My first Suite will be played in London this winter by August Manns.⁴ You know that I prefer to live rather solitarily, that is, not in too big a place: One enjoys life more. Do you know what I have in mind, "please don't faint": to live in Norway. That is 8 months in the year & 4 months in Leipzig or Paris. When I come to Norway I will look out for a nice place where I can live & work in peace. Perhaps you can help me to find somewhere like this. Streets & smoke distort our ideas. One must breathe pure air before one can think purely. I feel so well in mind & body when nature is beautiful. Please take care this winter &

do not exert yourself too [much][1] for the sake of Pounds Stirling. If you come to Paris I will care for you & promise that you will have a wonderful time. My uncle is a splendid fellow. I can't do anything sensible in Paris, the environment is just not suitable.

I hear from Sinding from time to time, he wrote to me a few days ago & is happy at the Brodskys, they are splendid people after all.[3] I am very glad that Brodsky has done this & has taken an interest in him. How he is going to get to Norway (he writes) "the Devil only knows". But something is bound to turn up. Well farewell, dear friend, & don't let me wait too long for your reply. Give my kind regards to your wife. I don't understand how I came to write Lina instead of Nina, I knew it perfectly well. My address is

43 Rue Cambon, *Paris*.
Stay well & write soon

Your friend
[Fritz Delius][1]

Autograph letter, signature missing, dated, written in German.

The original is in the Bergen Public Library.

1   A number of words are obliterated in the original letter.

2   August Manns (1825–1907): German-born conductor. He succeeded Schallehn as conductor of the Crystal Palace Band in 1855, later making it into a full orchestra and giving his immensely popular Saturday Concerts until 1901. He was knighted in 1903. Delius's hopes that Manns would perform his *Florida* suite were not to be realized, although the conductor's final reply did not arrive until the following March (see Letter 19).

3   'I am now staying at the Brodskys' and live excellently,' wrote Sinding to Delius on 6 October. 'They are odd people these Russians. With a kind of naïve idealism which puts them high above any other nation. I can well understand how nihilists and Turgenevs and similar phenomena appear there.'

(13)
Fritz Delius to Edvard Grieg

Chalet des Lilas
à la Chaumière
Ville d'Avray
(Seine & Oise)
[mid-November 1888]

My dear Grieg

Your letter gave me great pleasure & I thank you for your kind words concerning my songs.[1] Indeed, you do not know how glad I am that you have had some pleasure from my songs, especially as *you* have given me so much enjoyment & pleasure through your music. So I will try to pay you something back. I have been in Ville d'Avray for a week now, 35 minutes by train from Paris. I have rented a small 2-roomed cottage, it stands quite alone on the bank of a small lake in a wood. So I am at work again. Close by there is a small restaurant where I eat. It is really lovely here, not a soul & all around woods & hills. You would think a 100 miles from Paris. The concerts have already begun. Next Sunday your concerto is to be played at the Lamoureux by René Chansarel.[2] I shall of course be there & give you a report. When will you leave Bergen — surely not before Christmas? I would love us all to be together again like last Christmas. Have you received Paa Vidderne?[3] I have not looked through it carefully yet, & the songs too are the first sketches. I am already looking forward to next summer, do your gymnastics thoroughly & take care in London. I hope that the Pounds Stirling will flow in. I am tremendously sorry that you cannot come to Paris, you really would enjoy it, it is 10,000 times nicer here than in Germany, more free, no comparison at all. Perhaps I shall come to London for a few days but I don't know yet. It would be lovely if you were already there.

I have heard nothing at all from Sinding for some time. He hasn't replied to my last letter yet. But he likes it very much at Brodsky's. A young Norwegian Arvesen,[4] a violinist, is studying in Paris with Marsick,[5] I think you saw him in Leipzig. When you were in Aberdeen you will certainly have seen Halvorsen.[6] How is he?

Farewell now, write soon. I hope that you & your wife are in very good health. My best wishes go to both of you.

Your friend,
Fritz Delius

Autograph letter, signed and undated, written in German.

The original is in the Bergen Public Library.

1   Grieg had written on 6 November: 'on closer acquaintance I see your songs from a different viewpoint. The less flattering this fact is for *me*, the more it is for *you* and *your songs*. They show such fine feeling, and I shall never be so foolish as not to see that this is the main thing.'

2   René Chansarel: pianist at the Concerts Lamoureux and a composer of piano pieces. He was an early friend of Debussy, who dedicated the *Fantaisie* for piano and orchestra to him.

3   Grieg replied on 23 November: 'the score and the songs have arrived safely.' He commented, 'I liked the songs very much! Geibel's O schneller mein Ross! is excellent!'

4   Arve Arvesen (1869–1951): Norwegian violinist. He studied, together with Delius, at Leipzig and then continued his studies in Paris. Arvesen was for a while to

become conductor in Helsinki, Turku and Gothenburg, and he founded his own widely known Arvesen Quartet. From 1928 until his death, he was principal of the Bergen Conservatorium.

5   Martin. P. Jos. Marsick (1848–1924): Belgian violinist and composer. After studying at Liège and Brussels, he became a pupil of Massenet at the Paris Conservatoire, where he was subsequently to teach, and of Joachim in Berlin. Among his compositions are three violin concertos.

6   Johan Halvorsen (1864–1935): Norwegian composer, conductor and violinist, and a fellow-student of Delius at Leipzig, where he studied with Brodsky. He spent some time at Aberdeen as leader of the orchestra there, and had studied, taught and performed in several European centres before becoming conductor of the orchestra of the National Theatre in Christiania. Halvorsen was to write fresh incidental music for the production there in 1924 of Gunnar Heiberg's *Folkeraadet*, Delius having composed the music for the first production in 1897. He married Grieg's niece.

(14)
Edvard Grieg to Fritz Delius

Bergen, Norway.
9th December 1888.

Dear Delius, I really ought not to write to you today, for I am in very low spirits. I am doing so nevertheless (avoiding, of course, effusions of pessimism) as I should like to say a few words about the melodrama. I have read it and re-read it and in it have found splendid music indeed. A pity that the general run of performance would fall short of your intentions. You see, you have composed with an unbelievable lack of consideration for the declaimer, and I am convinced that this lack of consideration will exact a cruel revenge if ever you should put the piece to the test. In my opinion this is precisely what is unfortunate about melodrama: namely that one cannot make *music*, absolute music. All the time fantasy has to lie on a Procrustean bed. It is only if one does not disdain these considerations that one can make it effective, otherwise not. You have added a note,[1] which is sufficient proof that you have entertained some secret fear. But what are you to think, if the beautiful, passionate passages have to be played piano in order for the voice to be heard? You will not hear what you thought you would hear. I think that with regard to the way in which you have conceived the music, you ought rather perhaps to have taken a *singing* voice. Am I wrong? Possibly. But I do not think so, as far as my experience goes. In a melodrama[2] I took every possible consideration myself, and yet, – after the first orchestral rehearsal I had to make alterations. For the very *first* thing is: One must be able to take in the poem in an entirely natural and effortless way, otherwise the listener has no satisfaction. The battle between *voice* and *music* is frightfully unpleasant. And how *fantastically* little is necessary to mask the voice. How I wish we could hear a rehearsal together! One or two things will come over very well, — it is only as concerns the piece as a whole that I have my doubts. I hope that you will not only forgive me for speaking quite frankly, but that you will indeed expect it of me. Is this not so? For happily our friendly relationship rests on more than mere formality. And quite independently of this: whether rightly or wrongly: I have an aversion to kid gloves in any form!

How marvellously well you must have established yourself in Paris! Indeed it sounds quite ideal. Something like this I must do one day too. I heard from Sinding a few days ago as well. He certainly seems to feel quite at home at the Brodskys. But he doesn't mention his work there.[3] Of course he must come to me in the summer. All in good time, as we say. I have acquired a little old square piano for my lonely room in the "Troldthal",[4] on which he can hammer away. While on the subject of pianos: Just imagine my surprise: A few days ago the firm of Pleyel in Paris, which I do not know at all, sent me a wonderful grand piano as a present! The man must not be quite right in the head! I hope you will have the opportunity of admiring this beautiful instrument at Trold-haugen in the summer. It stands in my big room, alongside an old Pleyel grand, and really takes up far too much space. I hope I shall now be able to do a concerto for 2 pianos. I have just finished the instrumentation for a choral piece. It is really the first act of an opera, for which Bjørnson[5] wrote the text many years ago. I drafted the music immediately — and then I heard not a word more. In order to rescue this fragment I am turning it into a choral piece, and it is going quite well. It deals with the Norwegian king Olav Trygvason,[6] or rather with the Norwegian people awaiting this violent importer of Christianity.

At the beginning of January I move from here. From then on my address is: C.F. Peters, Thalstrasse 10, Leipzig.[7] That does not mean that I shall necessarily go to Leipzig quite yet, but the letters will be sent on to me.

Write soon. And forgive me: The pessimism that was to have been avoided has perhaps after all crept into my discussion of the melodrama!

  Kind regards
  Yours
  Edvard Grieg

Thank you very much for the letters, and for the news of the concerto performance.[8] When and where would you like the score of the melodrama to be sent?

Autograph letter, signed and dated, written in German. Envelope addressed: Mr. Fritz Delius./ Chalet des Lilas / à la Chaumière/ Ville d'Avray./ *Seine & Oise/ France*. Postmark: BERGEN (date obscured). Receiving postmark: VILLE D'AVRAY 15 DEC 88.

The original is in the Delius Trust Archive.

1   Delius's note at the foot of the title-page of the MS. of *Paa Vidderne* runs: 'The conductor is throughout particularly requested to take into consideration the strength of the reciter's voice & whenever necessary to reduce slightly the volume of orchestral sound.'

2   *Bergliot*, melodrama for orchestra (1871/1885), op. 42. The text was by Bjørnstjerne Bjørnson.

3   Sinding's principal preoccupation was his affair with Olga Picard, and much of his letter to Grieg (dated 20 November) was taken up in explaining the situation. Although Olga Picard was still not divorced, Sinding was in love with her and intended to marry her. It helped little that he had scarcely a penny to his name (cf. Rugstad, p. 57).

4   Grieg's 'lonely room' was a small wooden cabin some way below his house, at the lakeside. It was there that he did most of his composing.

5   Bjørnstjerne Bjørnson (1832–1910): Norway's great patriot poet. Together with Ibsen (with whom on most matters he roundly disagreed) he bestrode nineteenth-century Norwegian literature, not just verse, but also drama, the novel and journalism. His daughter Bergliot, studying with Mathilde Marchesi, knew Delius well in Paris, and introduced him to her father.

6   *Scenes from Olav Trygvason*, op. 50, for soloist, chorus and orchestra, performed for the first time, under Grieg's baton, in Christiania on 19 October 1889.

7   The address of Grieg's publisher. The house of C. F. Peters was founded in Leipzig in 1814.

8   Delius had reviewed Chansarel's performance of the Piano Concerto for Grieg in a letter to the composer written late in November.

(15)
Fritz Delius to Edvard Grieg

Chalet des Lilas
à la Chaumière
Ville d'Avray
(Seine & Oise)
[December 1888]

My dear Grieg,

Thank you very much for your kind letter & candid criticism. It pleased me perhaps a lot more than you think for it has shown me that you are the person I always thought you to be. How good it does one to discover that about someone whom one esteems – & loves. What you wrote about the melodrama I rather thought myself, especially after having heard a piece at the Theatre Francais, the music almost always pp. I must tell you that I had not seen a single work in this genre before I composed 'Paa Vidderne', for that reason I wrote the whole thing so that I could easily write a voice part for it. Please keep the score until you come to England & if you will be so good as to bring it with you I shall, I hope, come & fetch it myself. I should also like to ask you to bring the songs as I should like to make a copy, since they are the first ones, & I do not even have any sketches. I was so glad to hear that you have a small work ready, perhaps you will have it performed in London? & I hope I shall get to hear it then. Were you really serious when you wrote to me about writing a double concerto or rather a concerto for two pianos, that would be simply marvellous. I hope you have already started it. I think that you could get splendid effects. To get a grand piano like that as a present is not bad at all, you ought rather to say that Pleyel must be perfectly right in the head. I have a string quartet[1] ready & have sent it to Sinding to give it to Brodsky. In the summer Sinding & I will turn up in Bergen. How I long for the summer. It's pretty cold here & I've caught a fine old cold. It's marvellous in my chalet, but rather damp, & as I have just finished my quartet I am staying here for a few days. (Perhaps you don't know that I am at the moment at my uncle's in Paris) Please write to Ville d'Avray. I wish you & your dear wife a merry Christmas & *many* more New Years. Farewell & I hope to see you again soon.

Yours
Fritz Delius

Write a few lines soon. I think the only improvement that Christ & Christianity have brought with them is Christmas. As people really then think a little about others. Otherwise I feel that he had better not have lived at all. The world has not got any better, but worse & more hypocritical, & I really believe that Christianity has produced an overall sub-mediocrity & really only taught people the meaning of fear.

Farewell, dear Grieg.

Autograph letter, signed and undated, written in German on notepaper headed 23 RUE CHAUCHAT (crossed out by Delius).

The original is in the Bergen Public Library.

1   Only two movements of this early string quartet survive intact in the Delius Trust Archive. Delius had already mentioned the piece to Sinding, who wrote from Leipzig on 27 November: 'You are indeed a real devil for work. In addition to all you've already done this year – another quartet for strings. How did you hit upon this idea? I shall be very glad to see it if you send it here, and I shall do everything to get Brodsky to accept it.' Delius complied with his friend's request, and on 22 December Sinding acknowledged receipt of the work: it looked 'damned good', but Brodsky could not rehearse it before Easter. Sinding further commented, 'you have made quite a few errors of notation in it, and some stoppings are impossible to execute. For instance you have a few thirds

which have to be played on the same string.' Grieg, writing on 30 December, commented eloquently, 'And you have written a string quartet! What a wonderful time is this time of youth, when it just pours out of one's heart in one long stream!'

(16)
Fritz Delius to Edvard Grieg

Chalet des Lilas
à la Chaumière
Ville d'Avray
(Seine & Oise)
[31? December 1888]

My dear Grieg,

Just a few words to say "Happy New Year" to you & your wife & to wish & hope that you will enjoy very good health through the coming year, both of you. How time passes! a whole year has gone by since we were together at my place on the 4th floor in Harkortstrasse & drank Benedictine punch & the ringing of bells filled the room when we all clinked glasses, & we shall, I know, be together at many more New Years.[1] Let's see now whether I am not right. I might almost go so far as to say that I would eat "Beckling"[2] with pleasure if only I were up there in the North with you now. It is not impossible that I shall meet you in London "Beginning of February", didn't you say? & not impossible too that you may get to hear my symphonic poem "Hiawatha".[3] I have written to Herr Manns about it,[4] & I should very much like you to hear it. I am about to start on something about which I shall write rather later. In the meantime accept my very best wishes & give my kindest regards to Frau Grieg

Yours
Fritz Delius

Autograph letter, signed and undated, written in German.

The original is in the Bergen Public Library.

1 Grieg, too, was in a reminiscent mood when he wrote from Bergen to Johan Halvorsen on 31 December: 'I remembered too that last, splendid Christmas Eve we had together in Leipzig. That was surely once and for all. But – never mind! we'll fix a summer evening at Troldhaugen instead. Delius is coming. Sinding, don't know. . . . And Halvorsen will come too!' (autograph letter in the Bergen Public Library, written in Norwegian; 'never mind' is in English).

2 *Bøkling*: a type of smoked herring, whose strong flavour was evidently not to Delius's taste.

3   *Hiawatha*, 'a tone poem for Orchestra after Longfellow's poem'. The MS is dated '1888 Januar' and could well have been studied by Grieg in Leipzig.

4   Manns did not mention *Hiawatha* in his letter to Delius of 14 March 1889 (see Letter 19).

1889

Having spent Christmas and the New Year at his uncle's apartment in Paris, Delius returned to Ville d'Avray. He was now spending a great deal of his time with Arve Arvesen, his friend from Leipzig days, who was studying the violin in Paris. In March he took a break in Bradford and Ilkley, travelling to Manchester for a reunion with Grieg, who was performing in that city. He failed in an attempt to get an orchestral work at last performed, as *Florida* was rejected by August Manns, conductor of the Crystal Palace Concerts.

Returning to Paris in April, Delius again stayed briefly with his uncle before spending a few final weeks at his cottage at Ville d'Avray. According to a much later memoir of his, he left France on 20 June for a major tour of Norway, which was to include a stay at Arve Arvesen's family home at Hamar, visits to Christiania and Bergen – where he stayed at Troldhaugen with the Griegs – and an August tramp through the Jotunheim mountain region with Grieg and Sinding.

He was back in Paris in September, in time to visit the Universal Exhibition, and staying once again with his uncle. In the middle of October he moved to an apartment at Croissy-sur-Seine, where, once established, he was soon hard at work on composition.

Sakuntala, for tenor and orchestra (Drachmann) (RT III/2).

Seven Songs from the Norwegian (RT V/9). Nos. 1, 2, 3 and 7 completed; no. 4 begun.

Florida suite (RT VI/1). Revision of two movements.

Romance, for violin (RT VIII/2).

Two piano pieces (RT IX/5).

Idylle de Printemps, for orchestra (RT VI/5).

'Small piece', composed jointly by Grieg, Sinding and Delius (RT X(i)3). Jotunheim, c. August 1889.

Draft orchestral piece (RT X(ii)3). 'Aug. 1889, Leirungs Hytte, Jotunheim, Norge'. Incomplete.

'Chanson de Fortunio', song (Musset) (RT V/8). November.

Norwegian Bridal Procession (comp. Grieg) (RT X(i)2). Orchestrated by Delius in December.

Suite d'Orchestre (RT VI/6). May 1889. This includes 'Marche Caprice', revised in 1890.

[*Norwegian*] *Sleigh Ride* (RT VI/7). Orchestrated.

(17)
Fritz Delius to Edvard Grieg

Chalet des Lilas
à la Chaumière
Ville d'Avray
(Seine & Oise)
[January 1889]

My dear Grieg,

I was delighted with In Autumn, really delighted, & thank you very much for it: I was tremendously interested to look at the work in score form & how I should love to hear it: Many thanks too for P V. The songs can wait up there until I fetch them, I am in no hurry: I am very sorry that you have taken so much trouble about them; had I known this, I wouldn't have written to you about them, for whether I have them now or in 6 months' time is immaterial. The Tannhäuser score must be colossally interesting & I will be mindful to take a good look at it. That one can call a lovely Christmas present. I am delighted with Dr Abraham.[1] Please give him my regards. Just you come to Paris & try at least to get rid of your stomach complaint. Paris is splendid for stomach complaints & some very famous specialists live here. You must come; you won't regret it. I have a proposition to make: come here at the beginning of May; then we will see the World Exhibition as well; afterwards I shall travel to the North with you. But if you cannot wait so long, come as soon as you can & I promise to show you things which are really *only* to be seen here. Please write & tell me if you can come. Latterly I too have not been well & little inclined to work. Please give my regards to your wife & let me hear very soon from you with best wishes

Yours
Fritz Delius

Have you read "Brand" by Ibsen & "Beyond Our Power" by Bjornsen?[2] What a different interpretation of the same material. In my opinion Ibsen is one of the greatest minds of this century, if not *the greatest*. He is the *only one* who handles the Christian religion & its history without kid gloves & says what he really feels without beating about the bush & without regard for anything at all.

Autograph letter, signed and undated, written in German.

The original is in the Bergen Public Library.

1   Dr Max Abraham (1831–1900): head of the music-publishing house of C. F. Peters, and thus Grieg's publisher. Grieg had written to Delius on 30 December: 'Just imagine what Dr. Abraham has sent me: the score of *Tannhäuser* autographed by Wagner, (only exists in a few copies) but not only that, for this copy is a present from Wagner to a friend of his youth. Not only has he written in it himself, but drawn a picture of himself as a young man on the title-page.'

2   Grieg replied from Leipzig on 4 February: 'You ask me if I have read Brand. 20 years ago! And "Beyond Our Power"! too and I think about 5 years ago, when it came out. It is a work conceived in genius, but in its execution nothing like as superior as Ibsen in his dramas. His latest work is "The Woman from the Sea", an original, characteristically Ibsen thing, which must have a tremendous effect on the stage. And the strangest thing is: It has a mystical, almost romantic keynote, which is certainly at least influenced by Hypnotism.'
Delius's idiosyncratic spelling of Bjørnson's name persisted and has found its way into most of the published versions of his Bjørnson song settings.

(18)
Fritz Delius to Edvard Grieg

43 Rue Cambon
Paris.
[February 1889]

My dear Grieg

I was delighted with your letter: that you are well & had such great joy & success in Berlin. If one asks oneself just once?; What have the critics ever done that is great or good one must honestly say, Nothing, & they therefore have no significance: perhaps an apparent one but certainly not a real one.[1] It is like the gravy from a good roast hare, if it is good you leave it & eat it with the other meat, but if it is bad you can pour it away. The roast hare itself is always there. When I read about your dinner at the Panorama, the whole scene came back to me again, I played whist again, drank Benedictine & joined in our walks together along the Promenade.[2] What wonderful memories. Last Saturday Arvesen a violinist, & Soot[3] a Norwegian painter came to me at Ville d'Avray. We played your C minor sonata together, which also brought back many memories to me. At midnight we took a walk in the woods, there was very beautiful moonlight & a hard frost. I am now staying in Paris again for a few days to get rid of my cold, & am much better. I am looking forward to our meeting in Norway as never before. I should think it is quite certain that Sinding will come too. Yes, as you said, it is marvellous that he has had such a brilliant success, & it is also marvellous that you have done what you write to me about.[4] That is what I love about you Grieg & you do not know how highly I esteem you for such an act. I believe too that his success will have a great influence on his whole career. If only he can get an Author's Pension![5] I shall acquire Tolstoi's work.[6] If you have not yet read it, please buy *"The Conventional Lies"* by *Max Nordau*[7] right away. You *must* read the work, it is magnificent. Perhaps I am crazy, but I am writing incidental music for Emperor & Galilean.[8] I believe I shall work quietly in Ville d'Avray until, døde piene,[9] I sit myself down on the steamer to Norway.

I hope that your wife is better now. Was it the same kind of attack as she had in Leipzig? These damned Authorities always make me angry when I hear about them. They act as if they could do heaven only knows what & at the end they can do nothing. Find out oneself what one can & cannot put up with, live moderately, eat little meat, lots of fish & vegetables & I think one would seldom need a doctor. For these learned gentlemen only look wise & try one thing & another, until they try you into the grave itself. Adieu dear Grieg. Give my kind regards to your wife & Sinding as well, I will be writing to him too as soon as possible

Yours
Fritz Delius

Autograph letter, signed and undated, written in German.

The orginal is in the Bergen Public Library.

1   Grieg had taken part in two Philharmonic Concerts in Berlin on 21 and 29 January. The works of his that were given were *In Autumn*, the first *Peer Gynt* suite, the *Elegiac Melodies* for string orchestra, op. 34, and the Piano Concerto, with Erika Nissen as soloist. In fact, the critics had generally been appreciative after the first concert, and unreservedly so after the performance of the concerto in the second. But they clearly did not attain to that almost ecstatic enthusiasm usually recorded by Grieg's English reviewers.

2   Following the Berlin concerts, the Griegs had spent a fortnight in Leipzig, eating and drinking, as Grieg wrote to Delius on 4 February, 'good roast hare and bad red wine'.

3   Eyolf Soot (1858–1928): Norwegian painter. He studied with Bonnat in Paris in the early 1880s and painted in the St Cloud area, not far from Ville d'Avray, around this period. He had studied in Christiania, Berlin and Munich, and an interest shared

with Delius would have been the United States, where he had spent his childhood and adolescence.

4   Grieg applied in February 1889 to the Norwegian Parliament for an Artist's (or Author's) Pension (*Digtergage*) for Sinding, so that the latter might devote his entire time to composition. The main grant was not forthcoming, but the Parliamentary Grants and Pensions Committee was to agree in June that Sinding should instead receive a State Stipendium of 1500 kroner annually for two years (Rugstad, p. 58).

5   *Dichter Gage* in the original letter.

6   Grieg had asked if Delius had read Tolstoy's 'On Life'; an edition of this work was published under the title 'Über das Leben' in Leipzig in 1889.

7   Max Simon Nordau (1859–1923): born of Jewish descent in Budapest. Initially a physician, his *Conventional Lies of Society* (1883), a refutation of current ethical, religious and political principles, brought him a considerable renown. Two further works, *Paradoxes* (1886) and *Degeneration* (1893), also made a significant impact in their time.

8   *Emperor and Galilean* (1873), Ibsen's huge drama. Nothing remains of Delius's project.

9   *by Jove*. In Norwegian in the original letter (but more properly *død og pine*).

(19)
August Manns to Fritz Delius

TELEPHONE, NO.   *Crystal Palace Company*,
9320.   *Crystal Palace, S.E.*
                                                       March 14. 1889

Dear Mr Delius!

I examind my work now before me carefully last night, and found that I and my Orchestra are so very much required for all sorts of necessary work in connection with performances, that we cannot spare any time for rehearsing Music which is not required by the general daily Entertainments. Under these circumstances it seems best that I should send you your Florida at once.

    – Score and Parts will leave here this afternoon, and ought to reach you early tomorrow, Friday.

    I shall have a little more time in May and June for taking up MS works.

    With best wishes
    Yours sincerely
    August Manns

Mr Fritz Delius

Autograph letter, signed and dated, written in English on headed notepaper.

The original is in the Delius Trust Archive. One other letter written by Manns is preserved in the Archive; dated 15 June 1899, it is addressed to the Concorde Concert Control (see Letter 102, note 2).

Delius was now in England, and it seems that he attended the Philharmonic Society's concert in London on 14 March, when Grieg conducted some of his *Peer Gynt* music. Evidence is supplied in a letter from Grieg dated 24 February and in an invitation dated 14 March to Delius to visit him. While in London, Grieg again stayed in Clapham, at the home of his publisher's London agent, Augener (see Letter 6, note 1). Delius returned to Paris in April, staying initially with his uncle.

(20)
Christian Sinding to Fritz Delius

Leipzig 15 April 89.

Dear friend,

I am sorry now to have to return your string quartet unrehearsed. Brodsky and his colleagues have really been exceptionally busy all the time and have not been able to play it. And now Nováček[1] the viola player is going to Marienbad as leader of the Spa Orchestra. Rehearsals will therefore not be resumed until after the summer holidays. You can send the manuscript direct to Brodsky. I don't like to leave it behind, because I am going to Norway myself tonight and Brodsky is setting off for Russia afterwards. I have read through the quartet several times with great interest. It must sound very well – but it struck me that in some places you show far too little consideration for the instruments. You have even done some absolutely impossible things. I have altered a few places in the parts, as you wanted me to, because I hoped to be able to get a run-through for you. Look and see if you agree. But there are a few other things too. Do let Arvesen play through the parts. I lay emphasis on making the passages and chords as playable as possible, because I know what people are. There is always a certain prejudice against new things, and a couple of impossible chords are jumped at as a means of getting away from it. In this respect Brodsky is admittedly an exception, but still it is always better if the parts are correct.

I am having Grieg over this evening, and then I leave at 4 o'clock in the morning.

Yours   Christian Sinding

c/o Advokat G.Th. Mejdell,[2] Christiania
Norway.

Autograph letter, signed and dated, written in German. Envelope addressed: Monsieur / Fritz Delius / Chalet des Lilas / à la Chaumière/ Ville d'Avray / (Seine & Oise). Postmark: LEIPZIG 15 4 89. Receiving postmark: VILLE D'AVRAY 17 AVRIL 89.

The original is in the Delius Trust Archive.

1   Ottokar Nováček (1866–1900): Hungarian violinist and composer. He had been a fellow-student of Delius at Leipzig and was a sometime member of the Brodsky Quartet.

2   Glør Thorvald Mejdell: Sinding's brother-in-law. Himself a cousin of the Sindings, he had married Christian's sister Thora Catrine. A lawyer and a writer, he did a great deal to help the composer and his artist brothers, Otto and Stephan. In a letter to Delius dated 18 November 1890, Mejdell was to discuss his recent book, *Independence*, mentioning at the same time that he was writing another, *Man and Woman*.

(21)
Christian Sinding to Fritz Delius

Skisstad, Naesodden near Christiania   20 May 89

Dear friend,

Do forgive me – I was convinced that I had replied to your last letter right away. I did write, I know that much, but must have forgotten to post the letter: it is not the first time that this sort of thing has happened to me.

I can't say how much I am looking forward to our trip,[1] and even more so because I still don't know my own native country at all. Only one thing – I can't leave here as early as the middle of June, because first I have to earn some cash for the fare by manufacturing songs and piano pieces. I therefore prefer your first plan – to start off in the middle of July. Have also told Grieg that we'll arrive about this time, and he agrees. I have been asked to send you best wishes from him and his wife. They spent 2 days in Christiania passing through, and both looked very well. – Busoni[2] has written to tell me that he would like to come too, and Johan Svendsen[3] also intends to come. But Grieg was afraid it may get too uncomfortable to undertake the tramp through the Jotunheim if the party becomes too large. – My Author's Pension seems to be out of the question for the time being, but I'll probably get a two-year allowance. – I expect to have to stay in Norway until Christmas but I don't know anything for certain. – The summer is already here, and I have begun to bathe and enjoy life.

Remember me to Arvesen.

Yours –
Christian Sinding

Autograph letter, signed and dated, written in German. It had a chequered history
before reaching Delius: the envelope, which has survived and was originally addressed
to Monsieur / Fritz Delius / Chalet des Lilas / Ville d'Avray / Seine & Oise, was
readdressed to 43, rue Cambon, Paris. It also bears a printed stamp, MISSENT TO
NEW YORK. U.S.A. JUN 8 89, and has on its reverse a receiving postmark: VILLE
D'AVRAY 17 JUIN 89.

The original is in the Delius Trust Archive.

1   In correspondence with Grieg and Sinding, Delius was planning the summer's
Norwegian tour, which was to include his first visit to the Jotunheim.

2   Ferruccio Benvenuto Busoni (1866–1924): Italian composer, conductor, pianist
and teacher. Like Delius, he went to Leipzig in 1886, where the two students got to
know each other well. By now he was already a pianist of note.

3   Johan Severin Svendsen (1840–1911): Norwegian composer and conductor. He
studied in Leipzig in the mid-1860s. Like Grieg, he was one of the first Norwegian
composers to sound a genuinely national note in his music; unlike Grieg, he was
considered to achieve his best work in the larger forms, notably in two symphonies.
Best known for his *Carnaval à Paris*, Svendsen did, however, write a wide range of works
on a smaller scale. Any acquaintance he may have had with Delius is not documented.
Neither Svendsen nor Busoni were able to take part in the summer's walking tour.

(22)
Fritz Delius to Edvard Grieg

43, *Rue Cambon*
Paris
[early June 1889]

My dear, good Grieg

Your kind note made me feel happy: but you can't be happier than I am. For
months now our meeting in Glorious Norway has been my be all & end all.
How I long once again to wipe all the dust & dirt from my feet, & to set foot on
the fresh, fragrant moorland! How splendid if we can live for a while in this hut
& enjoy something of the uncivilized life. I will of course come direct to Bergen
from Christiania by sea & not overland.[1] It is a bit far to go via Hamburg from
here – but one can travel quite well via Havre or Amsterdam. I expect to travel
from here in about 10 to 14 days' time & spend a day or two in Christiania &
then stay in Hamar[2] for a few days with Arvesen the violinist. Then I shall go
direct to Bergen via Christiania &, if all goes well, arrive in the middle of July.[3]
I am just reading Peer Gynt for the 5th time, this time however in Norwegian
with the help of a dictionary, & am making good progress. Is Olaf Trygvason a
new dramatic work? I only know Landkennung,[4] although I have never heard

it. Where is the performance to take place? Just now I am busy with your C minor sonata (violin). I am going to play the first & second movements with Arvesen. It is already going well. This is a splendid work & the better I get to know it the more I like it. I myself have not been lazy. I have sketched out something from Emperor & Galilean. Then a little Suite d'orchestre in 5 movements[5] – Marche, Berceuse, Sckerzo, Duo & Tema con Var^{en}, which has come off quite well. Then I am completely revising my Florida Suite & have finished two of the main movements. It was clumsily done with many unnecessary orchestral brutalities in it. Only here do I feel I have really learnt how to orchestrate. I hope you & your wife will gladden me with your new songs. Farewell, dear Grieg, & my kind regards to your dear wife. Looking forward to the pleasure of seeing you again in the near future

Yours
Fritz Delius

Autograph letter, signed and undated, written in German on headed notepaper.

The original is in the Bergen Public Library.

1   Grieg had written on 1 June from Bergen to tell Delius that a Christiania friend, Professor Nicolaysen, had offered the party the use of his hut on Lake Gjendin in the Jotunheim. In that letter Grieg also offered considered advice on how to travel to Bergen.

2   Arvesen's family home was in the small town of Hamar, some 100 kilometres north of Christiania.

3   Sinding and Delius were consulting carefully on their arrangements: 'I shall be at Grieg's at Troldhaugen on the 15 July,' wrote Sinding from Christiania on 12 June. 'He wrote to tell me that he had advised you to go direct to Bergen. But if you can come here it will give me enormous pleasure.' By the time Grieg wrote to Dr Abraham on 13 July, all arrangements had been confirmed: 'The day after tomorrow Sinding and Delius are coming, a few days later Augener and then we are off by way of Laerdal to the mountains and Jotunheim' (cf. Elsa v. Zschinsky-Troxler, ed. *Edvard Grieg: Briefe an die Verleger der Edition Peters 1866–1907.* C. F. Peters, [Leipzig: 1932] p.26). For Delius's account of the tour, see Appendix IV and V.

4   *Landkennung (Landkjending)*: Grieg's op. 31, for male chorus and orchestra.

5   Of this *Suite d'Orchestre* (1889), only the first movement mentioned has so far been published, under the title *Marche Caprice*, in the version revised in 1890.

(23)
Edvard Grieg to Fritz Delius

Christiania, 6th October
1889

Dear Delius,

I have *three* letters from you, but not one contains what I deserved to hear: that I am a silly ass, who has not yet replied. So you are working again at full pressure! Well, one ought to work while the pressure is on. I imagine that the pressure will produce something à la Jotunheim. I have been here for 2 days and am preparing several things for performance, among them the Scenes from Olav Trygvason on the 19th. There will be a repeat on the 27th and then on the 15th November in Copenhagen. After that on to Brussels, where I have 3 concerts at the beginning of December. I come to Paris in the middle of January or a little later. Then in the middle of February to Stuttgart and afterwards Prague. As you see, I am using to the full the strength I gained in the Jotunheim. I have a frightful lot to do here, but I have the strength and so it should be alright. But most of all I should like to be, like you, in some quiet village, just to work! Oh well: the time must come. Then we shall go walking and philosophizing again!

Yours
Edvard Grieg.

I spoke to Sinding yesterday. All's well with him. He is going to Leipzig in November.

Autograph letter, signed and dated, written in German. Envelope addressed: Mr. Fritz Delius. / Croissy / Seine & Oise / 8 Bould de la Mairie / *France*. As with many of Delius's letters, the removal of the postage stamp has obscured the postmark. A receiving postmark, partially obscured, shows that the letter was received in SEINE ET OISE on 11 OCT.

The original is in the Delius Trust Archive.

(24)
Fritz Delius to Gertrude Rueckert

8 Bd de la Mairie.
Croissy (S & O) France
[7 December 1889]

My dear Miss Gertrude,

Just a few words to wish you a happy Christmas & a happy new year. How are you all getting on over in Danville? I should be very happy to receive a few words from you. Since a 1½ years I am living near Paris & like it very much. The Exhibition[1] is just over & was a great success. Do you keep up your music yet or have "Whispering Winds" whispered away into Ewigkeit? I may possibly pay a visit to America next year, if so I hope I shall have the pleasure of seeing you all again. Give my kindest regards to your father & mother. Does your father play as much as ever?

With kindest regards
sincerely yours
Fritz Delius

Greetings card, signed and undated, written in English. On the front of the card, which bears a flower design, Delius wrote 'Miss Gertrude'. Envelope addressed: Miss Gertrude Rückert / % Fred Rückert Esqre / Danville / Virginia / Etats Unis d'Amerique. A partially obscured SEINE ET OISE postmark bears the date 7 DEC. Readdressed: 1740 – 14th St, N,W, Washington D,C, the envelope bears a receiving postmark: WASHINGTON DEC 23 89.

The original is in the Delius Trust Archive.

1 Delius was back in Paris in September and visited the Universal Exhibition with his uncle Theodor. He moved to Croissy-sur-Seine around the end of the month, renting an apartment on the Boulevard de la Mairie.

1890

By 1890, as one perceptive onlooker put it, one had to be an Eskimo to succeed in Paris,* at least as far as the somewhat disgruntled indigenous artistic community was concerned. The city was full of Scandinavians – painters, writers, composers, performers – and it seemed that Delius was getting to know most of them. He certainly spent a hard-working winter at Croissy, but during the year his circle of acquaintances was clearly expanding and his social life was stimulated accordingly. It was around this time that he first came to know Edvard Munch. Grieg was in Paris in January (furnishing Delius, incidentally, with a letter of introduction to Vincent d'Indy), and Arve Arvesen was still there. Delius also associated with the Norwegian composer Johan Selmer, and his friendship with the Danish writer Helge Rode is first documented this year. More significantly, he had now got to know William Molard, half-Norwegian, half-French, an aspiring composer who was gathering around himself a wide-ranging circle of mainly Scandinavian friends and acquaintances in the city.

Although Delius appears to have spent the spring largely at home, he made excursions to Paris and to the surrounding countryside, for he was a great explorer and never happier than when alone with nature. 'I go for long walks every day & am remarkably well & fresh,' he wrote to Grieg on 1 April. Around the end of May he undertook a trip to Leipzig, which was to last for more than three weeks, and while there he again met Sinding, Selmer and the conductor Iver Holter, among others. In Leipzig he also took the opportunity to conduct some of his works informally with a rehearsal orchestra. The summer he spent mainly in Jersey, Normandy and Brittany, in spite of exhortations from Norwegian friends to join them in the mountains: 'How sad', wrote Grieg on 11 August, 'that you are not coming to the Jotunheim.' As in the summer of 1888, he found himself working particularly well while staying in the St Malo area.

Delius returned to Croissy in the middle of October, and again settled down to work. His considerable output during these early years after Leipzig is

---

* Kjell Strömberg, *Svenskarna i Frankrike* (Örebro: 1953), p. 58.

testimony to the fact that he was learning his craft thoroughly. And now, at least, he was a published composer; for Augener, in London, had issued his *Five Songs from the Norwegian*.

Seven Songs from the Norwegian (RT V/9). Nos. 4, 5 and 6 completed by or in 1890.

Irmelin, opera (RT I/2). Begun.

Three Small Tone Poems (RT VI/7). The 1889 orchestration of *Sleigh Ride* is included in a MS. dated 1890, which contains two further pieces, *Summer Evening* and *Spring Morning*.

A l'Amore, orchestral fragment (RT VI/8) (1890?)

Petite Suite d'Orchestre (RT VI/9).

Légendes (*Sagen*), for piano and orchestra (RT VII/2). Draft incomplete.

Two piano pieces (RT IX/5). Completed 1890?

'Skogen gir susende, langsom besked', song (Bjørnson) (RT V/10). 1890 or 1891.

Four Heine Songs (RT V/11). Begun.

Paa Vidderne, symphonic poem (RT VI/10). Begun.

(25)
Fritz Delius to Johan Selmer

8 B^d de la Mairie
Croissy (S & O)
le 9 Avril 90.

My dear Selmer,

Through Molard[1] I have had the opportunity to see one of your scores, "The Spirit of the North"[2] & I have taken the liberty to take it home to get better acquainted with it. The work pleases me enormously & must make a great impression & I would like hereby to express to you my great admiration for your masterly score.

  With kind regards
  Yours sincerely
  Fritz Delius

Autograph letter, signed and dated, written in German.

The original is in the Oslo University Library, Oslo, Norway, where one other letter from Delius to Selmer is preserved (see Letter 26).

Johan Peter Selmer (1844–1910): Norwegian composer and conductor, generally considered to have been first exponent of programme music in his country. He was a pupil of Ambroise Thomas in Paris and of Richter and Paul in Leipzig. Among his colourful orchestral works, in which the influence of Berlioz is discernible, are the *Carneval flamand*, *Prometheus* and *Nordisk Festtog (Nordic Festival Procession)*. As a result of his having taken part in the Commune uprising in 1871, a year which inspired his *Scène funèbre* (*L'Année terrible*), op. 4, he was forced to flee to Norway. Now, however, he was once again living and working for a time in Paris.

1   William Molard (1862–1937): French civil servant and composer. Married to the Swedish sculptress Ida Ericson (1853–1927), he was part-Norwegian by descent. As a composer, his expenditure of effort seems to have been sporadic, if not desultory: 'The whole of his life he worked on incidental music to Hamlet. It is said that when on one occasion he was going to get the work performed, all the parts were different, making it impossible to play' (Almqvist, p. 8). The Molards' studio, in the rue Vercingétorix in Montparnasse, was very much a centre for Scandinavian artists as well as for friends from many other countries; among the frequent visitors during the 1890s were Delius, Gauguin, Strindberg and Munch. It is unlikely that Delius had known Molard for very long when this letter was written, since this appears to be the earliest reference to their friendship. Much later (in 1908?), it seems that a 'Marche Nuptiale' by Molard, dedicated to his stepdaughter, Judith, was performed in England at Delius's expense (cf. Almqvist, pp. 8–9).

2   *Nordens Aand*, op. 5 (1872). This was among the works performed at the Nordic Music Festival in Copenhagen in 1888.

(26)
Fritz Delius to Johan Selmer

Café de la Régence [Paris]
le 18 Avril 90.

My dear friend,

I unfortunately missed my train & only arrived at the Café de la Regence at 7.10. You had just left. I went to the 10 Marmites & then came back here hoping to find you I brought your Scène Funèbre[1] & also some of my own music & will give it you on Sunday instead. I should like immensely to hear your Scène Funèbre. It must make a grand effect. As it is I can only get half an idea of your worth. I think your orchestration is admirable.

   With kindest regards to you & your wife

   Believe me
   Sincerely yours
   Fritz Delius

Autograph letter, signed and dated, written in English.

The original is in the Oslo University Library.

1   See Letter 25, note.

(27)

Fritz Delius to Edvard Grieg

8 B^d de la Mairie
le 26 Mai 90.
Croissy (S & O)

My dear Grieg

I suppose you will be in Troldhaugen again now: I hope that you and your wife
are well. I am sending with this post a volume of songs.[1] In a few days I am
going to Leipzig for a couple of weeks in order to hear various things there You
will probably be doing a lot of bathing & fishing now. I have got a devilish
wanderlust again & would like to see the sea again. Farewell, my dear Grieg. I
am sending a few lines herewith to your wife.

> Yours
> Fritz Delius

Please give Franz Beyer my best wishes ogsaa hans Kone.[2] I shall send him a
volume of songs too.
> If you have time, write me a few lines
> Poste Restante
> Leipzig

Autograph letter, signed and dated, written in German.

The original is in the Bergen Public Library.

1   *Five Songs from the Norwegian*, published in London by Augener in 1890.

2   *also his wife*. In Norwegian in the original letter.

(28)

Fritz Delius to Nina Grieg

Croissy le 26 Mai 90
8 B^d de la Mairie

My dear Frau Grieg

I am sending you today an album of songs:[1] You know them already. I have
taken the liberty of dedicating the album to you & I should like at the same

time to express my thanks for all those lovely days we have enjoyed together. When I first became acquainted with Grieg's music, it was not only that it made a deep impression on me, it was as if I was hearing something quite new, a curtain went up. So it was too when I heard you sing. I had never heard anyone sing like you, it was also something quite new to me. My very best wishes to you, Frau Grieg. With kind regards I remain

>   Yours sincerely
>   Fritz Delius

Cordial greetings to your sister[2]

Autograph letter, signed and dated, written in German at the same time as (and enclosed with) Delius's letter to Grieg of the same date.

The original is in the Bergen Public Library.

1   Nina replied from Troldhaugen on 6 June to thank Delius for the 'beautiful' songs, adding, 'Good that you are going to Leipzig again, I have always thought that it was a little too lonely for you in Croissy. I do not know if this was really the case, but at the time in Paris I definitely had that impression.'

2   Tony Hagerup: Nina Grieg's sister, who often lived with the Griegs at Troldhaugen.

(29)
Johan Selmer to Fritz Delius

Leipzig-Gohlis, den 21/6 1890

My dearest freind & collegue

I hope you do not feel to much offended by my behaviour today.[1] Trusting in your friendship and noble colligality I dared to do it.

You see — as I have explained — Mr Jason[2] has years ago promised me a repetition. And you now yourself, whow difficult it is to profit of his promises. It is not *my* mistake, that he had asked me to be here at 11 oclock. If I not was obliged to go away tomorrow perhaps (or Thursday), I should'nt have been so interested in this case. I should be very sorry if you do'nt excuse me being such an unagreeable intruder. At least, I hope, that you have not lost *too* much time by my playing my short, modest composition.

>   Dear freind!

>   Summa summarum,
>   "Forgive me!"

But I can scarcely *forgive you*, that you did'nt invite me to hear your orchestra-pieces. I would'not stay without this permission.

Yours
Joh Selmer

Autograph letter, signed and dated, written in English on the headed notepaper of the Restaurant und Café, / Waldschlösschen, / Leipzig-Gohlis.

The original is in the Delius Trust Archive. It is the first of five letters written by Selmer to Delius in 1890 and 1891 and in 1908 that have been preserved.

Both Sinding and Selmer had for some time been encouraging Delius to return to Leipzig. 'Don't lose more time than necessary,' wrote Sinding from Leipzig on 23 May. 'A Wagner cycle has just begun.' Selmer, writing the following day, announced, 'We are waiting for you impatiently. Molard *must not* miss "Meistersinger", which will be given on 30 May.' Whether William Molard actually did accompany his friend has not been established.

1   Delius was indeed offended by Selmer's behaviour. Having arrived in Leipzig, presumably towards the end of May, he arranged to buy some time with a rehearsal orchestra in order to play through some of his music. A letter he sent to Grieg from Jersey some time in July gives the reasons for his understandable pique with Selmer. The original of this letter, which was written in German and is carefully preserved in the Bergen Public Library, is in poor condition and many words are obliterated. However, the following extract will convey its sense:

I wanted to have a rehearsal [. . .] & had to pay 50 marks for it, which is quite a good idea, for one can rehearse better [. . .] I intended to arrange things so that I could rehearse for at least 2½ hours, as I had 5 things to try out. Selmer had already rehearsed a Finnish March or some such thing 2 or 3 times. For all that, he came to me & asked me if he could rehearse his March at my rehearsal, he wanted heaven knows what of it, to make it popular etc! I said no, for I only had time to rehearse my own things. So I went out to Gohlis where [. . .] wanted to play; The orchestra was an hour & a half late & just as I was about to begin, along comes Selmer & asks me if he could play his [. . .] once through. I said "You know what I already told you", so he takes the baton & [. . .] begins to rehearse. Not just playing through, but the violins alone, the violas alone etc, taking 25 minutes of my time which was already short. When he went away he said to me, "You know everyone must fend for himself" Afterwards he wrote me such a creeping letter in which he apologized in such an abject way. It is quite [. . .] that this sort of thing happened for I have never liked him. I was quite contented with my rehearsal, as far as the orchestra was concerned. I just had time to play the things through.

2   Presumably a reference to Salomon Jadassohn (see Letter 5, note 2).

(30)
Gudmund Stenersen to Fritz Delius

Skogadalshø 12.7.90

Dear friend!

I schould try to write in English, but do not know how it will go. Long I have thought to send you some lines to inform you about my voyage home, that was very good, and how I intended to spend the summer. But coming home I found my studio so snug, that it was impossible to leave it; further, my mother and family was very glad to have me home, and then I am first now gone out into the "wide wide world". A little trip with my father to Utladalen and then back to Vik in Sogn will be all my excursions this summer.

The "fører"[1] Sulheim, whom I think you know, promised "very god veir"[2] but veiret had another manner and fog and rain hindered the magnificient views we should have had tant pi.[3] My father is to wit going to take out a saeter for horsebreeding in Utladal and then I think to stay in Skogadalshø for two days hoping for good weather. My sketchbook is longing for the pencil you know, but is impossible to make sketches in rain, though the effects when fog is driving over the "fons"[4] is very pictoresque. I should like very much to stay among those big mountains for a summer to make høifjeld[5] directly after the nature. – And you, what are you doing at Croissy, you work and take from time to time a little trip to Paris. *Come* here and *feel the fresh wind from the fons and be like me a new man.* O, how I cheer. Now I can better understand Ibsens Brand and Peer Gynt, when I have seen those wild tracts, that are knit to his poems it is magnificiently done. Painted? yes I have finished three motivs at Stavanger, with which I am satisfied for the first, as I in those things see, the progress I have done. At Vik I will meet with Gronvold[6] and Frk Steinegger, who have been there already for a long time.

There you have Sulheim [two pen and ink sketches] a type on a Norwegian tindebestiger[7] Hurra! I have seen the blue heaven, and hope but hope.

I hope to see you here in Norway this summer.

Adieu mon chere ami
Au revoir
Ton ami
Gudmund Stenersen.

—
Vik
Sogn

Autograph letter, signed and dated, written in English and containing two pen and ink sketches. Envelope addressed: Mr. Fritz Delius / 8 Boulevard de la Mairie 8 / Croissy

(S S) / Paris. The removal of the postage stamp has obliterated an 1890 postmark, but the receiving postmark is PARIS 20 JUIL 90. On the reverse of the envelope is a crude pen and ink sketch of a mountain peak, and the footnote Envoyé p / Stenersen Vik. Sogn. Norvège.

The original is in the Delius Trust Archive. It is the only extant letter from Stenersen to Delius.

Delius had left Leipzig by early July, travelling to Jersey, where he stayed until the end of the month. Neither Grieg, Sinding nor Stenersen in the event succeeded in persuading him to go to Norway, for, after short intervals in Paris and Croissy, he returned to the northern shores of France, beginning around the middle of August a two months' stay in St Malo. Writing to Grieg on 14 September he related, 'I have been bathing almost the whole summer; here in St Malo it is absolutely splendid & suits me & my work very well. . . . The next time we meet I will really show you something, as I have done a lot: I shall soon publish a further album of songs.'

Gudmund Stenersen (1863–1934): Norwegian painter. He studied under Bonnat (1889–90) and Cormon (1891–2), after which period in Paris he made a study trip to Italy (1893–4). Stenersen was not considered to be a great colourist, but a fine draughtsman and illustrator.

1   guide. In Norwegian in the original letter.

2   weather. In Norwegian in the original letter (veiret means 'the weather').

3   tant pis. Stenersen's French seems to be as erratic as his English.

4   snow-fields. In Norwegian in the original letter.

5   Literally high fell (mountain region). In Norwegian in the original letter.

6   Perhaps Marcus (1845–1929) or Bernt (1859–1923) Grønvold: Norwegian painter brothers. Both studied in Munich, lived mainly in Germany and are represented in Norway's National Gallery.

7   alpinist, mountaineer. In Norwegian in the original letter.

(31)
Edvard Grieg to Fritz Delius

Copenhagen 22nd Decbr
90.
Hotel König v. Dänemark.

Dear Delius,

I have been intending to write for so long and then came your kind letter this evening.[1]

I am very moved — a few hours ago I was told in the street that *Gade*[2] was dead, (he had visited me the day before) I hurried to his home — and there lay the handsome old man, stiff and cold, but he looked gentle and happy. Carried off quite suddenly by a thrombosis. —

I have been travelling for 2 months, conducted a few concerts in Christiania and am now living here quite quietly without giving any public performances. Whether we shall go anywhere south in the spring is still undecided. I should love to hear your overture "På Vidderne" — and what about the opera material?[3] It must surely contain much that is capital. Ibsen is in Munich and has just enriched the world with a play. — It is called: Hedda Gabler and is in some respects a masterpiece, but — too cold and carefully calculated. No matter, it's marvellous that the old man can still produce something of this quality.

Farewell, my dear chap! And a thousand Christmas greetings and New Year dittos from my wife and from your

Edvard Grieg

The new year must see us in Norway, mustn't it?
Write soon!
How are your prospects for the future? I am very eager to hear about them.

Autograph letter, signed and dated, written in German. Envelope addressed: Monsieur Fritz Delius. / 8 B*d* de la Mairie / Croissy / (S & O.) / France. The removal of postage stamps has obliterated a Copenhagen postmark. Receiving postmark: CROISSY 25 DEC 90.

The original is in the Delius Trust Archive.

1   The letter referred to has not survived. It must have contained the first reference by Delius to his having taken up again Ibsen's *Paa Vidderne*, now using it as the inspirational source for a symphonic poem.

2   Niels Wilhelm Gade (1817–90): Danish composer. He succeeded Mendelssohn briefly as conductor at Leipzig after the latter's death. Among his major works are eight symphonies and a number of cantatas and overtures. Grieg had sought out Gade's advice in Copenhagen and had particularly appreciated his encouragement. The strong bond of sympathy had continued, but Grieg tended to disapprove of his mentor's early rejection of a Nordic style, which had led Gade to take a more typically German romantic path in his compositions.

3   The subject is again Ibsen, and Grieg was referring to Delius's apparently abortive project for *Emperor and Galilean*.

(32)
Fritz Delius to Emma Klingenfeld

8 B^d de la Mairie
Croissy (S & O)
France
[c. 1890]

Dear Fräulein,

A short while ago I wrote to Herr Henrik Ibsen on the subject of my plan to adapt *"The Feast at Solhaug"*[1] as a lyric drama. He replied to me saying that I should apply to you & that you own the German publication rights.[2]

I take the liberty herewith of asking if you will permit me to adapt your translation to music. I could arrange to be in Munich for a short time to discuss it with you, should you feel it possible to agree to my proposal.

I remain,
Yours faithfully
Fritz Delius

Autograph letter, signed and undated, written in German.

The original is in the Oslo University Library. No further correspondence between Delius and Emma Klingenfeld has been found.

Emma Klingenfeld (1848–1935): Ibsen's German translator. Nuremberg-born, she also translated from Danish, Swedish and French. Her version of *The Feast at Solhaug* was published in Leipzig in 1888.

1 There is some evidence in one of Delius's surviving notebooks and in a draft of a choral song that the composer had experimented at some stage (or stages) between 1887 and 1890 with *Solhaug* material. However, since Hugo Wolf was actually commissioned to write incidental music to *Das Fest auf Solhaug*, completing it between 1890 and 1891, it seems likely that Delius was refused permission by Klingenfeld herself. On the other hand, she was later to collaborate with him by undertaking the German translation of his opera *The Magic Fountain*.

2 Ibsen's letter does not appear to have survived.

1891

A second busy winter in Croissy was rounded off by a visit in March to Bradford and London. From April to June, Delius remained based at Croissy, but then gave up his apartment there to travel once again to Norway, where he had arrived by early July. In the meantime, his Norwegian friends in Paris now included Bergliot, daughter of Bjørnstjerne Bjørnson. Delius's acquaintance with her, at a time when she was studying singing with Mathilde Marchesi, resulted in an invitation to spend a week at her father's home at Aulestad.

In the event, Delius spent four months in Norway. He visited the Griegs and the Bjørnsons; undertook another mountain tour, with Iver Holter as a travelling companion for part of the time; had a long, if interrupted, stay at Fredriksvaern at the mouth of the Christiania Fjord, where in their turn the Griegs visited him and where he also enjoyed the companionship of the painter Hjalmar Johnsen. At the same time he developed a warm friendship with Randi Blehr, wife of the Norwegian prime minister. During the winter he had completed his symphonic poem (or 'concert overture') *Paa Vidderne*. The fact that Holter had agreed to perform it would have been one of the main reasons for Delius's protracting his stay in Norway at least until 10 October, when the work was given in Christiania under Holter's baton. Another reason for his long stay may well have been an *affaire de cœur*, hinted at occasionally in the letters of Nina Grieg, who was ever curious to hear about Delius's romantic attachments. It was not until 4 November that he left Norway, returning to Paris via Sweden and Copenhagen, where he took the opportunity to spend an evening with the author Helge Rode.

On his return to Paris, Delius probably stayed for a short time with his uncle before moving into a small rented apartment in the rue Ducouëdic, in the Petit Montrouge quarter. For the next few years this was to be his main home. Once again he settled down to the city's musical life, and at Christmas he wrote to the Griegs that the season's concerts were the best yet: 'Lamoureux twice gave a symphonic poem by Richard Strauss, there were splendid things in it but some frightful echoes too of the Tannhäuser Bacchanalia. It was *Don Juan*.'

Irmelin, opera (RT I/2). Continued.

Four Heine Songs (RT V/11). Completed.

Maud, five songs for tenor and orchestra (Tennyson) (RT III/3).

Three Shelley Songs (RT V/12).

'Lyse Naetter', song (Drachmann) (RT V/13).

Paa Vidderne (RT VI/10). Revised.

(33)
Iver Holter to Fritz Delius

Kristiania 19/3 91

My dear Delius,

I just don't know how I can possibly find an excuse for myself. I had better leave it because there simply isn't one, and my only hope is that I can proclaim with Tannhäuser: "der Gnade Heil ward dem Büsser beschieden" when I ask you sincerely to forgive me. But you must not think that I have not written because I did not like your overture; this is not so. On the contrary I have a very good impression of the overture, which for one thing will sound good, and for another is musically both interesting and beautiful. In spite of this I have not been able to perform it this season; it arrived too late for the last concert before Christmas, and since Christmas we have only had two large concerts, one of them was completely rearranged because of Gade's death, and for the last concert we had decided on a large choral work, Te Deum, by Anton Bruckner, which would exclude any other new music. May I now keep the score and the parts until the autumn? I shall then have it performed at once. –

How are you otherwise? I hope we shall see each other this summer, don't you? We shall take up the overture then.

Sinding is soon coming home.

With kind regards

Yours
Iver Holter

Autograph letter, signed and dated, written in German.

The original is in the Delius Trust Archive. It is the first of two letters written by Holter to Delius that have been preserved; the second is dated 1902.

Iver Holter (1850–1941): Norwegian conductor and composer. Among his compositions were the symphony in F major and an orchestral suite, *Götz von Berlichingen*. He conducted the Christiania Musikforening from 1886 to 1911 and was to conduct the first full public performance of a Delius orchestral work, the symphonic poem *Paa Vidderne* referred to in this letter, at a concert given by the Society on 10 October 1891. Delius had certainly known him for some time, since Sinding, in a letter dated 29 April 1890, passed on Holter's regards.

(34)
Christian Sinding to Fritz Delius

Christiania 16 April 91
c/o Advokat G. Th. Mejdell, Christiania

Dear friend,

Thanks very much for your letter. Had the best intentions all winter of writing to you, but never got down to it. It's terrible how one's own petty interests claim all one's attention. But I have in fact got through so much that it nearly got too much for me. It's over now though, I've come into somewhat calmer waters, and in the future I shall take care not to venture too far into unknown regions. He who restricts himself reveals himself the master, says our Gehte;[1] I haven't been ready enough to appreciate this. But in one respect it's right: if one wants to accomplish or attain something, one has to be careful not to dissipate one's energies in too many directions. I have always admired you for knowing so well how to keep to your main plan without letting yourself be influenced too much by external circumstances.[2] By God, this is difficult. – As you see, I am now in Norway, and am waiting for the decision of the Storting[3] as to whether I shall get an allowance again. – I don't know yet what I am going to do in the summer. Grieg, who has just arrived, proposes that we all go into the mountains again. The Brodskys will perhaps come here too, and Grieg is naturally anxious to show him the splendours of Norway. I don't know yet if I can take part, as I have awfully much to catch up with so that I'll be prepared for the winter. My chances of making a name for myself have increased so much, in spite of everything, that it is no longer quite impossible. But it is a matter of not losing again what has already been won. So it is possible after all that I shall settle down in peace somewhere to get some work done. – I should very much like to go to Paris next winter, but this depends on how things go for me in the Storting. Have no great desire to return to Germany in any case, it would rather be Vienna. Leipzig and Munich I know almost too well, and Berlin from my stay there last winter. Berlin seems to me smaller and more petty than I had imagined. In spite of its million inhabitants, it really does not make much more of an impression than, say, Leipzig. Gossip flourishes there in the greatest profusion. If somebody farts in the street the whole town knows it at once. In the course of four months I only went to the opera once, to hear Meistersinger,

otherwise there were only two Walküre performances. The rest of the programme was Oberon, Tannhäuser and Lohengrin, and not much else. Bülow
did not have a particularly interesting programme. Only once was I very taken
with a symphonic poem "Tod und Verklärung" by Richard Strauss. That was
grand. I will not even mention his technique of instrumentation etc., but he
had great ideas and an astounding ability to give his ideas form. That impressed
me. I have seldom enjoyed myself so much. – It is strange to see how youth
absorbs almost with its mother's milk what the old ones have achieved with toil
and trouble. And yet the old fools dare to offer advice and give themselves airs
with their authority. One should not live too long. Regards to Arvesen. The
Griegs and Holter ask to be remembered

Yours   Chr. Sinding.

Autograph letter, signed and dated, written in German. Envelope addressed: Monsieur
/ Fritz Delius / 8, Boulevard de la Mairie / Croissy (S. & O.). The removal of postage
stamps has obliterated the postmark. Receiving postmark: CROISSY 19 [AVRIL] 91.
Delius pencilled a list of numbers on the reverse of the envelope.

The original is in the Delius Trust Archive.

1   A misspelling of 'Goethe'.

2   Writing from Bradford to Grieg on 10 March 1891, Delius had confirmed, 'I have
been very busy the whole winter.' He added, 'Really you know very little of mine, apart
from my earliest efforts. I must bring a few scores with me to Norway.'

3   The Norwegian Parliament (see Letter 18, note 4).

(35)
Fritz Delius to Edvard Grieg

Fredrichsvaern [Norway]
16 July 91.

My dear Grieg

I arrived here yesterday from Aulestad[1] where I spent a very pleasant week at
Bjørnsen's. Holter isn't here but on a sailing tour, & I expect him back any day.
I fear that I haven't enough money to come to the Jotunheim with you this year.
Are you quite sure that you are going there? I really don't know what to do. If I
could perhaps spend a few days with you when you come back from the
Jotunheim, then I would stay on here quietly until then. Please write a few
lines to me at Wasilhofs Hotel. I should so much love to see you again & to stay
with you for a while, I have much to tell you & much to show you. Write & tell

me how we can best arrange it,[2] I am staying for a fairly long time in Norway this year in order to hear the overture of mine[3] which Holter wants to perform. Best wishes to you & your wife & Troldhaugen

Yours
Fritz Delius

Wasilhofs Hotel
Fredrichsvaern

The Björnsens send their best wishes & hope to see you soon at Aulestad.

Autograph letter, signed and dated, written in German.

The original is in the Bergen Public Library.

1   Aulestad was the home of Bjørnstjerne Bjørnson, and Delius's visit would have been arranged by the poet's daughter Bergliot.

2   Letters written later in the year show that Delius did link up with the Griegs while in Norway that summer. 'How often I think of our companionship in Fredriksvaern,' wrote Nina Grieg on 16 November, 'it still seems like a fairy tale to me, a wonderful one.' Also at Fredriksvaern Delius met Randi Blehr, wife of the Norwegian prime minister (see Letters 37 and 40).

3   *Paa Vidderne*.

(36)
Fritz Delius to Bjørnstjerne Bjørnson

Troldhaugen
Hop Station
Bergen
le 29 Juillet 91

Dear Mr. Björnsen,

The English flag will very soon arrive at Aulestad, but please use it with care otherwise you will be overrun by English tourists. I will always think back with pleasure on my delightful stay at Aulestad and I thank you and your wife for your kind reception.

With best greetings,
I remain,
Your devoted
Fritz Delius

The Griegs send many greetings[1]

Autograph letter, signed and dated, written in German.

The original is in the Oslo University Library, together with a musical autograph. The latter consists of the first four bars of Delius's setting of Bjørnson's poem 'Skogen gir susende, langsom besked' and is signed *Fritz Delius. Aulestad. le 11 Juillet, 91*. Bjørnson had sent the poem to his daughter in Paris the previous year, on 30 March. Written long before, it had just been found among his papers by his wife. 'Isn't it beautiful?' he wrote to Bergliot. 'Someone should set it to music.' Delius promptly did (cf. Bjørnstjerne Bjørnson, *Aulestad Breve til Bergliot Ibsen* [Kristiania & Copenhagen: Gyldendalske Boghandel, Nordisk Forlag, 1911], p. 151). No further letters between Delius and Bjørnson are believed to exist.

It seems likely that Delius's acquaintance with the Bjørnsons had come about through Arve Arvesen, whose father, a distinguished pedagogue, was a good friend of Bjørnson. Bergliot Bjørnson, at this time studying singing with Mathilde Marchesi, spent a lot of time in Paris with Arvesen junior.

1   Grieg had written to Bjørnson a few days earlier: 'I have just had one of your guests in my home. – The Englishman Delius, a talented and modern musician – something of an idealist. I am now going with him to the Jotunheim' (cf. Gunnar Hauch, ed. *Breve fra Grieg: Et Udvalg* [Copenhagen: Nordisk Forlag, 1922], p. 86; the original letter, dated Troldhaugen, 23 July 1891, may be seen in the Bergen Public Library). Grieg had announced the Jotunheim trip, and the fact that Delius might be accompanying him, in a letter to Dr Abraham dated 11 June 1891. In the event, his travelling companions were Frants Beyer and Julius Röntgen; Delius did not go.

1892

A February visit to London took Delius to the home of the poet Richard Le Gallienne, where the two men sketched out the plot of an opera based on the legend of Endymion. The project was before long abandoned. However, Delius was to complete *Irmelin*, begun some time in 1890, later in the year. By the beginning of March he was back in Paris, renewing contact with Christian Sinding, who had come to stay in the city for a while.

The pattern of alternating summers, in the Brittany/Normandy area and in Norway, continued. Based in St Malo, Delius made a lengthy stay on the coast, to the considerable disappointment of the Griegs, who had hoped to see him at Troldhaugen again. Some time in October he was back in Paris, soon making the acquaintance of Isidore de Lara, an English composer whose star over France was very much in the ascendant and whose social circle was wide and varied. At all events, titled ladies in Parisian society now began to figure in Delius's life, even if he was perhaps more at home with the Molards' largely Scandinavian circle.

Meanwhile, Augener published this year two more volumes of his songs, the *Seven Songs from the Norwegian* and the *Three Shelley Songs*. And, in the United States, the early piano piece *Zum Carnival* made an appearance. It was published in Jacksonville, Florida, just possibly in a second edition whose first has not been traced.

Irmelin, opera (RT I/2). Completed.

Paa Vidderne, symphonic poem (RT VI/10). Revised and completed.

Sonata in B major for violin and piano (RT VIII/3).

Légende, for violin and orchestra (RT VII/3). Conceivably completed as a work for violin and piano in 1892, and orchestrated in 1895.

String Quartet (RT VIII/4). Probably begun in 1892.

(37)
Fritz Delius to Randi Blehr

33 Rue Ducouëdic
Montrouge
le 3 Mars 92.

Dear Frau Blehr,

Many thanks for your card & also for the drawings by Sigurd,[1] they are really original, he must become a painter. How old is he?

You have been very ill, I hear, what was the matter? I am very happy to hear that you are better —

I have been in London, that is why I have not been able to write; I had so much to do — Today I send you some songs, soon others will be published which I will then send to you.[2]

Have you seen Frøken Sandströme? I will send her some songs too, but she will have to wait some time as I am waiting for further copies. Give her my best regards if you should see her.

You asked me when the compositions promised at Fredriksværn will be ready? Well! You must be patient with me. It isn't done in a hurry & I am now taken up by a larger work.[3] Sooner or later you will get something.

It has been very cold here for some time & I am freezing, but spring will soon come & I shall thaw out again. Indeed, it's only in spring and summer that I really live. I have heard now & then from Johnsen.[4] He is a very kind man & his letters are full of feeling: his brother has also sent me his poems. Unfortunately I don't understand them very well. Sinding arrived in Paris a fortnight ago to see some Parisian life.[5] He seems to like it very much here.

Write to me very soon & farewell. Forgive this uninteresting letter. I could *never* manage an interesting one.

Until we meet again!
Your very devoted
Fritz Delius

Autograph letter, signed and dated, written in German.

The original is in the State Archives, Oslo, Norway (Privatarkiv nr. 233 [O.A. og R. Blehrs archiv] kasset 116). It is the first of nine letters written by Delius to Mrs Blehr between 1891 and 1893 that have been preserved.

Randi Blehr (1851–1928): *née* Nilsen in Bergen. She married a prominent liberal politician, Otto Blehr, in 1876. He was now serving his first term (1891–3) as Norway's prime minister. Randi Blehr was a pioneer of women's rights and was president for many years of the Norwegian feminist movement. Only one letter from her to Delius

PLATE I Fritz Delius in the mid-1870s. (*Photograph W. Höffert.*)

PLATE 2   Pen-and-ink sketch by Fritz Delius, 26 March 1885.
(Coll. Jacksonville Public Library.)

PLATE 3   Fritz Delius, 1888. (*Photograph Atelier Hermann.*)

PLATE 4   Card party at Leipzig, 1887: Nina and Edvard Grieg, Johan
Halvorsen, Fritz Delius, Christian Sinding.

PLATE 5   Gertrude Rueckert. (*Photograph A. H. Blunt, Danville.*)

PLATE 6 Delius in Bradford with four of his sisters.

PLATE 7   Christian Sinding, 1890. (*Coll. Andrew Boyle.*)

PLATE 8   Edvard Grieg, 1893.

PLATE 9   Edvard Munch, 1891, by Christian Krohg.

PLATE 10   Fritz Delius: an early sketch by Edvard Munch.
(*Coll. Munch Museum.*)

PLATE 11   Pen-and-ink sketch of mountain guide Sulheim
            by Gudmund Stenersen (inset).

PLATE 12 (a) Iver Holter (*coll. Andrew Boyle*); (b) Johan Selmer, *c.* 1886 (*coll. Andrew Boyle*); (c) Bjørnstjerne Bjørnson; (d) Olaf Thommessen, 1884, by Christian Krohg.

PLATE 13   Delius and companion (Dagny Bjørnson) at Aulestad, 8 July
1891 (see p. 401). (*Coll. Grieg Museum, Troldhaugen.*)

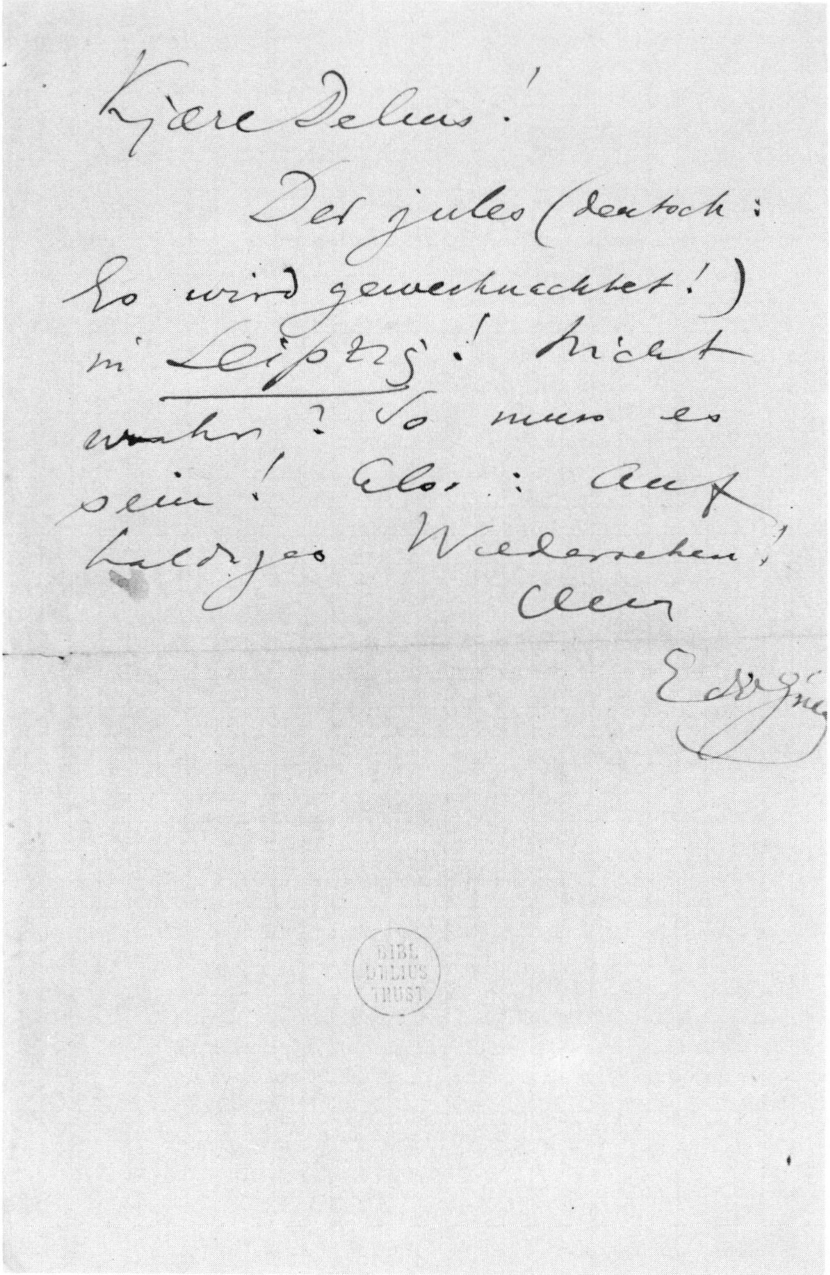

Kjære Delius!

Det jules (deutsch: Es wird geweihnachtet!) in Leipzig! nicht wahr? So muss es sein! Also: auf baldiges Wiedersehen!

Ihr

Edv. Grieg

PLATE 14 Letter from Grieg to Delius, 20 October 1892 (see p. 69).

PLATE 15   (a) Georges-Daniel de Monfreid: self portrait (*Cliché des Musées Nationaux, Paris*); (b) Isidore de Lara; (c) Emma Calvé.

PLATE 16   William Molard, *c.* 1894, by Paul Gauguin.

has been preserved, probably dating from late 1891, which is written in markedly warm and friendly terms.

1   Randi Blehr's young son.

2   The songs actually sent would have been the *Five Songs from the Norwegian*, and those promised, most probably the *Seven Songs from the Norwegian*. Both sets were published by Augener, in 1890 and 1892 respectively. Another group was published by Augener in 1892: the *Three Shelley Songs*.

3   Delius was preoccupied with the composition of his opera *Irmelin*, and a letter from Nina Grieg on 1 April seems to indicate that he was having difficulties with the libretto: 'Why do you not write the text yourself? You spoke about this much earlier and surely one then works much more freely?'

4   Hjalmar Johnsen (1851–1901): Norwegian painter. A sailor, he began to paint in 1875, particularly in the region of his birthplace, Stavanger. For a time he was associated with the much more widely known Norwegian painter Frits Thaulow. His brother, Peter Rosenkranz Johnsen, was a journalist. No Johnsen to Delius letters are extant.

5   Sinding had written early in February to ask Delius to meet him at the station and book him into a hotel near the rue Ducouëdic. And Nina Grieg, in a letter to Delius dated 2 March, was anxious that while they were together they should agree on a summer tour in Norway.

(38)

Nina and Edvard Grieg to Fritz Delius

Troldhaugen 29*th* June.
92.

Dear Delius,

Well then, quelque chose plus fort que les montagnes! "I fear I shall *not* be coming to Norway" is the long and short of it! There is a saying that goes man's sweetest of dishes is that which he wishes, and perhaps it is true: Your sweetest dish at the moment seems to be "3 rooms and a kitchen" ————!¹ But, – joking apart, we felt *very* sorry that you intend to leave us in the lurch this year, I had looked forward enormously to being able to wander around "on the Vidder" with you again. Another time is a mischievous thing to say and I am pessimistic enough not to expect much from the future, it is very dangerous for us human beings, who must inexorably drift along with the stream, to put things off till tomorrow. Mais – nous verrons! – I don't wish to be indiscreet, so I won't ask you *why* you are not coming, you can speak if you wish, if you prefer to stay buttoned up – "haughty", I shall certainly not pry into your innermost self. –

Thank you very much for your greetings on our wedding anniversary. It turned out to be a real festival with sunshine from morning to evening, with thousands of happy people, with fires on the islands in the Nordåsvand[2] and with masses of boats on the calm water. Up at Troldhaugen as many guests as possible in the house and garden, singing and "skåls" long into the wonderful brightly shining summer night. Finally a beautiful song by Sinding to the most moving words of Jonas Lie.[3] Bergen presented us with a beautiful Steinway, Christiania with a Werenskjold[4] and a splendid bear skin. Do you still remember the bear skin you fell in love with last year in Haukelia? This one is much more beautiful and bigger, I can stretch out full length on it – goodness, I have to laugh when I think how little is needed, – but I am certain that it is big enough for you too and that says more. Just come and try it yourself. You would not at all recognize our simple living room any more, it is all so fine and splendid here, really far too elegant for us. – I don't yet know what we shall do this summer, whether we shall go to the mountains somewhere together, or whether just Edvard will visit the Saeter-jentene[5] with Fr. Beyer. If by any chance you have changed your plans and come to Norway after all, please write to us at once, so that we do not miss each other. In the autumn we are certainly going away, but *where* we have not yet decided. I am glad that we are not going to spend another winter here, life is not so long that one can afford to be wasteful with it. – Finally many hearty thanks for the songs.[6] I am very fond of them, the last one especially appeals to me. Only it's a pity for me that they are so *highly* erotic, and it just doesn't work, to transpose Love.

– Now farewell, dear Delius, let us hope that we shall meet up with each other again in life somewhere; I would not like it to end with this, we are too fond of one another for that, aren't we?

– Many thousand greetings from your very sincere

Nina Grieg.

The Engdronninge[7] are beginning to blossom again. –
Holter spent a week here, perhaps he will be coming again, I don't know.

Dear friend,

I am not at all pleased that you are not coming to us this summer! I cannot show you any new music, the only new thing I have available is this cursed gout in my feet, which has been plaguing me since February and has driven off the urge to work. But if you come and bring summer with you, then the gout must go, I am quite sure. Some Norway would do you a lot of good. And you would find here a friendship that will be just as new as it is old! Think the matter over. At any rate we are staying here for the whole of July and the first half of August.

A thousand greetings!
Yours
Edvard Grieg

We must talk further about your songs. There are some very lovely things in
them. I feel however that in some respects you are treading dangerous ground.
But one cannot put these things in writing.

Autograph letter of Nina Grieg, signed and dated. Autograph letter of Edvard Grieg,
signed and undated, follows on. Both are written in German.

The original is in the Delius Trust Archive.

1   Delius presumably had indicated contentment with his apartment in the rue
Ducouëdic.

2   The fjord at Troldhaugen.

3   Jonas Lie (1833–1908): Norwegian author and poet. He lived in Paris from 1882
to 1906 and was very much the doyen of Norwegian writers there. He was a friend of
both Grieg and Strindberg.

4   Erik Werenskjold (1855–1938): Norwegian painter. After studying in Munich
and Paris, he became one of the foremost Norwegian artists of his day, with strong
elements of realism and Norwegian nationalism in his work. Werenskjold became
justly celebrated for his illustrations to Asbjørnsen and Moe's *Norske folkeeventyr* (1876–
87), and was to execute a number of portraits of Grieg.

5   *Saeter-girls* (farm-girls, milkmaids). In Norwegian in the original letter.

6   Presumably this is again a reference to the *Seven Songs from the Norwegian*, published
in 1892 and dedicated (like the *Five Songs* earlier) to Nina Grieg. However, Augener
also published Delius's *Three Shelley Songs* in 1892, the edition number being slightly
earlier than that of the *Seven Songs* (see Letter 37, note 2).

7   *meadowsweet*. In Norwegian in the original letter.

(39)
Fritz Delius to Olaf Thommessen

le 1 Juillet 92

Passage Plougastel-Daoulas
Finisterre
Bretagne.

My dear Mr Thomasson

This is to introduce to you a friend of mind Mr *Philippe Augier*[1] a talented young
french poet, & journalist of the *Journal* des *Débats*

His intention is to go to the North Cape, Tromsoe, Bodoe, Hammerfest, &
to make a literary account of this journey.

If you are able to give him any introductions to those northern towns which might be of help to him, I should be greatly obliged to you. You will I am sure find him also a very fine fellow.

I am staying this summer in Bretagne & hope next summer to be able to come to Norway again & of course hope to meet you well & healthy.

Give my kind regards to Mrs Thomasson

Thanking you in anticipation

I remain,

Sincerely yours,

Fritz Delius

Autograph letter, signed and dated, written in English.

The original is in the Oslo University Library (U.B. Oslo, Brevs. nr. 100). No further correspondence between Delius and Thommessen has been found.

Olaus [Olaf] Anton Thommessen (1851–1942): Norwegian journalist and author. He became editor of the Christiania daily *Verdens Gang* in 1878, and under him it became a leading organ of the left. On leaving the paper in 1910, he was to found another, *Tidens Tegn*. This sole letter to Thommessen is an early indication of an acquaintanceship that was to prove useful to Delius rather more than five years later, when *Verdens Gang* supported him strongly throughout the furore surrounding *Folkeraadet* (see Letters 73 to 76 for details of this episode).

1   Delius had clearly written 'Augier', an odd way to misspell the name of 'a friend of mind [*sic*]', Philippe Auquier. A connection between Thommessen's circle and Auquier is certainly hinted at in a letter preserved in the Oslo University Library (U.B. Oslo, Brevs. nr. 466) from William Molard to his friend in Christiania Karl Vilhelm Hammer, joint proprietor of *Verdens Gang*. It is dated Paris, 1 October 1892, and Molard wrote, 'I don't see Auquier very often because his occupations as a journalist detain him until 2 o'clock at night.'

(40)

Fritz Delius to Randi Blehr

Au passage
Plougastel-Daoulas
Finisterre
le 7 Août 92

My dear Frau Blehr,

I very much enjoyed your long & interesting letter. You must forgive me for replying only now.

I have been very busy, that is why you have had to wait so long for a reply. I have now been in Brittany for 6 weeks, on the coast, rather like Fredriksværn. It was impossible for me to come to Norway this year. Next year, however, I hope I will be able to come. I am glad you like the little songs. Soon I will send you more.

I did not know you had been so ill & I am very pleased to hear that you are well again. Perhaps you will come to Paris next spring, it will give me great pleasure to see you. The political situation in Norway seems to be rather confused. I am afraid I have no opportunity to read the papers & to follow events. If you could give me some news about it I would be very glad, for I am very interested in Norway – not just in politics, but in the development (spiritual) of a country I am so fond of and where it seems that gigantic forces in art and science are slumbering. It seems to me that politics do not quite accord with Norway's other interests and as things are now everything must surely come to a standstill. Why not straight away have a revolution and become a republic, quite independent of Sweden. You will have to explain something of this to me as I still do not really know what is going on. This Consul question *alone* cannot really provoke such a crisis. *All or Nothing*, you see; if the politicians would only understand. A people would follow eagerly, we have already seen this. But a people usually has no real trust in its leaders and where there is suspicion, there is no liberty; and no real devotion. Then we have this old story about interests, you see in Norway, just like here and elsewhere, there are so few disinterested politicians. That is why great events happen with bloody revolution in spite of their leaders, who hardly dare to do anything on account of their interests. Now we will see if things will develop as I told you at Fredriksværn. I don't want to set myself up as a prophet. I am completely ignorant. But I have observed a great deal, even if I am only 29 years old. I have met many different people during my life & they are all the same. *The All or Nothing* people, the *Nothing* people & the *Something* people, or those who are satisfied if they can eat & drink well during their life, in short the people who want to insure their life, the real egoists. The *All or Nothing* appear infrequently & are only to be found among artists, great criminals, anarchists like Ravachol, politicians like George Washington, Gambetta, Danton, Wm Bradlaugh. Now the time is ripe for such a man to appear in Norway. *Will he arise?* and *be bold enough*. You seem to worry a lot about what is right & what is wrong. You are really a *strange* person. You say you do *not* want to preach *freedom* to your children. Why do you want to preach at all? Your children will follow their own nature, as surely as anything. If you bring your children up well, that is explain to them fully all worldly affairs & bring them up so that they follow the vocation they bear within themselves, develop their talents & help them with sympathy, they would look after themselves & act in the way they *must* act, *given their natural inclinations*. It is a problem that slowly solves itself right up to death. In this respect I too am a *fatalist*. Right is what you *can* do. Wrong is what you *cannot do*. One must know.

Adieu, dear Frau Blehr, farewell & write to me again very soon. Give Blehr my regards

I remain
Your friend
Fritz Delius

P.S. No-one has the right to tell you what is right or wrong. Everyone has to find out for himself, often with quite sad results. However, if one is born under a favourable star, one has some chances of coming through relatively unscathed.

Tusend hilsen[1]

Autograph letter, signed and dated, written in German.

The original is in the State Archives, Oslo (see Letter 37, note).

1 *A thousand greetings.* In Norwegian in the original letter.

(41)
Christian Sinding and Edvard Grieg to Fritz Delius

Christiania 20 October 92.

Dear friend,

Thank you very much for the letter and for the news of yourself. God these opera texts! What a rotten business! It's a damned nuisance to be so dependent on others in this sort of thing. To do the text oneself would of course be easiest; I would do it too if I were able to discern the slightest talent in myself. Absolutely nothing there. – I shall probably go to Berlin next week, to see if it's possible to get anything done there. I had really intended to give a concert here, but tiresome matters interfered, and I got fed up with it all. It really isn't worth the candle. – Can't you come to Germany too? The Griegs will probably come to Leipzig later; it would be so marvellous if we could all spend another winter together again. – Do give my greetings to the Molards and the painter.[1] Have forgotten his name. Do you know Mons Lie's[2] address?

Yours
Chr. S.

c/o
Advokat Mejdell
Christiania

Kjaere Delius!

Det jules³ (Christmas will be spent!) in *Leipzig*! Won't it? It must be so! Well then: Here's to seeing you again soon!

    Yours
    Edvard Grieg

Autograph letter, signed 'Chr. S.', and dated, written in German. Grieg's signed note, also written in German, follows on.

The original is in the Delius Trust Archive. See plate 14.

1   Probably Charles Boutet de Monvel.

2   Son of Jonas Lie, the Norwegian writer (see Letter 38, note 3).

3   In Norwegian in the original letter (Grieg himself then supplying the translation).

1893

The earlier part of the year appears to have been spent busily at work in the rue Ducouëdic. Delius's only publications so far had been of songs and of a piano piece, and he must have envied Christian Sinding's being taken up by the firm of C. F. Peters in Leipzig: Dr Abraham paid a handsome fee for Sinding's symphony and promised to publish other works of his. Sinding apparently visited Delius in mid-March, and after briefly returning to Norway was later to make his way to the Riviera with the Griegs and Dr Abraham. Meanwhile he dispatched the Norwegian poet Vilhelm Krag to Paris with an introduction to Delius. Both Sinding and Grieg had set a number of Krag's poems to music, and Delius in his turn was now to make one Krag setting.

New acquaintances were Harold Bauer and Serge Achille Rivarde, who rehearsed and played to Delius his newly composed Sonata in B major. And an interest in occultism and astrology becomes evident as Delius began to cast horoscopes for various of his friends, who by now included the celebrated Emma Calvé. For a while, at least, this curious new interest provided something of a diversion from the more serious matter of composition. Delius's range of French acquaintances was now growing. He probably got to know the young Florent Schmitt this year, and his setting of Jean Richepin's 'Nuages' may well be accounted for by his presumably meeting the poet at the home of their mutual friend, William Molard. And it was early this year that the painter Daniel de Monfreid, confidant of Gauguin, made a pastel portrait of Delius.

Delius was back in Norway by the end of June, staying for most of the time with Sinding at Drøbak. September saw him once again in Paris. His interest in the occult had now led him to associate with Papus, a leading figure in this fashionable field, and before long the two men were to put together an odd booklet exploring the mystic properties and characteristics of the orchestra. Now, too, Paul Gauguin and Alphonse Mucha had settled down nearby in Montparnasse and were taking their meals in a little crémerie in the rue de la Grande Chaumière. Here painters, poets and musicians would meet, and it was probably around this time that Delius himself began to frequent Madame Charlotte's extraordinary eating establishment and enjoy long conversations with its various luminaries. At all events, he seems to have had less success at composition this year, as the works that have survived and can reasonably be assumed to date from 1893 are sparse indeed. Perhaps a real pointer is supplied in general terms by another friend, Richard Le Gallienne, who was later to write of this period: 'here was not so much the ending of a century as the beginning of a new one. Those last ten years of the nineteenth century properly belong to the twentieth century, and, far from being "decadent", except in certain limited manifestations, they were years of an immense and multifarious renaissance.' The creative energy packed into the decade was 'almost bewildering in its variety. So much was going on at once, in so many directions, with so passionate a fervour. A three-ringed circus gives but a small idea of the different whirling activities'.*

For a while, at least, Delius was caught up with the circus.

_____

'Jeg havde en nyskaaren Seljefløjte', song (Krag) (RT V/14).

'Nuages', song (Richepin) (RT V/15).

Over the hills and far away, 'fantasy overture' (RT VI/11). Begun? Completed 1897?

String Quartet (RT VIII/4). Completed?

(42)
Nina Grieg to Fritz Delius

Leipzig 21*st* Jan.
93. –

Dear Delius,

I have a feeling that it is a long time ago since I wrote to you, but perhaps it is not really so. I should like to know how you are, whether you are hard at work again and whether the opera has made good progress? I hope you spent a pleasant Christmas with your friend Arvesen and that you slipped into the New Year softly and imperceptibly. I hope it will bring you some of the things you wish for, everything – no, there must always be something left over to wish and long for.

We are middling. Edvard is still not well, he just does not feel his real self. For a time things can go quite well and we just begin to believe it is real, but how long was Adam in Paradise, one fine day things are bad again and we cannot understand why. But he is certainly better than he was in Norway and I am determined not to lose hope. It is our intention to stay in Leipzig until the end

_____

*   Richard Le Gallienne, *The Romantic '90s* (London: Putnam, 1926), pp. 102–4.

of February and then to go somewhere where the air is mild and pure. We are thinking about Merano, on the Riviera perhaps, but shall let things come as they may and shall make no plans. Do you know that Edvard has been made a Doctor at the University of Cambridge? He is to receive this "new honour" at the beginning of June and so he must go to Cambridge and conduct something there as well. But we shall probably go first to London, where he will perhaps also give some music if he is fit enough to carry it off. So it will be very late before we shall be able to greet our beloved mountains again, but perhaps that is just as well, some time it must be summer again in the north. God knows what it looks like up there now, – snow, stretching to infinity over the Vidder, the great, silent loneliness, swept only by the wild wind that freezes everything to ice. That is probably what it is like now up on Haukelid Fjeld.

Adieu, dear Delius, may you have much joy from life, and think of us now and again.

Many thousand greetings from Edvard and your

very sincere
Nina Grieg.

Sinding was here recently for a couple of days. We dined together in the "Panorama" again, but I am afraid we had all become blasé, we did not like it any more. Holter and the Musikforening[1] – yes, that didn't *look* good, but it is difficult to judge of course.

We spent Christmas in Berlin, even had a Christmas tree in the "Hotel Kaiserhof", but it was nothing like the old times here in Leipzig.

Address still:
C.F. Peters, Thalstrasse 10.

Autograph letter, signed and dated, written in German.

The original is in the Delius Trust Archive.

1 *Christiania Music Society*. In Norwegian in the original letter.

(43)
Max Abraham to Fritz Delius

C.F. Peters.

LEIPZIG, 28/2 1893
Thalstrasse 10.

Dear Herr Delius,

If I have not answered your friendly lines of the 11 Feb. & returned the Sonata[1] you kindly sent until today, it is because Grieg, who was not really very well here, has only just given his judgment. He says it is a work full of talent, in particular that the Adagio is wonderful, but that the Sonata would have to be written out differently, because the musical orthography is such that even first-class musicians would have difficulty in playing from the manuscript.

As far as I am concerned, I regret that I cannot publish the Sonata, because the form is too free, the key is changed too frequently & the first & last movements are so difficult to play that reasonably large sales for the work are unthinkable.

I would not write to every composer in this way, but I have the honour of knowing you, & I know also that you want frankness on my part.

The day after tomorrow I am going with Grieg to the Riviera & perhaps I shall return at the end of March via Paris. In that case I shall look forward to the pleasure of visiting you & in the meantime I remain with kindest regards

Yours truly
Max Abraham

Autograph letter, signed and dated, written in German on the headed notepaper of C. F. Peters.

The original is in the Delius Trust Archive. It is the second of two letters from Dr Abraham that have been preserved. The first, dated 2 February 1891, is a kindly but firm rejection of songs: 'I take the liberty of advising you against publication of songs for the time being. Once you have made a name for yourself with other works, piano pieces or *short* chamber works, then will be the time to publish songs too, but to make one's début with them does not seem to me to be practical.'

1   Sonata in B major (1892).

(44)
Christian Sinding to Fritz Delius

Christiania 11 April 93.

Dear friend,

Vilhelm Krag[1] is leaving for Paris this evening. I have given him your address, and promised him that he will find in you extremely pleasant company. I promise you the same — you will certainly not regret it if you receive him

Regards from the Gades[2]

Yours   Chr. Sinding

Autograph letter, signed and dated, written in German.

The original is in the Delius Trust Archive.

1   Vilhelm Krag (1871–1933): Norwegian author and poet. His début as a lyric poet of quality came at the beginning of the 1890s. 'We are sending you a little book of poems by a young Norwegian called Kragh,' Nina Grieg had written to Delius on 21 December 1891. 'There is so much feeling in them.' Grieg set Krag's lyrics, as did Delius just once in the case of 'Jeg havde en nyskaaren Seljefløjte' (1893?), although the original poem seems never to have been published by Krag. Almost certainly Krag wrote the poem specifically for Delius during this visit to Paris, but the poet's original manuscript has not been found and the piece itself only exists in Delius's score. Krag's later work included tales and novels, which like some of his poetry derived much from his native countryside of Sørland. He also wrote plays and a series of lively and good-humoured memoirs, and he was director of Norway's National Theatre from 1908 to 1911.

2   Sinding had known Frederik Georg Gade (1855–1933), a distinguished Norwegian physician, and his wife, Augusta, since 1890, if not earlier, often staying with them at their home in Drøbak. Delius, too, had stayed there. After the Gades' marriage broke up, Sinding at the age of forty-three married Augusta, three years younger than himself, in 1898.

(45)
Isidore de Lara to Fritz Delius

[Paris, 13 May 1893]

My dear Delius

The Princesse Brancaccia is in a great state of anxiety about her horoscope. She is coming here today at 2, could you come & meet her . . . I shall be also happy to shake hands with you, as I am telegraphed for to go to London tomorrow – I have been absolutely [. . .][1] here by rehearsals with artists: if I dont see you remember that at 4 Portman Mansions Baker St London you have a devoted friend, who appreciates & Believes in you

   I de Lara

Autograph 'letter-telegram', signed and undated, written in English. Envelope addressed: *M.*ᵒⁿˢ Delius / 33 Rue Ducoüedic / Avenue D'Orleans / *PARIS*

The original is in the Delius Trust Archive. It is the first of three items of correspondence from de Lara to Delius that have been preserved. The two later items are undated.

Isidore de Lara (1858–1935): English composer and pianist. He studied at the Milan Conservatory, and his operas, the best of which were written (and performed) in the 1890s, are his main claim to fame, although he greatly enjoyed singing in the salons of the period. He cultivated aristocratic patrons and played a part, after their first meeting in the autumn of 1892, in introducing Delius to a number of useful people. These probably included the American-born Princesse Brancaccia, who, like Delius, was a frequent guest at de Lara's table at this time and whose horoscope Delius was expected to cast. Delius's interest in astrology, and, indeed, in occultism generally, became a feature of this period of his life.

1 A corner of the page is torn, and a word is missing.

(46)
Emma Calvé to Fritz Delius

TALBOT HOUSE,
WARWICK PLACE,
GROVE END ROAD,
[LONDON] N.W.

8 July 1893.

Dear Sir and Friend:

I was born in *1858* on the *14 August*, at *noon*; in a small town in the south of France.
    Three years have been the highlights of my life:
    1877. 1882. 1889.
    Thank you from the bottom of my heart for all the trouble I am giving you.
    I send you my best and most sincere regards.
    Emma Calvé.

Next week I shall be singing the opera by your good friend de Lara, "very anxious and exited at this moment". You should write a nice letter to him, because I know he likes you a lot; and you have the power to do him a lot of good. I am staying here until the 25 July; then I shall be leaving for Paris, where you should please address your reply to *34 Rue Marbeuf*.

Autograph letter, signed and dated, written in French on headed notepaper.

The original is in the Delius Trust Archive. It is the second of four letters written by Emma Calvé to Delius between June 1893 and November 1894 that have been preserved.

Emma Calvé (1858–1942): French soprano. A pupil of Mathilde Marchesi, she made her début in *Faust* in 1881 and was later to make the role of Carmen very much her own. The de Lara opera she was to sing in was *Amy Robsart*, which was performed at Covent Garden in 1893 and later at Monte Carlo, and which was written for her. Calvé had already written to Delius, with whom she was acquainted, to remind him of a promise he had made to cast her horoscope — their mutual friend de Lara having passed on Delius's address to her. It is clear that Delius had written back to ask her for more information to help him in this curious task.

(47)

William Molard to Fritz Delius

Concarneau 17 August 1893

Dear Friend,

Since yesterday we have been installed Ida, Judith, Monvel, Bob and I[1] in Concarneau (Finistère) Boulevard Bougainville N° 16 in a detached house with garden situated 2 minutes from the beach where we have our bathing cabin.

We have just come from Pont-Aven where we left Gans who had come from Paris with us as well as Eriksson,[2] whom we left at Quimperlé from where he made his way to Loctudi near Pont l'Abbé where the Wallgren[3] family are living.

We might perhaps have gone to Dröbak[4] if Mors Lil[5] had got the free trip for us he promised from Anvers to X[ia],[6] but having heard nothing not even a letter, we weren't able to wait any longer because of my leave which I have been compelled to take in August and so we chose Brittany, attracted by the cheapness of Pont-Aven where you can live for 3[f] a day each food and lodging included.

Pont-Aven is a pretty village, really quaint, with a river the Aven flowing through it, which is affected by the tide and this brings in the salt sea water twice a day, but the lack of a sandy beach makes bathing very difficult, and it is this that made us decide to leave it for Concarneau, seeing that the doctor has advised sea bathing for Judith, and fresh water is not as beneficial as salt water.

Ida does the cooking for us; she has just this very moment come back from the port where she had gone with Judith to buy some fish, she's brought back some fresh sardines and a lobster which we have just tied up and which we shall soon throw into the pot when the water boils. Ida dares not drown it in such a treacherous fashion and it will be for Monvel or me to do the job of executioner.

Up to now I have still done nothing, what with all the to-do of our trip, which began on the 10th, and before that we had all the rushing about to buy various things before leaving, but today – now we have a *home*,[7] I shall get down to the business of copying my music, as I am still far from having finished this disagreeable and very long job.

Monvel is doing botany in his room, as this is his current craze and Judith is nibbling at a bunch of grapes. We take our meals in the garden which is delightful, isn't it. Remember us to Sinding

We are staying here until the 2nd September next. If by chance you'd like to write to us, you have our address

Tibi
Molard

Ida & Judith send their love, Charles is going to write to you, and Bob offers you his paw, all this moving about from one place to another quite perplexes him.

Autograph letter, signed and dated, written in French. Envelope addressed: Monsieur / Fritz Delius / Drøbak / ved Christiania / Norwège. Readdressed: Aasgaardstrand. Postmarks on the back of the envelope indicate a probable receiving date of 24 August.

The original is in the Delius Trust Archive. It is the first of eleven letters and postcards written by Molard to Delius between 1897 and 1908 that have been preserved.

1   The ménage was composed of William and Ida Molard, Ida's daughter (by her earlier liaison with the Swedish opera singer Fritz Arlberg) Judith, Charles Boutet de Monvel and the Molards' dog, Bob. Boutet was a prominent member of the Gauguin circle in the early 1890s. Four letters that he wrote to Delius, of which one only is dated (1889), are preserved in the Delius Trust Archive.

2   Christian Eriksson (1858–1935): Swedish sculptor. A close friend of Ida Molard since her student days in Stockholm, he had a studio in Paris in the artists' quarter at 59, avenue de Saxe. I have been unable to identify Gans, his travelling companion to Pont-Aven.

3   Possibly the Finnish sculptor Ville Vallgren (1855–1940), who lived in Paris for a large part of his adult life. He had a studio at this period on the avenue du Maine, close to the Molards, and he and his wife often stayed in Brittany in the summer. It is of some interest that Vallgren had come to know Grez-sur-Loing (Delius's later home) well in the early 1880s during the period when his friends August Strindberg and Carl Larsson had lived there together with various other luminaries of Nordic art and literature. John Boulton Smith has written of him: 'No other Finnish artist so completely represents international Art Nouveau' (*The Golden Age of Finnish Art* [Helsinki: Otava 1975], p. 50).

4   Delius was staying, with Sinding, at Drøbak in Norway. This was the home of Sinding's friends the Gades.

5   *Mother's little boy* (perhaps Sinding). In Norwegian in the original letter (but more properly *Mors Lille*).

6   Christiania [Kristiania], the earlier name for the city of Oslo.

7   In English in the original letter.

1894

The event of the earlier part of the year was a performance at the end of February of *Paa Vidderne* (*Sur les cimes*), reworked and presented at Monte Carlo in a concert of British music. It brought Delius a favourable, if brief, notice in *Le Figaro* and no doubt impressed his uncle, who had supported the venture financially, as it certainly impressed that notable patron of the arts, Princess Alice of Monaco.

Meanwhile, in Paris the studio of William and Ida Molard in the rue Vercingétorix was becoming ever more lively. At the beginning of the year Gauguin had moved, taking the studio above theirs, and was soon holding his weekly 'at homes'. An extraordinary array of artists and eccentrics came and went, Grieg joining the company on at least one occasion in the spring when the nineteen-year-old Maurice Ravel, a student at the Conservatoire, was also present. Delius was a frequent and welcome visitor in both households and seems to have been considered as a leading light in these circles, even if Gauguin was very much the focus of attention until his final departure for the South Seas. Other French musicians involved included Florent Schmitt and Léon Moreau. The painter Daniel de Monfreid was another of the main figures in the circle, and one important source of information on his life and work mentions that his close friend and fellow-artist, Aristide Maillol, was also a friend of Delius.* Finally, late in the year, August Strindberg, who had arrived to stay in Paris in the summer, began to frequent the gatherings at the rue Vercingétorix and at Madame Charlotte's *crémerie*.

On another plane, a renewed friendship in Paris was with Jutta Bell, who had been a neighbour some ten years earlier in Florida. She now re-entered Delius's life as a collaborator on the libretto of a new opera, *The Magic Fountain*, the one work which began to preoccupy him from the middle of the year. Delius probably stayed mainly in Paris until July, before setting out on a trip to Bayreuth and Munich, returning early in September. During the autumn it would seem that his energies were mainly devoted to his new opera.

---

*   Jean Loize, *Les amitiés du peintre Georges-Daniel de Monfreid et ses reliques de Gauguin* (chez Jean Loize, 1951), p. 30.

The Magic Fountain, opera (RT I/3). Begun mid-1894.

Anatomie et Physiologie de l'Orchestre, booklet by Delius and Papus. Published 1894.

Florent Schmitt makes a piano arrangement of *Irmelin*. May.

(48)

Princess Alice of Monaco to Fritz Delius

Feb^{ry} 26th [1894]

PALAIS DE MONACO

Dear Mr Delius,

Let me tell you how fine I thought your "Sur les Cimes"[1] yesterday. It is splendid music, very highly pushed – and I would be very much surprised if you don't attain "Les Cimes" of glory – for you have great science coupled to great art, & it is such a hard [?] alliance that something great must be born of it – When you have written any more, send it to me, for I shall have it given here, where you have a good orchestra. De Lara was very pleased also & thought you very far gone in art.

Believe me

Yours sincerely
Alice de Monaco

Autograph letter, signed and dated, written in English on the headed notepaper of the Palais de Monaco.

The original is in the Delius Trust Archive. It is the only item of correspondence from Princess Alice to Delius that has been preserved.

Princess Alice of Monaco (1857–1925): the second wife of Prince Albert of Monaco from 1889 to 1922. The American-born Alice Heine had first been married to the Duc de Richelieu, but was widowed after a comparatively short time. Her marriage to Prince Albert lasted for twelve years until its dissolution in 1902. She was a devoted patron of the arts, and in bringing the impresario Raoul Gunsbourg to the Theatre at Monte Carlo in 1892, she helped give fresh life to the musical and theatrical establishment of the principality and was instrumental in forging Monaco's reputation as a brilliant centre for the performing arts.

1 *Sur les cimes* was a revision of the second *Paa Vidderne*. It was given in the seventh international concert of the Monte Carlo season on 25 February in a programme devoted entirely to British works. No circumstantial evidence has yet come to light to prove that Delius was present at the concert, but it is almost inconceivable that he was not there.

(49)
Léon Moreau to Fritz Delius

[Paris, 22 May 1894]

Dear Delius

Schmitt[1] is very busy doing your reduction for you. But as for me I am taken up every evening of the week. Could you come tomorrow Wednesday – Schmitt and I will be at home from 3 to 6.

Yours
L Moreau

Autograph *carte-télégramme*, signed and undated, written in French. Addressed: Monsieur Fritz Delius / 33 rue Ducouëdic. Postmark: PARIS 22 MAI 94.

The original is in the Delius Trust Archive. It is the last of three items of correspondence written by Moreau to Delius, all dated 1894, that have been preserved.

Léon Moreau (1870–1946): French composer. A fellow-student of William Molard under Pessard, he was to win the Prix de Rome in 1899. It seems likely that he met Delius through Molard, possibly at one of the many soirées in the Molards' studio at 6, rue Vercingétorix.

1   Florent Schmitt (1870–1958): French composer. A winner of the Prix de Rome (1900), he had entered the Paris Conservatoire in 1889. By the time he was reaching compositional maturity in the early 1900s, he had prepared vocal scores, commissioned by Delius, of four of his friend's operas: *Irmelin*, *The Magic Fountain*, *Koanga* and *A Village Romeo and Juliet*. Schmitt was now presumably at work on *Irmelin*.

(50)
Fritz Delius to Edvard Grieg

33 Rue Ducouëdic
le 15 Juin, 94.

Dear Grieg,

I am glad that you are getting on well at Grevsen's Bad.[1]

I am glad too for Molard & Leclercq,[2] that Dr Abraham has at last agreed to 35 francs: they have taken a hell of a lot of trouble and it cannot be better translated.[3] Molard has a very fine nature: I think highly of him both as friend and artist. We have now quite finished one act: now we are working on the second. At the end of this month or at the beginning of July we will, I think, be finished. Many thanks for writing to Levi.[4] I am leaving here on the 25 July.

If you write to Dr Abraham, please tell him he could send an advance now to Molard. I think it would be very welcome.[5] He hasn't got much to manage on either.

Write to me again soon & give my greetings to the splendid summer nights & forests and to your dear wife too. Farewell, & have a complete rest

Yours
Fritz Delius

Autograph letter, signed and dated, written in German.

The original is in the Bergen Public Library.

1   Grieg was recuperating from an illness at a spa near Christiania.

2   Julien Leclercq (1865–1901): French author and poet. A devoted follower of Gauguin, he was one of the most frequent visitors to the studios of both Gauguin and Molard at 6, rue Vercingétorix. Delius knew him well, but did not particularly like him.

3   Grieg had been in Paris, as well as in London, in the spring and had for the first time associated with the Molard circle as such. However, letters that are preserved in the Bergen Public Library show that he had known William Molard for a considerable time, and that Molard had first offered to help him in some way in 1887, if not a little earlier. Grieg had written from Troldhaugen on 21 January 1887 to Molard in Paris: 'I remember your father well. . . . I also remember going into his music shop in Kristiania, (Akersgaden) to buy music paper. Most likely it was then that I talked with you and your wife.' (But Molard did not marry Ida Ericson until 20 August 1891.)
     Since Grieg had written to Molard from London on 19 May, thanking him and Leclercq for 'Solveig's Song', 'a masterpiece of translation', it seems from the context of Delius's letter that with some help from Delius himself the two Frenchmen were producing a French translation of *Peer Gynt*. Letters between Grieg and Molard from May to July discussed the work of translation and contained messages of goodwill from Grieg not only to Delius but also to Ida Molard, Julien Leclercq, Léon Moreau and 'all in your friendly little circle'.
     Grieg's intervention with his publisher over the matter of payment for Molard and Leclercq came at Delius's instigation and was instantly effective. Gauguin, too, was interested in seeing the matter solved; now at Pont-Aven, he wrote to Molard, 'It is a great pity that the Grieg translation has come to a stop; it means that I shall not have the pleasure of seeing you this summer.'

4   Hermann Levi (1839–1900): German conductor. He studied at the Leipzig Conservatorium, was court conductor at Munich from 1872, and became general musical director in that city in 1894. Grieg had written to Levi on Delius's behalf earlier in June. However, writing from Reichenhall to Delius on 31 August, Levi apologized for the fact that he would be unable to see him in Munich, suggesting instead that Delius play his work there to Richard Strauss: 'I am at the same time writing to Herr Strauss, asking him to give an hour to you.' This was to be early in September.

5   I must here take the opportunity to correct an error in my *Delius – The Paris Years*, where I mistakenly state on page 59 that these lines were written by Grieg.

(51)
Herman Bang to Fritz Delius

> St. Germain en Laye, Rue des Coches 17bis.
> Friday.
> [July ? 1894]

Dear friend,

Do not be angry because I have not sent you the fifty francs and still cannot do so. You see, I am very ill and I am not allowed to do any work. I can only have milk – *only* milk – and that is going to last six weeks. How am I going to be able to live during these six weeks? God only knows. I cannot earn anything and I have absolutely nothing.

Do drop me a line to tell me how matters stand with Hennings.[1]

Your friend
H. B.

Autograph letter, initialled and undated, written in German.

The original is in the Delius Trust Archive. It is the second of two letters written by Bang to Delius in 1894 that have been preserved.

Herman Bang (1857–1912): Danish author and actor–playwright of the first rank. He wrote a wide range of stories and novels in the Naturalist style. Living in Paris in straitened circumstances, he was acting as consultant and stage director for Lugné-Poe, founder of the Théâtre de l'Oeuvre (see Letter 161, note 2). Bang was instrumental in getting Lugné-Poe to present Strindberg's *Creditors*, his own play *Brothers* being given on the same bill, on 21 June 1894.

It seems likely that this letter was written some time in July, as Strindberg recorded on 1 September that Bang was on his sick-bed in Denmark (*Strindbergs Brev*, X, 2927), having left Paris for his home country in August after a year and a half in France. Strindberg was, in fact, to move into Bang's rooms in Paris for a time later in the year.

One other letter from Herman Bang is preserved in the Delius Trust Archive. It is undated, but written from his usual address, 14, rue de l'Abbé de l'Epée (Hôtel des Américains), shortly before this note; in it Bang told Delius that he had written 'a long letter' to Hennings.

1   Henrik Hennings (1848–1923): Danish music publisher and concert promoter. He studied at the newly founded Copenhagen Conservatorium and composed songs and piano pieces. Becoming manager in 1880 of the Kongelig Musikhandel, a company he himself took over in 1887, Hennings published the work of a number of leading

Scandinavian composers. Furthermore, he was now responsible as concert arranger for bringing many celebrated foreign conductors and soloists to Copenhagen. Another brief reference to him is found rather later in Grieg's correspondence with Delius, demonstrating a positive, if short-lived, interest by Hennings early in 1896 in *The Magic Fountain*.

(52)
Fritz Delius to Jutta Bell

33 Rue Ducouëdic
le 11 July 94.

My dear friend

Your letter just received — I am really most happy that you now see things in the right way and put all feelings of the ordinary woman aside. I feel also that for the first time a woman understands me thoroughly — Believe me when I tell you that I understand you also and have the greatest admiration for you — Dont search any more for the truth. It will come to you in working for a great cause — Why you never found it was, simply, that you did not look in the right direction — You looked for it in the castle of Rolf instead of in the arms[?] of Irmelin.[1] The people that surround one in everyday life are equally groping in the dark Or indifferently frittering away their lives in little enjoyments. Surely you would not find it there — You say you have never been able to work with anyone — no doubt — because most people — even artists — have no special aim or direction — You will however be able to work with me. I can see that by the way you have understood my idea of Watawa — I am very pleased with the stanzas you sent me — And it would have been in that strain I should have attempted to make her think. When you send more verses please write on a large sheet and only on one side, with a large margin I can then put any remarks I like and return it you for approval. After the 8th line you have

> Say what is it
> All this anguish.

It might be better there perhaps to put —

> What can it be
> This strange, vague anguish.

As you repeat Say what is it in 18th line. Of course only a little detail. It might be more powerful the question she puts herself first. Instead of

> Let me end it
> Let me kill him

I think

> Why not end it?
> Why not kill him?

More forcible. All these lines are very fine and powerful and characteristic of the
hot blooded Indian girl. In the lines

> And Watawa
> by her fathers
> for ever more be blest

"Should" is not necessary. You have put "would then have rest" above which
will apply to the rest. For Quick! yes quick! etc. I think we might put –

> Quick and sure
> into his heart
> I will plunge
> My pointed knife.

The lines following I think you might express more vividly, more hesitatingly.

> No, ah! No.
> Although I hate him
> I cannot – cannot
> take his life

I find a little bit abrupt. Something to this effect might be better: but I leave it
to you to find the most appropriate lines.
— A pause —

> But just as surely
> will the fountain –
> now so near,
> fulfil my revenge –
> Patience – tarry –
> Why such hurry.
> Let me trust in providence.

Here dont you see, she is trying to make a concession to her feelings. She is half
hoping that something may turn up to prevent his death. which she feels is her
duty to accomplish – but her feelings have become different – She continues
admiring the scenery and the weird beauteous sounds of nature –

> How different the harmonies of nature
> To the discords in my heart.
> The airs breath[e] love and peace.
> And I nurse thoughts of murder.
> So far now have I come
> I cannot retrace my steps:
> I would betray my blood.
> The fountain! The fountain –
> He will drink and die.
> And then? _____[2]

Then can come –

> Still another night must vanish

The rest to the end is very fine and powerful and just what I want. Improve on the lines that I have scribbled down on the spur of the moment.
After

"Take my life!"

Solana enters from the swamps returning after searching for the fountain He sees Watawa standing in the moonlight and cries with great tenderness

Watawa! Watawa!

Then her feelings become clear to her. She fights with herself. He rushes forward and clasps her in his arms. She half resists and half gives way. Then a love scene of great tenderness and passion. She tells him all her hate gradually turning to love etc and now for a moment they are happy. And sink to sleep In the meantime the mists rise and reveal the fountain. Mystic voices fill the air. Solana wakes with a start. Then Watawa. Solana in rapturous joy sees the fountain which now takes the first place in his mind. Watawa remembers again his fate and the terrible danger to one she loves, above all on earth. (You see all this no doubt vividly.) In terror she tries to hold him back   he understands not. Not knowing the danger. At length seeing all is lost she rushes to the fountain and drinks, dying slowly in his arms. Singing a kind of death plaint — Please keep this letter and put the thoughts down as you find them good. — I will look after the house for you. The address is 30 Rue de Clamart

Fontenay-aux-Roses

Ever your friend
Fritz Delius

— Please send the book —

Autograph letter, signed and dated, written in English.

The original is in the Jacksonville University Library, Jacksonville, Florida. It is the second of fifteen letters, dating from 1894 to 1899, written by Delius to Mrs Bell that have been preserved.

Jutta Bell (1857?–1934): *née* Mordt, of Norwegian extraction and distantly related, by marriage, to Grieg. She had been a near neighbour of Delius during his Florida days. Married at that time to a lieutenant in the Royal Navy, she, like Delius, had lived on the St Johns River near Picolata. The Bells moved to England around 1886 and, before long, separated. Jutta remained in Europe, seeing Delius both in London and in Paris; she was studying with Mathilde Marchesi and was later to make a name for herself (as Madame Bell-Ranske) teaching singing and voice production. Her letters to Delius have, unfortunately, not been preserved, but those he wrote to her in 1894 show that she was working with him on the libretto of *The Magic Fountain*. The references in this letter are to the hero and heroine, Solana (later to be renamed Solano) and Watawa.

The first extant letter from Delius to Mrs Bell, dated 29 May 1894, discusses a possible scenario (unrelated to *The Magic Fountain*) based on a poem by Matthew Arnold. The letter ends, 'Please tell me some more fairy tales. I love them as much as you do, and we might weave some together for our purpose. I should, as I said before, like to give all my works a deeper meaning. I want to say something to the world very serious & music & poetry are only my means. You might really be of great help to me, as I see in you a sister nature to mine. You are about the only woman that understands a little what I am driving at. But I want to tread in Wagner's footsteps and even give something more in the right direction. For me dramatic art is almost taking the place of religion. People are sick of being preached to. But by being played to, they may be worked upon.'

1   The reference is to Delius's earlier opera, *Irmelin*.

2   At this point Jutta added in her own hand, 'I dont like this at all in her present mood she would see no peace & love in nature!'

(53)
Robert Phifer to Fritz Delius

July 27th 1894

Dear Friend

It has indeed been a long time since any of us here in Danville have heard aught of you & I send this to tell you we still remember you and think of you & speak of you. – The last news we had was when you sent the set of songs published by Augener to Miss Averett. We all admired them greatly and hope yet to make acquaintance with other of your works. Kindly let me know the title of some of your recent productions that I may obtain them & recall the talented young friend of the old years in North Danville.

Many things are changed since you left us & many things are not. The old school still keeps going but Mr. Jack Averett is no longer the "principal" as his health is very feeble now. The Averetts live up on Green street near the flower-garden. I often go there – there have been no marriages in the family – Miss Pattie A. is still my assistant at the college. For several years past she has gone North during vacation to study voice culture. She sings very beautifully as of old. – For the past seven years I have lived in Danville – I live on Main St not far from the house where Miss Jean Arm[i]stead (now Mrs. Venable) once lived when you gave her harmony lessons. The town has grown much & presents a much better appearance than when you were here. Many of the modern dwellings are quite handsome. – Of course we have electric street cars. North Danville has changed its name & is now known as Neapolis. It is a town of more than 5000 inhabitants now. There are very large cotton mills on that side of the river. One building, up by the upper bridge (wooden) is 900 feet long & three stories high. Midway between the upper & lower bridge is a stone dam which catches the surplus water from above & a large canal feeds another handsome cotton mill below the lower bridge almost just at the North Danville depot where Hoppe & I took leave of you upon your departure. They also have street cars in N. Danville. I have learned nothing of Hoppe of late. I believe he now lives in Richmond & is married. Old Man Wilson is dead — His daughter Annie married a Mr. Rover James & they live at "The Burton" a handsome modern hotel built on the site of the old "Arlington". Summerfields building (the hotel for down town) was burnt & some lives were lost.[1] New buildings have been & are being erected all along there making the street much more handsome. I am the Organist at the Episcopal Ch. & have a fine choir (the best in town) Mrs. Jean Arm[i]stead Venable is Organist at the Pres. Church. — Willa my daughter is a hansome young woman of over 19 yrs now. She still has the bangle on her bracelet with your name on it. Tommie my son is now a lad of 16 & is taller than I am. My other children you would not know of. — Gitt still has his drug store in North D. but all that part has been rebuilt after a fire — There is a continuous line of stores from Flippins (just across from Gitts) down to the Railroad in North D. — Rhodes has a barber shop on this side I merely mention his name to aid you in recalling persons & places. Tom Averett is still a Book Man. Bill Averett — still Shoe-man. Tom Lee of North D. died — Left big estate — Widow remarried — money about all gone. Old Dr Martin (Presbyterian) still alive. Ditto — Dr. Dame. With me the world wags just as of old. Going up Main St. & keeping to the left at the Fork then crossing the railroad bridge ("Dry Bridge") & continuing about ½ mile there is now a large military school. I attended a picnic out there today — Beautiful wooded dell just like the one I showed you & Hoppe once over in North D. where the Kalmias grew. Numbers of the young people make excursions up the river to the "House Rock" — The Rhododendrum was especially beautiful up that way this year. Do you remember the time we all went on the boat ride up there. Miss Averett & I were speaking of it & of you some days ago. But see what a scrawl I have written you. Receive it such as it is for the sake of the old days — Still think of us sometimes & when opportunity allows write us a few words

Yours sincerely
Robert S. Phifer
629 Main St.
Danville Va

To
Mr. Fritz Delius
Claremont
Bradford
Yorkshire

Autograph letter, signed and dated, written in English.

The original is in the Delius Trust Archive. It is the first of two letters written by Phifer to Delius, the second dated 1910, that have been preserved.

Robert S. Phifer (1852?–1912): professor of music at the Roanoke Female College (now Averett College), Danville, Virginia. He had studied at the Leipzig Conservatorium and settled in Danville in 1878. Phifer was Delius's closest friend during the composer's stay in the town in 1885–86, and this letter is included in this collection for the unique insight it gives into the community of which Delius had so recently been a part.

1   In his letter dated 16 February 1910, Phifer conveyed a piquant query from Summerfield: 'Say Telius does you make much money out of your composing pisness.'

(54)
Frederick Delius to Jutta Bell

33 Rue Ducouedic
29 July 94

My dear friend

It is really very kind of you to send me the "Gypsies"[1] and I appreciate very much your gift, but much more your friendship.

My intention is to write a musical work on the Gypsies that is why I wanted it. It was not for the present work: I have a vague idea of writing 3 works : One on the Indians, one on the Gypsies and one on the Negroes & quadroons.[2] The Indians I am doing at present. But as I told you once, I always have another work which I think of in the entracte of the present one. Thanks for the verses I like them very much. You understand thoroughly Watawa and the sentiment of the whole. As soon as I have a little time I will write out what I have done in the 1st & 2nd Acts and send it you.

Since you left I read the Last of the Mohicans & Lake Ontario by Fennimore Cooper. There are some very fine things in the works of this man. The descriptions of Nature are really praiseworthy. I read also, The Natchez, then Atala by Chateaubriand. Should you come across anything interesting about the Indians let me know. I read all I can on the subject which I am treating. And then treat the subject in my own way. I want this work to be essentially Indian I want the Indian Characters to be the most important. For this reason I dont want much of the Spanish element it would complicate the subject without adding to the conciseness. The first Character is Watawa then comes Tamanūnd the magician and Solana who in the end almost becomes an indian himself and quite disappears – or loses his individuality in the last act. He and Watawa become one with their surroundings and Nature. He is no more Solana but the love of

Watawa, who has not changed one iota since the beginning. Her nature I mean.
Solana is an adventurer and gradually the surroundings & the beautiful Watawa
make him forget all his past life: that is why I make him drink of the waters
seeing & knowing this fatal effect. He does not want to go back to his native
land or people The nature of the great Spirit is very good, but it must be only
used by the Indians Solana knows it by the name of the fountain of Eternal
youth, "La Fontaine de Jeunesse" I have got the outline of the drama very firm
now. I have worked a good deal at the 1st & 2nd Acts. After the wreck Solana lies
on the beach. Watawa comes down to bathe and is startled by the sight of the
white man who now begins to move. She runs back again into the bush and tells
the indians what she has seen. In the meantime Solana comes to himself and
endeavours to understand his situation which slowly dawns on him as he sees
the wreck out at sea. The indians now are seen looking out of bushes at him and
slowly and cautiously they run down on to the sands. A sachem speaks to him
and tells him to follow them to the Wigwam where he will find meat and drink
– Solana having asked for water – As the Indians never fought or attacked – in
those days – helpless or unarmed men this is alltogether motified. The Indian
maiden however is not pleased with this. She expected to see him killed. At the
camp fire Solana asks about the Fountain & finds out about the Seer Tamanūnd
who dwells in the forest alone. The Sachem cannot give him a man guide as on
the morrow they undertake an expedition against another tribe. But he thinks
of Watawa – He proposes this to her. And she then tells him her thirst for
revenge. Why does the white man still live? The Sachem tells her of his intention
to send her as guide for Solana to Tamanūnd – the hereditary hate of the Indian
and recent struggles make him wish the death of Solana and he sees the
convenient instrument in the shape of Watawa. He gives her a knife and places
the fate of Solana in her hands thereby also clearing his own conscience He
artfully confides to her a mission to Tamanūnd – He wants the advice of the old
prophet. This motivates much in the 2nd Act. I will let you have it later.

I have received a little money for my journey to Bayreuth.[3] But thank you
from the bottom of my heart for your generous & friendly offer. Should I need
any I will apply to you with the greatest confidence. Goodbye! dear friend My
address in Bayreuth is Wahnfried Strasse 7. 1 étage c/o Frau Medizinalrath Dr
Berr

Autograph letter, unsigned and dated, written in English.

The original is in the Jacksonville University Library.

1   Delius had written on 20 July: 'I should very much like the Gipsies of Lelande if
you can afford to send it to me. I am yet *stone broke* but will pay you back later.'

2   The 'Indian' work is *The Magic Fountain*; 'Negroes & quadroons' are to be the subject
of *Koanga;* and 'Gypsies' were ultimately to be transformed into the vagabonds of *A
Village Romeo and Juliet*.

3   Delius had been luckier than Sinding, who had written to him from Drøbak on 26
June: 'If only I had the money' for the trip to Munich.

(55)

Fritz Delius to Jutta Bell

München, den 12 August 1894

Schiller Strasse 26ª II etage

Dear friend

I received your letter on the point of starting for Munich. In Bayreuth I heard
"Parsifal" twice and Tannhaüser once. Parsifal is magnificent: the finest work
of Wagner The orchestra and theatre are perfect. I am really very glad I came
here, it will no doubt be of great benefit to me. Before leaving Munich I shall
hear the Nibelungen 3 times, Tristan und Isolde 3 times and the Meistersingers
3 times. On my return to Paris I will read you all my sketches for Watawa and
shall not give the final form to the poem before being settled down again. I
change and alter and rewrite a great deal. Therefore I dont like to shew my first
sketches. The whole however is very clear before me now and in a fortnights
work I shall be able to give the proper poetic form. Your ideas & verses in the
last act will be of great use to me and they are all very good and felt. However
we will talk all this over together when I return. When you have ideas write
them down for yourself and shew me them. We will then decide together what
can be used etc. Only a woman could have conceived Watawa like you have
done, therefore all your thoughts will be of great value to me. I want to make
the poem very *concise*, not a word to much philosophical or phsychological – as
the drama – as I have conceived it – requires. My sketches of the first and 2nd
Act are nearly complete. Although I have altered again since writing you last –
Today I dined with Bjørnsen his daughter and wife who I met yesterday in the
street they invited me to come to them at Schwaz in the Tyrol, which I may do
for a few days.[1] Levi I met in Bayreuth and shall shew him my Lyric drama in a
few days.

    Now dear friend, write me a few words, and tell me if you find all comfortable
Rue Ducouedic.[2] The address of my friends is 6 Rue Vercingétorix. Monsieur
Molard. I told them about you and you will be welcome. I dont go very much
now – there is a man named Leclercq who I dont care for much and he seems to
have taken root there.

Believe me
Ever your friend
Fritz Delius

Autograph letter, signed and dated, written in English.

The original is in the Jacksonville University Library.

1   Bjørnson and his wife had been in the Tyrol since May. In a later reference to his Bayreuth trip, Delius made no mention of a venture into Austria. He returned to Paris around 7 September, and a letter from Sinding dated 11 September indicates that Delius had indulged in typically *gemütliche* Bavarian practices: 'I am very glad indeed to hear that you have made such good progress in beer drinking and cigar smoking.'

2   Delius had lent Mrs Bell his apartment in Paris.

(56)
Irma [?] to Fritz Delius

[mid-1890s?]

My dear Fritz

I love you with all my heart, you are the only friend in whom I still trust and the only one who means anything to me — Rest assured that as long as I live you have in me a real sister and a sure friend. How tired I am today I cannot say here Have fetched my old lady to accompany me —

I must dash away — I shall come early on Tuesday like today —

Work well and remember you are not alone and can work at peace with yourself as long as I am there

Yours
Irma [?]

Autograph letter, signed and undated, written in German.

The original is in the Delius Trust Archive.

The identity of the writer of this letter has so far remained a mystery. A mid-1890s — or earlier — date is postulated. The signature is not particularly clear, and no surname is given, nor are any further communications from this source preserved. The letter is included in this selection as evidence of Delius's romantic attachments during this period. To my knowledge the only Irma known to Delius was to be Victor Thrane's younger sister (see Letter 72, note), whose first language would almost certainly have been English. A memoir preserved in the Oslo University Library indicates that she associated with Delius and Munch in Aasgaardstrand in 1906. (See also Letter 77, note.)

1895

By June *The Magic Fountain* was finished. The winter and spring had certainly seen their diversions, as Strindberg and Gauguin were now playing their interesting parts in Delius's life. He would take meals with them at Madame Charlotte's *crémerie*, talk with them at the rue Vercingétorix, and take walks with Strindberg and Mucha in the Luxembourg Gardens and the Latin Quarter. *La vie de bohème*, however, exacted its price, often unfortunately high, if commonplace at the time. Early in the year Gauguin contracted syphilis. Some time that same year secondary syphilis was diagnosed in Delius. There is evidence that more than one course of treatment was prescribed until 1900, after which Delius's health was to remain stable until neurological problems occurred some ten years later. Perhaps not surprisingly, very little correspondence has survived from this year, and a line from Sinding in September – 'You don't seem to be exactly cheerful?' – takes on a wry significance.

As if this were not enough, there were family and financial problems. For some years, Delius had been supported by a moderate allowance from his father, but it is clear that the family was singularly unimpressed by his seeming lack of progress. Composition was earning him no money, and the only larger work to have had a public performance since his arrival in Paris in 1888 was *Paa Vidderne*, just twice, in 1891 and 1894. His father's business was, furthermore, in deepening trouble; and at the same time Delius had fallen out with his uncle, with Theodor now resolutely refusing a request for money to help get *The Magic Fountain* performed.

Delius's movements during the year remain poorly charted, and the only evidence of a major excursion from Paris shows him in Berlin in November – perhaps looking for a contribution to his upkeep from members of his family there. The year had probably started brightly enough, but unquestionably by the autumn, 1895 must have proved to be the bleakest year so far in the life of the gradually maturing composer.

Delius was certainly attractive to women in his younger days, a fact that is hinted at in just a few surviving letters. Nina Grieg displayed a coquettish interest in his love life, and in the sequence of letters preserved by the Griegs one or two, which the recipients may have judged it discreet to destroy, are missing. Clearly, there were Norwegian affairs during those early, long summers in the north. Camilla Jacobsen wrote to him and then met him in Christiania in the summer of 1887, according to his travel diary. How close was his relationship with Charlotte Bødtker, another Norwegian acquaintance? Delius's own remaining letters to Randi Blehr are circumspect, but the dreamily romantic tone of one letter she wrote to him, if innocent, is still indicative of his ability to charm.

In Paris itself, the early years have bequeathed only little evidence of his sentimental affairs, but there was certainly an 1890s relationship with the Princesse de Cystria.

Then some time in 1895 he was informed that he had contracted syphilis, a disease that could almost be termed an unfortunate commonplace in the Paris of his day. The circles in which he moved were well aware of the risks so easily run at the time, and there was a concomitant and often morbid fear of contracting the disease. Treatment, and sometimes diagnosis, was not notably successful at this period, and the considerable diagnostic and medical advances in the field of sexually transmitted disease in the first decade of the new century were still to come. At all events, there would certainly have been a hiatus in Delius's *vie sentimentale* until the symptoms ascribed to syphilis disappeared.

Early in 1896 Delius began the friendship with Jelka Rosen, whom he eventually married in 1903. Whatever their early relationship, it never became sufficiently binding for him not to seek occasional pleasures elsewhere, to Jelka's inevitable distress. Even the young Louise Chadwick, a near neighbour in Grez, felt real alarm, convinced that Delius was trying to seduce her some time after he first came to live there. She was probably around seventeen at the time. That life in Grez assuredly did have its intimate pleasures at this period is hinted at in in a letter Delius wrote from Berlin to Ida Gerhardi: 'I am glad that you kept my bed sacrosanct from Serena [Jelka's mother] – I hope you, too, dreamed sweetly in it – Many fond memories lie hidden there – Serena wouldn't have got off to sleep easily in it – or might have had another heart attack.'

Several of Jelka's friends would come to stay at Grez during those early days, but Louise Chadwick (later Louise Courmes) remembered that Delius gradually 'took their place and drove them away'. The last to go was Ida Gerhardi, who until 1904 had always found a welcome there; but an earlier casualty was Maud Ede, an English painter. There was, indeed, a woman called Maud in Delius's life for a while (see Letter 77), but it is not clear whether she was Maud Ede. Another artist who did not stay long at Grez was the German painter Julia Wolfthorn. Delius did have a relationship with a German woman at some time in the 1890s (see Letter 56), but this probably had no connection with Grez. We have, therefore, the picture of Delius steadily clearing the household at Grez of Jelka's friends, Jelka clearly being much in love with him and in consequence unable or unwilling to check what must on the whole have been for her an unhappy sequence of events.

In short, it can probably be said that in the 1880s and early 1890s Delius had a number of more or less conventional young love affairs, and that after the fearsome setback of 1895, his attitude to sexual matters gradually became more cynical and perhaps exploitative. He was to become no stranger to Parisian houses of ill repute, and Halfdan Jebe's letters allude to his taste for oriental girls. He seems to have made little secret of such dalliances to his closer friends, Alfred Hertz remembering an occasion in the early 1900s when Delius had taken him to see 'six whores' in Paris before inviting him home to dinner with Jelka. By then there had come a gradual acceptance of a life spent with the plain but loving Jelka, with its corollary of extra-marital affairs. And yet, as Percy Grainger succinctly put it: 'Fred set out to enjoy life, did so, & did not regret paying the price it cost.'*

_____

The Magic Fountain, opera (RT I/3). Completed.

Deux Mélodies, songs (Verlaine) (RT V/16).

'The Page sat in the lofty Tower', song (Jacobsen) (RT V/17). 1895?

Légende, for violin and orchestra (RT VII/3). Orchestrated 1895?

Florent Schmitt makes a piano arrangement of *The Magic Fountain*. 1895?

(57)
Christian Sinding to Fritz Delius

Christiania 25 June 95.

Dear friend,

I was very glad to hear from you, and most impressed that you have already produced a new opera.[1] Lord, how I should like to have a crack at something like that, – but I can't escape from the song and piano piece factory. I recently finished a violin sonata – the biggest thing I have been able to do for a long time. Damned money – it runs away just like through a sieve – can't keep it at all. But I admire your energy for getting on with things without stopping – in spite of family and uncles. Eventually you must have a lucky break. Then you will be able to enjoy your family being friendly again. – I don't know what I am going to do in the winter yet – it's a long time till then. If I can raise enough

_____

* Letter to Eric Fenby, 6 December 1936.

money, I wouldn't mind going to Vienna. In any case I must live in a big city —
bigger even than Berlin.

Farewell for now. Thanks for your letter.

Yours
Christian Sinding

Permanent address: Brödrene Hals.
                    Christiania.

Autograph letter, signed and dated, written in German.

The original is in the Delius Trust Archive.

1   *The Magic Fountain*. Although little correspondence survives from 1895, it is quite
evident that Delius had been busy during the winter and spring months, working on
the opera whose completion is signalled by this letter from Sinding. This, too, had
been the period when Delius had been associating with Gauguin and Strindberg in
Paris, both of whom he had met in 1894. Gauguin, however, had recently left Paris —
and France — for good, and was to live out his last years in the South Sea Islands.

(58)
Christian Sinding to Fritz Delius

Christiania 1 September 95.

Dear friend,

My plans for the future are very vague. In any case I shall go — probably this
week even — to Berlin. My Symphony is to be played this season at a symphony
concert given by the Opera orchestra under Weingartner,[1] and until then I shall
certainly remain in Berlin. Would certainly like to go somewhere where one
doesn't freeze, e.g. Algeria, if only I can escape from the need for cash. God
help me, Amen!

You don't seem to be exactly cheerful? And yet you have at least had time and
peace to finish two such big scores. If only you knew how songs and piano pieces
can embitter the life of a poor devil. And the worst of it is — time goes so awfully
quickly — carefree youth is over my boy. — I hope for your sake that your uncles
etc. will not demand that your opera be performed within a fortnight or so. I
know how it is — it takes an eternity before one gets a reply. — If you don't
mind a comment from me — I think it would be a very good thing if you could
get a publisher first, and pass over the unpleasant job of placing the opera to
this slave. For these people locked doors are opened. But it depends a great deal
on whether the text "pleases". I know a big opera publisher in Berlin — I can't
remember his name just now — I admit it's only a very superficial acquaintance,

but perhaps I could be of a little use to you after all. We can of course talk about this later. —² It's been a a bad summer with endless rain and rheumatism.

Yours
Christian Sinding

Addr. C.F. Peters. Thalstr. 10. Leipzig.

Autograph letter, signed and dated, written in German.

The original is in the Delius Trust Archive.

1   Felix Weingartner (1863–1942): Austrian conductor and composer. He studied at the Leipzig Conservatorium, became a protégé of Liszt and went on to achieve great distinction as a conductor both in Europe and in the United States.

2   Although no precise indication has so far been found of Delius's movements during the summer, a further letter from Sinding, written from Berlin later in the month, gives evidence of Delius's own intention to travel, probably in October, to Berlin; hence Sinding's reference to being able to talk about an 'opera publisher' later. Delius was certainly in Berlin in November.

1896

Financial problems continued, and Delius now contemplated selling his valuable violin. Immediate worries about his health had receded, at least for the time being; his illness had been treated, and its major symptoms would by now have subsided. Life was returning as far as possible to its normal course. Undaunted by the failure of *Irmelin* and *The Magic Fountain* yet to appear on any stage (although for a time it had seemed that the latter would be given in Prague), Delius began work on a third opera, *Koanga*, again consulting Jutta Bell on the libretto. In January he had made the acquaintance of a German painter, Jelka Rosen, who was studying at Courtois's academy in Paris. The friendship blossomed, and they began to spend more and more time in each other's company. In the spring Jelka introduced him to the village of Grez-sur-Loing, near Fontainebleau, where she often painted.

An old friend, Edvard Munch, was now in Paris, and Delius spent a good deal of time with him, Molard, de Monfreid and, occasionally, Strindberg, who was still living in Paris and was finally to leave in the summer.

Delius returned to Norway around the beginning of June, staying for nearly three months; for much of the time he was settled in Valdres at work on the first act of *Koanga*, but later in July and early August he took himself off with knapsack and Norwegian guide to the Jotunheim mountains. He returned to Paris by way of Denmark and Germany around the middle of September.

The autumn was spent in Paris at the rue Ducouëdic. He continued to work on *Koanga*, his largest musical score yet, and by Christmas, which was spent at the family home in Bradford, he had regained much of his confidence, was working well, planning performances, and now looked forward to a return trip to the United States at last, early in the new year. He had also seen five of his songs published in Paris by the firm of L. Grus fils.

Koanga, opera (C. F. Keary) (RT I/4). Begun.

Appalachia, American Rhapsody for Orchestra (RT VI/12). An early version of the later orchestral variations.

Romance, for cello and piano (RT VIII/5).

(59)
Fritz Delius to Jutta Bell

33 Rue Ducouëdic
le 9 Fev 96 —

My dear friend —

I am really awfully sorry you have had trouble with your house,[1] and am glad
you got out quick — Bad drains can kill a barrack full of soldiers, to say nothing
of a small family. It is really extremely good of you to take such trouble about
my things and be such a good friend — There is in spite of everything something
big about your nature which not only commands my respect but also my
greatest sympathy. I believe you are after all about the best woman I ever met.
I am sending you the copies of my songs which I possess — 4 copies. If you want
more get them from Augeners'[2] & I will repay you for them — Johannes Wolff
wrote to me for the full score of my "Legende"[3] So you will have the opportunity
of hearing it shortly in London — I am writing another opéra — *Please keep this
quite to yourself* — I am taking the story of Bras-Coupé — in the Grandissimes[4] —
Read it and tell me what you think of it — I will send you shortly the libretto
and no doubt you will be able to give me some help. I am getting all the
Southern flavor in the music. The first act is fully sketched out & part of the
2nd. It will make a strange effect on the stage —. I am keeping the whole in the
character of the negro melody. Palmyre & Bras Coupé are the two chief characters
— I am not yet certain about the end — I must change the real end. Make Bras
Coupé kill himself & Palmyre or something of that sort — However you will
see.

Write me again soon. My Violin is not a small one — It is full sized & worth
about £200 this would of course be too much for your friend. It is a genuine
Cremorna instrument.[5] Good bye [?] dear friend for the present &

Believe me
ever your friend
Fritz Delius

I am *also working* like a *negro & with* negroes

Autograph letter, signed and dated, written in English.

The original is in the Jacksonville University Library.

1   Mrs Bell was living in England.

2   Augener's three albums of Delius's songs had been published in 1890 and 1892.

3   Delius may have made the acquaintance of the violinist Johannes Wolff through the Griegs. Nina Grieg had written to Delius on 1 April 1892 describing Wolff as a 'fantastic player'; he had come to lunch at Troldhaugen two days earlier and had then played to them until late in the evening.

4   George Washington Cable, *The Grandissimes*, first published in the United States in 1880. 'The Story of Bras-Coupé' forms an episode in the novel and provides the subject-matter for Delius's opera *Koanga*.

5   Delius seems to have had little success in selling his violin. In 1907 there came a polite note from Arve Arvesen declining to buy it (see Letter 222).

(60)
Fritz Delius to Jutta Bell

33 Rue Ducouëdic
le 25 Fev 96.

Dear friend —

I send you today my libretto of Bras Coupé — I wrote the music and the words at the same time. You will see about the color — I find I must really get some one to work with me — My literature is not on a level with my music — And I believe in Colaboration a greater effect may be attained — Please advise me — As you see I have not decided about the end Shall I make a 3rd Act or only the 2 — You see the 2nd Act is much shorter and might have 2 parts. I thought of an epilogue like the prologue ie. bringing the scene back to the old negro — his tale now finished — I want a finale — Have you an idea? a dramatic one? Do you think you have time to help me in this? I think the music is a success — It is more of an opera than the last one — with quartetts Trios, quintettes & chorus — If you undertake it make it as varied as possible — Do not fear not being realistic — I dont believe in realism in opéra — Fantasy & poetry Please write and let me hear your idea about this — I own my style & language is sometimes so vile that it shocks me as a musician — I hope you are well & getting on in your work — There is some talk of Watawa being given in *Weimar*.[1]
    I am employing the Banjo in my orchester. The effect will be strange —
    Good bye, dear friend

Ever yours
Fritz Delius

Autograph letter, signed and dated, written in English. Envelope addressed: Madame / Jutta Bell / 9 Cranley Gardens / Londres SW / Angleterre. Postmark: PARIS 26 Fevr 96.

The original is in the Jacksonville University Library.

1   *The Magic Fountain* was to remain unperformed in Delius's lifetime.

(61)

Fritz Delius to Jelka Rosen

33 Rue Ducouëdic
le 1 Mars 96 –

My dear Miss Rosen –

I thank you very much for your kind note and will, as you propose, come on
Monday night.

The masquerade was a great success – a tremendous entrain – I got home at
7.30 a m – this morning –

Your sympathetic words about my music gave me great pleasure and I hope
you will soon come again and give me the opportunity of playing you something
else –

Believe me
Sincerely yours
Fritz Delius

Autograph letter, signed and dated, written in English.

The original is in the Grainger Museum, Melbourne University, Melbourne, Australia.
It is the first of some 300 communications addressed by Delius to Jelka between 1896
and 1921 (including those dated 1897 and 1898 which have been found in copy form
only) that are preserved in the museum.

Helene ('Jelka') Sophie Emilie Rosen (1868–1935): born in Belgrade of Schleswig-
Holstein parentage, into a family which was distinguished in legal and diplomatic
circles. Her mother, Serena Anna (1830–1902), a daughter of the composer and pianist
Ignaz Moscheles, was the widow of Consul-General Georg Rosen (1820–91). She was
now living in Paris with her daughter, Jelka, who was studying painting there. For an
account of Jelka's first and subsequent meetings with Delius, see Appendix VII.

(62)

Fritz Delius to Jelka Rosen

33 Rue Ducouëdic
Samedi
[March 1896]

Dear Miss Rosen –

I shall be unable to leave before Tuesday, so am sorry that I cannot accompany
you – but will come on Tuesday morning 11.50. I shall first stay a night at
Bourron to speak with Keary[1] about our work – at least I think so – as I do not

know how far Bourron is from Grez[2] – I hope the weather will be fine so that we can walk about in the country.

I am glad our talk helped you – perhaps you will be able to help me on another occasion –

With kind regards
I remain
Sincerely yours
Fritz Delius

Autograph letter, signed and undated, written in English. Jelka later added 'March Spring 1896'.

The original is in the Grainger Museum.

1   Charles F. Keary (1848–1917): educated at Marlborough and Trinity College, Cambridge, the author of a number of novels and of historical and philosophical works. It was in his role as poet that Delius turned to him for the libretto of *Koanga*, which the composer had originally worked on with Jutta Bell. Keary was again to collaborate with Delius, on the libretto of *A Village Romeo and Juliet*, although his version was to be discarded as unsatisfactory and the circle completed by Delius finally writing his own text. A distinguished numismatist, Keary had for some years been a member of the Department of Coins and Medals in the British Museum; and a shared interest with Delius is indicated in a book which he published in 1892, *Norway and the Norwegians*, following on other works he had written on Nordic history and mythology. A delightful, if irreverent, characterization of Keary is to be found in a letter written to Delius over a decade later by their mutual friend the artist Guy Maynard: 'He always reminds one of those dark planets that are supposed to circulate about the moon; giving forth no light, but gloomily circulating all the same.'

2   For several summers Jelka had had the permission of the Marquis de Carzeaux to paint in the garden of a house which belonged to him in the hamlet of Grez-sur-Loing, near the Forest of Fontainebleau. With the help of her mother, she was to buy this property in May 1897. Keary himself was living in neighbouring Bourron, and the first clear record of Delius's visiting Grez is contained in a letter written to Jelka on 11 April [?]: 'Keary and myself go long walks every day – Yesterday we went to Barbizon – We passed by Grez the other day – Not a soul there.'

(63)
Ottokar Nováček to Fritz Delius

[Berlin] 7. [May 1896]

My dear Delius,

I have been to Prof. Mannsteadt's[1] twice; he is now in Christiania, and his wife could not find the music,[2] but telegraphed her husband about it – so I ought to be able to send you your piece in 3–4 days.

A few days ago I went with your Elegy to Ries & Erler[3] – "but the piece is much too complicated and difficult for it to have a large circulation, we regret" etc . .

Thank you for your Anatomy & Physiology of the Orch;[4] – I was not able to translate everything, but I personally feel myself to be a stranger to your views. –

How is your opera going? Give my kind regards to Sinding, when I meet him again I have some more new "*Experiences*" to relate to him. –

Dear Delius, you must forgive me for not yet having sent you what I owe.[5]

On the 15th inst. I am going to Nauheim, a spa near Frankfurt, to take a cure.

Best wishes from the two girls, as also from Busoni & his wife, and especially from me

Yours
Ott. Nováček

My piano concerto is *not* going to be played at Düsseldorf. –

Autograph letter, signed and dated '7', written in German. Envelope addressed: Herrn / *Fritz Delius* / *Paris* Montrouge / *33 Rue Duconëdic.* The removal of the postage stamp has obliterated the postmark. Receiving postmark: PARIS 8 MAI 96.

The original is in the Delius Trust Archive. It is the first of three letters written by Nováček to Delius, two dated 1896 and one dated 1899, that have been preserved.

Nováček was apparently writing from Berlin. The Sinding correspondence shows that Nováček and Delius were in touch in January 1896, although for what purpose we are not told.

1   Franz Mannstädt (1852–1932): German conductor and pianist. He was at this time conductor of the Berlin Philharmonic Orchestra.

2   Nováček wrote again on 18 May: 'I had to leave without getting your piece, but have written again to Prof. Mannstaedt telling him to send the symph. poem direct to you.' The only full-scale 'symphonische Dichtung' Delius had composed to date was *Paa Vidderne*, which he had earlier dubbed a 'concert overture', but whose MS bears the clear title 'Symphonic poem'.

3   'Elegy' may be a slip of the pen for *Légende*, whose version for violin and piano was written some time between 1892 and 1895. Ries & Erler was a Berlin firm of music publishers. The third movement (Adagio cantabile) of Delius's early Suite for Violin and Orchestra was originally headed in MS 'Elegie'.

4   Delius et Papus, *Anatomie et Physiologie de l'Orchestre* (Paris: Chamuel, 1894). In this curious essay, one of Paris's leading occultists, Dr Gérard Encausse (Papus), attempted with Delius's aid 'to find a new orchestral system'.

5   See also Letter 105.

(64)
August Strindberg to Fritz Delius

[Paris, Wednesday, May ? 1896]

I feel that the time has not yet come for me to disclose my discovery — Strindberg.[1]

Telegram, the original of which has remained untraced. Its content, which would originally have been in French, was recorded by Delius in his memoir 'Recollections of Strindberg', first published in *The Sackbut*, 1, No. 8 (December 1920), pp. 353–4 (see Appendix VI).

August Strindberg (1849–1912): Swedish author. By the 1880s he had achieved fame in his native country. Now his plays, in particular, were becoming widely known and performed in continental Europe, especially in his favourite stamping-grounds of Paris and Berlin. His interests were extraordinarily wide: medicine, chemistry, philosophy, painting, acting, music, journalism — he had tried his hand at them all. Now almost at the end of his sojourn in Paris, Strindberg's precarious mental balance coloured his life darkly. He tended to remain secluded in his apartment, driven there by a morbid distrust of most of his friends and a quite paranoid fear of those he felt were his enemies.

Of Strindberg's acquaintance with Delius, almost the only record is provided by Delius's memoir, republished as an appendix to this volume. Strindberg was unlikely to have heard any of Delius's music, unless informally at the Molards'. However, he certainly enjoyed music, even to the extent of trying his hand at writing songs, some of which are extant. Very fond of Grieg's Piano Sonata, Strindberg grew to hate Wagner, whom he described as 'the musical personification of Evil'; he loved the story of Tristan, but abhorred its most celebrated setting, just as he abhorred operetta, too, as a musical form. His favourite instruments were, he claimed, the organ, piano and violin, and he played the guitar quite proficiently.

1   Delius had invited Strindberg to his rooms in order that an 'eminent chemist' friend could meet the Swede, who claimed to have perfected a method of making gold. Although time and place had been agreed, Strindberg characteristically changed his mind at the last moment. Delius referred in his memoir to 'a certain Wednesday afternoon', but he did not give the exact date. However, three chemical analyses by Léon Padé, director of the Laboratoire de la Bourse de Commerce, Paris, are dated 3 Juin 1896; now preserved in the Delius Trust Archive, they relate to Strindberg's experiments, although the covering envelope (like the analyses) is addressed to the Princesse de Cystria (see Letter 99). Delius had just left Paris and had no doubt arranged payment, amounting to 100 francs, by his wealthy patroness in order to help Strindberg.

It was in his letters of this particular period — around June 1896 — that Strindberg made most frequent references to analyses of the results of his chemical experiments: 'Many chemists are working on the material and we await their conclusion' (to Mathilde

Präger, 12 June 1896); 'You understand that the analysis has been done and approved'
(to Torsten Hedlund, 18 June 1896); 'it is acknowledged by chemists *here*. . . . The
final difficulty with the analysis has now been overcome' (to Mathilde Präger, 19 June
1896); and 'This is considered by many chemists here to be gold' (to Karin, Greta and
Hans Strindberg, 29 June 1896). Delius left for Norway at the beginning of June, so
assuming he made the appointment with Strindberg shortly before Padé was to
undertake his analyses, we can probably postulate a (Wednesday) date for this telegram
of 20 or 27 May.

(65)

Jelka Rosen to Fritz Delius

Félicité
Grez par Nemours
S. et M.
[20th June 1896]

Dear Mr Delius,

Of course you did not write; I thought you were'nt going to so I was not very
disappointed; only I am rather curious to know where you are, and what
happened at Copenhague.[1] This letter is supposed to reach you just on the
longest day: the 21st, I think? I hope you will enjoy that long twilight; but
here it is beautiful too in our solitary garden, all full of oldfashioned roses, and
birds and "Hollunder büsche".[2] It is so intoxicating! I don't know whether you
feel all this rich summer beauty, glow and perfume as I do, but I always hear it
in your music, much more than in anybody else's. I love the accompaniment of:
Nur schneller mein Ross;[3] it is just my summer Stimmung, and I manage to
play it, a desperate effort, but so exciting! Il pleure dans mon coeur[4] is beautiful
too, but more in town, or perhaps in autumn when one feels like that.

My mother met Mottl[5] in London; they talked about you. My aunt[6] said très
ingénument whether he had heard of you, and that all the very musical ones in
Paris were quite excited about your music. He said he had never heard or seen
anything of yours. Augener would only tell *you* how many songs there are still:
Panzer[7] wants to know; he also wants to know, whether they may print the texts
of the songs; They think it would make it a great deal easier to understand, as
the people then glance at the words beforehand. It would cost about 25 frs
which you would have to pay. Will you send me a line to say? I really pity you:
business following you even to the midnight sun! But what *shall* I do?

We made a séance at the Chadwicks[8] the other night; and a slate, after
jumping on my lap about 50 times at last alighted on my head. Madame was
not touching so I have to suspect him. But we don't often go there – it is much
nicer to have an exhilerating ride on the wheel at dusk and then come to the
dark garden. I wonder whether you are composing Nietzsche? I am longing for

that. I have discovered several other poems of his, and send you a little one: the others are all longer. Would you like copies? I hope you may feel inspired for this one! The big ones are very fine: Dionyssos—Dithyramben.

Miss Gerhardi[9] sends you this sketch of my hands after the last chord of Plus vite mon cheval; she says she enjoys it. This is a piano from Fontainebleau in an empty room, and she sits there and we took our pillows too, so as to lessen the sound.

Au revoir!   Jelka Rosen.

Venedig (1888)

An der Brücke stand
jüngst ich in brauner Nacht.
Fernher kam Gesang:
goldener Tropfen quoll's
über die zitternde Fläche weg.
Gondeln, Lichter, Musik –
trunken schwamm's in
     die Dämmrung hinaus . . .

Meine Seele, ein Saitenspiel
sang sich, unsichtbar berührt,
heimlich ein Gondellied dazu,
zitternd vor bunter Seligkeit.
– Hörte jemand ihr zu? . . .

Fr Nietzsche[10]

Autograph letter, signed and undated, written in English. Jelka later added '20th June 1896'.

The original is in the Grainger Museum. It is the first of 78 communications from Jelka to Delius, written between 1896 and 1920, that are preserved in the museum.

1   Delius, now in Norway, had seen Hennings in Copenhagen to discuss The Magic Fountain. He was 'just as pleasant as ever and just as uncertain'. Stavenhagen, conductor at Weimar, was considering the work, too; by December he had the score, but nothing was to result from this.

2   elderberry bushes. In German in the original letter.

3   'O schneller, mein Ross!' ('Plus vite, mon cheval'): a song composed by Delius, to a poem by Emanuel von Geibel, in 1888, and published in Paris by Grus in 1896.

4   'Il pleure dans mon coeur' (Verlaine): another of the 5 Chansons published by Grus in 1896.

5   Felix Mottl (1856–1911): Austrian conductor and composer. He studied at the Vienna Conservatorium and conducted at Bayreuth and then at Karlsruhe, where he was to become general musical director. Delius had tried to interest Mottl in his music late in 1895, and was shortly to send him the score of *The Magic Fountain*.

6   Grete Moscheles, *née* Sobernheim, wife of the artist Felix Moscheles (1833–1917), who was the second son of the composer and pianist Ignaz Moscheles, and brother of Serena Anna, Jelka's mother.

7   There are several references to Panzer or to the Panzers in the letters of this period. It is presumed that Jelka and Delius were discussing the pianist Rodolphe Panzer and his singer wife, Térésa Tosti, that the Panzers were proposing to perform some of the early songs and that the song-texts were required for the printed programme of their recital.

8   Francis Brooks Chadwick was an American artist whose wife, Emma Löwstädt, was a Swedish painter. They had settled at Grez, having earlier rented the Marquis de Carzeaux's property there for some years before Jelka bought it. They had been prominent members of the largely Scandinavian circle around the Swedish painter Carl Larsson in Grez in the early 1880s.

9   Ida Gerhardi (1862–1927): German painter. Jelka's friend since early days in Detmold, and now a fellow-student at Courtois's academy in Paris. She was to become an artist of great distinction, executing over the years a number of portraits of both Jelka and Delius, although the sketch referred to here has not survived. She lived for some time at Grez, sharing the house with Jelka, Frau Rosen and, occasionally, other of their friends. She was shortly to effect the introduction of Delius's music to Hans Haym (see Letter 74, note 2), conductor at Elberfeld, near her native town of Hagen. In doing so, she effectively set Delius on the path to fame in Germany.

Only a week earlier Ida had written to her mother and described Grez: 'Here it is almost like being in an enchanted paradise, – it is a little village: Grèz, near Fontainebleau & Paris. We live in an idyllic little house, the home of 2 seamstresses mother and daughter Félicité. . . . Just think, an old Marquis has lent us a garden, which is so lonely & hidden and overgrown that only the priest, if he were to climb the church tower, would be able to see in – we work there in quiet tranquillity, nobody is allowed in here but us & we moreover gather the fruit, climb up cherry trees & pick wonderful bouquets of roses with which we decorate our delightful studio. At the bottom of the garden flows the river & we bathe there in the morning and in the evening, the weather is so heavenly. . . . We have a piano too, – Jelka sings wonderfully.'

10   There is no indication of Delius setting this Nietzsche text, although he wrote to Jelka from Valdres at the end of June, 'The verses you sent me are beautiful many thanks – I shall compose them.' More significantly he also wrote, 'I am orckestrating the 1st Act of my opera & it is getting on very well – . . . almost all my time here I spend on my opera.'

(66)
Fritz Delius to Jelka Rosen

Haugen
S/Aurdal
Valders 8 July 96

Dear friend—

I am glad to learn from your letter that you are having a good time in Grez doing some work & enjoying your beautiful little garden with Marcelle[1] in it I can almost see her nude form amongst those long white flowers & Bamboos with you & Miss Gerhardi painting away with tremendous energy, very lightly dressed & with paint all over your gowns. Your description of Felicité[2] amused me very much. She must be a darling — all suchlike have the "santé très forte" I know several like that — I think I shall leave here about the 20th or 25th inst & go first to Drontheim to visit a friend & then via Copenhagen to Germany. I want to go & see Mottl in Karlsruhe — Could you find out for me whether he will be in Karlsruhe at the end of August — or if not where he will be. I might go to him —[3]

I hope the Panzers are having success — where will they be at the end of August? I really did not smile when I said "all my efforts to be heard" For me they have been really efforts — at least what I consider efforts. But I know that I am not very gifted in such matters & that makes me doubt whether anything I may do in the "Effort" line, will be successful Keary has written to me quite often, fine long letters; he has also sent me the 2nd Act of the new opera — So musically things are all right. The word you could not read must be *Synthétique*.

So you are going to *Plougastel-Daoulas* — the best way is to take the train to Landerneau (*Montparnasse*) & drive to Plougastel-Daoulas — If I can manage it I shall come also. It depends on my work — as a piano is out of the question at Plougastel. Unless one has one brought from Brest. Are many people at Grez? I suppose Chadwick wondered why I did not come to live there in June! I dont know when the song is coming in L'aube, as I have not received the proof sheets yet.[4] — The weather here is lovely — warm & sunny. They are now making hay & the smell is delicious — I send you a little flower which grows only in Norway & Sweden & has a very sweet perfume when fresh. Please write to this address when you write & tell me when you expect to be in Plougastel-Daoulas —

Give my kind regards to Miss Gerhardi & when you have a little time write to me again.

Believe me
Sincerely your friend
Fritz Delius

Autograph letter, signed and dated, written in English.

The original is in the Grainger Museum.

1   An artists' model, Marcelle was a frequent subject of both Jelka and Ida Gerhardi in drawings and paintings.

2   Daughter of the seamstress in whose cottage Jelka and Ida were staying.

3   Mottl was to post back the *Magic Fountain* score (which had been sent on to him by Hennings) on 17 September. Although it seems to have interested him, he was not prepared to recommend a Karlsruhe performance.

4   Delius's Verlaine setting, 'Le ciel est, par-dessus le toit,' was first published in the Parisian journal *L'Aube* in July 1896.

(67)

Fritz Delius to Jutta Bell

Haugen
S/Aurdal
Valders
15 July 96

Dear friend

Your letter was forwarded to me from Paris. Since the beginning of June I have been in Norway, living on a farm in Valders & working at my new Opera.[1] The text was rewritten by C.F. Keary, an English writer of much merit; and also a new friend who I value much. Please dont say anything about this opera to anyone — what it is about or anything — We shall make efforts to have it given in London perhaps next season. My other Opera "The magic fountain" is, as it appears, on the list at Weimar: when it will come on I dont know — 5 of my songs have come out in Paris, of which 2 new ones I send you one today, as soon as I return to Paris I will send you the others. At present all goes well. I am working on a work which I believe will be *unique* in its way.

I am so glad to hear of your success & that you are making so much money I must not tell you but my money matters are just as bad as ever, nay! even worse. I cannot sell a song; It seems ridiculous when one comes to think of it but I cannot make a fiver — I should be very happy to let you have my rooms but I am afraid I shall be back in Paris by the end of August, but I hope to see something of you when you come. I shall be happy to be of use in other ways. When your letter reached me I was just on the point of writing to you.

I shall leave Norway about the 24 or 5th of August[2] & hope by then to have fully finished & orchestrated the 1st act — Let me hear from you when you have time and Believe me

yours ever
Fritz Delius

Autograph letter, signed and dated, written in English. Envelope addressed: Mrs Jutta Bell / 117 Gloucester Road 117 / Stanhope Gardens / London SW / England. Postmark: SØNDRE AURDAL 17 VII 06.

The original is in the Jacksonville University Library.

1   *Koanga.*

2   After a tramp through the Jotunheim mountains, Gudbrandsdal and the Rondane hills, Delius went back to Valdres in the middle of August. On 15 August he wrote to Jelka, 'I expect to leave here for Christiania the 20 or 21st thence to Kopenhagen Berlin Weimar Karlsruhe where I hope to meet Mottl and also Keary & then, Vive la France, to Paris –.' He returned to Paris around the middle of September. There are no references in the letters Delius sent to Jelka from Norway to the 'concert tour' claimed by Jelka to have taken place in the summer of 1896, Delius being accompanied by his friend Halfdan Jebe (see Letter 68) and Knut Hamsun. Beecham's embellished account (*Frederick Delius*, pp. 84–5), although in part based on a conversation with the composer, largely relies on Jelka's reminiscences written down for him after Delius's death (see Appendix VII). Delius was likely to have met Hamsun in Paris in 1893, when the Norwegian writer came to live in a little hotel in the rue Vaugirard, near the Luxembourg Gardens.

(68)
Fritz Delius to Jutta Bell

Claremont
Bradford
Yorkshire
[23? December 1896]

My dear friend

Your letter was forwarded to me here and I was very glad to hear from you again.

I arrived in Paris a few days after your visit to my rooms & was very sorry to have missed you

You are certainly a wonderful woman & your energy seems boundless! I am sure you will accomplish all you undertake. I most likely shall soon come and live in London and make efforts to have at least my new opera performed – I have been working on it for the last 12 months and am about halfway thro', having written and orchestrated the 1st Act and half of the 2nd It ought to be wonderfully effective & original and is full of color & contrast – I think I told you that C. F. Keary wrote the libretto – We worked together & the result is all that I could wish. I have written also an "American Rhapsody"[1] for Orchestra which is probably going to be played here in Bradford. The bigger & better orchestras of England are unreachable for me at present and I have neither wish nor energy enough to go kicking around the ante chambers of well known Conductors & as I feel quite certain that one of these days they will be kicking their heels in my ante chamber I give myself no trouble about them. Johannes Wolff is playing my "Legende" for Orchestra & Violin in London in January.[2] Please look out for it. I am sailing on the 9th January for New York en route for Florida where I intend spending 2 months to settle up that unfortunate grove business[3] – I have chosen the 2 worst European months for my stay over there & shall take my work with me. A first rate Violinist[4] is coming with me & we may give a few recitals – Send me the address of your mother & I will call upon them on my way thro' Jacksonville. I shall stay a couple of days in town on my way to Southampton so of course you must give me a rendez-vous. It seems to me that you are infinitely better off separate from Bell – a man so unartistic in feeling & with tastes diametrically opposed to yours – Watawa is at present in Weimar awaiting its performance – when?! I dont know. I am sure I should be delighted if your daughter would sing Watawa one day. I think it will be a grateful role. Otherwise I have not much news for you – I will send you some of my new songs when they arrive from Paris. I have written 5 songs to J.P. Jacobsen's poems[5] – I think they are good. However I cannot find a publisher who will pay me & I am not going to publish anything more gratis, even if I die of starvation.

I shall be delighted to give a concert with you later on in the Season. Say in June, with Johannes Wolff –

I wish you a happy new year & also a merry christmas

Believe me – as ever
Fritz Delius

Autograph letter, signed and undated, written in English.

The original is in the Jacksonville University Library.

1   *Appalachia*, American Rhapsody for Orchestra. Composed in 1896, this early version of the more familiar *Appalachia* variations with chorus exists in an autograph manuscript in the Delius Trust Archive. There is no record of its having been performed in the composer's lifetime.

2   Delius had told Augener of the performance, and Augener had written on 19 November: 'I will endeavor to hear your Légende in January.'

3   Delius's orange plantation, Solana Grove, had been – and continued to be – a constant source of worry, with crops failing and land taxes falling due. His Negro foreman, Albert Anderson, had written to him on 16 December: 'I will again write you and give you a liss of things in the house. Mary Furgison have been here, and seem to want to take possion. of things and have been tanalizing me for quite a while I do not care to be bothed by Mary. I will have evry thing ready for you Jan. 25.' Anderson added a short inventory of the furniture still in the house on Solana Grove.

4   Halfdan Jebe (1868?–1937): Norwegian violinist and composer. He studied in Christiania, Leipzig, Berlin and Paris, where he played in Colonne's orchestra from 1894 to 1897. After a series of world-wide travels he played and conducted in the United States for a number of years before settling in Mexico, where he taught the violin, piano and composition. He was the dedicatee of Delius's *An Arabesk* (1911). He was to be orchestra leader at the Delius Orchestral Concert under Hertz in London on 30 May 1899. See also Letter 160, note.

5   These are five of the *Seven Danish Songs*, written around the mid-1890s. Six are settings of Jacobsen, and the other is Holger Drachmann's 'Lyse Naetter' ('Summer Nights').

1897

More than one explanation has been put forward for Delius's second visit to the United States. The most prosaic and the most likely is that Solana Grove and its deteriorating condition represented a continuing worry for him, as well as a drain on his meagre resources, and that he now needed to see if anything useful could be done with it. The most exotic is that he went in search of his Negro mistress, a story eagerly averred by Percy Grainger: 'The "Negress" story is quite true, for Delius told it to me himself, several times. He had a negro mistress while in Florida & she had a child by him.' According to Grainger, Delius sailed for America 'merely to try & find . . . her & his child. But she (the Negress) thinking he might want to take the child away from her, fled. So Delius couldn't find her, his trip was for naught, & he never heard what became of her & the child.'* Yet a third contributory factor to his departure from Europe is supposed to have been his desire to escape the attentions of the Princesse de Cystria, understood to have been his mistress in Paris. Even this failed, since she arranged to sail on the same ship, only disclosing her presence to Delius and his travelling companion, Halfdan Jebe, when they were well out to sea; and Delius was, anyway, to continue to associate with her in Paris. Under such pseudonyms as 'Mr Lemanoff' and 'Madame Donodossola', Jebe and the princess gave recitals together with Delius during the course of what must be labelled one of the more eccentric of European artistic excursions into the New World.

Whatever may have happened in the course of the quasi-fairy-tale that made up the first half of 1897, taking in Solana Grove, Jacksonville and Danville for the second and last time, Delius was back in Paris by the end of May and was assessing the realities of a situation which now seemed to hold distinct promise for him. Jelka had bought the property in Grez, and the opportunity beckoned for him to move there. Before long he did so. In that summer of 1897 Ida Gerhardi painted in the garden her first portrait of him, and Gunnar Heiberg, the Norwegian dramatist, came along with a commission for incidental music

---

* Letter from Percy Grainger to Richard Muller, 5 October 1941 (Library of Congress).

to his latest play, *Folkeraadet*, which was to be produced in Christiania in the autumn. Delius left Paris towards the end of September to supervise rehearsals and spent a spirited month in Christiania, with controversy raging about the play and more particularly around his music to it. His return to France was by way of Denmark and then Germany, where on 13 November he attended the first performance of his orchestral work *Over the hills and far away*. It had been Ida Gerhardi who in September had been instrumental in effecting an introduction for Delius's music which was to be of inestimable value to the composer in at last getting his work onto the German concert platform, for this performance was conducted by Hans Haym, musical director at Elberfeld, who was subsequently to pioneer many of his works in Germany.

The *Folkeraadet* incidental music and *Over the hills and far away* marked the end of a long apprenticeship. He had attended frequent rehearsals and performances of the former and would certainly have arrived well in time to hear the latter rehearsed in Elberfeld. As a consequence, a certain coarseness in his orchestration, most notably in his writing for brass (as evident in *Paa Vidderne*), is clearly modified in the works dating from 1898 onward.

Koanga, opera (RT I/4). Completed early in 1897.

Piano Concerto in C minor (first version entitled *Fantasy for Orchestra and pianoforte*) (RT VII/4). Florida, spring 1897; completed Paris, late 1897.

Foldkeraadet, incidental music to Gunnar Heiberg's play (RT I/5). Summer/autumn.

Seven Danish Songs, with orchestral or piano accompaniment (RT III/4). Largely completed in 1897.

Florent Schmitt makes a piano arrangement of *Koanga*. 1897/8?

C. F. Keary prepares a draft libretto for *A Village Romeo and Juliet*.

(69)
Fritz Delius to Jelka Rosen

Solana Grove
Piccolata
St Johns Cº.
Fla.
[April 1897]

My dear friend,

Your letter was forwarded to me here. I left in January for Florida and have been basking in the sunshine and enjoying this lovely place for the last three months. [1]

The climate and the flowers are extraordinary and the situation of my grove is lovely and right on the beautiful S! John's River. Mr. Jebe came with me and enjoys his stay very much. We have caught a young alligator about a yard long and have it in a barrel in front of the house. I am bringing a lot of snake skins back that I have killed and am sorry I cannot bring some of the flowers or a piece of the moonlight nights or some of the magnolia blossoms and orange blossoms. The sunsets here are something remarkable and always different varying between the most delicate colours on some nights to the most lurid and ferocious hues on others. The scenery is lovely and I should say remarkably well adapted for a painter. There is a nice little house on the place with a broad verandah facing the St. John's river and standing in the middle of the orange trees. In front of the house is a garden with gardenias hibiscus and a few other tropical flowers of which I do not know the names. Over the veranda an enormous honey-suckle creeps and in front of the house to the right and near the river an enormous live oak stands and shades a sort of lawn of very green grass. We have had the most delicious weather all the time and I have enjoyed my stay immensely. I have not written about the songs, I will put it off until I get back. Many thanks for thinking about them. I suppose I shall find some editor some day. Well good-bye, I leave here at the end of the month and shall be in Paris middle of May. Write Rue Duc.

  Ever yours, Fr. D.

Handwritten transcript in English in the Grainger Museum, dated by the copyist 'April 1897'.

Although most of the letters from Delius to Jelka in the Grainger Museum are originals, there are a number, dating from 1897 to 1898, which have so far come to light only in the form of handwritten transcripts. Because of their intrinsic interest, several of the transcripts from this period are printed in this selection, even though they may be inaccurate and incomplete. This letter is of especial interest, since it provides the only contemporary and first-hand account by Delius of Solana Grove. No letters written during his first stay in Florida (1884–5) have yet been traced.

1 A short memoir by Mrs Henry L. Richmond is preserved in the Jacksonville Public Library, Florida. At Solana Grove on 7 May 1942 she interviewed Edward (Ned) Colee of Bakersville: 'Says he remembers Delius in 1897 period. . . . Delius was always pleasant and kind and full of fun. Mr Colee said he remembers Elbert Anderson rowing Delius out to mid-river, to catch the steamer Crescent; also remembers that "a lady was with Mr. Delius, too"; is positive that the lady stayed in the cottage also, "didn't know if they were married". Says Anderson said that Delius composed a piece of music while at cottage in 1897.' (The lady is presumed to have been the Princesse de Cystria, introduced to him, according to an affidavit in the Jacksonville Library, by Jutta Bell in Paris; the piece of music would have been the first version, completed by the end of the year, of the Piano Concerto.)

Mrs Richmond also talked with Julia Sanks, Albert Anderson's sister-in-law: 'She and her family were not house servants, but she remembered Mr. Delius: said Solana Grove was a happy place, they all loved to go there.'

A letter from Halfdan Jebe to the composer in 1905, proposing a 'great Pacific journey', refers obliquely to their American trip of 1897: 'the important things are: good planning, no follies, no princesses and no false names – ours are good enough.'

(70)

Fritz Delius to Jelka Rosen

[33 Rue Ducouëdic
Late May 1897]

Dear friend,

I arrived yesterday in Paris and found your letter awaiting me. So you have really settled in Grez[1] – how nice! – and how wise of you – if I were a painter I should surely live out in the country and in the open-air. I am thinking of coming down there soon for a day or two to see you and then I will tell you all about my travels and doings. I had a lovely trip back again and am only sorry that my plantation is not in Grez instead of Florida. Let me hear from you soon.

Believe me sincerely your friend
Fritz Delius.

Handwritten transcript in English in the Grainger Museum, dated by the copyist. The original was presumably undated, and the home address is not as Delius would have written it: the copyist's actual heading being 'End of May, 1897 / 33, Rue Duc. (Paris)'.

1   The sale was confirmed in a letter from Ida Gerhardi to her brother Karl-August, dated Grez 20.5.97: 'At last the purchase of the enchanted garden & the house has now been concluded.' She and Jelka were moving furniture from Paris, and an English friend, Maud Ede, was staying with them.

(71)

C. F. Keary to Fritz Delius

65 B^{vd} Arago [Paris]
Saturday
[Summer 1897]

Dear Delius,

For the moment I am stuck with R. & J.[1] I dont see this 2nd (or rather 1st) act satisfactorily. If you have any suggestion to offer send it. I cant come down &

discuss it because that w' make too much of a break in my own work, onto wh. I have got rather well just at this moment. But if I come to a full stop in that, I will run down to Grez.

I have written Act 2 (1) after a fashion; but I dont care for it; I put in an auction, because you said that w' work well musically. It don't literally. Howbeit I'll keep it, unless you think of something better. 1st Vreli alone – voices from village girls & boys outside – then Sali & Vreli – then Manz (or Marti, I forget wh. is father of wh.) – He comes in, threatens Sali – then some older villagers come on & are followed almost immediately by the *Maire* or other officials from neighbouring town with auctioneer – Manz' land is sold by auction – then?

Tu me parais tres sensible. What I shd. have guessed about the press is that unless you advertise in certain papers to a certain extent they wont send a representative to a concert. They have similar ways about reviewing publishers books – though of course it is never acknowledged. But my dear chap I cd. not think any the better of you if you had a press as good as De Lara's nor the worse if you had had a bad one. Not even if yr music *was* disagreeable to the majority of hearers. The only thing I think of is if a person has the creative stuff (Stoff) in them. I have a *flair* for that – at least I flatter myself so. There are plenty of painters, authors, &c whose production I like very much of its kind, but who have not the creative stuff, so as anybody could supply their place I wd not go out of my way to help in their work.

Of course a good press like any other advantage that comes is a thing to be *used*. And the use for you is *tout indiqué* viz. to get yr people who can afford it to relieve you of all cares for yr bread & butter.

You know the Bruces[2] asked me to take these rooms, & keep on their servant. Of course it is v. convenient for me & also convenient for them But (alas!) Bruce has not left his standing easel which I was looking forward to as something always ready to work off ones brain irritations upon I meant to repaint some *pochades*[3] once in this country.

I recall what I said about running down to Grez. It is not likely I can afford such a break as that. But I am sure to have blocks in my work when I will go on with R. & J. I dare say there is not much to be done I know I thought so the other day.

You say nothing about going north. It is too late to go now for the best time.

I believe I wrote *les dessus* instead of *les dessous* in my last letter.

Toutes mes amitiés

C.F. Keary.

Autograph letter, signed and undated, written in English.

The original is in the Delius Trust Archive. Two other letters preserved from Keary to Delius are dated 1908.

1   Keary's libretto for *A Village Romeo and Juliet* was ultimately to be jettisoned. This was first indicated in a recently discovered letter from Ida Gerhardi to her brother Karl-August, written from Grez and dated 20 September 1897: 'Do you know Gottfried Keller's Romeo & Julie auf dem Dorfe? Delius has long had it in mind to use it as an opera & now he is negotiating with an English writer (Keary) who has done the text of the opera for him, and is finishing it about now.' Meanwhile, Jelka had suggested that Delius set the opera to a German libretto instead, and Ida had proposed her poet brother for the task: 'To begin with Delius would like to know your feelings about R. & J., – it must be short . . . he is always very much for the dramatic approach & in this the Engl. writer Keary can't do a thing, for this reason alone it would be good already to put him aside, – he uses wonderful words in which nothing happens, – he is a good observer of detail & a great admirer of Zola's marvellous gift of observation, – everything must always be true & realistic to an extreme, – but that is so dreadfully unmusical & reduces Delius constantly to despair. After he read Romeo & Juliet, i.e. Keary, he found it to be a quite banal commonplace sentimental German love-story, rather à la Auerbach & all the others of this genre.'

Although there was further correspondence on the subject, and Karl-August Gerhardi was at some stage sent a manuscript text in English for Act 1, in Jelka's handwriting, the idea was finally dropped, and Delius was later to write his own libretto for the opera.

2   See Appendix VII. Both Daniel de Monfreid and Edvard Munch lived for a time in this same picturesque group of artists' studios.

3   *rapid sketches*. In French in the original letter.

(72)
Victor Thrane to Fritz Delius

SEASON OF 1897–98.

MR. VICTOR THRANE.

_____

DISTINGUISHED ARTISTS.

CONCERT TOURS.

33 WEST UNION SQUARE,
NEW YORK, Aug. 17, 1897.

My dear Delius:–

Pardon my neglect in acknowledging your very kind favors of July last. I am glad you had a delightful trip across the ocean. The young ladies have often spoken of you. You win the bet. Sorry!

I enclose herewith check which Mr. Fitzhugh sent me. I sent him my check for $3.00, but he never acknowledged receipt of same; of course, if he *did not* receive my check, I would probably have heard from him.

I returned yesterday from a six weeks vacation out West. Enjoyed it immensely. I spent three weeks at Grand Rapids with my fiancee. I enclose
herewith a clipping from the Eau Claire paper. We expect to get married in
January or February — that is, if I make enough money to pay my laundry bills
until that time. However, the crops are very good this season, and there is a
general aspect of prosperity all over the country; I expect to do a good business
this season.

Have you met Sieveking yet?[1] Do not fail to call upon him, and give me your
impressions of his playing. His address is — 10 Rue du Guet, Sevres, Seine et
Oise, France. I think you will like him very much.

The tile business is still undeveloped. I am disgusted with the capitalists
here. Before giving up everything to them, I will let the whole thing go to the
dogs.

Before returning to New York I spent three weeks at home with the family;
it was the first time since seven years we had a complete reunion. They all
wished to be most kindly remembered to you, and sent their best wishes for
your success. Sister Ella was disappointed that she did not even hear from you
during your sojourn here.

Seidl[2] will return to America next week, when I shall learn what I am to do
in regard to his orchestra. If you will send me the orchestral scores, I shall have
your works played by his orchestra in New York City. Please do not delay, as he
will undoubtedly commence to make up his programmes within a *few* weeks.

Mr. Frederick Chapman,[3] the young gifted man, whom you write about, has
not yet called; I shall certainly be glad to make his acquaintance. Am planning,
if my season is successful, to go to Paris next Spring, and certainly expect to see
you then. How is the Princess? I had a great time satisfying the curiosity of the
family in regard to Cyril Grey and the Princess.[4]

Now, old man, let me hear from you soon. I shall do all I can for your songs.
Mlle. Verlet has already promised to put your songs on her programmes.[5]

With kindest regards, believe me,

Very cordially yours,
Victor Thrane.

Typed letter, signed and dated, written in English on headed notepaper.

The original is in the Delius Trust Archive. A total of six letters written by Thrane to
Delius between 24 February 1897 and 20 March 1899 have been preserved.

Victor Thrane (1868–1936): American impresario, of Norwegian origin. From 1893
to 1900 he was a concert agent, managing Ysaÿe and Pugno among others, based in
New York. Later he was to move into the timber business in Michigan (cf. Randel,
'Frederick Delius in America', p. 362). According to Beecham (pp. 73–4), Thrane and
Delius were in touch prior to 1897: already interested in Delius's compositions, Thrane

had visited Solana Grove during the course of his travels and had urged Delius to return to the plantation to put it in order, so as to derive some income from it. A short memoir by his daughter, Irma Thrane Schmidt, which is preserved in the Oslo University Library, quotes a Chicago newspaper's description of Thrane: 'Tall, well built and bronzed by the long hours in the sun, Mr. Thrane gives every evidence of his love of nature. He is unassuming in manner, easily approachable and an entertaining companion.' He is also described as 'a violinist of some skill'.

1   Martinus Sieveking (1867–1950): Dutch pianist. He studied with his father and with Julius Röntgen, beginning his career as an accompanist in Paris. From about the mid-1890s he lived mainly in the United States.

2   Anton Seidl (1850–98): Austro-Hungarian conductor, noted for his interpretation of Wagner's music. From 1885 he conducted mainly in New York.

3   Frederick E. Chapman: a respected teacher, he was supervisor of music at this time at the high school in Cambridge, Massachusetts (cf. Edward Bailey Birge, *History of Public School Music in the United States* [Ditson, 1928], pp. 136 and 167). In collaboration with Charles E. Whiting, Chapman 'compiled and arranged' *The Apollo Song Book for Male Voices*, published in 1910 by Ginn and Company, and including two arrangements of his own. Thrane was to write to Delius on 21 April 1898, 'I like Mr. Chapman immensely; he is one of the most charming fellows I have ever met. He is a very loyal friend of yours and has done a great deal to interest people in your work.'

4   The reference is presumed to be to the Princesse de Cystria and Halfdan Jebe, both of whom adopted unusual pseudonyms during the American tour with Delius.

5   Alice Verlet (1873–1934): Belgian soprano. Her fine voice was much in demand in Brussels and Paris at this period, and she was later frequently to perform in the United States.

(73)
Gunnar Heiberg to Fritz Delius

22-9-97
c/o Verdens Gang
Chr*a*

Dear Delius,

Conductor Winge[1] asked me to write to you and say that the theatre orchestra only has 2 corni, 2 trombe and 1 trombone. This mystical message I hereby convey to you

The rehearsals begin on Saturday. And the intention is to put the play on in the middle of October.

Within the next few days the 400 frcs will be sent to you from the Gyldendalske Boghandel in Copenhagen[2] I hope you will excuse the slight delay. It is because of bungling on my part

I am looking forward very much to seeing you again. But it is unlikely to be in the paradise-garden in Grez. It will probably be in Paris.

Much is expected of the play. And that is all very well. But Christiania is no fun as a town and I am longing to get back to Paris.

Give the kind ladies many friendly regards from

Yours sincerely
Gunnar Heiberg

Autograph letter, signed and dated, written in Norwegian.

The original is in the Delius Trust Archive. Three further letters from Heiberg to Delius, one dated August/September 1897 and two dated May 1899, are preserved.

Gunnar Heiberg (1857–1929): Norwegian dramatist and fine essayist and critic. He directed many plays, notably in Bergen, where he mounted the first productions of Ibsen's *The Wild Duck* and *Rosmersholm*, and then in Christiania. His own plays, particularly such fine pieces as *Aunt Ulrikke* and *Love's Tragedy*, enjoyed considerable success in their day. He was for a while Paris correspondent of the Norwegian daily *Verdens Gang*, whose editor, Olaf Thommessen, Delius already knew, and he was acquainted with members of the Molard circle in Montparnasse. It must have been some time in the summer of 1897 that he asked Delius to write incidental music to his new play, *Folkeraadet* (*People's Parliament*). Delius had written to Jelka at the beginning of July: 'Gunnar Heiberg, the poet, will come to Grez for a short time.' That the visit actually took place is confirmed in a subsequent letter (probably written in August) from Heiberg, in which he sent regards to the 'kind ladies' and asked Delius, 'how are you down there in le beau, faux paradis'.

1   Per Winge (1858–1935): Norwegian conductor and composer. He conducted the Christiania Theatre Orchestra from 1893 to 1899.

2   The publishers of Heiberg's *Folkeraadet*.

(74)
Fritz Delius to Jelka Rosen

Oct. 16th Christiania.

Dear friend,

Thanks for your post-card – since I wrote you last I have been very busy with rehearsals and day after tomorrow, the 18th, the première comes off. Christiania is in suspense and there will very probably be a "manifestation". At the theatre they are afraid that my music will cause trouble as I have employed the *National hymn*.[1] What interests *me* the most is that the orchestration is just as I thought it and sounds fine. I have had an orchester rehearsal alone and now, considering the orchester (only two horns and one bassoon) I cannot hope for better. They managed to get four trombones. On the whole I am *very glad*, *very glad* I came; I know now where I am: and this affair is of the greatest importance for my future work. As long as they don't lynch me or stone me too badly I don't mind. I spent a few hours day before yesterday with Ibsen who was very much interested and promised to be there. The tickets are put up to ten Kroners and the house is already sold out for the first night. Pecuniarily of course, Heiberg gets the money and I very little perhaps two hundred Kroner. It will pay my ticket back however, which is useful as I am running short. Please write me about Elberfeld if it is decided and when I must be there? How much it costs for "Stimmen" and Dr. Haym's address.² I long to be back in Grez, the life here is stupid. People drink, drink and drink and do nothing else.

Is Keary in my place? Write me how you all are and what you have been doing.

I will send you papers. I wrote here the Einleitung to the first Act.

Yours as ever,
Fritz Delius.

Give my love to Frl Gerhardi and Marie.³

Handwritten transcript in English in the Grainger Museum. The date is as written by the copyist.

1　Heiberg's play *Folkeraadet* was an amusing and trenchant satire of the Norwegian parliamentary system and its politicians. In consultation with Delius, Heiberg had originally decided that three preludes (to Acts 2, 3 and 5) were needed; in fact, Delius added a short overture after arriving in Christiania about the beginning of October, and there are also a few bars of purely incidental music during the stage action. In its context the music is lively, imaginative and perfectly appropriate to the subject. Its full impact, however, can be discerned only if one is familiar with the theme (and the usual setting) of the Norwegian national anthem, 'Ja, vi elsker dette Landet', and to some extent with the tide of nationalist emotion flowing in Norway at this period.

2　Hans Haym (1860–1921): German conductor and composer. He conducted at Elberfeld, in succession to Julius Buths (see Letter 112, note 1), from 1890, and was now to give, at Ida Gerhardi's instigation, Delius's *Over the hills and far away* on 13 November. Ida had written from Grez to her brother on 20 September: 'I wrote to Haym in Elberfeld to ask if he couldn't perform an orchestral piece by Delius sometime & he wrote me a charming letter back to say that I should send him something to look at in the middle of Sept., – we are now anxiously waiting to see what he will write. It is at least as difficult to place music as it is with books and pictures & you can imagine what it means for a composer at last to hear something of his played by an orchestra. Delius's songs are making quite good progress in Paris & England, but of course he still longs for something else.'

From this time on, Haym's enthusiasm for Delius's music knew no bounds, and Elberfeld was to hear the first performances of several of the composer's larger works during the next few years.

3 Marie Blandel, who came from Brittany, was Jelka's cook–housekeeper at Grez.

(75)
Fritz Delius to Jelka Rosen

[Christiania, 20? October 1897]

Dear friend,

Well! the first two performances have been and the result is tremendous, they hissed and had a real demonstration against the piece and especially against the *music*. But more than half applauded. So you can imagine the row: the left political party is furious. I have been ordered out of the hotel where I lived – *just fancy* – the second night there was more applause than hissing and the piece will be a success I think, every place was sold. All artists were for me and all the other bourgeois were furious – they thought I wanted to make fun of their national song. But all I care about understood at once. It was a furious evening. I have sent you some of the papers – others will follow.

Write me when I must be in Elberfeld. I am longing to get out of this place and back to Grez. Give my love to Miss Gerhardi and Marie,

Yours as ever,
Fritz Delius.

Handwritten transcript in English in the Grainger Museum, dated by the copyist. The original was presumably undated, the copyist's actual heading being 'Oct. Oslo. 1897'.

(76)
Fritz Delius to Jelka Rosen

Holmenkollens Turisthotel[1]
[22 October, 1897]

Dear friend,

No one speaks any more of Heiberg's piece, now it is only my music. Chriania is divided into two camps – for or against – *all* the good artists are for. All the bourgeois are against. I have been with Ibsen quite a good deal and he was delighted and congratulated me most heartily. Every night in the theatre there is a pitched battle when the music begins. Hissing and hurrahs. There was some talk about lynching me but no one has as yet dared to attack me in the street. I am too big and Englishmen have the "renommée de pouvoir boxer" here! It is a furious affair but in spite of all I hope to arrive sain et sauf in Paris the 15th of November — I leave here tomorrow evening for Copenhagen. The students hold a protestation meeting tomorrow night[2] — in the streets there are also manifestations. Tonight in the theatre there will be sixty police and when the hissing begins the gong will sound and the police will arrest the manifestors. It is all very amusing for me, I can tell you. Write to me poste restante, Copenhagen. Give my love to Miss Gerhardi and Marie,

> Yours as ever
> Fritz Delius.

Handwritten transcript in English in the Grainger Museum. The original was probably written on headed notepaper, and the transcript is dated 'end of Oct. 1897'.

1 A well-known and picturesque hotel on a hill some 7 kilometres north of Christiania and overlooking the city.

2 The Christiania Students Union meeting, which was also attended by a number of the city's leading artists and actors, was held late in the evening of Saturday 23 October. An original motion condemning the theatre management was withdrawn after some argument, to be replaced by one requesting Delius — who himself had just withdrawn his music — to return his manuscript to the theatre. The motion was adopted, being carried by 158 votes to 78. The debate was widely reported in the capital's newspapers. Delius was present, so he could not have left for Copenhagen as intended.

(77)
Maud [?] to Fritz Delius

16 rue d'armaillé
[1897/8?]

Dearest —

Just a line — Mrs Smith & I leave next week — Monday I think for St Moritz — or Dinard — perhaps Hombourg or Trouville — she does not know but *go* we go —

Sweet one. I think constantly of you. We have one tremendous interest — your work. I'd make every Every sacrifice toward it for you. even if it meant losing you, baby — Sweet love — promise me not to worry — pin your faith to me & you are sure to win. I want to see the dear eyes lose all that troubled look — & they *will* too in time. Ask Miss Rosen for me if she does not want two of those photos. I am sending over now & a dozen come cheaper. 12 shillings a dozen.

Dont forget my moustache. Dont think it small — it is not; it means something to me that I cant put into words. I should think you w'd understand that when I had first loved you like that, that I long to see you so again — (Hateful stub pen)

In mad haste —

Your own —
Maud.

Autograph letter, signed and undated, written in English.

The original is in the Delius Trust Archive.

This is the second of two letters in the Archive filed at one time under the heading 'Unknown Female Admirers' (see also Letter 56). It is possible that the writer may have been Maud Ede, an English artist who was sharing the house at Grez with Jelka Rosen and Ida Gerhardi earlier in the summer of 1897. I recently found further mention of her in the Gerhardi family correspondence in the possession of Frau Malve Steinweg. A number of photographs taken in the garden at Grez during this period were also found, and the reference to 'two of those photos' may concern these. It must, however, be conceded that there are one or two seeming Americanisms in the text of this letter.

1898

In Paris in the early part of the year, Delius busily revised a number of pieces, including *The Magic Fountain*. Busoni and he were spending a lot of time together; indeed, Busoni was now exploring Delius's music thoroughly, particularly the Piano Concerto and the Nietzsche songs. In April, in Grez, *Koanga* in its turn was undergoing some revision.

Grez was now providing for Delius the calm atmosphere in which he could do his best work. And in Jelka and Ida it harboured disciples of a fervour he had not known before. In a letter Ida wrote to her brother, Karl-August Gerhardi, on 7 April from Grez, something of that fervour is evident:

'If only I knew someone who would take an interest in Delius in Elberfeld – You may be quite sure that he really is the only personality among all the well-known modern composers who is producing something outstanding, – Jelka & I are musical & intelligent enough to comprehend his great talent; it is difficult to say whether it is genius, one would have to be a consummate musician to give a judgment on that, – but you feel, when you live with him in this way & hear him creating, that there is something altogether particularly beautiful in this music & Jelka & I want to do everything just to help him get on. I am now reading Wagner & Liszt to see how to make composers famous & of course the more they produce & the greater it is the worse it is. D.'s field is opera. You would be astonished if you could hear (& that we must hope) what he is composing now – a negro opera from Florida'.

Delius seems to have divided his time between Paris and Grez, and there is no record of any major excursion in the summer. At all events, his compositional activity was evidently busy and diverse. The death of his uncle Theodor, with whom he had recently been reconciled, caused new paths to open up. Armed with the knowledge that a fairly large sum of money (25,000 francs) was to come his way as his inheritance, armed too with various letters of introduction, Delius set off in mid-November for London. He was determined to sponsor a major performance of one or more of his works, preferably *Koanga*. He visited the family home in Bradford, and then spent Christmas with his sister Clare 'near the Wuthering Heights', not far from Skipton, in Yorkshire.

Two other significant events occurred in 1898: Delius's acquisition of Gauguin's painting 'Nevermore' (see pp. 138ff.) and the publication of C. F. Keary's novel *The Journalist* (see Appendix VIII, pp. 416–19), in which the character Sophus Jonsen is in part based on the composer.

The Magic Fountain, opera (RT I/3). Minor revision.

Koanga, opera (RT I/4). Some revision.

Seven Danish Songs (RT III/4). Some revision/completion?

Four Nietzsche Songs (RT V/19). Completed early 1898?

Mitternachtslied Zarathustras, for baritone solo, male chorus and orchestra (RT II/1).

'Traum Rosen', song (Marie Heinitz) (RT V/18).

'Im Glück wir lachend gingen', song (Drachmann) (RT V/20).

La ronde se déroule, symphonic poem after Helge Rode (RT VI/13). Begun.

---

(78)
Fritz Delius to Jelka Rosen

33, Rue Duc. (Paris)
Jan. 25th 1898

Dear friend,

Many thanks for your letter and the little flower which gave me a great longing for Grez. I received Miss Gerhardi's letter, thank her kindly for it. I wrote to her brother asking him to have the opera sent here to Paris as I want the piano-score and also to look through the thing again.[1] I am having my Fantasie Ouverture copied and in a day or two shall take it to Chevillard.[2] I am altering the cadenza of my concerto Fantasie and annihilating the alterations I had made for Falke.[3] I shall go and see Harold Bauer[4] tomorrow and see what I can do with him. Falke is no artist, of that I am now thoroughly convinced. I hope to arrive in Grez on Feb. 4th. In the meantime I re-orchestrated a little Serenade for Jebe's orchester and have sent it to him to play when Heiberg's "Balkongen" is given.[5] I am sorry to hear your influenza is not over yet. The good air of the country ought to take it away. But perhaps the bacteria of Paris are more destructive to the influenza bacteria. I am quite alright again. Give my love to Miss G. and Marie,

Your affectionate friend,
Fritz Delius.

Handwritten transcript in English in the Grainger Museum. The address and date are as written by the copyist.

1   Karl-August Gerhardi had retrieved on Delius's behalf the score of *The Magic Fountain* from Weimar (see Letter 65, note 1, and Letter 68).

2   Camille Chevillard (1859–1923): French conductor and composer. He was deputy conductor at the Concerts Lamoureux, succeeding Lamoureux on the latter's death in 1899. The work referred to is *Over the hills and far away*.

3   Delius had made some alterations to the first version of his Piano Concerto for the Franco-German pianist Henri Falke, a Premier Prix du Conservatoire, and they had played the work together in a four-handed arrangement at a private home in Paris.

4   Harold Bauer (1873–1951): English pianist. He had initially studied the violin, but then turned to the piano, studying with Paderewski in 1892 and making his début in Paris the following year. For a time he shared an apartment there with the American violinist Serge Achille Rivarde, and it was there that Delius had a rare opportunity to hear his Sonata in B for violin and piano, composed in 1892. Bauer had spent quite a lot of time with Delius during this period and now visited him from time to time in Grez, where they would often play tennis together in the summer months. From 1900 on he was to live more often and tour more frequently in the United States, finally settling there during the First World War.

5   Jebe had written earlier in January to tell Delius of his appointment as conductor of the orchestra of Christiania's Centraltheater: 'Heiberg's "Balcongen" is to play in a month's time at our place. (rejected at Kristiania Theater) I have proposed that we use music by you for it. And Fahlström and Frau F. who are both of them young, spirited people, have accepted the idea with a bravo. Please send me what you have as quickly as you can. Do you feel like doing an overture?' He went on to enumerate the instruments at his disposal. (Johan Fahlström was the theatre's director.) The result was that music by Delius was again heard in the Norwegian capital: 'The orchestra played a Serenade by Fritz Delius' (*Morgenposten*, 4 March 1898), and *Dagbladet* (2 March 1898) confirmed that it was played as an entr'acte.

(79)

Harold Bauer to Fritz Delius

26 rue Washington
Paris 22 April [1898?]

My dear Delius

Thanks very much for your letter and enclosure from Thrane[1] which I return. I did not answer you at once as I wished before doing so to show Mr Thrane's letter to my impresario Mr Strakosch and to consult him on the matter – I shall be very glad to meet Mr Thrane through you when he arrives in Paris, and to have a talk with him respecting the American tour. Meanwhile I can only say that I should be quite disposed to put myself in his hands, if we can make satisfactory arrangements, as I have received the best accounts of his success as a manager. I have told Strakosch to communicate with him.

I am very much obliged to you for the interest you have shown in the matter,[2] and also for having spoken of me to de Lara. I really dont know how far the latter means what he says, for he told me years ago what he repeated to you i.e. that I could easily get an engagement at Monte-Carlo by application and that he would use his influence in that direction at the same time. I can assure you that it is not for lack of application that I have not yet been engaged! and I am anxious to get there not so much for the one or two concerts that it represents as for the fact that it is the best centre and starting-point for the south of France and Italy and it would facilitate matters towards arranging a series of concerts in that direction if I could first commence there.

You have done all that was possible and I am very grateful to you. Let me know when you come into town or come & see me without letting me know. I should like to have an evening with you.

I remain
Very sincerely yours
Harold Bauer

Autograph letter, signed and dated (but no year given), written in English.

The original is in the Delius Trust Archive. Two other letters preserved from Bauer to Delius are dated September 1898 and October 1898.

1   None of the letters which are preserved from Thrane to Delius makes any mention of Bauer.

2   Bauer was again to comment on Delius's selflessness in a letter written during his Florida retirement to Percy Grainger, and dated 19 February 1945. Other remarks in this letter are of particular interest: 'I remembered that my first impression of Delius, when we met in Paris, was that he was an intelligent amateur who derived a large income from orange plantations . . . – an impression which was soon revised, since I discovered almost immediately that he was anything but wealthy . . . and that his attitude towards music was as far away from that of the "amateur" as could be conceived.

'At least, so he thought and said in his frequently expressed contempt for the individual who imagines that a superficial acquaintance with the art gives the right to deliver snap judgments.

'Fritz's judgments were quick and often quite unexpected – unhampered by prejudice or academic reasoning – In that, he was, to my mind, a great deal closer to the true amateur (or *lover of art*) than he would have been willing to admit. He was also pretty close to the amateur in his habit of neglecting his own work when his interest was attracted to the work of some other artist.'

(80)
Alfred Hertz to Fritz Delius

Frankfurt a/M. 27.8.98.
38 Niedenau

My dear Herr Delius,

I would have written to you long ago if I had not been travelling so much this summer; I have hardly been here. I have been to Vienna, Munich, & have travelled about all over the place in Switzerland, & definitely thought I would be coming to Paris too, but it did not turn out that way this time. Therefore, in apologizing for the delay in sending you these lines, I should like to pay you a *most genuine* compliment on your opera.[1] I studied it in detail right through, & was quite frankly inspired by some of its beauties. The whole colouring of the music is so original, & the conception of the whole so poetic, that really my boldest expectations were exceeded. Now, if in spite of this I do *not* perform the piece this season, the reason is as follows. I am fully aware of the importance and consequence of an absolutely first performance; I twice had an opportunity to initiate operas in Elberfeld. On both occasions the Director, doubtful of success, sanctioned no money for the decor, & on both occasions the operas, in spite of musical beauties, were buried. Now, in your work a characteristic setting, changing scenery, etc. etc. are in my opinion an *integral part* of the whole, & if this is not all staged really handsomely, then it is impossible for the piece as a whole to produce the desired effect. Now Elberfeld is not the place for it. The Director hasn't a free enough hand to take so great a risk with the work of an author who is as yet unknown, & if it is *not* properly staged even a musically good performance can only do you harm. *Next* year, however, as I have been engaged by a very large theatre, the name of which I may not yet reveal, I may be in a position to procure for you a performance *which will do you good*, & I shall then most certainly try to carry it through, but I do not think I can advise Elberfeld for the *very first* performance in spite of my full appreciation of all the beauties & qualities of the work. So please find enclosed with my best thanks the material & rest assured of my fullest interest in the work.

With cordial greetings
Yours truly
Alfred Hertz

Autograph letter, signed and dated, written in German.

The original is in the Delius Trust Archive. Three further letters from Hertz to Delius are dated March 1899 and April 1899; also preserved in the Archive are three letters of introduction Hertz wrote on Delius's behalf.

Alfred Hertz (1872–1942): German-born conductor. He studied at Frankfurt and conducted in various European centres in the 1890s, including Elberfeld from 1895 to 1899 and London in 1899, where he had charge of the Delius Orchestral Concert. From 1902 he was active in the United States, conducting successively the orchestra of the Metropolitan Opera and the San Francisco Symphony Orchestra.

1 *The Magic Fountain*. Ida Gerhardi had written to her brother on 7 April: 'Kapell-meister Hertz will receive on the 15th. at Frankfurt, where he probably wants to recuperate after his Wagner performances – Delius's opera, which you succeeded in getting back from Weimar, – he did the libretto himself 4 years ago, it is very poetic & charming. God willing, Hertz will like the music & the opera will be performed in the autumn-winter.'

(81)
Helge Rode to Fritz Delius

[Copenhagen] 14-9-98.

My dear Delius!

It is rather difficult for me to answer your Letter. I wrote to ligthly about the matter, preferring to talk about it when we met. The question had no real Actuality as "Dansen gaar" and Dramas of the Mind shall and must have no Music. (Another Thing is that every Drama kan and perhaps ougth to have an Ouverture and kan have Music between the Acts)

But on the whole I felt certain Fears for Difficulties and Unpleasant Things arising of working together when living in different Countries.

Now about Nationalism. Dont think I want a little Country to think itself something grand. I quoted the Line : Nur die Lumpe sind bescheiden, thinking it would remind you of a Conversation we had about all this Denmark Nation-alism and "zu viel Bescheidenheit".

Nationalism is not pure Stupidity, there is something in it of Necessity and therefore Rigth. Small Nations feel this perhaps in a different way from great ones. We must try to do something good to feel our Rigth of Eksistence and Danes have for some Time been so far from Chauvinisme that this was much like Self contempt, and this will hurt everybody who wants to do something. But I think this is over now. The great nations seems not only admirable and enviable.

After all – as you know me – Nationalism is not on the Bottom in me. It sometimes occupies my Mind more than other Times but certainly never in a chauvinistic Sense. I could well fancy a Patriot, whose chief Wish for his Country was, that it migth produce a good lot of Cosmopolites and out of this world people.

By the way : If Nationalism was at the Bottom of the Dreyfus question still this was no Proof that Nationalism was merely bad Humbug. Sensualism is at the Bottom of Love as at the Bottom of less beautiful Phenomenons. But I think the Bottom of the Dreyfus Affair is Crime, Crime and personal Hatred, which misuses Nationalism.

Well no more about this today.

Now about "Dansen gaar" Suppose one had written an Ouverture to it and Music between the Acts one Difficulty was, that the Drama was accepted at the Theatre months before it was printed and no "Solidaritet" therefore possible between Author and Musician. Probably the Theatre would say : We want no Music, it is uneccesarry. more Work and more Money. And if it was a Foreigner who had made the Music, perhaps the[y] would further say: "Why not at all Events a Dane. We have young Komposers, "who want to try their Power."

Now let me suppose, *you* had written this Music of course I would have felt very pleased. Of Course and I would have done anything I could to get it played. But I would have felt sorry if I had not succeeded. I have myself here to begin with had some Difficulties to get my Plays performed and understanding, that your Music is a personal one, which not everybody likes at first, there *migth* arise Difficulties, which I would feel painfully especially on account of my utterly Want of Knowledge in musical Matters. These were some of my Thoughts when I wrote. Now you see, I know nothing whether you have or have had a Mind or Time to write an Ouverture to "Dansen gaar" but if you have felt it so and if that little Tune of Irritation in your Letter, which made me sorry, not least because I in certain ways found it justified, was due to this, then I sincerely ask you: Do make it! Of Course I shall be very glad, and I hope the Theatre will play it – I would find it very remarkable if they would not – An Ouverture is allways played before the Performance (only Music between the Acts would be something ecceptional and therefore more difficult to get accepted) But here too I migth be wrong. The Theatre *migth* appreciate as I, that a Foreign Komposer took the Interest in a danish Drama. Do you know Johan Svendsen. (I seem to remember you did not like him and perhaps he neither likes you.) I know nothing about this and only want you to see Things as they are here before you do anything.

After all – there is not much for you to loose. Perhaps "Dansen gaar" will be performed in Berlin too: It is not settled yet. – (With Kongesönner[1] I am disappointed till now). – At all Events if you made Music you had the Music if my Play was never performed and nothing was lost.

Well perhaps you never thougt of Doing anything of the Kind, but if you have the Mind – Send it – an Ouverture – as I said – would very likely be received with Thanks. But if you like, I shall ask before. As for the Future when (if) I write a Work which more than this *wants* Music we will talk about it. – I assure you, there is something national. I *migth* write something to which you would say: "No let a Dane do this." Only *he* can – And I migth write something with which you would feel more than any Danish Komposer I know. The last is perhaps most probable.

And now dear Delius I shall be glad to hear from you. And about your greater Things too. I sincerely hope, that you will succeed in your Attempt with your new Opera in London I understand the immense Difficulties of Course not to be compared with those in small Places. The greater the gain. Not knowing your Work and not able to have any Opinion about it, I believe in it, because I know you and not least because I know that you never "write a Line for the Public". Neither do I. No real Artist does — because he cannot — he has something else to do. But when we talk we want the present People to listen and it is easier to get Silence in a small Place than in big ones because the Noise is not so tremendous.

Sincerely yours
Helge Rode.

The other Day I had a little one act Piece played at the Dagmartheatre — "Kain and Abel" — to this some Music was made of one Rosenberg. The Director of the Theatre engaged him to do it, I think, chiefly because he could do it in a Hurry and cheaply. — This not to blame him — I believe he is a sincere Musician — but you see I am not allied with or obliged to any danish Musician.
Dansen gaar will come on the Stage in January or February, I suppose.

Autograph letter, signed and dated, written in English.

The original is in the Delius Trust Archive. One further letter preserved from Rode to Delius is dated 28 February 1899. His eccentric spelling of 'might', etc., persists.

Helge Rode (1870–1937): Danish poet, essayist and dramatist. He was the author of *Kongesönner* and *Cain and Abel*, the plays mentioned in this letter. His play *Dansen gaar* (*The Dance Goes On*), published in 1898, had interested Delius, and finally *La ronde se déroule*, after Rode's piece, was completed by the composer in 1899; it was subsequently twice revised, to become the more familiar *Lebenstanz*.

   Still flushed with the fame — or notoriety — that he had achieved with his *Folkeraadet* score in Norway, it is apparent from this letter that Delius had tried to interest Rode in incidental music to *Dansen gaar*. In the event, he went ahead instead with his 'overture', which he later styled 'symphonic poem'. It was first given in the opening half of the London concert in May 1899.

   As a matter of interest Delius was shortly to introduce Harold Bauer to Rode. Bauer wrote from Copenhagen on 21 October: 'I duly presented your letter to Rode on my arrival here. I find him a most charming and interesting fellow and have seen a good deal of him.'

1   Evidence of a meeting with Rode in Berlin little more than two years later is furnished in a letter written at the time by Delius to Jelka from that city: 'Rode was here for 4 days — a play "Kongsønner" was given in the Secession Theater but had no success — he is a dear fellow — '.

(82)
Fritz Delius to Jelka Rosen

Oct. 13th 1898.
Paris.

Dear Jelka,

How kind of you to send me the roses and the grapes — they are beautiful — many thanks. I shall come out on Tuesday morning twelve train as I go to dinner at Robin's[1] on Monday and want to see Robin about Lady de Grey.[2] It appears I only get 25,000 francs,[3] the rest goes to my father — 50,000 for each child, and we get it at his death. What a nuisance. I have written him and told him he must give me this sum at once. I shall probably spend 25,000 on my opera in London.[4] If I can have it played I shall not hesitate. Love to Marie and "Koanga",[5]

Yours ever,
Fritz Delius.

Handwritten transcript in English in the Grainger Museum. The date is as written by the copyist.

1   Dr Edouard Charles Albert Robin (1847–1928?): eminent French surgeon and professor of the Faculty of Medicine, Paris, as well as a patron of the arts. He occasionally figures in the correspondence between Delius and Edvard Munch; and at least one letter of introduction which he wrote on Delius's behalf is preserved in the Delius Trust Archive. It is not known to whom it was originally addressed, but dated '24 nov 98' it describes Delius as a composer of great talent and of great individuality.

2   Lady de Grey: noted patroness of Covent Garden at the end of the 1890s. She was largely responsible for the first real attempt for some time to bring grand opera back to London.

3   Delius's uncle Theodor had died. Almost the first thing that Delius did with his legacy was to use a part of it to buy *Nevermore*, a painting by his friend Gauguin, purchased for 500 francs.

4   This is the first indication of the project which resulted in Delius's 1899 concert, in which parts of *Koanga* were given a concert performance. Delius used up much the larger part of his inheritance in order to finance the venture.

5   'Koanga' was the name given to the tame jackdaw which had adopted Jelka's home at Grez.

(83)

Arthur Krönig to Fritz Delius

Berlin, 24th October 1898.

My dear Fritz,

I thank you very much for your letter. I hope that you have recovered more quickly than my mother[1] and Aunt Collmann, both of whom were seriously ill, even before the terrible news arrived. Mama is completely disconcerted by the fact that such a shining light of mankind, such an exemplary human being − all the Deliuses of the previous generation are angels − had to die so young. She herself is now 75 years old and most desperate that she is no longer active as a youngster. About your father she said a short while ago: "Heavens, isn't it too terrible that he has to be wheeled in a bath-chair at the age of only 78". I have been wheeled for already 6 years; that appears to her quite natural and she is always greatly surprised that I am not as cheerful as I used to be in the days of my health. Indeed, such people as the Deliuses are will not be met again anywhere in the world. We, of course, do not belong to the family. Meanwhile, the dear departed Uncle is doubtless already united with the saints, flying in the Beyond in white garments and singing hymns. After all, he was so very musical. The whole family will be reunited there, but without the children.

I greatly regret that your musical plans have not yet made any progress. Perhaps you might use part of the large inheritance for this purpose. Then a stage will soon be found, even if it is not a Court Theatre. We will [study] your fine new songs[2] with great pleasure. I consider Nietzsche quite unsuitable for musical treatment. He is not sombre enough. I, for my part, have not touched a piano for eighteen months, except for composing a few songs which did not turn out well. No [good] texts can be found anywhere in the world. My wife sends her love.

Your cousin Arthur.

English typescript, dated, in the Delius Trust Archive. The original German letter, of which this is a translation, has been lost. Of a total of fourteen letters and postcards known to have been written by Arthur Krönig and his wife, Marie, to Delius around this period, five originals are extant, while the remainder have been found only in typescript translations.

Arthur Krönig (1853−1900): son of August Karl Krönig and Albertine Delius, he was first cousin to Fritz and held the post of *Amtsgerichtsrat* in Berlin. He was the dedicatee of the *Mitternachtslied Zarathustras*, composed this year. In this letter he wrote of the death of Theodor Delius.

1   Albertine Johanne Caroline Krönig, *née* Delius (1823−1913): sister of Julius Delius, Fritz's father, she lived in Berlin.

2   The four *Songs to Poems by Friedrich Nietzsche*, composed this year.

(84)
Fritz Delius to Jelka Rosen

25, Montpelier Street, S.W.　　　　　　　　　　　　　　　London.
　　　　　　　　　　　　　　　　　　　　　　　　Nov. 20th 1898.

Dear Jelka,

I had a quiet passage and arrived on Tuesday morning. Keary received me very kindly and got me lodgings close to his own. I feel awfully out of my water here, and pretty hopeless. I shall do all I can, and present all my letters of introduction. Bispham,[1] the singer, is in America, Mrs. Maddison[2] (Mrs. Robin's brother's introduction) is in France. I have three from Equsquiza[3] to Mrs. Joshua,[4] Mrs. Woodhouse,[5] and a manager Curtius[6] which I shall present tomorrow and day after. The concerts, it appears, are all made up for this season etc, etc. Percy Pitt,[7] my friend who is organist at Queen's Hall dines with me on Tuesday, and I shall show him some of my things. Yesterday at 12 midi it was without exaggeration (as to spelling I am mixed) as black as night. All lamps and electric lights lit but as black as night. I was on the top of an omnibus going to Piccadilly and it looked like the gates of Hell — how can art flourish here? Well! I will not give it up yet. Write me when you have time, and give my love to all,

　　Your affectionate friend
　　F.D.

Handwritten transcript in English in the Grainger Museum. The date is as written by the copyist.

1　David Bispham (1857–1921): American baritone, noted for his wide operatic repertoire. From 1891 he sang at Covent Garden.

2　Adela Maddison: composer and patron of the arts, she was for a time Fauré's intimate. See Letter 99.

3　There are a number of references to Equsquiza, Paris-based impresario, in the Delius letters, indicating that he showed interest in the composer for a time. Some years later the pianist Theodor Szántó (see Letter 198) was to write to Delius thanking him for an introduction to this influential figure.

4　Like Lady de Grey (see Letters 82 and 85), Mrs Joshua was a patron of the arts. Neither however seems to have been of much help to Delius.

5　Violet (Kate) Gordon Woodhouse (1872–1948): English harpsichordist, clavichordist and pianist, and dedicatee in 1919 of Delius's 'Dance for Harpsichord'. Delius found her, as he wrote to Jelka on 28 November 1898, 'a very musical and charming woman'.

6   Alfred Schulz-Curtius (1853–?): German-born concert director and impresario. A friend of Percy Pitt, he was naturalized as a British subject in 1896. He was impresario of the famous Wagner Concerts at the Queen's Hall from 1894 to 1900.

7   Percy Pitt (1869–1932): English conductor, composer and organist. He had studied at Leipzig while Delius was there and was now organist, accompanist and *répétiteur* at Queen's Hall. From 1902 he was to become increasingly engaged in the opera house, becoming conductor at Covent Garden and later with the Beecham Opera Company and the British National Opera Company. In 1924 he became director of music at the BBC. 'I shall be awfully interested to see your latest things,' he had written to Delius on 24 October.

(85)
Fritz Delius to Jelka Rosen

Dec. 19th 1898.
London.

Dear Jelka,

No good news to tell you – I went twice to Lady de Grey in vain – they told me at the door that her ladyship was very busy this week but would write to me – since then no news – Mrs. Joshua was a great disappointment – a pretentious stupid woman spouting morals, philosophy, political economy in one breath – no artist and arrogant as hell – I came to loggerheads with her over Nietzsche. She is a disciple of Schopenhauer and Wagner to a degree which approaches idiocy – I don't suppose anyone ever spoke to her as frankly as I did, and she no doubt expected something quite different. She seems to be surrounded by a worshipping clique, you know I am not of that race. Mrs. Woodhouse is a nice, artistic, unpretentious little woman who I like. I have two people at least already very enthusiastic about my opera, one a musician Clutsam,[1] who has played my work and would do so whenever I required an audition, another is a concert manager Norman Concorde[2] – we have an idea of starting a theatre of our own to give new operas of every description as long as they are good. We want £4000 to run us a month. Shall we get it? The miracle might happen. When everything has failed here I shall go to Germany – I hope your nose is alright again. Of course a frame could not fall on anything else, could it? I have seen Mrs. Bell. She is getting on very well, and may be of use. I see there is a great opportunity here, but the difficulties are frightful – for that reason they doubt that my music should be worth anything. However if I could get a hearing I should be alright. If! Well good-bye. I sent you the book.[3]

Best love,
Your affectionate friend,
F.D.

Handwritten transcript in English in the Grainger Museum. The address and date are as written by the copyist.

Delius's letters to Jelka during this period are lively and descriptive, even if the tone is predominantly pessimistic. He had written the previous day to inform her that in spite of Clutsam having played parts of *Koanga* to Hedmondt, of the Royal English Opera Company, who had been 'very much struck with it', things were not going well: 'What a rotten life I lead here! What a city! What people! No wonder Nietzsche went mad.' He had evidently not succeeded in manipulating people in London as he had hoped with such confidence when writing still earlier to Jelka (on 28 November): 'the people here are a weak-headed lot — at least in the things I care about — I have a certain feeling of power here amongst them — if I could only get my fingers on the strings I could make the marionettes dance.' At least there were old acquaintanceships to be rekindled, with Busoni writing from London to his wife on 11 December: 'The first person I met here was Delius. He was very delighted, and exceedingly warm' (Busoni, *Letters to His Wife*, p. 29). In a letter to Jelka on 20 December, Delius too recorded this meeting.

1   George H. Clutsam (1866–1951): Australian composer, pianist and critic, domiciled in London. He was to become best-known, as a composer, for his light operas.

2   R. Norman-Concorde: impresario who was, as director of the Concorde Concert Control, to organize the Delius Orchestral Concert in London the following May.

3   Delius had written to Jelka on 28 November: 'Keary's book is very good. He has taken an awful lot of sayings out of my mouth for Johnson, but the characters are alive and artistic upon the whole. I will send it to you.' The novel, just published, was entitled *The Journalist* (London: Methuen, 1898) (see Appendix VIII).

(86)
Fritz Delius to Ida Gerhardi

25 Montpelier Str
London S. W.
[December 1898]

Dear Fräulein Gerhardi —

I have received your letter & postcard — Why rack your brains so? I sent this letter to Frl Rosen to whom I was just writing when I received this letter — Do you know me so little — I am quite astonished at your friendliness & interest in this unfortunate plantation[1] & in my music — Do as you wish, you know that I already agree — Perhaps something will turn up! Perhaps however my brother will go to Florida with some capital in order to settle the whole business —

But this is *secret* — You must say nothing about it & so far nothing is certain — In this case, if Peters does not get a move on I would have once again to withdraw my proposition — because somebody must be there before the middle of January — Perhaps, too, Peters could work together with my brother.

I shall send you my Zarathustra with parts in a few days' time[2] — London is hell & the [most] inartistic city in the world — Whether I will have my opera performed here is very doubtful — if not, I will come to Germany to try there — The English are simply not musical — Shall I address my music to Lüdenscheid? I hope you are well — Give my regards to Haym & his wife & fare well

With kind regards
Yours
Fritz Delius

Autograph letter, signed and undated, written in German.

The original is in the collection of Frau Malve Steinweg, Lüdenscheid. This collection includes, apart from a number of letters from Delius, some correspondence from Jelka addressed to Ida Gerhardi and to her sister Lilli.

1   Ida was acting as Delius's intermediary in a project to lease Solana Grove to Willy Peters, a young German.

2   The score had been requested by Ida in order that she could pass it on to Hans Haym in Elberfeld.

Nevermore
(purchased 8 November 1898)

Paul Gauguin to Georges-Daniel de Monfreid: Tahiti, 14 February 1897
I am trying to finish a canvas so as to be able to send it with the others, but *will I have the time?* I strongly recommend you to observe the vertical when you put it on a frame; I don't know if I'm wrong but I feel it's good. I wanted with a simple nude to suggest something of a barbarian luxury of the past. The whole is submerged in colours that are by design dark and gloomy; it isn't silk, nor velvet, nor cambric, nor gold that produces this luxury but simply the material enriched by the artist's hand. No nonsense . . . the imagination of man alone has enriched the dwelling by means of his fantasy.

As a title, Nevermore; not the raven of Edgar Poe at all, but the bird of the devil which is on the watch. It's badly painted, (I am so nervous and I work in fits and starts,) no matter, I believe it's a good canvas — A naval officer will send you everything in a month, I hope.

Gauguin to de Monfreid: Tahiti, 12 March 1897
No, don't put them at Molard's who hasn't got any room and who doesn't receive any buyers.

Gauguin to de Monfreid: Tahiti, November 1897
Schuff[enecker] tells me that Leclercq has abandoned Bing's so as to set himself
up as a picture *dealer*; I do hope you won't entrust any canvases to this rascal, no
more for Norway than for anywhere else.

De Monfreid: Notebooks
Tuesday, 8 November 1898: After lunch visited by Borel; then Delius comes with
a Norwegian lady. He buys Gauguin's femme couchée (Never more) and I go
with him to a picture framer's.
Thursday, 10 November 1898: After lunch, visited by Delius.
Friday, 11 November 1898: At 11 o'clock visited by Delius who brings me 500
fr. for Gauguin price of the picture he has bought. After lunch I write to
Gauguin.

De Monfreid to Gauguin: Paris, 11 November 1898
Herewith you will find two cheques.* . . . The second cheque is the price that
Delius, our English friend, offers you for one of your best works: "Nevermore",
the woman lying on the bed with a yellow fabric under her head. He can't give
you more than 500 francs for it; but knowing that you wanted to put this canvas
by to sell at a high price, I only let him have it on condition. If the amount
seems too low to you, he'll let you have the canvas back for the price he paid for
it. Like Lerolle. However, I think I did well to let him have this fine piece; for
it will be seen by the *very numerous* well-connected people cultivated by Delius.

* To Vollard 4 canvases for 600 fr = 1 cheque for 578 frs, charges for the said cheque
12 frs, carriage 10 frs = total 600.
  To Delius, one canvas for 500 frs = 1 cheque for 488,60, charges 11,40 = total
500 frs.

De Monfreid: Notebooks
Monday, 14 November 1898: Delius came this afternoon & brought me 50 fr for
his frame ordered at Dubourg's. I send him his Gauguin canvas in the evening
through G. Belfils who comes to dinner.

Saturday, 19 November 1898: Paid for Delius's frame with the money he brought,
i.e. 50^f.

Gauguin to de Monfreid: Tahiti, 12 January 1899
You did well to let Delius have the picture "Nevermore". He pays more than
Vollard. Once this Vollard bought from Bernard some pictures of mine, from
Brittany, for more than he's paying now. Never mind, it's better to sell cheap

than not at all. You remember you reproached me for having given a title to this picture: don't you think that this title *Nevermore* is the reason for this purchase – Perhaps!

Whatever the case, I'm very glad that Delius is its owner, seeing that it isn't a speculative purchase for resale, but bought because he likes it; then some other time he'll want another, especially if callers compliment him on it or get him to talk about this subject.

De Monfreid to Gauguin: Saint-Clément, Pyrénées-Orientales, 11 March 1899
I'm glad you don't disapprove of the sale to Delius. As a matter of fact he's a lad who likes your painting, and especially this canvas. Not because of the title; he told me that himself. But because it is a *beautiful painting*. An opinion which I fully share. Yes, my dear Gauguin, paint fine pieces like that often, generously, abundantly, with love: I am sure that everyone will appreciate the richness of such works.

* * *

Gauguin to de Monfreid: Marquesas Islands, 25 August 1902
M . . . writes to tell me that he hopes to make a major exhibition of my works next year. Perfect!! I'm not particularly keen on a large number of canvases but I am keen above all on *quality*, (lucky that you're there to supervise matters). If possible, the *big canvas* which is at *Bordeaux*. From Z . . . I would think only the *woodcarving* – If possible the picture *Nevermore* at Delius's – Nothing from Brittany . . .

* * *

De Monfreid to Delius: Saint-Clément, Pyrénées-Orientales, 14 September 1906
Perhaps you already know that the exhibition of Gauguin's works at the Salon d'Automne is definitely fixed, and this exhibition will be opening at the end of the month. May we count on your picture "Never More"? I hope this beautiful canvas won't be absent from this solemn reunion of the works of the great artist, to whom justice is at last being done. Please be so kind as to tell me if you will be at Grez on the 26th or 27th of this month, the date on which we must assemble all the works to be shown. I intend to be there so that I can personally look after the transport, hanging, etc. in order to avoid all damage. At the same time, therefore, I hope to have the pleasure of seeing you.

If you should not be at home at that time, could you give the necessary orders for the picture to be entrusted to us? Once I am in Paris I shall see about the best means of transport.

* * *

De Monfreid to Delius: Paris, 9 May 1910
Your picture has still not come back from the restorer; though I wrote to him two or three days ago. But I don't think he'll be much longer now; as he promised to let me have it for the end of April. He is a very painstaking and

skilful man, but he is exceedingly slow. I think one of these days we could ourselves bring the canvas to you, in our little motor car.

De Monfreid to Delius: Paris, 17 June 1910
Your Gauguin picture is back from the restorer's. It is now *waxed* with all possible care; I think you will find, as we did, that these repairs have improved it considerably.

* * *

Paul Gauguin (1848–1903): French post-impressionist painter. Apart from 'Nevermore', Delius is also known to have possessed a number of wood carvings by Gauguin. In need of money, Delius was to dispatch 'Nevermore' in 1920 to London, where it was finally bought by Samuel Courtauld, industrialist and patron of the arts. Jelka painted a copy of it beforehand, and this the Deliuses retained at Grez. It now hangs in the Grainger Museum. The original is in the Courtauld Institute Galleries, London.

Georges-Daniel de Monfreid (1856–1929): French painter, sculptor and engraver, and confidant of Gauguin. He was an intimate friend of Delius in the 1890s, and in early 1893 he executed a pastel portrait of the composer. A well-liked and respected member of the Molard circle, he had a calmness of character and an innate good taste that probably particularly endeared him to Delius. He was seldom to return to Paris after 1900, retiring to the family *propriété* at St Clément in the Pyrenees, where he continued to paint.

1899

Delius's stay in London had not been in vain. He had involved himself in a scheme to found a 'London Permanent Opera', largely, no doubt, with a view to seeing *Koanga* performed in the capital. His main partner was to be the impresario R. Norman-Concorde, with whom Delius throughout this year engaged in a busy correspondence relating to the major concert on 30 May of his works (in the event, only parts of *Koanga* were given, in a concert performance). The correspondence grew acrimonious in its later stages as the bills began to come in; they were considerably larger than Delius had perhaps naïvely expected, and he showed a marked reluctance to pay some of them. During the build-up to the concert there was much discussion on the subject of conductors and soloists: Henry Wood, it was asserted, would be the only English conductor likely to have any sympathy for Delius's 'new' music, although Hamish Mac-Cunn was at one stage mooted. But Wood was not available. Delius, therefore, had to look abroad, and asked Alfred Hertz to take up the challenge. Halfdan Jebe was to lead the orchestra.

Delius arrived in London on 20 April and started on an exhausting round of visits to performing artists and to likely patrons, helped Norman-Concorde to assemble a chorus, took part in rehearsals — and dutifully visited Jelka's relatives. The concert was widely reviewed — a tribute to the Concorde agency's gift for publicity — and was unquestionably the major talking point of the day in musical circles. A sufficient number of the reviews were favourable, some notably so, for the enterprise to be judged a success. 'It is the first powerful ray of sunshine shed on English music,' wrote the singer Fischer Sobell to Delius after the concert.

During most of the rest of the year Delius divided his time between Paris and Grez, apart from an excursion to Norway in July and then to Denmark and Germany for a few days in mid-August in an unsuccessful attempt to interest publishers in his music. He was now fretting on account of having spent so little time on composition in recent months. In November, however, he was at last hard at work in Grez on a new opera, *A Village Romeo and Juliet*.

La ronde se déroule (RT VI/13). Completed.

Paris, Nocturne (The Song of a great City) for large orchestra (RT VI/14).

A Village Romeo and Juliet, opera (RT I/6). Composition substantially begun towards the end of the year.

(87)
Fritz Delius to Jelka Rosen

25 Montpelier Str
S.W.
[5 January 1899]

Dear Jelka —

I received your letter this evening on my return from Stone Gappe[1] — at the same time one from Miss Gerhardi where Peters puts off his journey again Of course I cannot wait any more for him — I leave here on the 10th & shall be in Grez about the 15th — We will try and translate Koanga together — Keary does not seem to jump at the idea of it being performed in Germany — He thinks I ought to return in a year to London and try again — However, translated it shall be & Germany tried first. Afterwards I can try England again — I think I shall write Romeo myself — we might do it together —[2]

I shall bring a book back which you will like better than Keary's — Journalist — "The Story of an African farm" by Olive Schreiner — Temperament[?]! So glad you sold your pictures — If you have money to spare send me 250 francs to come back with — I suppose I shall get my 25.000 on my return & can then return you the frs 500 — My stay here has not been useless as I have interested a certain milieu & a result may come later — I dont feel up to going anywhere else just now I am working at my Overture,[3] in my head, & dont want to knock it out — When I return I think I shall get it quick on paper — I shall either leave Jebe in my rooms or bring him to Grez[4] — he can stay at Charlots — altho' I dont think he will want to stay in the country long — I am so glad you have had a little success with your pictures — How is my poppy garden getting along? & the moonlight Stimmung? The "unexplainable" What a strange conflict there is between our inner & outward natures — I think that, the most extraordinary thing in human life — My inner nature is contrary to all my physical nature wants to do & wins always in the end. I think before I am thro' I shall become an absolute ascetic. I felt the greatest physical attraction to my youngest sister on seeing her again Strange, Eh! very seldom felt greater. Did Marie & Koanga get my cards? I hate London artistically — & I understand that everything fine & free must wither here — Well! goodbye! & au revoir give my love to all & Believe me

Your affectionate friend
Fritz Delius

Autograph letter, signed and undated, written in English. Jelka later added '5.1.99'.

The original is in the Grainger Museum.

1   The Yorkshire home of Delius's favourite sister, Clare, with whom he had spent Christmas. Her relationship with him is charted interestingly, if not always accurately, in her *Frederick Delius: Memories of my brother*.

2   In a letter written during the Christmas holiday at Stone Gappe, Delius had told Jelka, 'Keary is awfully slow and takes a fearful amount of warming before he gets a-going. He does not seem to have got any further with "Romeo and Juliet" and has no more "Stimmung" about it — you have to put it all into him. He asked me to play the themes of it to him to inspire him, but I have no themes yet — . . . I am afraid he is too old to do anything. I could not base my future work on him — he goes too slow —'.

3   In a letter written from London to Jelka on 18 December, Delius had proposed, 'I could come back for a month or two to finish my overture to "Dansen Gaar".'

4   'Jebe is coming to Paris,' Delius had written from London on 18 December. 'If he turns up look after him a bit. He is the only one that is worth something and the only man I really love — I told him to visit you in Grez.'

(88)
Fritz Delius to Jelka Rosen

33 Rue Ducouëdic
Monday
[January 1899]

Dear Jelka —

Unless Peters turns up tomorrow Tuesday I shall come out by the 5 train with Jebe — Please get him a room at Charlots — Miss Gerhardi, I am afraid, has muddled our meeting frightfully — However, tant pis; I am longing to get to work again & for our walks —. I went tonight to "Les Revenants" Henrik Ibsen — Theatre Antoine — It sounded a bit old fashioned to my ears — I want much more now — and certain things cease to interest me — The piece is however good — "The Wild Duck" is better — Yes! Our niveau is higher I think than we are ourselves aware of — Tant mieux — Am anxious to see what you have been doing since I was away — You are certainly the highest woman I have met — The others are not free & too dependent — Altho' very pleasant pour un quart d'heure — My Gauguin is now framed[1] & hanging in my room —

yours ever
Fritz Delius

Autograph letter, signed and undated, written in English. Jelka later added '1899 End of August'; internal evidence, however, points to a January 1899 dating.

The original is in the Grainger Museum.

1   As early as 8 November 1898, Daniel de Monfreid had recorded in his diary: 'Delius
. . . buys Gauguin's femme couchée (Never more) and I go with him to a picture
framer's.'

(89)

R. Norman-Concorde to Fritz Delius

The Concorde Concert Control,
186, Wardour Street,
(Corner of Oxford Street,)
London, W.
26 Jan. 1899

Dear Delius

The press notices still continue to pour in, and as we have no-one to consult, we
do not like to make any move. We wish that you were here in order that you
might formulate a strong plan of action. Messrs Clutsam and Keary are too
occupied with their own affairs to call here and discuss matters and so practically
the whole thing is in our hands. All the press notices seem to indicate that the
scheme is simply visionary, and the sooner we can put it on some practical basis,
the better. There is a good office below us, which will be vacant in a few weeks,
and which we could obtain for the reasonable rent of £30 (thirty pounds) a year,
and we think it would be a good plan to have such an office and devote it entirely
to the London Permanent Opera. The expenses of furnishing would not be more
than £8 or £9.

We think that before issuing the prospectus to the public another strong
circular should be sent out criticising the press and the position that they have
taken. The question is: – Is the press influenced by artistic merit, or is it only
dazzled by moneyed names.

We have not asked for any contributions from the public in our circular! The
only things put forward for criticism are the artistic ideas set forth in the
circular. When do you think you will be here again? We see plainly that the
whole matter will rest with you and us, and its success depends upon the energy
with which we work things. We are more confident than ever and are sure that
as soon as you are on the spot we shall make headway.

To those people who inquire as to the moneyed status of the concern it is
sufficient to say that we have all that is required to put the scheme before the
public and that when the proper time comes the financial basis will be shown
to the public.

In haste.
Yours ever
R.U.B-N.

Fritz Delius Esq.

Typed letter, with MS additions, initialled and dated, written in English on headed notepaper.

The original is in the Delius Trust Archive. It is the third of forty-five letters written by Norman-Concorde to Delius between 24 January 1899 and 1 August 1901 that have been preserved. Norman-Concorde's letters to Delius are signed, or initialled, in various ways, often virtually illegibly. However, his first extant letter to the composer, dated 24 January 1899, on paper that includes in its printed heading the legend

MR. R. NORMAN-CONCORDE ⎱ DIRECTORS
MRS. F. NORMAN-CONCORDE ⎰

is signed R. U. Brunel-Norman. A rather later letter-heading includes an advertisement for 'Mme. Adey Brunel's RECITALS'.

Norman-Concorde, in collaboration with Delius, had issued a circular to promote a 'London Permanent Opera'. Operas were to be produced in English, and 'English artists, both vocal and instrumental, will receive every encouragement'. Delius obviously saw the whole project as a suitable vehicle for getting *Koanga* onto the London stage. It is debatable, however, whether his motives were entirely selfish: some years later he was to see himself in a similar role, promoting English music in England under the banner of the short-lived Musical League.

In spite of Delius's earlier misgivings, this London visit was not to prove abortive. There were several enquiries about his works, addressed to Norman-Concorde and others, and two of his songs were programmed for a concert at Queen's Hall on 14 March.

It seems quite possible that the introduction to Norman-Concorde and the Concorde Concert Control came about through Jutta Bell, since she figured in the agency's advertisements at this period as Mme. Jütta Bell-Ranske, who gave 'Lectures on Voice Production, illustrated by her daughter Tullik Bell-Ranske (aged 10) and Miss May Warren (aged 16)' (cf. *The London Musical Courier*, 7, No. 18, 4 May 1899, p. 282).

(90)
R. Norman-Concorde to Fritz Delius

The Concorde Concert Control,
186, Wardour Street,
(Corner of Oxford Street,)
London, W.
25 Feby. 1899

Dear Delius,

In reply to your letter received this morning the expenses of your concert will of course vary according to the amount you expend on chorus, etc, but the certain expenses will be: —

Hall		25 guineas		
Attendance, police, etc.	about	£ 7		
Gratuities	"	£ 0	10	0
Printing	"	12	0	0
Bill-posting		1	0	0
(unless you have large bills up on the hoardings)				
Sandwichmen	each per day	0	2	0
Postage, according to the amount of circulars you wish sent out				
Advertisements	at least	30	0	0
Orchestra	between	£70 & £80		
according to your requirements				
Stationery, etc	about	0	10	0
Press cuttings		1	guinea	

We certainly think the Queen's Hall would be the most suitable place. We have an extremely good baritone, who would sing for nothing, namely Mr. Homer Lind.[1] You will see by the accompanying programme the class of artist he is. Bispham ought to sing for nothing for a thing like this, Busoni also should play for nothing, as the piano firm will give him a fee, and we will see what we can do towards getting you a good tenor and dramatic soprano on the same terms. As soon as we settle the matter I will start paragraphing the press with a "forty engine power", and my partner, who will be in Paris, will probably be able to collect facts from you which would be useful for this purpose. We will make inquiries about a chorus and see if it can be got for very low fees. We would also make special arrangements with the orchestra to give two or three rehearsals, instead of only one, as is usual. We will see Clutsam[2] and ask his opinion as to whether it would be best to do the second or third act of KOANGA.

London Permanent Opera.

If this circular is issued next week, we will, as soon as we get inquiries from the press, let them know that you are connected with it, as we think it is time that the information was given to them. It will also advertise your name for the concert.

Our kindest regard
Yours Ever
R U N-C

Fritz Delius Esq.
Grez sur Loing.

Typed letter, initialled and dated, written in English on headed notepaper.

The original is in the Delius Trust Archive.

1   Homer Lind: had been principal baritone at the Stadttheater, Mainz, and with the Carl Rosa Opera Company. As a teacher he specialized in training for English and German opera, including stage deportment, and in the interpretation of German *lieder*.

2   Clutsam had, furthermore, been able to inform Delius, only three days earlier: 'Madame Fischer is singing your "Abendstimmung" and "Venevil", on March 14th at Queen's Hall.'

(91)

Percy Pitt to Fritz Delius

211, Camden Road N.W.
12/3/99

My dear Delius,

Pleased to hear from you again & I shld. have answered sooner but for a beastly lot of work. With regard to your concert, I had already sounded Wood[1] re conducting when your letter & that of Concorde Agency suddenly arrived. I fear that the fact of your having placed the arrangements in C.'s hands will prevent Wood from doing your thing as Newman[2] will step in & refuse permission.

You see, Wood is retained solely by Newman & cannot accept outside engagements. Had you waited, I was going to write you – in fact I had done so but happening to call on W. before posting same, found the two letters. I had advised you to write Wood personally, applying for him & the Queen's Hall Orchestra. This would have been placed before Newman & I believe that between W. & myself, a favorable result wld. have been arrived at. As it stands however, I don't believe you will be able to do much, for it will not be possible for you to have our men & all the other good players will be required for Covent Garden. I wld advise you to put off the concert for present, take it out of Concorde's hands & wait until the Autumn. If you will then write Wood, I daresay we can arrange with Newman for the Orchestra *and* the Male Voices of our Chorus. This is a thing you did not bear in mind – it is most difficult to pick up a Choir off hand!! Let me know what you intend to do.[3] I also want to ask a favor & that is for you to get me Mrs. Maddison's Paris address as I must write her about something.

Hope you are well & hard at work. I have written a sort of "Ballad" for Male-Chorus & Orchestra which will be performed here in May. Many kind regards from

Yours always sincerely
Percy Pitt

Autograph letter, signed and dated, written in English.

The original is in the Delius Trust Archive. It is the second of three letters preserved from Pitt to Delius dated 1898 and 1899.

1   Henry J. Wood (1869–1944): English conductor. Studying initially with his parents, he became an organist, then a student at the Royal Academy of Music. He conducted with the Carl Rosa Opera Company in 1891 and 1892, but his fame rests on his conducting at the Queen's Hall Promenade Concerts from 1895 and on his continuing championship of newer music.

2   Robert Newman (1859–1926): English bass and impresario. Although he had studied at the Royal Academy of Music, he turned his back on a singing career in 1893, becoming concert manager at the Queen's Hall, and organizer from 1895 of the Promenade seasons.

3   Delius was to write a few days later to Norman-Concorde to say that he could secure Alfred Hertz as conductor for his concert. In the event, Queen's Hall was already let for the whole of May, and on 17 March he was informed by Concorde that 'we will have to take St. James's Hall'.

(92)
Fritz Delius to Jelka Rosen

33 Rue Ducouëdic
[March 1899]

Dear Jelka –

Thanks for your letter which I thoroughly understood – Dont ever think that I dont understand you – I do – and that's why I hate myself so much sometimes. The truth however is – that my artistic aspiration has drowned & smothered everything else in me – Am I going to the devil or not? I dont know, but I must go after my art & I know you understand it & want it so. Still we are human beings & every now and then other things come up in you & me. They are not important –

  Gabriel Fauré[1] & a few of the best young french musicians played my opera at Mrs Maddisons[2] this afternoon – Prince & Princess de Polignac[3] & a few other musical people were there. And I think I may say they were quite enthusiastic – it gives me a little more confidence for London Farewell – love to Koanga & Marie & you –

yrs
Fritz Delius

Autograph letter, signed and undated, written in English. Jelka later added 'March 1899'.

The original is in the Grainger Museum.

1   Gabriel Fauré (1845–1924): French composer, at this period teaching at the Paris Conservatoire. He began his career as an organist, and achieved distinction as such. From 1905 to 1920 he was director of the Conservatoire. It is possible that Delius had met Fauré in the context of Theodor Delius's wide circle, which had included one of Fauré's closest friends, André Messager.

2   Delius had earlier sent a postcard – from Paris on 8 March – to announce to Jelka: 'Am lunching with Mrs Maddison on Saturday –'

3   Distinguished patrons of the arts, the Prince and Princesse Edmond de Polignac held elegant court at their salon and helped younger musicians in France for many years. Ravel's *Pavane pour une Infante défunte*, completed this year, was originally commissioned by the Princesse de Polignac. Of all the Paris salons, hers was that of the avant-garde. Fauré was its frequent guest of honour, and many of his works had their first hearing there.

(93)
Alfred Hertz to Fritz Delius

Elberfeld 30.3.99.
22 Wasserstr.

Dear Herr Delius,

When do you intend to go to London then? I should like to come at the end of the season (16th April) to Paris, where I could stay with my uncle (Emile Hertz Rue Spontini 18); you seem however to live right outside the city. Where is "Grez" then? But in any case it would be important for me to get acclimatized to some extent in London beforehand & to get some practice in speaking. On the other hand I consider it of great moment that we should go through the things together for a while, as it is *your* conception that I would wish to express. At all events could you not send me at least *one* score in the meantime? You will understand how inquisitive I am. I can only comment on the programme, which incidentally seems colossally long to me, when I know the things. Do please let me hear from you again in more detail.

   Cordial greetings
   Yours truly
   Alfred Hertz

———————

Autograph letter, signed and dated, written in German.

The original is in the Delius Trust Archive.

(94)

Gabriel Fauré to Fritz Delius

[April 1899]

Here, dear Sir, are letters of introduction[1] to three people who I am sure will receive you very well, and who will in no time be delighted to make your acquaintance.

Bon voyage and all success

Yours sincerely
Gabriel Fauré

Please tell Percy Pitt that I am having great difficulty in rousing my publisher Hamelle on the subject of the songs. He is a man who always changes *the subject* when he does not wish to make a decision!

Autograph letter, signed and undated, written in French.

The original is in the Delius Trust Archive. It is the sole item of correspondence from Fauré to Delius that has been preserved.

1   One of Fauré's three letters has certainly survived (the other two were to Leo Schuster and to John Singer Sargent); addressed to Lady Lewis, wife of the solicitor Sir George Henry Lewis, it was written, in French, from 154, B^d Malesherbes, and like Fauré's covering letter to Delius it is not dated:

'Will you permit me to recommend to you a Composer of very much talent, Mr Delius, who intends to have some of his works performed in London shortly?

I would be very glad if you could possibly help act as a patron for him. . . .'

(The original of this letter was sold in 1974 by Winifred A. Myers [Autographs] Ltd, London.)

Since 1896, society circles in London had opened to welcome Fauré warmly, and apart from Schuster, Sargent and Lady Lewis, other particular friends in the centre of the London scene were Lady de Grey and Adela Maddison.

(95)

John Singer Sargent to Fritz Delius

Tuesday [2 May 1899]
33, TITE STREET,
CHELSEA, S.W.

Dear Mr Delius

Before meeting you tomorrow at Lady Lewis' let me make my excuses to you for having delayed so long in thanking you for having sent me the songs, which I have greatly enjoyed (especially those which I am able to play!)

I have been so busy lately that I have not only not been able to carry out my wish of proposing an evening to you for dining together and adjourning to the studio, but (but) I realise to my great regret that I have been lacking in courtesy in not having written to you – and I beg your indulgence. –

Lady Lewis has allowed me to be associated with her in a plan to become acquainted with some of your works before the Concert – and to have our friends hear them at her home.¹ I hope that tomorrow we will be able to talk it over –

Believe me
Yours sincerely
John S Sargent

Autograph letter, signed and undated, written in English.

The original is in the Delius Trust Archive. Three letters and one telegram from Sargent to Delius are preserved; they are dated April 1899 and May 1899.

John Singer Sargent (1856–1925): American painter. He lived for most of his life in Paris and London and is best known for his fine portraits – as, for example, a head of Fauré, of whom he was the apostle in England. Percy Grainger vouched for the artist's devotion to music and musicians: 'Sargent used his great prestige as a unique social as well as artistic "lion" in London, to benefit those musicians he considered worthy of help or fame. He had only to announce his approval of any musician for hostesses to spring up ready to engage these protégés, hoping that the performance of these musicians at their "At Homes" would guarantee them Sargent's coveted presence – which it usually did' (as quoted in Evan Charteris, *John Sargent* [London: Heinemann, 1927], p. 150).

1   Delius was to write to Jelka on 7 May: 'Lady Lewis is getting up a musical party for me – so we may get a few people in the house –'.

(96)
Fritz Delius to C. F. Keary

6 Colosseum Terrace
Regents Park
[8 May 1899]

Dear Keary –

I have been so overwhelmed with work & worry that I had no time to write before – We have had 2 chorus rehearsals & the orchestral rehearsals take place on the 23rd – 25 – 29th inst We shall have the programme in the papers on Wednesday or Thursday As soon as the literature is printed I will send it – In the "Synopsis" you have made a few slight mistakes — How did you get hold of the name of Washington Cobb? & then the story takes place in Louisiana & not in Florida — Please look in the *Grandissimes* & see the correct name of Cable Georg W I believe[1] — I have already 3 of the solo singers & hope to engage the other 2 today —

I met the Duke of Manchester yesterday who is much interested — I invited him to come to one of the orchestral rehearsals Could you send me a box of plates[2] — which are between the steps going upstairs — as I shall require them — You might get a man to nail them up & take them to a bureau d'Expediteur — If too much trouble dont bother If you send the plates — please send to 184 Wardour Str
Concord Concert Control

　　Yrs F D.

Autograph letter, initialled and undated, written in English. 'May 1899' was added by another hand.

The original is in the Grainger Museum. It is the only letter from Delius to Keary in the museum's collection.

1　Keary evidently had been requested to write a synopsis of the action of *Koanga* (whose original plot had been taken from a section of George Washington Cable's novel, *The Grandissimes*). The credit, however, for the 'Analytical Notes' printed in the concert programme went to Joseph Bennett, Keary simply being named as *Koanga*'s librettist. A note in the programme runs: 'Owing to the absence on the Continent of Mr. C. F. Keary, the libretto and proofs have not been submitted to him for correction.'

2　Presumably photographic plates required for publicity purposes.

(97)
Fritz Delius to Jelka Rosen

6 Colosseum Terrace
Regents Park
[9 ? May 1899]

Dear Jelka —

Your letter & little flower were very welcome in this Pandemonium I am frightfully busy with Chorus Rehearsals & making visits — dining out & going to Receptions So you can about understand what state of mind I am in — I dined last night with your uncle & Aunt[1] & went afterwards with them to a big party at Carl Meyers horrible! horrible!

Your Aunt is very kind-hearted & nice — The artists that are going to sing are Ella Russel (Palmyre) Andrew Black — Koanga Miss Tilly Koenen a new dutch singer with a charming voice — Clotilde Mr Vanderbeeck — Simon Perez — Mr Llewelyn Don José Martinez and Mr Douglas Powell Zarathustra[2] —

The Chorus has now swelled to about 150 but we are trying to get still more men — they are the weakest part of the whole thing De Lara was here for a week & introduced me to a lot of useful people — amongst which, the principal critics.[3] The concert will cost 300 pounds — I suppose the orchestra is as good as can be had in London The first rehearsal is on the 23rd then 25th & 29th Lady Lewis has been very kind — She gives a big reception on the 26th & sends out invitations to meet me — my songs will be sung & the "Legende" played — Bispham asked 40 guineas to sing! — Ella Russel — whose price is 40 guineas — sings for 20 & Andrew Black also 40 guineas sings for 15 — the others offered to sing for nothing — Farewell & write soon — Hoping you are all well

yours always
Fritz Delius

Autograph letter, signed and undated, written in English. Jelka later added 'May 1899'.

The original is in the Grainger Museum.

1   Felix and Grete Moscheles.

2   A number of these artists were normally handled by the Concorde Concert Control, including Tilly Koenen, G. A. Vanderbeeck and William Llewellyn.

3   One such critic, B. W. Findon, reminisced briefly many years later: 'I was much interested in the work [Koanga], and more so in the man. One night we had a supper party at the Hotel Cecil, and those present included Delius, Isidore de Lara, and Andrew Black, and Delius provided the chief amusement of the evening by his palmistry; he was exceedingly good at it" (cf. Play Pictorial, 43, 261, London 1923, p. 109).

(98)
Jelka Rosen to Fritz Delius

THE GRELIX,
80, ELM PARK ROAD,
S.W.

[26 May 1899]

Dearest Fritz —

I am thinking all the time of your music — It is so beautiful and I am so intensely happy that I can understand and love it so well. I can't express, what I feel —

you must try to guess it – A sort of fresh joy and courage *through* it and *for* it. Art and nature are what is fine – the rest seems so small now.

Life is beautiful like that – I think I owe all this to you, my best friend –

Yrs always
Jelka

Just got your card. We will be delighted to see you both[1] on Sunday at 1.30.

Autograph letter, signed and undated, written in English on headed notepaper.

The original is in the Grainger Museum.

A letter from Ida Gerhardi to her friend Elisabeth Gebhardt, written from Lüdenscheid on 19 June 1899, shows that Jelka and Ida had travelled to London for the concert and had stayed at the home of Jelka's uncle, Felix Moscheles, while the latter and his wife were attending the Peace Conference at The Hague. 'Delius is a genius,' wrote Ida, 'whose fame is just beginning, his concert was a magnificent revelation, apart from Jelka & me there was of course really no-one who knew this music so well, – but with orchestra it was a million times more beautiful than we could have dreamed, so that we were quite overwhelmed.'

1   Delius had proposed to bring Alfred Hertz to lunch.

(99)
Adela Maddison to Fritz Delius

157 rue de la Pompe [Paris]
29 Mai [1899]

Dear Mr Delius

I have been *so terribly* occupée with all this move, and getting settled! I have *four* pensionnaires, & the large household & responsibility at present are terrible – but later it will be all right I am sure!

I am so glad Fauré's letters were of use & that London has welcomed you *as you deserve*! – I wish I could be present at the concert – I shall search anxiously for the critiques, & think of you tomorrow – *how exciting it will be*!

Ravel's "Schérézade" was played yesterday at the Société Nationale Concert. It was interesting, but too "décousu", & fearfully cut up of course in the papers today! That means nothing! –

On *Sat*: I have some music here – at 10 oclock – but I fear you won't be back? if you are I shall expect you at 10 — till minuit! P*cess* de Cystria[1] is coming – & Fauré & Polignacs & others.

Have you seen my friend Mrs Bolten?
You will tell me all news when we meet?

Yrs very sincerely
Adela Maddison.

Autograph letter, signed and dated, written in English.

The original is in the Delius Trust Archive. It is the first of four letters written by Mrs Maddison to the Deliuses, the last dated 1909, that have been preserved (see also letter 84, note 2).

1   Princesse de Cystria (1866–?): Marie-Léonie, daughter of the Duchesse de Trévise. She married the Prince de Cystria in 1888 but preferred the social and musical life of Paris, where she spent most of her time, to that of Guadeloupe, where her husband managed his estate. Introduced to Delius by Jutta Bell, she is understood to have been his mistress and also to have accompanied him and Jebe – much against the composer's will – on their trip to the United States in 1897. One edition of the song 'O schneller, mein Ross!', printed in Paris in 1896, bears a dedication to her.

(100)
Fritz Delius to Jutta Bell

Grez sur Loing
Seine & Marne
Tuesday [6 June 1899]

Dear friend –

Here I am again & glad to be back again I can tell you – I was sorry I did not see more of you – the work I had was quite too much for a man who is accustomed to quietness – The concert[1] turned out far better than I had expected & may be called an artistic success – I was sorry not to have been able to meet you after the concert & gather your impressions – I was overwhelmed by receptions & had to rush away from London[2] – I am sending over my signature to Norman in order to stamp each copy of my songs[3] both those published by Norman & those to be published by Stanley-Lucas on a royalty – Will you undertake to stamp them for me & keep my stamp? I must see that my works begin to bring me in a little money – With kindest remembrances

I remain
yours always
Fritz Delius

Autograph letter, signed and undated, written in English.

The original is in the Jacksonville University Library.

1   The Delius Orchestral Concert, organized by the Concorde Concert Control, had at last been given at St James's Hall, London, on Tuesday, 30 May at 8.30. The 'Orchestra of 95 Performers and Full Chorus' was conducted by Alfred Hertz.

2   Norman-Concorde had written from London on 4 June: 'You have had a magnificent success far far greater than could have been hoped for. . . . I was extremely sorry that you had to go – it was a business mistake as you w^d have been the lion of the season . . . & w^d also have made many useful musical & moneyed friends who w^d probably have subscribed to something in the future – However I am glad for your happiness & your arts sake that you went. London was telling on you.'

3   The *Seven Songs from the Norwegian* and the *Three Shelley Songs* were to be stamped with a facsimile of the composer's signature.

(101)

Fritz Delius to Edvard Munch

Grez sur Loing
Seine & Marne
12 June 99

Dear Munch

I am back again from England & I am sorry not to meet you in Paris – I am thinking of coming to Norway at the end of July to go some way into the mountains – Will you come with me to the Jotunheim or paa Hardanger Viddern? I could be quite a good guide – How are the etchings of the sick girl coming along?[1]

Write me a few lines to let me know whether I can count on you for the Jotunheim

Farewell

your friend
Fritz Delius

Frl Larsens[2] is here in Grez for a few days and is kindly sending this letter with hers.

Autograph letter, signed and dated, written in German.

The original is in the Munch Museum, Oslo. It is the first of thirty-four letters and postcards written by Delius to Munch between 1899 and 1934 that have been preserved.

Edvard Munch (1863–1944): in due course to become the most celebrated of all Norwegian painters. Munch apparently met Delius while painting in and around Paris about 1890. They met many times over the years and were to remain firm friends until Delius's death.

1   *The Sick Child*, particularly in its various graphic versions, occupied the artist much in the mid-1890s. It was an image from his own family experience to which he often returned, using a series of techniques: lithograph (sometimes coloured), etching, pastel and oil.

2   Mathilde (Tulla) Larsen (1869–?): Norwegian artist, and Munch's mistress from the late 1890s until 1902. In 1903 she married another Norwegian painter, Arne Kavli. Letters from Delius to Jelka early in May 1899 indicate that Tulla Larsen was already in Grez, together with Charlotte Bødtker's (see Letter 175, note 2) sister, fru Mowinckel: 'I cannot stand Mrs Mowinckel – she is tactless & stupid (almost) it was all I could do not to be rude to her in Paris – She is the sister of Charlotte Bödtker the one in Chili – Miss Larsen is better & more natural – If you dont like them send them to Hell! – not much in either of them.' He wrote again, 'Don't be bothered too much by the Norwegians.'

(102)
Fritz Delius to Jutta Bell

Grez sur Loing
Seine & Marne
[mid-June 1899]

Dear friend –

My expenses for the Concert were simply awful – double what Concorde stated at first – Please get my stamp from him & stamp all his copies & also those coming out with Hatzfeldt.[1] I am beginning to understand how hopelessly unpractical I am – These business people have a laudible way of explaining anything they do but which is entirely false – Up to the present I have paid 344 pounds for what was estimated at £200 – I think I shall absolutely refuse to pay any more –. The Concert of course has done me an immense amount of good & has placed me amongst the first composers of today[2] – The german papers also have long articles.

My Opera will be given in Breslau next season[3] – I should be delighted if you would act as my agent in England –

Farewell & write soon again

Yours as ever
Fritz Delius

Autograph letter, signed and undated, written in English.

The original is in the Jacksonville University Library.

1   The firm of Stanley Lucas, Weber, Pitt & Hatzfeld Ltd. It has not yet been established whether this company did in fact issue any of the songs (cf. Threlfall, p. 98).

PLATE 17 Fritz Delius, 1893. Pastel portrait by
Georges-Daniel de Monfreid.

PLATE 18   Madame Charlotte, by Christian Krohg
(in *Verdens Gang*, 29 November 1898).

PLATE 19   (a) Madame Charlotte's living room, above the crémerie:
most of the paintings are by the artists who dined below; (b) Madame
Charlotte's crémerie, showing 'Strindberg's table'.

PLATE 20   (a) August Manns; (b) Jutta Bell; (c) H.S.H. The Princess
Alice of Monaco; (d) Herman Bang, 1899, by P. S. Krøyer.

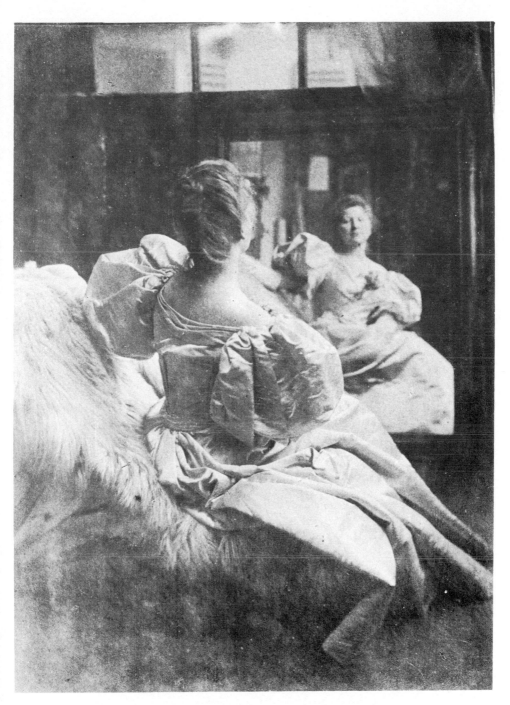

PLATE 21   Jelka Rosen. (*Gerhardi/Steinweg Collection.*)

PLATE 22 Grez-sur-Loing. (a) Jelka's house centre left, immediately
before the church (*photograph Coffin*); (b) the church and house from
across the River Loing (*Gerhardi/Steinweg Collection*).

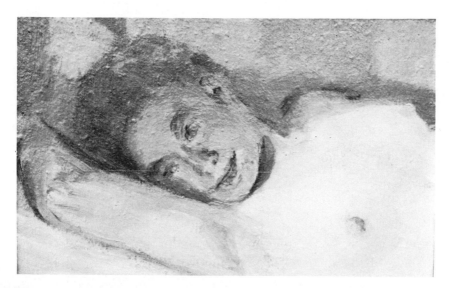

PLATE 23   Marcelle, artists' model, painted and photographed at Grez by Ida Gerhardi. (*Gerhardi/Steinweg Collection.*)

PLATE 24   Halfdan Jebe. (*Coll. Andrew Boyle.*)

PLATE 25   (a) Grez-sur-Loing, summer 1897 (?): Maud Ede, Ida
Gerhardi, Jelka and Serena Rosen at the garden door; (b) Maud Ede, by
Ida Gerhardi; (c) Jelka Rosen, by Ida Gerhardi.
(*All Gerhardi/Steinweg Collection.*)

PLATE 26   Fritz Delius, 1897. (*Gerhardi/Steinweg Collection.*)

PLATE 27   Fritz Delius, 1897, by Christian Krohg.

PLATE 28 'Two of the homeless'. *Constable* (to *Folkeraadet*'s author and composer, who are roaming homeless about the streets on the night after the first whistling concert): 'Now, now, you'd better come along to the station with me; you can't wander about here all night!' (Cartoon in *Vikingen* (Christiania), November 1897.) (*Coll. Andrew Boyle.*)

PLATE 29   (a) August Strindberg (Paris, mid-1890s); (b) Henrik Ibsen;
(c) Helge Rode, 1898, by Edvard Munch (*coll. Munch Museum*);
(d) Gunnar Heiberg, 1890, by Christian Krohg.

PLATE 30 'Nevermore' by Paul Gauguin.
(*Courtauld Institute Galleries.*)

PLATE 31   Ida Gerhardi in Lüdenscheid.
(*Gerhardi/Steinweg Collection.*)

PLATE 32 Fritz Delius, 1897, by Ida Gerhardi.
(*Gerhardi/Steinweg Collection.*)

2   Even August Manns had been prompted to look at Delius's works again. He wrote to the Concorde Concert Control on 15 June: 'I will examine the *Orchestral* works (no Choral Scores, please) of M Delius, although I see but little chance of introducing any of those works just now: From what I have read in the London Journals about M. Delius Compositions, I gather that they are prominently "radicalistic" and require a very large modern Orchestra for doing them justice.'

3   The reference is to *Koanga*, and yet another project for its production that was to prove abortive.

(103)
Edvard Munch to Fritz Delius

Aasgaardstrand 24/6 99

Dear Delius, Thank you for the letter – I would of course have very much liked to go to the mountains – and I am sure we two would have got along very well together – but unfortunately there are several obstacles. Firstly I don't know if I will be well enough – perhaps you know I have had influenza which has lasted a long time – then there is my work – which may possibly force me to stay here – In any case I hope we will meet – it may well be possible for me to go with you – if not up to the high mountains then at least part of the way –

I am living in my little house at Aasgaardstrand.[1] Unfortunately my guest room is not ready yet – otherwise you could have stayed there for a while – until you went off to the mountains –

This house of mine was really a brilliant idea – I walk around in my garden here in a free and easy way – just like in a little paradise – You must anyway come down here for a few days.

– Your success in London delighted me and I congratulate you from the bottom of my heart –

Write and tell me when you will be coming –

If you see the Mollards, give them my regards and tell them that I was so sorry that I could not visit them – I was so poorly and nervous that I could not ask them to come to me either. I did not meet anyone –

If only we could work out that plan, with engravings and music – and I.P. Jakobsen?[2]

Until we meet again   Your friend

Edvard Munch

Autograph letter, signed and dated, written in Norwegian.

The original is in the Delius Trust Archive. It is the first of thirteen letters and postcards written by Munch to Delius between 1899 and 1907 that have been preserved. A further number of draft letters, which Munch did not send, are preserved in the Munch Museum. See plate 35.

1   A small fishing village on the Oslo fjord, some 60 kilometres south of the capital. Then, as now, it was a popular summer resort. Munch's cottage still stands and is preserved as a museum.

2   Jens Peter Jacobsen (1847–85): Danish author. His novel *Niels Lyhne* (1880), with its psychological insights, was a pioneering work in its day and exerted a considerable influence on contemporary German and Scandinavian writers. It was to form the basis of Delius's last opera, *Fennimore and Gerda* (1909–10), but the composer's interest in Jacobsen's work was already well in evidence in the mid-1890s, when he began to set a series of Jacobsen's poems to music.

    This is the sole reference to a project which, had it come to fruition, would have been the only creative artistic collaboration between Munch and Delius.

(104)
R. Norman-Concorde to Fritz Delius

THE CONCORDE CONCERT CONTROL,
186 WARDOUR STREET
(*Corner of Oxford Street*),
LONDON, W.
30 June, 1899

Dear Delius

Your letter was a terrible shock to me, but in re-reading it I see that it is only half serious. You keep on speaking about the enormous expenses of the concert and you do not see that all the extra expense is for things that you yourself required.[1] My estimate of between £70 or £80 for the orchestra was for the ordinary orchestra of about 60 and not an orchestra of 95 with *three* rehearsals, and the same with *all other* items, if you will look into them. At *every turn I did all I could to save expense.* Had I carried out all your instructions literally, as any other agent would have done, the expenses would have between £600 or £700. I have also in order to make matters lighter for you taken *the tickets*, *and* the responsibility of the analytical notes, *and* Powell, *and* many other items not in your account. Besides this instead of ordinary *routine* management I gave up my entire days and evenings to the working of the concert, and everyone who is in the know will tell you that I created more interest in the affair than there was for any other concert. *But this work* took me away from my ordinary work, so that I am *quite* £200 out of pocket from neglect of the Society work & orchestra engagements I should have got had I attended to it, but which I quite neglected. With *me* of course the question of whether I am paid or not is one of *life* and *death* not of adv[t] & enlisting sympathy. If *I were to break, my business would go* for *ever* and I should have wasted all my time and energy, and be without *a hope of doing anything again*. *As it is* I have had to borrow money at a high rate of interest to satisfy creditors. I *do not, as you see, ask for nearly what I have spent*, and besides this I have published the songs and am advertising them, but shall not of course see my money back. I don't know what to do from day to day to keep off those who only call for what they have a right to get and which they will soon enforce. *Would you send me a cheque* by *return* and let me communicate with your uncle **Mr Daniel Delius**, who seems greatly interested, saying nothing about your having paid & asking him if he would advance the balance of the account, and then when I get his cheque I would send it on to you.

I certainly shall see what I can do towards arranging a concert in the autumn and shall apply for subscriptions to get sufficient capital. I shall see some of the critics on the subject during next week & issue circulars ————

Please do not fail me by return with a cheque − you do not know the anxiety you are causing me and the dreadful consequences which will result if I put off further payment with my creditors. *To me debt* is a *disgrace* and *ruin*.

Yours Ever
RNC

Typed letter with MS. additions, initialled and dated, written in English on headed notepaper.

The original is in the Delius Trust Archive.

1   For a month or so following the London concert, Delius and Norman-Concorde carried on an intense and often heated correspondence as the bills poured in. Concorde's letters clearly demonstrate that Delius (whose letters have not so far been found) was angry and aggrieved over a number of unexpectedly heavy financial demands. The final cost of the concert appears to have been around £450.

(105)
Ottokar Nováček to Fritz Delius

[Summer 1899]

Dear friend,

On Sept. 15th I am going to New-York again, have been engaged there as solo viola and am getting 60 Dollars a week.

I am telling you this because I am in difficulty as to where to find the money for my passage, and forgive me for asking you even though my old debt still stands, but once I am in America I shall be able to pay you back.

Please be so kind as to tell me at once whether you will be able to lend me 500 M. for 3 months at the most; you would save me from a crisis, because it would really be too ridiculous if I could not take up my appointment because I could not find the fare.[1] Busoni has "nussing at all" – Brodsky too is broke.

I was very pleased to hear of your extraordinary success in London, and similarly it was very pleasant for me to hear that you liked my string quartet in Manchester.

I shall have to put off composing for the time being and earn money in America – it is very sad. Cordial greetings and forgive me once more for having to ask you.

Busoni and his wife also send greetings – incidentally it was he who suggested you as the only other way out of my difficulty.

> Ottokar Nováček
>   Berlin S.W.
>   Teltowerstr. 3,[II]

Autograph letter, signed and undated, written in German.

The original is in the Delius Trust Archive.

1   It is not known whether Delius was able to help Nováček. On this occasion the mounting costs of his concert may have prevented him from making a loan, although we may assume from his reputation by this time that he would have done so if possible to help a friend in need. The unfortunate Nováček, with a history of heart trouble, had less than a year to live. He died in New York on 3 February 1900.

(106)
Fritz Delius to Jelka Rosen

Hotel Phønix
Copenhagen
14 August 99

Dear Jelka

I arrived here last night & leave tonight for Bünde[1] – After looking up the railway guide I can go, probably, as far as Osnabrück – I saw Hansen[2] today & mentioned my songs but he did not seem anxious to publish them Said he had so many things in hand etc – So of course, I let the subject drop – I really am no good vis à vis Editors[3] & am sure only make an indifferent or bad impression – I think I shall travel thro to Paris & get to work again – I am longing for my work & am quite sick of doing nothing – Heilbronn is a devil of a distance from Cologne – Mainz is on the way – but as I have no music & do not even know whether the *Chief* of Schott's is there – most probably not at this time of the year – I shall let the matter drop & send my music after I have written – As I have just had my hair cut very short – it was so hot – my chances are still less – I think – on the whole – Verleger better not see me as I have – nichts Geniales – in my appearance – On my return to Grez I will answer Aibl's[4] letter – We can talk the matter over – I shall be in Grez then say on the 18th – How long will you stay away? I could stay so long in Paris if you like – but want to get to work badly Have bought the danish books. I saw Jebe just before leaving Christiania he is vegetating – or waiting for something to turn up – Give my kind regards to Miss Gerhardi & Believe me

your sincere friend
Fritz Delius

Autograph letter, signed and dated, written in English.

The original is in the Grainger Museum.

1   Delius was due to interview another young hopeful in connection with Solana Grove. The prospective farmer was the son of a prominent cigar manufacturer in Bünde. Ida Gerhardi seems to have engineered this arrangement, writing from Grez to her sister Lilli on 18 January 1901: 'Young Fröhlke has now decided to take over Delius's farm & moreover together with a friend in the tobacco business Nicolas from Minden. . . . Delius is awfully glad.'

2   Wilhelm Hansen, music publishers, Copenhagen and Leipzig. Delius's music was rejected by many a publisher at this period, and Hansen, who had declined *Folkeraadet* in 1897, was to refuse yet another (unspecified) work in 1903.

3   Delius frequently used the term 'editor' for 'publisher'.

4   Jos. Aibl Verlag, music publishers, Munich. Delius had sent a selection of reviews of his London concert to Aibl, Richard Strauss's publisher. Aibl, however, was not prepared to take the risk of publishing works by a composer who was 'new in Germany'. As with Hansen, Delius was to try Aibl again in the summer of 1903, only to be met with a further refusal.

(107)
Fritz Delius to Ida Gerhardi

Grez sur Loing
Seine & Marne
21 dec/99

Dear Fräulein Gerhardi

You are really marvellous & I do not know how to thank you for all that you have done for me[1] – You are a good friend indeed & I am touched – which does not happen very often — So I will hope again — with such co-operation all should go well — I am also very glad to hear about the jolly meeting with Herz & that he is the same fine old chap.[2] I hope all three of us will soon be sitting again in the first row of the stalls of the Breslau Stadttheater and then all four in a good restaurant having a good meal & quaffing champagne Bougre de merdre —

When I put on the cravat you gave me I always think of the Courbet.[3] Strange isn't it how things connect — Farewell & paint Nikisch nice & sweetly[4] —

I & Jelka send our best wishes

Your friend
Fritz Delius

Autograph letter, signed and dated, written in German.

The original is in the Gerhardi/Steinweg collection.

1   Some time earlier, Ida had asked her brother to write an original German libretto for the first act of *A Village Romeo and Juliet*, after Keller, Delius having decided to set the opera in German. However, writing from Grez on 13 November, Ida told Karl-August, 'Delius has done his own libretto for Romeo & Juliet — after having talked & corresponded with an English writer for a whole year & then having finally received an English text from him, found that it was not at all what he himself felt & wanted. A few days after I arrived he sat down suddenly & wrote a delightful text. . . . He is now composing all the time & I believe it will be a ravishing masterpiece, it sounds utterly enchanting when he plays it at night. . . . I am sorry that you had all the work with your text in vain.' See also letter 71, note 1.

2   Ida had been in Breslau some time after Delius's visit to Hertz there. The composer himself had discussed with Hertz the possibility of staging *Koanga* in the city.

3   Brief references in other letters indicate that Delius owned at some stage a painting by Courbet (see also Letter 123, note 1), as well as one by Félicien Rops. His collection also contained a portrait of Balzac, but it is not known by which artist.

4   Ida was staying in Leipzig, where she was at work on her portrait of Artur Nikisch (see Letter 108). Several months later she was to report to her sister meeting Busoni on a Berlin street. He had praised her work inordinately, especially the Nikisch portrait, which he had just seen in an exhibition (perhaps the *Alte Sezession*), going on to ask if she would paint his own portrait and travel with him and his wife to Weimar. As a matter of interest, Busoni too had considered writing an opera based on *A Village Romeo and Juliet*, but had rejected the idea as impractical owing to the difficulty of representing the couple at different ages of their lives.

1900

The earlier part of the year was spent in Grez, with Delius at work largely on *A Village Romeo and Juliet*. For whatever reasons, certain frictions became evident in the household at Grez, and Jelka suffered a period of depression.

Delius returned to Normandy and Brittany for a late summer holiday; he possibly spent some time there with the Molards, perhaps joined by the French artist Achille Ouvré. He undertook a part of his tour by bicycle along the coastline. Early in October he took to his bicycle again, this time with Jelka and Ida Gerhardi joining him on a tour of the Loire valley. Then, later in the month, he left for a long stay in Germany, meeting Julius Buths, conductor in Düsseldorf, and then Hans Haym in Elberfeld. Soon after arriving in Elberfeld, he attended a rehearsal by Haym of *Paris*, which he found disappointing and led to doubts about Haym's ability really to understand his music. He next visited Breslau, where Alfred Hertz gave him letters of introduction to three further conductors. Other ports of call were Berlin and Leipzig. In Berlin he spent some time with Busoni, got in touch with Nikisch, and tried to interest publishers in his work.

At home, in the meantime, both Jelka and Ida (who was once again staying in Grez), had in Paris made the acquaintance of Rodin, and the next few years were to see a considerable correspondence and a number of meetings between them.

Once in Berlin, Delius set about recultivating family links and exploring more seriously the possibility of financial support from his relations. Marie Krönig, widow of his cousin Arthur, was paying his rent, and he now tried to get a monthly allowance from his aunt Albertine. A former allowance was renewed by his father, and he settled in Berlin for a winter which had so far been almost entirely lost to composition. He had at least been promoting himself and his work as actively as possible.

La ronde se déroule (Dansen gaar) (RT VI/13). Undergoes revision.

A Village Romeo and Juliet, opera (RT I/6). Continued.

'The Violet' and 'Autumn', songs (Ludvig Holstein) (RT V/21).

(108)
Fritz Delius to Ida Gerhardi

Grez sur Loing
Seine & Marne
4 Jan 1900

Dear Fräulein Gerhardi

It is splendid of you already to have got Nikisch[1] interested in my music – I am
sending today to your address Lützow Str 67. Dansen Gaar "Und Weiter geht
der Tanz" in German – If you can find a better title it would please me to hear
– Please then fetch Zarathustra from my cousin Dr Arthur Krönig 9 Landgrafen
Str & please try especially to get this played – I like it best myself – Dansen
Gaar is an Impressionistic mood and one ought to know the play to be quite
clear about it: it is symbolic of the Dance of Life just as Helge Rode has depicted
it in his play – I am now writing to my cousin – Farewell & many thanks for
your kindness I am glad that Nikisch is such a nice fellow – Jelka & I send our
cordial greetings

    I am hoping that I shall have to come to Germany soon –

    Your
    Worthless
    Fritz Delius

Autograph letter, signed and dated, written in German.

The original is in the Gerhardi/Steinweg collection.

1   Artur Nikisch (1855–1922): Hungarian conductor and violinist. From 1895 he
was conductor of the Leipzig Gewandhaus Orchestra and the Berlin Philharmonic
Orchestra. He had great charisma, toured widely in Europe and the United States, and
was a noted interpreter of Wagner's operas.

(109)
Elise Delius to Fritz Delius

Bradford Jany 13' 1900

Dear Fritz!

Your letter, to say the least, astonished me. You say we left you alone just when
you require help; that is a simple untruth. Papa has spend more money on you,

than he ought to have done. That you went to Virginia was your blessing, as that was the only time you made a living. Then you were send to Leipzig which again cost hundreds, with the intention to make a degree and go back to Amerika to get on better. Instead of that you choose to remain in Paris where for 5 years got 120£ a year. Even Uncle Theodore told us you ought to go back to America.

Then for more years you got 60£ a year and all your travelling expenses paid. Then *you* wrote that, if Papa would send you the deeds of the Grove, you could do whithout more help. Now you want money again, though Uncle left you 1000£. on whose interest you might have lived in some other town.

What you write about lessons is simply nonsense. How about Halle, Bethoven, Mozart, Paderewsky, Rubinstein etz. Where there is a will there is a way. You will have to do something on your future fame you can not live. Go back, as we have told you over and over to America, *there* you have a future, as I know of other musicians

You speak of your share of Uncle's money, you have no share, as we have consulted a lawyer and he also says that the money is left to mon frère Julius[1] it only mentions 12 parts as he is getting so much more than his sister. She also keeps the money.

Max[2] has *not* gone bad because he could not do as he liked, but because he has been entangled with low people, and did not stick to business. *Every* father here says when a boy is 21 not 36, that he now has to make his own living. Papas fault has been is kindness. Paper never *lost* his money but his children you, Minnie, Rose etz cost too much.

We have always been careful and I dont choose to begin to retrench [?] with the three girls as I am getting old.

So more money for you is quite out of the question. Go to America or remaine it is the same to us. We shall be pleased if you become famous and hope so, but *we* have done our share towards it and *nobody* can say that we have not. I told you that we loose now 7000£. much more than Clara would ever get. In Papa's *new* will, he left all to me, as long as I live. From his Uncle he got 2000£ to establish himself, from Ernst[3] 25,000£. and from Theodore about 16,000£. that is 40,000£. and 12 children to educate and losses etz. you see where the money is. Alas in the last years people who were rich have lost every thing. The Warehouse & house cost 11,000£ which is sunk capital Now I think I have explained all to you my dear, and never write to us on the subject again. Not another penny we shall give to anyone again. If you were to go to America I daresay Papa would pay your journey again there once more. You say also what should you give lessons in, in what you learned piano or violin as you did in Virginia. I can say no more, if you are not manly enough to see it yourself then you must shift for yourself. My believe is that Paris has spoiled you altogether. Arthur Krönig is dead.[4] He also told us, as well as Tante Albertine, you ought to do something besides composing. You know dear Fritz, it is very sad for me to have to write to you such letters, to you, who has always had so much done for him.

Papa must under no condition be bothered any more, I want him to have piece.

Your loving Mother

Autograph letter, signed and dated, written in English.

The original is in the Delius Trust Archive. One earlier letter to Delius from his mother, written on 4 June 1899, is in the Archive; and a later letter is preserved in the Grainger Museum (see Letter 116).

Elise Pauline Delius, *née* Krönig (1838–1929): the composer's Bielefeld-born mother. In 1855 she had married Julius Delius, who, having emigrated from Bielefeld, was already settled in Bradford.

1 'mon frère Julius' is evidently a quotation from the will drawn up in Paris by Theodor.

2 Max was the composer's favourite brother. Unsuccessful in a business career, he emigrated and died relatively young of cancer in Canada on 23 October 1905.

3 Julius Delius's elder brother.

4 Delius's cousin had died on 7 January.

(110)
Fritz Delius to Ida Gerhardi

Grez sur Loing
Seine & Marne
[16 February 1900]

Dear Fräulein Gerhardi

I have received your letter & card — The news of Novaçek's death saddened me much he was a dear friend & a man of excellent talents — I would like to know how & where he died, perhaps you can find out from Frau Busoni. You do the "impossible" for me, my dear friend, & I begin really to believe that my works will soon be heard. Do you feel that I should write to Busoni now or should I wait to hear from him? I ask for advice as what I do myself is usually wrong — I am delighted that you have already made good friends with Marie:[1] She is indeed one of those people with a natural goodness of heart. I hope that Frau Busoni is now "out of the family way"[2] & is well on the road to good health.

We had a big wind storm yesterday with extraordinary clouds — it was wonderfully beautiful I am working on Romeo & Juliet & have just finished the First Act — We did not get ourselves anything new from B.M., but are busy reading a very interesting poison story — I have received all the catalogues, many thanks — I hope that your portrait of Nikisch has come off well. I cannot quite understand why such a good musician should be scared by Zarathustra It shows how difficult it is to get the atmosphere & mood before a good performance — therein lie the great difficulties of a composer. I sent an authentic Parisian postcard to Hertz

Something like that but more daring
Perhaps it will put him in a good mood again — Jelka thanks you for [illegible] & Quickbumbum³ Strindberg does not exactly shine in it — He has become triste & boring.

Looking forward to seeing you again soon in Germany — fare well

Best wishes —
Your friend
Fritz Delius

Autograph letter, signed and undated, written in German. Envelope addressed: Mademoiselle / Ida Gerhardi / pr adr Fräulein Dᵣ Bluhm / Lützow Str 67 / Berlin W / Allemagne. Postmark: Grez-S-Loing 16 FEVR oo.

The original is in the Gerhardi/Steinweg collection.

1   Ida, now in Berlin, had visited Marie Krönig, widow of Delius's cousin Arthur.

2   In English in the original letter.

3 *Quickborn*: German periodical, edited by Emil Schering, appearing briefly in 1898 and 1899. It died without further trace after the fourth issue (of January 1899), which was devoted to Strindberg and Munch.

(111)
Fritz Delius to Ida Gerhardi

Grez sur Loing
Seine & Marne
[28 July 1900]

My dear friend –

I hear that you are still not quite well yet – Pack up your things and come to Grez for a good long time. Then we will go to Germany together – You can paint Busoni in the winter & then Frl Rosen needs you – She is terribly depressed[1] & out of sorts – She keeps saying she thinks she is going mad. Don't say that I have written to you but come as quickly as possible – I consider it absolutely necessary that Jelka has her friend at home with her – Everything else is of little importance compared with this – Write & tell her that you have decided to come to Grez to get well – I think I was rather foolish to move into the house here – But now it is a matter of finding some way to help our friend –
    Farewell & come as quickly as possible

Your loyal friend
Fritz Delius

Autograph letter, signed and undated, written in German. Envelope addressed: Mademoiselle / Ida Gerhardi / Lüdenscheid / Westphalie / Allemagne. Postmark: GREZ 28 JUIL 00.

The original is in the Gerhardi/Steinweg collection.

1   Jelka was now suffering deep depression, and it is likely that her feelings for the ever-errant Delius were at the root of the trouble. Some indication of the constancy or otherwise of his affection is given in a letter he wrote to her the following month while on holiday in Norway, containing a tentative suggestion that while gradually recovering she might care to join him there. As soon as it seemed likely that she would come, however, he promptly wrote in an attempt to dissuade her, proposing that she take a break with Ida Gerhardi instead. Lamely, he wrote later, 'I am afraid I do not understand the nature of a woman which seems to be so entirely different to a man's.' All seems to have returned to normal by October, with the three of them making an apparently good-spirited bicycle trip down to the Loire.

(112)

Fritz Delius to Jelka Rosen

Elberfeld
Thursday [25 October, 1900]

My dear Jelka —

I arrived here at 2.30 am after a rather unpleasant journey: the train was overcrowded — The Emperor of course had arrived the same day & the place was beflagged & illuminated & everybody entzückt & gerührt Before leaving Paris I received the enclosed letter from Buths[1] — I saw Haym today & shall see him again tomorrow[2] — "Paris" had not arrived & I am at a loss what to do. Leave it with Haym I suppose — But the Stimmen? They are heavy to carry about — I suppose I better leave them with Marie — I went to Düsseldorf this afternoon & had a chat with Buths, who is a very nice man. He promised to look at my things later on in the season but his programmes were already settled for this season — I took Zarathustra with me & will send it to him later on — I shall probably leave for Berlin day after tomorrow — I hope no more of my letters have gone to Rue Leopold R.[3] Will you kindly send *Thamar* a Poème Symphonique by Balakirew, a partitur which is on the music stand near the piano, to Florent Schmitt 49 B^d Pereire — Haym sends his best love to Ida, & so do I. I hope you both enjoyed yourselves in Paris I will write again when I have more news —

In great haste
yrs ever
Fr D.

Autograph letter, signed and undated, written in English. The date '26.10.1900' (a Friday), added in Jelka's hand to the original, may have been taken from the receiving postmark. The envelope is no longer extant.

The original is in the Grainger Museum.

1   Julius Buths (1851–1920): German conductor, composer and pianist. He was conductor at Elberfeld from 1879 to 1890 (when he was succeeded by Hans Haym), and subsequently became musical director at Düsseldorf, being appointed principal of the Conservatorium there in 1902. Delius had sent him the score of the *Mitternachtslied Zarathustras*, probably initially on Haym's advice, and in his letter (also preserved in the Grainger Museum), Buths had asked him for more time to study the work.

2   Delius was distinctly disillusioned with Haym after the *Paris* parts had arrived and the work had been rehearsed with a forty-member orchestra. 'Everything went wrong', Haym did not understand the music, and he was 'too slow & of absolutely no significance', as Delius wrote to Jelka and Ida from Berlin on 1 November. The composer was

to revise his views over the succeeding years, as the Elberfeld conductor immersed himself in Delius's music and introduced in Germany one new work after the other.

3   The rue Léopold-Robert, in Montparnasse. Delius occasionally stayed at this address when in Paris about this period. Before finally returning to Grez in April 1901, at the end of his long stay in Germany, he spent two days there.

(113)

Fritz Delius to Jelka Rosen

HÔTEL DE PRUSSE
Leipzig, den [9.11 1900]

Dear Jelka –

I arrived here last night: before leaving Breslau I spoke with Director Loewe[1] who was very amiable – but seemed to know nothing about my Opera (Pose of course) he said he would interest himself in it however – We will see! I believe Hertz will do his best – but when it will be given Koanga only knows – In Breslau I made the acquaintance of Otto Singer[2] & Maszkowski[3] both Capell-meisters – Singer arranges Strauss' things for 2 pianos & is a very nice & intelligent man – he was much interested in "Paris" but only has a small orckestra & is helping Maszkowski who is very ill – Maszkowski said he would have time to look at it in a few weeks & would play it if he could – I went today to Nikisch who was *verreist*[4] & comes back tomorrow – I asked for Mrs Nikisch – the girl went in again & presently came out & asked my name which she took in to Mrs N. She then returned and said she could not receive me!!! I asked when I could see Nikisch – she said that Der Herr Director was nie zu sprechen or some such nonsense – After I had however insisted a little while she said that I better go to the Gewandhaus on Sunday morning when he had a Probe[5] – This does not look hopefull – I will go to the Gewandhaus on Sunday however but as far as I can judge everything is *shut up* & there is nothing to be done but give a Concert – My only hope is Breslau – Everything else seems absolutely hopeless – No one seems to have the slightest interest in anything but money – Marie wrote me to Breslau that she had spoken with Albertine and Albertine was not "gesonnen viel für mich zu thun"[6] I think it was unwise of Marie to ask her so soon – She is kind hearted & nice but one of the old school all the same – If she only had a 100th part of Ida's brains & cleverness I dont hope anything from this quarter – there would be only one way to work it & that I dont propose to do & to hell with em all It is always the same thing over again – Gracious! how small people are – M. has still a little "Glanz" of Arthur & that is all otherwise she too is a Philister more or less although I believe she does her best not to be one – Arthur! what a change since *he* is no more here. The color

seems to have gone out of everything – I begin to see – certain people color
things with the fine gloss of their own rich natures – when they are gone the
old gray[7] *not Grez* dull leaden color returns – I suppose one must not be angry
with the world – they are so rich & still so poor & they dont know really what
they do; as far as I can see before I am also catalogued & stamped I have not the
slightest earthly chance – not the slightest – only a miracle can push me thro'
– I hope you are all well in Grez give my love to Ida – Marie & Koanga
I hope you are having a better time of it than I am If I only could keep from
worrying I would not care – but I worry all the same over all these things & all
these people – But again – to hell with them all –

I shall leave for Berlin on Sunday night & hire a room somewhere – I have
not decided what to do yet, whether to stay in Berlin or come to Leipzig & give
a Concert with my last means – all the editors[8] are here – Well – farewell – I
will write again as soon as I have something new –

your friend
Fritz Delius

Autograph letter, signed and undated, written in English on headed notepaper. Jelka
later added '9.11.1900'.

The original is in the Grainger Museum.

1   Theodor Loewe (1855–1936): director of the Stadttheater in Breslau. Delius had
written slightly earlier (5 November) to Jelka from Breslau: 'The libretto does not
please the Director & It is not sentimental enough Es mangelt an Liebe etc.'

2   Otto Singer (1863–1931): German choral conductor in Leipzig and Berlin. He was
also a gifted arranger, notably of opera scores, making vocal scores of Wagner and
Richard Strauss operas. His piano score of *Appalachia* was published in 1907.

3   Raphael (Rafal) Maszkowski (1838–1901): Polish conductor. He studied the violin
at Vienna and Leipzig and then conducted various German orchestras. In 1890 he
succeeded Bruch as conductor of the Breslau Orchestral Society. Busoni had furnished
Delius with a letter of introduction to him.

4   *gone away*. In German in the original letter.

5   *Rehearsal*. In German in the original letter.

6   *of a mind to do much for me*. In German in the original letter.

7   Delius had first written *grez*; the *not Grez* which follows was added in the margin.

8   See Letter 106, note 3.

(114)

Fritz Delius to Jelka Rosen and Ida Gerhardi

26 Winterfeldt Str [Berlin][1]
18th Nov 1900

My dear Girls

I am now in my new lodgings: a nice large room: Of course my landlady is a
jewess but everything is very nice and clean. This morning I went to the
Hauptprobe of the Philharmonisch C – the overture to Lalo's "Le roi d'Ys" –
medium – A very slow Concerto by Saint Saëns for pianoforte, Clotilde Mieberg.
Written in 4 or 5 different styles – Bach – Mendelsohn & Meyerbeer – And
then "Til Eugelspielgel" – Richard Strauss – I like this piece more & more &
it was admirably played – It is so light & fantastic & so full of humor. The
public is certainly the most easily pleased that I have ever seen – They applauded
everything with frenzy – except "Til Eugelspiegel" the only thing worth
hearing –

Here they were Nüchtern Das Deutsche Publicum kann sich ja nicht alles
gefallen lassen – nur das Schlechteste![1] There was also the C minor Symphony
of Old Ludwig but I did not stop for it – knowing it too well – I shall go to
Ochs[2] tomorrow morning with Zarathustra – But really hope for nothing here
– The worst of it is that I cannot work here – the place has the most despondent
effect upon me & then it is always raining & as dark as London in a fog – Marie
is just as kind & nice as she can be – It appears that Albertine is a very hard nut
– a real Delius & was stingy even with Arthur – Marie thinks she would give
me something if I asked – but not much – When does Ida propose to come
here? Heinitz[3] a friend of Maries wants to play Koanga to Muck[4] – I wrote
Hertz to send me the piano score as soon as he sees no possibility of a performance
this season – At the theatres French Vaudeville "Die Dame von Maxim [?]" etc
Von Ibsen keine Spur[5] – At the opera house up till now no opera of Wagner –
but Wilhelm Tell – Barbier of Seville & Figaros Hochzeit – Cavelleria & other
such immortal works – Deutsches Theater – always Rosen monntag – ein
Officiers drama – which I have not had courage to go & see – Die Jungfrau von
Orléans (Schiller Theater) & Die Welt wo man sich langweilt etc. Up till now I
have received no impression of any modern movement or feeling – I went with
Marie to see some pictures Pissaro Monet – Cezanne Lovis Corinth – Leisti-
kow Fritz Klimsch – Very poor with exception of Cezanne who had several
very fine "nature morte" & Monet a good impression of the seacoast – I wish I
could get to my Opera again – but I find this place so unsympathetic that my
muse does not budge I hope you are both hard at work and having a more
profitable time of it The best things in Berlin are the Variétés There we have the
real taste of the people as the musical taste can scarcely be called a taste but is
an indiscriminate swallowing of everything "déjà entendu" "Sie spucken nur

das Gute aus"[6] My health is better again — I have a little brochitis as usual but with such weather nothing better can be expected — The people who occupy two other rooms in the house — one next to mine are expecting "a biby" The woman is "in the family way" so I have a treat in store for me — I will report anything interesting — My love to you all — Have you translated Paris?[7] altho' I dont suppose I shall want it — Farewell!

yours always
Fritz Delius

Autograph letter, signed and dated, written in English.

The original is in the Grainger Museum.

Delius intended to stay in Berlin for some time. His cousin Marie had insisted on paying the monthly rent for his room, and he was furthermore pressing his aunt Albertine Krönig for a monthly allowance.

1   [Here they were] *reserved{.} The German public cannot of course put up with everything — only the worst!* In German in the original letter.

2   Siegfried Ochs (1858–1929): German conductor, composer and teacher. He was conductor in Berlin of the Philharmonischer Chor. Marie Krönig had suggested in March 1899 that Delius send his *Zarathustra* to Ochs. Now, unfortunately, he was 'out of town', as Delius wrote to Jelka on 30 November.

3   Franz Heinitz: Berlin solicitor who was shortly to marry Marie Krönig. He was to act for Delius in 1907 in the matter of the conveyancing of Solana Grove to the composer under the terms of Julius Delius's will.

4   Carl Muck (1859–1940): German conductor. He studied at the Leipzig Conservatorium, and conducted widely in Europe before becoming conductor in 1892 at the Berlin Opera.

5   *Of Ibsen no trace.* In German in the original letter.

6   *They spit out only what's good.* In German in the original letter.

7   This is presumably a reference to the words by Delius which preface the autograph full score of *Paris*.

(115)
Fritz Delius to Jelka Rosen

26 Winterfeldt Str[1]
14/12/1900

My dear Jelka

I am glad you liked the things I sent — Did you not get my two last letters? you do not mention them — Alas! Ich habe keine Kasse gesprengt[1] & Albertine's

will take a devil of a lot of sprengen I can tell you — She will never forgive me
those 2000 M & grudges me now every mark. Even Marie mentioned it again
with "What a pity" etc "we all knew they would be lost" etc I dont think much
help will ever come from Berlin — As I wrote you she offered me 100 M for 3
months — but every month I have to ask for it again — Today I asked for it again
You should have seen her face — She said nothing but pretended to be ill. Herz-
Klopfen[2] etc. What funny people — If this continues I think I shall prefer to be
without it — I leave my room on the 20th & go to 43 Eisenacher Str[IV] bei Frau
Müller — it is cheaper also & quieter — 30 Marks — as I told you in my last —
there is a violinist & 2 singers in the present place — I am altering "Dansen
gaar" a little[3] as I cannot work at my opera until I am quiet — Tell me what Ida
would like for Xmas I should like to give her something. I sent my brother[4]
50 Marks today — he is hidden in London & absolutely without means — his
woman wrote me & he also — He stupidly ran away when they made him
bankrupt — he is as soft as cheese poor chap it is not his fault — People think he
is in America — I begin to see things in a funnier light now — It is silly to take
these sort of people too seriously — Everything is really more comic than tragic
— Albertine is monumental — a dried up little thing sitting on over a million &
using nothing & getting Herz Klopfen every time she gives a 100 marks away
— Marie is too weak & "unbedeutend"[5] to ever do anything really useful or big
for me — She will probably marry Heinitz & be very happy in another way this
time — Ida was right: She is Maslowa but a sentimental one — As far as I can see
I have absolutely no chance here — Strauss plays his own things — Weingartner
plays his own things & Nikisch plays nothing new — The last Concert was a
Haydn Symphonie — Mendelsohn Violin Concerto & a slow ungifted Dramatic
Overture by Scharwenka "beaucoup de bruit pour rien" Strauss of course is
always interesting — but as I am here I might as well stay a bit & hear as much
new as I can — I hope your work at least is going well & that you are busy — I
am glad you like Rodin so much[6] it is always interesting & often helps one to
be in contact with real artists & they are fewer than we really believe — Here it
is awful what mediocre talents hold the ropes, in Music, painting & sculpture.
A real genius would be hopelessly lost unless he had means — They only applaud
the most awful rot — the "pfennig Gefühle"[7] & the most sickly sentiment
brings down the house — Well, it is so & cannot be altered just now — My love
to you all — I hope you are all working hard at the garden & are in good health —

> yours as ever
> Fritz Delius

Autograph letter, signed and dated, written in English.

The original is in the Grainger Museum.

1   *I haven't broken any bank*. In German in the original letter.

2   *palpitations*. In German in the original letter.

3   The manuscript full score bears the date 1899.

4   Max. See Letter 109, note 2.

5   *insignificant*. In German in the original letter.

6   Jelka and Ida had recently made the acquaintance of the great sculptor, visiting him often in his Paris studio. I have documented this relationship in detail in 'Jelka Rosen Delius: Artist, Admirer and Friend of Rodin. The Correspondence 1900–1914', *Nottingham French Studies*, 9, Nos 1 and 2 (May and November 1970), pp. 16–30 and 81–102.

7   Literally *the penny feeling*. In German in the original letter.

(116)

Elise Delius to Fritz Delius

Claremont.

[Late December, 1900]

My dear Fritz!

Thank you for your good wishes for a happy Cristmas which I return. It is not like the olden times where your children were all at Home. I asked Papa to let you have again 5£ a month for a time and he said he would. We stopped as you know by your sugestion, when you got that Grove. I would sell or let it. We were only wishful for you not to have too much charged to you. You have had 1269£ allready, and you know all will be charged to everyone. The elder children have had 15,000£ allready. Clare has got every penny she will ever get. But enough of this, you know best what to do! About *I* speaking ill of you that is of course an impudent lic. Do me the favour and tell me who told you. First I never heard that Lady's name in my life before, then is it likely I would speak ill of my own son? In Berlin I saw nobody but Tante Albertine & Marie and we did not even mention your name. Do tell me dearest I dont like to be stabbed in the dark. Does it perhaps come from Jack? You know your old Averdieck[?] is dead? Apropos do you know that Daniel Delius has 100£[1] for you if you require it? I will tell Shaw[2] to send you 5£ regulary. I am only sorry that we are not rich people or by God I would give you anything. That money from Oncle Theodore dwindled down to very little. We don't know what has become of it. Now goodbye dear I wish you good luck in your career and remaine

   your loving Mother.

May promised to tell you of Grandmama's death.

Autograph letter, signed and undated, written in English.

The original is in the Grainger Museum. It was enclosed with Letter 117, written by
Delius to Jelka on 29 and 30 December 1900.

1   Jelka added a note in her own hand: *Evidently Arthurs money*.

2   William Shaw: employee of (and subsequently executor for) Julius Delius in the
firm of Delius and Company, Bradford. Beecham described him as the secretary of the
company.

(117)
Fritz Delius to Jelka Rosen

49 Eisenacher Str [Berlin]
29/12/1900

My dear girl —

At last the packet of fruit & cakes has arrived & I am eating every morning 2 or
3 of the delicious biscuits and also a little fruit — A thousand thanks once more
for the nice present — The news from Fröhlke[1] is splendid — but I will wait a
little before I dare to hope anything I have written to Fröhlke & this afternoon
he wired me — "Komme morgen in Ihrer Privat-Wohnung mit Nicolas um
Elf"[2] What I shall arrange I really cannot even surmise as yet — Dont you think
if I asked 25% of all he makes & give him the plantation free of rent it would be
reasonable? It is strange that the news came the very day I had removed — the
number is 49 where I live — (13)le numero fatadique!! Ah! Ah!

Strange also that I received this morning a letter from my mother in answer
to one of mine wherein she informs me that they will now give me £5 a month
regularly — Not so bad — I enclose you her letter — I told her about her having
said that about you, my best friend — you will read what she says — are you
sure? I am working at "Dansen gaar" and it is becoming twice as good as before
— I received the book today — many thanks I saw Gerhardt Hauptmann's new
piece yesterday "Michel Kramer" it is splendid & the best thing he has done I
went with Busoni & wife — After the Frohlke & Nicolas interview I will write
again —

yrs ever
F D.

Sunday

Mr Nicolas has just left — He is a nice young fellow & full of go — He is going
to try & persuade young Fröhlke to go out with him — it appears F. always
regretted not having gone — Well! Nicolas goes back tonight & is having a
contract drawn up wherein he gets a hypothek[3] on part of the land in order that

in case of his death – his brother may profit on what has been laid out & can continue the work – I told him he must at least take 6000 Marks with him. If Fröhlke goes he will also take 6000 Mks –

Should I become partner with the other two & give my plantation as my part of the affair? – This would leave them proprietors with me & they would have more interest in the concern – & would stay there – as it is the plantation is worthless to me – I feel very much inclined to do so – I like the looks of Nicolas & I am sure Frohlke is a solid fellow & hard worker – A Happy New Year to you & a prolific artistic one – Wish Ida the same & love to you all.
yrs ever
Fritz Delius

Autograph letter, signed and dated, written in English.

The original is in the Grainger Museum.

1   Adolf Fröhlke: son of a cigar manufacturer in Bünde, Westphalia, he was introduced to Delius by Ida Gerhardi. In a letter to her sister Lilli, Ida, writing from Grez on 18 January 1901, confirmed the good news: 'Young Fröhlke now intends to take over Delius's farm, in fact together with a friend in the tobacco business [Paul] Nicolas from Minden, they are putting in 10,000 M. working capital & both run the farm jointly, everything has been done contractually & they are leaving at the end of the month, – we have been matchmaking for this farm for 3½ years & at last a fitting suitor, – Delius is awfully glad.' Minden and Bünde were centres for the German tobacco industry. See also Letter 106, note 1.

2   *Coming tomorrow to your private residence with Nicolas at eleven.* In German in the original letter.

3   *mortgage.* In German in the original letter.

1901

Still trying to advance the cause of his music in Berlin, Delius kept an eye on London in the hope that another concert of his works, perhaps even an opera, might now be arranged. Good news to reach Berlin from another source was that two of the *Danish Songs* with orchestra were to be performed in Paris in March. On the other hand, a projected performance in the German capital of *Paris* and the Piano Concerto by Busoni was cancelled owing to Busoni's falling ill. Delius's company in Berlin was as varied as ever, and early in March it included such visitors to the city as Busoni himself, Ida Gerhardi and Halfdan Jebe.

Delius returned to Grez in the middle of April and was soon back at work after what might well be called a winter of compositional discontent. Very little had been achieved. A high point of the summer was Rodin's short stay at the house in Grez in June. A bicycling holiday Delius took in the Loire valley with an artist friend followed in early July.

The death of his father took Delius back to Yorkshire early in October. His next major excursion was to Elberfeld, where he and Jelka joined Ida Gerhardi to attend the first performance of *Paris*, given on 14 December by Haym. This was the first time that a major work of Delius's had been given in Germany since Haym's *Over the hills and far away* four years earlier. Less encouraging, though, must have been evidence of sporadic – if apparently not too serious – health problems, to which a notably restless and perhaps not too productive year may have contributed.

A Village Romeo and Juliet, opera (RT I/6). Completed.

Lebenstanz, symphonic poem for large orchestra (RT VI/15). Now completed in its first version, this was a substantial reworking of the earlier *La ronde se déroule*.

'Black Roses', song (Ernst Josephson) (RT V/22).

'Jeg hører i Natten', song (Drachmann) (RT V/23).

Margot la Rouge, one-act opera ('Rosenval', i.e. Berthe Gaston-Danville) (RT I/7). Begun late 1901?

(118)

Fritz Delius to Jelka Rosen

49 Eisenacher Str
Schöneberg
Berlin
[4 January 1901]

Dear girl –

Your letter just to hand I knew my mother to be one of the largest liars but I, now, also think she is one of the falsest women, her letter does not ring true to me either – However, let us get all the money we can from that quarter. Fröhlke wrote me today that he has decided to go out to Florida with his friend Nicolas & that I have to meet them next Sunday in Hannover – I shall make them partners in the Grove: That will give them more interest. I hope this turns out well – I will write you as soon as all is arranged – Ida wrote me you are both deeply interested in Marie Grubbe[1] – It is one of the best books I have ever read – Ida asks me why I did not write sooner about Marie – I wrote you ever so long ago that she was over nervous & over strained – Hysterical – but otherwise I dont think she is very ill[2] – Albertine bothers her a great deal, She is so unfree & is obliged to keep the old woman company which is not very pleasant for a young woman – As I also told you she is a good warm hearted woman but at heart oldfashioned & unfree – not intellectual – In other words I should not be able with pleasure & peace to see her every day – She reminds me too much of all I hate – Bruch & all these people could never do her any good Hertz lets me know indirectly[3] that Koanga must be retranslated before it can be given! What to do now – He told me so in Breslau. I dont think any of these people can help me   I must work quietly in a corner & then things will go all alone – This sort of life paralyses me & I am unable to work – in other words my time is entirely lost – Best love to you both – 19 degrees of cold on the top of it all –

always yrs
F D

Tell Ida I cannot go to Nikisch on Sunday, as I go to Harmonie – [4]

Autograph letter, initialled and undated, written in English. Jelka later added '4.1.1901'.

The original is in the Grainger Museum.

1   *Marie Grubbe*: historical novel published in 1876 that first brought fame to Jens Peter Jacobsen.

2   Marie Krönig had left Berlin in the middle of December troubled by a nervous complaint and was now recuperating in a sanatorium. She was to return home early in February.

3   The conductor Otto Hess had written to Delius with this news on 1 January.

4   Harmonie Verlag, Berlin music publishers.

(119)
Fritz Delius to Jelka Rosen

49 Eisenacher Str
24/1/1

My dear Jelka

Many thanks for your letter & the sweet little flower − it still had some perfume − I still am in the dark as to what I have done − what things have I done not equal to my nature? & which you compare to mind − As far as friendship goes I also have never given you cause for suspicion − In the other things I dont suppose I shall ever be different.[1] My dearest girl − I am not living up to any standard − I am trying to live so that I can accomplish something in art − *that is all* − The mere fact of my being able to work so well in your home ought to speak for itself − When I suddenly wake up to the fact that you are suffering a sort of hell then only have I ever thought of leaving − Tripps are not the only ones talking about us − All your friends do. Lobach etc − The people I call my *friends* never do − I have written & written to Runciman[2] for my score & have received nothing − I telegraphed yesterday to send them to de Bréville[3] so that they might be sung at the société Nationale[4] − Will he send them? I own there is something strange about his conduct. The score ought to have been handed in last wednesday. I am afraid I am now too late. Try to come to the concert[5] & we will go back together − I can send you the money − I have really been nowhere − Bamberger[6] is a friend of Marie & very nice − I will send you the translations − Keep at your work. You will succeed − Give my love to Ida & Marie − Did you find the violet in the garden?

yrs ever
Fr Delius

Did you get Simplicissimus?[7]

Autograph letter, signed and dated, written in English.

The original is in the Grainger Museum.

1   Delius had written to Jelka in similar vein on 14 January: 'I am not affectionate − and regret it also. but cannot alter myself − My nature is so & very strong so that I cannot change − but I defy you to put your finger on anyone who is more himself &

herself – Please follow me thro' your friendship['s] eyes where I am always to be found – Thro' loves eyes, no doubt, I become hazy & indistinct.'

2 John F. Runciman (1866–1916): English critic. In a letter from Rouen dated 25 December 1901 he told Delius that he had in fact left this score (of the *Danish Songs*) in the care of Madame Bret, 12, rue de la Grande Chaumière, the Paris address of mutual friends. Somehow misrouted, it is clear that Runciman's letter did not reach Delius in Berlin.

3 Pierre Onfroy de Bréville (1861–1949): French teacher and composer.

4 Two of the *Danish Songs* were, in the event, conducted by Vincent d'Indy at the Société Nationale de Musique, in Paris, on 16 March 1901. The soloist was Christianne Andray.

5 Busoni was scheduled to play the Piano Concerto on 3 April, and *Paris* was also on the programme.

6 Translated the *Danish Songs* into German. He was shortly also to make some revisions to the German translation of *Koanga*.

7 German satirical magazine, founded in Munich in 1896 by Strindberg's friend Albert Langen.

(120)
Fritz Delius to Jelka Rosen

49 Eisenacher Str
Berlin
Schöneberg – 1 Feb. [1901]

Dear Jelka –

Many thanks for the nice letter. If Ida is still in Grez thank her also & tell her that what she writes about Nikisch is all very true – at the same time – I want her to know that I have written twice to Nikisch without any answer – I also went twice to his hotel without being received. When I next hear from Nikisch or meet him will be time enough to tell him about my things being played. I dont owe Nikisch any gratitude that would oblige me to inform him of my plans – as to writing or going to see him – that is out of the question – If he were merely polite he ought to have answered my letters – I belong to no clique – not even Busoni's – But I never knock more than twice at a door & I must think a great deal of somebody before I write 3 letters without receiving an answer – Nicolas & Fröhlke have sailed – a friend of Bamberger helped me with the contract – My Danish songs will be sung in Paris at the Societé Nationale on 16 March – Next time you go to Paris I will ask you to send the parts to the address I will send you in a day or two – Andray sings them – I

cannot come but D'Indy conducts[1] I dont know whether Runciman has sent
the score yet! Please send me the new address of Norman Concorde What do
you think if I gave another concert this spring in London? I might get N.C to
give it at his own risk or perhaps get Newman of Queen's Hall to give one – I
am going to propose to Busoni that we give one together. I ought to go to
London again, dont you think so – Why dont you take some of the earth at the
bottom of the garden near the river for the new garden? It would scarcely be
missed & it is splendid.
With love to all

 I remain
 affectionately
 Fritz Delius

Autograph letter, signed and dated, written in English.

The original is in the Grainger Museum.

1 A little later in the month Delius wrote urging Jelka to get a ticket for herself to
the concert, which was to take place in the Salle Erard; his own two tickets he would
probably have to give to Molard, who had translated the songs into French.

(121)
Fritz Delius to Jelka Rosen

49 Eisenacher Str
Berlin
Schöneberg. 8/2/1

Dearest friend – Many thanks for your letter & pretty flower – The thing now
is to get "Paris" back from Nikisch. I will try and see him after his next concert
Busoni left for Belgium & London last Tuesday. He returns at the end of March
– I hope he will at least be a friend & turn up in time for the concert on the 3rd.
It is strange that in spite of all his protests of sincerity etc I dont believe in him
– He has such false eyes & such an amiable way of speaking to everyone in order
to try & make himself popular. I dont believe he is what he wishes to appear –
I think he is a true Italian & superficial at heart – Well I'll hope for the best,
but if I am not mistaken in my instinct – Paris will be the only work in the
programme on April 3rd.[1] I wrote to Newman & am awaiting his answer.[2] If he
does not enter into my ideas – there is only two things for me to do. one is to
come back & get properly to work again & forget the world & pianists: the other
is to go to London & hire a theatre and mount one of my operas – I would really
risk it & the very man is at hand who would undertake the whole affair at ½

[h]is own risk – He is an American:[3] a sort of Jim Pinkerton – Energy & undertaking & invention enough for 20 others. He would find the theatre, Capital & company I would look after the rest – You perhaps would help with the scenery & decorations – Well more of this shortly – Please send the parts to M[r] Demets 20 Rue des Marais – The concert is in the Salle Erard – I am glad your work is going well – Give my love to Ida & Marie – I am looking forward to Ida's coming – Jebe is also coming here – that will be nice – I have only this piece of paper left – will write more shortly – Marie comes back in a few days – There are fewer real people in the world than I even thought

yrs
F D.

Autograph letter, initialled and dated, written in English.

The original is in the Grainger Museum.

1 See Letter 124.

2 Before long Delius was to inform Jelka, 'Newman replied that all his engagements for this season were filled up' and 'It is too late for a concert in London & the Queen's death knocks out everything.'

3 Probably Victor Thrane, Delius's New York impresario friend.

(122)
Jelka Rosen to Auguste Rodin

Grez sur Loing
S. et M.
21.2.1901

Bien cher maître

I think so much about you – it saddened me to see you so worried by so very many unpleasant matters, to be unable to do anything for you. Only my thoughts are with you, wishing to surround you with a magnetism strong enough to banish all these cares –

I am completely alone here; I have only the old Breton woman who looks after me. It is delightful, almost intoxicating, this peace, this life in my dreams, from which none can draw me. My work thrills me, in spite of the fact that it is still not at all good. Perhaps I love my picture[1] as mothers love their crippled children. I am painting my garden in full bloom. An extraordinary abundance of red flowers in the shade and at the tops of the trees a yellow setting sun. In the sunshine there are beings who are mad with joy and with life and in the shade the eternally unfulfilled woman – fallen there – fanatical – driven to despair – I have studied and worked on this for two years and I am putting my whole being into it. But how insipid is reality beside what I wish to express!

When I saw your exhibition it gave me new courage. I know how you have struggled and I saw your soul in your works I found it so beautiful, naked before me. You have been able to express the things which I have felt, which I have sought in vain in our painters and you have worked all your life, as I wish to do – How grateful I am to you!

Will you forgive me for this long letter? I know you so little and it seems to me that I have always known you. You are so rich in kindness and so unaffected, that I forget that I am really nothing myself. And in the great silence of this big and empty house and the quiet and dead garden I feel even smaller.

Your devoted
Jelka Rosen

Autograph letter, signed and dated, written in French.

The original is in the Rodin Museum, Paris. It is the third of thirty-five letters written by Jelka to Rodin between October 1900 and April 1914 that are preserved in the museum.

1   Possibly *Un jardin*, one of the five works exhibited by Jelka at the Salon des Indépendants (see Letter 146, note 3) in 1903.

(123)
Fritz Delius to Jelka Rosen

49 Eisenacher Str
Schöneberg
Berlin 14/3/1

Dear Jelka –

The 13th seems to be a good number for me. Yesterday the 13th. 2125 Marks suddenly arrived for the Courbet from Elberfeld[1] – Ida was quite as astonished as I was & as the day was warm & spring like we took a walk to the Disconto Gesellschaft & I deposited 1900 Marks – I am working a little now in Frl Bluhm's appartment My second Act is done – and I am at my American Rhapsody again – Last Tuesday we all – (Jebe's, Ida & I) went to a Concert at the Philharmonic & heard Tchaikowskis – Pathetic Symphonie – There are some very fine things in it – altho' the work is uneven – The 3rd movement is wonderful. I wrote to Molard & told him to give you one of his tickets.

On Saturday I shall go & hear Verdis Requiem – I heard also Falstaff[2] at the Opera: it is a wonderful work & full of humor – There is really quite a good deal going on here in the musical line & one could spend a couple of months very profitably here. I have given my scores to Rebicek.[3] One of these days I shall go & see Wolf[4] again – No doubt things are looking spring like in Grez & the garden must be budding out – I shall return 2 or 3 days after the concert & hope to be in time for the bulbs in the garden – Ida is well & sends her best love which I join to mine –

yrs ever
Fritz Delius

Did you get Simplicissimus

———————

Autograph letter, signed and dated, written in English.

The original is in the Grainger Museum.

1   It is obvious from this letter that Delius must have owned an original work by Courbet. No record, however, exists of its provenance, acquisition, subject matter or – apart from here – resale and buyer. See also Letter 107, note 3.

2   On 1 March Ida Gerhardi, in Berlin, had informed her sister, 'sometime we are going to hear Verdi's last & grandest work: Falstaff, – composed at the age of 80, Delius says it's wonderful & the only really great thing he has composed.' She also wrote, 'Delius now always works here [at the home of her friends, the Hackers] & I am glad to hear his beautiful sounds again from near & afar. . . . This evening Delius & Jebe & I are invited to the Busonis, Busoni is here for 4 days from England.'

3   Josef Rebicek (1844–1904): Czechoslovak-born violinist and conductor. Since 1897 he had been conductor of the Berlin Philharmonic Orchestra.

4   Hermann Wolff (1845–1902): German concert manager, music editor and composer. His agency, founded in 1880, ran the Berlin Philharmonic concerts.

(124)
Fritz Delius to Jelka Rosen

49 Eisenacher Str
[Late March, 1901]

Dearest Jelka –

Excuse me for not answering your letters. I have been a good deal bothered with this Concert which does not come off (and as you know I never believed it would)[1] Busoni is sick in London & has indeed not played at a Philharmonic St

James' Hall on account of sickness. In every case I shall never count on him again.[2] I shall leave here directly after Easter – Should Hertz come here – Ida has just written him – then I might be a few days later. Ida wants me to give a Concert here in October Hertz to conduct – The whole affair does not smile to me – I am sick of losing time over concerts, when they are not absolutely necessary for my developement. I dont care a d— for fame of any sort & would rather be at my work – Nothing disturbs me so much as this sort of thing – The last 6 months are absolutely lost – Perhaps Albertine might do something but I even doubt that – Well – dear girl, I am glad all is well in Grez & I am looking forward to being there again in its quiet atmosphere. I absolutely can do nothing here. Ida is well & sends you her love –

Give my love to all in Grez[3] &

believe me
your friend
Fritz Delius

I wonder what the surprise is? Ida's Picture of you is very good indeed.[4] But Koanga disturbs the whole – In every case he ought not to be on the floor he draws the eyes from the face.

Autograph letter, signed and undated, written in English.

The original is in the Grainger Museum.

1 Even *Paris* was to come off the programme, with Delius writing to Jelka on 20 March to tell her that the *Folkeraadet* suite would be played 'instead of Paris which required too many rehearsals'.

2 On 28 March Busoni wrote to his wife from London: 'I wonder if it will be possible to console Delius so easily? I am very unhappy for his sake for I know how much depends on it for him. He should try to get a later date. But if the worst comes to the worst, the *whole thing can stand as it is for next autumn*. . . . Please greet Delius and give him my apologies' (cf. Busoni, *Letters to His Wife*, p. 46). Busoni arrived in Berlin around 6 April, and he and his wife invited Delius and Ida Gerhardi to supper on the next day.

3 For at least part of the time Delius was away, Maud Ede had stayed at Grez with Jelka.

4 Ida's portrait of Jelka, dated 1901, is a large oil painting. She had painted a smaller, delicately impressionist oil of Jelka in 1897. 'Koanga' is the pet jackdaw.

(125)
Paul Nicolas and Adolf Fröhlke to Fritz Delius

Solana Grove, March 1901

Dear Herr Delius,

We were very pleased to get your letter of the 8th inst.

In answer to your enquiry, let us say first that as far as farm implements are concerned we have in the meantime come across 2 ploughs and 1 harrow; the rest we have got new. We cannot find your brushes, I think it best we do not enquire after them. As I have mentioned before, we have found a good support in Anderson and we are convinced that in all respects his intentions towards us are honourable. That we are naturally always looking to our advantage you can take for granted.

We have had a difficult job with the seed-bed, we chose as a site the dampest spot – (not the one you took before, but further back towards the swamp) – enough to plant about 40 acres, in other words big enough beforehand for all eventualities. The site and the field behind were completely overgrown with bushes, thick scrub and trees. You cannot at all imagine how wild it has grown since you were here 4 years ago. As I was saying, the hotbed i.e. the seed-bed, after it had been well manured with cotton-seed meal, was ready a fortnight ago and the shoots are already coming through. We planted 2½ ounces of Sumatra and 2½ ounces of Vuelta Abaji, which we got from Herr Dzialinsky in Jacksonville. This gentleman wrote very kindly to us, and as soon as the tobacco is up he is coming over to take a look at it and help us with all the advice he can. We shall be planting out the seedlings from the middle to the end of April, in other words in about 4 weeks' time.

We are now busily engaged in cultivating the overgrown land and will have to hurry to get it finished, as we have not too much time left; Anderson thinks, and we are all of the same opinion, that everything will be ready for planting out in 4 weeks. Everything we can do in the way of clearing land will be done, as you can imagine, but as we came too late and the land, as I have said, was too overgrown, we do not think we shall be able to cultivate 20 acres this year or season; we consider that if we are to do things properly we shall have to be content with 15 acres. The main thing is – and it is a principle of ours – that whatever we do must above all be *well* done. If the 15 acres turn out well, we shall have quite a nice yield. Next year, or rather this autumn and winter, we shall have time enough to bring more land under cultivation and it is of course our aim to extend the plantation as far as possible.

The drying-house will have to be improved and provided with a good new roof, perhaps we shall have to build a new one, we have made enquiries of Herr Dzialinsky on this matter.

The fence also looked in a very bad way, very dilapidated, we spent almost a week putting it in order again, so that the many pigs cannot do any damage.

Tomorrow we intend to dig out and repair the ditch which leads to the river, so that the heavy rains which have come down in the last few days can run away and shall not do any damage to our seed-bed.

So one job leads to another and as you can see, we have only very little time to finish what we want to do. –

We have set ourselves up quite well so far; as far as household and cooking utensils were concerned, we had to get new ones. Anderson got his wife's sister for us as cook, a very clean and honest girl she seems.

Physically we are all well and cheerful so far, and we hope to remain so.

So as not to become ill through the drinking water we have bought ourselves a pump and had it sunk 25 feet into the ground.

Up to now everything has gone according to our wishes and it would please us, Herr Delius, if we could always report to you news as good as this from here.

We hope you are well too, and remain with best wishes

Yours truly
Paul Nicolas

Dear Herr Delius, Herr Nicolas has told you everything so far. We are endeavouring to make straight for our goal, and hope that we shall succeed in every respect.
Greetings from

Yours truly
Adolf Fröhlke.

N.B.
Kind regards to Fräulein I. Gerhardi

Autograph letter, signed, written in German. Nicolas's handwritten date simply reads 'den März 1901', a short space having been left blank for the day of the month.

The original is in the Delius Trust Archive.

(126)
Jelka Rosen to Auguste Rodin

28.4.1901
Grez
s/ Loing
S. et M

Mon maître,

You have had the great kindness to send me a few charming lines and an invitation to the varnishing.[1]

I should have loved to come and shake you by the hand — it seems an eternity since I saw you. All this sumptuous spring has invaded my garden and my life — The joy of living and breathing has made me neglect my work, the soil demanded all my care and all these plant friends needed me. I am only sorry that you will not see them. The lilacs are in bud — will they bring you here?

Can I tempt you by telling you that there is a *very* artistic musician here who is a fervent admirer of your art, a great enthusiast of your Balzac, who would be *very* very happy to make your acquaintance?[2]

As for me, you know that you are always in my heart, you and your sublime works. Thus: absent or near me you always give me joy and I bless you for the beauty you have given to my life.

Your utterly devoted
Jelka Rosen

Autograph letter, signed and dated, written in French.

The original is in the Rodin Museum.

1 As president of the Société Nationale des Beaux Arts, Rodin had sent Jelka an invitation to the opening of the society's exhibition at the Grand Palais, which was to take place on 21 April. A covering note told her that he still hoped to come to see her 'and breathe in the spring' in her garden.

2 Delius had arrived in Paris on 13 April and made his way back to Grez two days later. His admiration for Rodin's controversial statue of Balzac was certainly not shared by the majority of the French critics of the day.

(127)
Jelka Rosen to Auguste Rodin

Grez 11.6.1901

Mon ami

You wanted me to write and in my thoughts I am always still with you, but so sad that I no longer have you[1] — If you only knew just how I drank with an ardent heart what I so much thirsted for, your great and true words, the beauty of all things seen through your eyes, your infinite gentleness. A joy radiates from you and sings in my heart and I remain alone to preserve this miracle — something holy and superb, unforgettable. I want to enfold you with my fond thoughts in this life which takes you away and then I am a little ashamed of my selfishness which prevented me from doing *more* for your happiness — ?

I am going to immerse myself in my work and study as you told me to I kiss your fine, magnificent brow and your dear hands and I am yours ever

Jelka,
or Hélène² if you prefer.

Delius talks so much about you and asks me to pay his repects to you.

Autograph letter, signed and dated, written in French.

The original is in the Rodin Museum.

1   Rodin had just left Grez, having stayed for two days at Jelka's home.

2   'Jelka' is a diminutive of 'Helene', by which name she was baptized.

(128)
Fritz Delius to Jelka Rosen

Lundi 8 Juillet [1901]

Having a delightful time –
Ot as ell
But alls well   Yrs. F D. –

Picture postcard, initialled 'F D.', and dated, written in English, of the *Château d'Amboise. – Vue Générale*. Addressed: Mlle Jelka Rosen / Grez sur Loing / Seine & Marne. Postmark: AMBOISE INDRE-ET-LOIRE 8 JUIL 01.

The original is in the Grainger Museum.

Delius was on a cycling tour of the Loire Valley with an artist friend, Guy Maynard, and this is one of nine postcards they sent to Jelka.

(129)
Auguste Rodin to Jelka Rosen

[Paris 10 July 1901]

Mademoiselle mon amie

Your 2 letters gave me great joy. And I thank you and beg you to write me more. Your charm as a writer gives me pleasure.

I am still reading Nitsche and I find a man of genius, very often obscure, but one may sometimes guess. I envy your having reached his level.

Write to me I hope to come and see you the day I visit Mirbeau,[1] who lives nearby

My regards to Monsieur Délius.

In homage I kiss your hand
A Rodin

Autograph letter, signed and undated, written in French. Envelope addressed: Mademoiselle / J. Rosen / a Gretz sur loing / par Bouron / S. et M. Postmark: PARIS 10 JUIL 01.

The original is in the Delius Trust Archive. It is the seventh of seventeen communications written by Rodin to Jelka between October 1900 and December 1904 that have been preserved. See plate 38.

1 Octave Mirbeau (1848–1917): French dramatist, novelist, critic and journalist, and a passionate admirer of Rodin's work. He lived 'nearby' at Veneux, a few kilometres north-west of Grez.

(130)
William Molard to Fritz Delius

Herewith our address: Eygurande d'Ussel
(Corrèze)

Eygurande 5 September 1901

My dear Friend,

I am writing to you on a very dirty sheet of paper, but it is all I have at the moment in my possession and in the country, you know, you don't always do what you want and you don't always find what you look for.

Yes, finally I'm on the heights of the Plateau Central, taking the cure d'air which according to my doctor is essential to my complete recovery. And as a matter of fact it's doing me a lot of good, because with the help of my feeding-up diet, I have put on two Kilograms and reckon to reach a weight of 67 Kilos before I leave, tallying with my height; before leaving Mantes[1] I only weighed 63 Kilos.

This would be your sort of country here, very picturesque, very varied, covered with streams inviting one to go for walks, and there are numerous interesting trips you can make into the surrounding countryside. There is even a very remarkable Lunatic asylum admirably situated at the foot of the Chavanon gorges which is well worth a visit, but women are not allowed in, so as not to excite the involuntary bachelors confined there. Our tragi-comedy. I had a letter from Boutet[2] yesterday telling me that the sacrifice has been consummated and that he is my Colleague; he and his wife are just now not far from the département de la Corrèze, staying with friends who have a property in Haute-Vienne. In the property itself, which is a château, if you please, there is a chapel and he dreams of nothing but decorating it with frescoes, you can see he's still the same, enthusiastic and full of projects. Our friend Daniel[3] has written to me too about Gauguin who is leaving Tahiti to live on the Marquesas. Daniel tells me that he himself is battling with the difficulties which always beset a man of property, as they are managing his mother's estate, but that he is going to leave all his worries behind him and stick to his painting alone from now on, and he's right because he is a man of talent, with an artistic nature that is susceptible to influence and impulsive.

Alquier[4], who is at La Rochelle at his family's, tells me that he has started to tackle a symphony and that just now he's composing his first movement. And you, what are you up to, I'd be glad to hear something on this subject and to have a little of your news. Me, I'm doing nothing, the far niente, but recommended, and I'm getting used to it nicely. Ida & Judith[5] send you their best wishes and I shake your hand with affection

Will.

I shall be grateful if you will be kind enough to give our best regards to Mademoiselle Rosen.

Autograph letter, signed and dated, written in French.

The original is in the Delius Trust Archive.

1   Molard's family home and place of birth.

2   Charles Boutet de Monvel (see Letter 47, note 1), who has evidently just married.

3   Georges-Daniel de Monfreid.

4   Maurice Alquier: French composer.

5   Judith, Ida Molard's daughter (see also Letter 47, note 1).

(131)
Fritz Delius to Jelka Rosen

Harrogate
Oct 9. 1901

Dearest Jelka

I really have not had time to write before & even now not the necessary quietness to give you an idea of the state of things here in Bradford[1] – The only one who has any (any) brains at all in the family is my sister Clare with whom I am staying now. We buried the old man on Monday and indeed he died just in time to save the whole family from ruin — I will postpone particulars until I return — on Monday next very probably — I leave for London tomorrow Friday — Is Runciman still in Grez? if so I had better come thro' instead of staying in London uselessly. My brother is a soft headed mope & broke down at the grave altho I know he has been waiting 18 years for this event & really did not care a straw. I was also surprised to see him kneel & do a bit of praying when the Parson drawled out his prayers — What a crowd of white livered fools they all are here — and not even honest at that. I am longing for Grez & my work again — To Hell with them all — as I really could see these sort of people wiped out by thousands with the greatest equanimity

With best love
I remain
as ever yours
Fritz Delius

Drop me a line if you have any address to Kings Cross Hotel
London

Autograph letter, signed and dated, written in English. The fact that Delius mentioned 'tomorrow Friday' would indicate that the letter was actually written on 10 October, a Thursday, in spite of its bearing the date Oct 9.

The original is in the Grainger Museum.

1   Delius had returned to England to attend the funeral of his father, who had died on 4 October. His first letter from the family home in Bradford, written a few days earlier, had told Jelka, 'The funeral is on Monday & will be a terrible affair as the town is making it a public funeral. . . . This is a terrible place & I shall stay as short as possible.'

(132)
Hans Haym to Fritz Delius

[Elberfeld, 6 December 1901]

Paris will be done![1] Six extra musicians & the second harp will probably be put on your account, the Concert Gesellschaft will be responsible for the rest. The first rehearsal is on Wednesday aft. at the latest. Hope you will be able to be there.

Best wishes!   Haym

Autograph postcard, signed and undated, written in German. Addressed: Herrn Fr. Delius / Grez sur Loigne / Seine et Marne / Frankreich. Postmark: ELBERFELD 6.12.01.

The original is in the Delius Trust Archive. It is the first of some fifty-six letters and postcards written by Haym to Delius between 1901 and 1910 that are preserved in the Archive. A postcard from Haym to Jelka, dated 5 October 1919, is preserved in the Grainger Museum.

1   Ida Gerhardi's efforts had succeeded, and Haym was to give *Paris* in Elberfeld on 14 December. A letter from Ida to Lilli Gerhardi, dated Kreuznach, 9 December 1901, and preserved in the Gerhardi/Steinweg collection, indicates that Delius arrived in Elberfeld on 10 December to supervise rehearsals, and that Ida and Jelka also arranged to attend the concert.

A pencilled note in an unidentified hand at the foot of Haym's card reads *Di{e}nstag Vorm. erste Probe* (Tuesday morn. first rehearsal).

1902

Delius spent January and February in Berlin, returning, it seems, in March to France. He was now at work on a one-act opera, *Margot la Rouge*, to be entered for the Sonzogno Prize. Much of the first half of the year was coloured darkly by the final illness of Jelka's mother in Paris, where she died on 11 June. Following this, the terms of her will caused some protracted wrangling among members of the Rosen family, with Delius himself keeping a sharp eye on Jelka's interests.

No major summer travels seem for once to have been undertaken, and Delius probably stayed for the most part in Grez. Now it was Jelka who had to be away in Paris and Berlin, helping to sort out matters connected with Serena Rosen's legacy. By late October they were both in Berlin, as Busoni was at last to give *Paris* there, on 15 November. Delius also wanted to be in Elberfeld for Haym's performance of the *Mitternachtslied Zarathustras*.

It was during the course of this year that Delius gradually stopped using the name Fritz. From now on he was to be Frederick.

Margot la Rouge, one-act opera (RT I/7). Completed.

'Summer Landscape', song (Drachmann) (RT V/24). April.

Appalachia, Variations on an old Slave Song, with final Chorus, for large orchestra (RT II/2). A reworking, begun this year, of the 'American Rhapsody' of 1896.

Florent Schmitt makes a piano arrangement of *A Village Romeo and Juliet*.

Maurice Ravel makes a piano arrangement of *Margot la Rouge*. Autumn.

(133)
Adolf Fröhlke to Fritz Delius

Bünde i[n] W[estfalen], 30 January 1902.

Dear Herr Delius –

I wrote to you yesterday from Löhne and shall now follow up my promise to give you some more precise information about your farm. As you can probably imagine, the land inside the fencing is ready for planting. The tall fir trees at the top, in other words near the entrance gate, have been left standing. The pump is under the cherry tree on the earlier old enclosure. There is hardly anything left of the landing stage; we used Pissetti's jetty further up the river. – Frl. Gerhardi also thought that if you wanted to sell your farm, now is the best time, before the farm becomes overgrown again. Have already written about the price yesterday. Land is very cheap over there because of the severe winters. E.g. I could buy your friend Douglas's[1] farm for 500 Dollars. Admittedly the farmhouse has been demolished, and the fencing too; but according to the reports of people like Armstrong the land is *very good*. The farm of Captain *Bell*,[2] your former neighbour, is also uninhabited and looks bare and desolate. Since the severe winters came to Florida, agriculture has fallen on very bad days, and hundreds of farms lie uncultivated on both sides of the river. – You will be able to get information about our work there from your acquaintances in Picolata, I expect. Nicolas and I were *the first* of those whom you sent to Fl[orid]a who have actually worked for you. I can tell you, dear Herr Delius, I have spent the hardest time of my life on your farm; in return for the money lost all I have brought back with me is experience. The uncertain livelihood, snakes, heat and, what is the main thing, again the shortage of money etc. induced me to go to my friends in Cincinnati, to take up work there. I was too weak to write all this to you in Paris. I should be glad to have a talk with you sometime; I hope your music will be played in Berlin in April or soon after, when I will visit you. – If Nicolas had not been the first to leave your farm, everything would still have been alright. – It is all over now. There is no point in complaining, as Frl. Gerhardi will tell you, for *nothing can be done without money*; on your part it means nothing but expense.

No more for today, so best wishes

Yours
Adolf Fröhlke

Autograph letter, signed and dated, written in German on the headed notepaper of ADOLF FRÖHLKE SÖHNE / Cigarren-Fabrik.

The original is in the Delius Trust Archive.

1   Presumably Charles Douglas, the Bradford friend with whom Delius sailed on his first trip to Florida.

2   Jutta Bell's husband.

(134)
Richard Strauss to Frederick Delius

Charlottenburg [Berlin], 2 March 1902

Dear Herr Delius,

I have read your score: Paris with great interest! I am afraid I cannot decide to perform the work for the time being: the symphonic development seems to me to be too scant, and it seems moreover to be an imitation of Charpentier[1] which has not quite succeeded – perhaps I cannot quite imagine the effect of the piece, and I beg you kindly to forgive me and in any case not to be discouraged if, with regret, I return your score to you unperformed.

Perhaps I shall have the pleasure of greeting you personally in Paris and of chatting to you at greater length.

With sincerest greetings

Yours
Richard Strauss.

Autograph letter, signed and dated, written in German. Envelope addressed: Monsieur *Frederik Delius / Grez sur Loing / Seine & Marne / Frankreich*. Postmark: CHARLOT-TENBURG 2/3 02.

The original is in the Delius Trust Archive. It is the only item of correspondence preserved from Strauss to Delius.

Ida Gerhardi had been in touch with Strauss around this period, as a rather haughty letter from Strauss to her, dated 23 May (and presumed to be from 1902), clearly indicates: 'I have not made any destructive judgment on Herr Delius, but only advised D[r] Haym to perform the work by preference in the winter, rather than at the Musikfest, where the public would make its customary demands of the piece, which Delius's composition would perhaps not, however, be able sufficiently to fulfil.

'Nevertheless the work shows evidence of talent, even if it does not exhaust the subject & is a little thin from a thematic viewpoint' (Gerhardi/Steinweg collection).

1   Gustave Charpentier (1860–1956): French composer. He studied under Massenet at the Paris Conservatoire and was a winner of the Prix de Rome. His opera *Louise*, completed in 1900 (that is, after the completion of Delius's *Paris*), told the story of a Parisian work girl and (like *Paris*) incorporated in its score street cries of the city.

The publishing house of C. F. Kahnt, Leipzig, were to echo Strauss when they wrote to Delius on 23 March 1905: *Paris* was 'a significant work which should certainly be published. . . . It reminds us of Charpentier's "Louise".'

(135)
Frederick Delius to Jelka Rosen

Grez sur Loing
Seine & Marne
[Spring 1902]

My dearest Jelka –

I am so sorry you are so miserable and advise you if you can to come down here
for a day or two. we can then go up again together – Why dont you send away
your cousin? Why can't you speak out to her and get rid of her – You suffer
from your own good nature – and weakness in not being able to say what you
think or feel for fear of offending people – Dont you see you will be eternally
imposed upon. Since I know you I have seen this going on with all your friends
& relations[1] – You know that I care for you immensely and am your real friend
– But you really ought to have somebody to love you in the way you desire – A
real strong man who could entirely absorb your nature – You will never be
happy otherwise. Thanks for writing to the Princess[2] I wrote also – I hope
when you see Ouvré[3] you will tell him what you think about him I dont
understand how Miss Warwick[4] can write a nice letter after such behaviour –
Please explain! I wrote a hell of a letter to Ouvré & asked him for an explanation.
Marie will make up the packet and send it off tomorrow if you dont telegraph.
The post has been a disaster for this country. Our rose dinde[5] are mostly frozen
and many sauge[6] – but we have lots more Sauge. Dont get low spirited: try to
come out here – Maud Ede is the only decent friend you ever had – I might
have sent the Sparkasse book direct to the bank! I suppose they'll end by taking
the rest!! There are two sorts of people in the world – one kind resembles the
Hammer, the others the Anvil or the Hammered – In every case come out here
for a day – It is as cold as heaven here! – I am well

ever your friend
Frederick

Autograph letter, signed and undated, written in English. Jelka later pencilled in
'Spring 1902'.

The original is in the Grainger Museum.

1   For reasons that are not entirely apparent, Delius was also trying to put to an end
Jelka's friendship with Ida Gerhardi. Several undated letters he wrote to Jelka in the
spring and early summer are testimony to this:
    'I enclose a letter from Bamberger – I suppose Ida has been up to her little games
again At all events from this moment I cease to take the slightest interest in what she
does say.'

'I don't see how Ida can dismiss such an assertion . . . – especially as you wrote expressly to ask her again – No my dear girl that will not go down with me – Let us drop Ida – she is really too dangerous – Bamberger of course has nothing to write on the subject – He denies it & that settles it for ever – She has done this now so often that I have no further illusion about her.'

'Ida interests me no more – If I were you I would gradually cease any correspondence with her – it only bothers you.'

One letter is dated 2 April 1902: 'Ida sent the Vorspiel of R & J. translated I have scarcely looked at it yet, but have already seen 2 or 3 things which I dont like.'

2   Presumably the Princesse de Cystria.

3   Achille Ouvré (1872–1951): French illustrator and engraver. He executed many portraits, most notably of writers, painters and musicians; among the latter Delius, Ravel, Szántó and Molard all figure. It is not established what part Ouvré was playing in the Warwick affair.

4   The only other reference to Miss Warwick in the correspondence of the Deliuses is in a letter written by Jelka to Rodin on 7 April: 'A young Creole, Mlle Warrick who seems *very* gifted to me has done a statue of the poor Thief on the Cross. In the middle of her work she fell ill, which has put her behind. She is so poor that she only has this one year in Paris, and her whole future in America depends on this: To have exhibited at the Salon. Her art is her life and she is so full of enthusiasm that I wanted to help her.' Jelka begged Rodin to use his influence to get the work accepted.

5   A variety of marigold. In French in the original letter.

6   *sage*. In French in the original letter.

(136)
Frederick Delius to Jelka Rosen

Grez sur Loing
Seine & Marne
[May/June 1902]

Dearest Jelka

I have just received a card from Schmitt asking for the 3rd Act[1] – Please send it off if you have time to Florent Schmitt, Villa Medicis, Rome – D'Humieres[2] has just left. He is going to translate R & J & also do the "Requiem"[3] with me – He is a most delightful man and as soon as you are out here again we will ask him out again. I am sure you will like him immensely – Everything was very nice and comfortable and he regretted going away so soon – The thrushes are thriving wonderfully and beginning to pipe & jump about in their cage – Unfortunately it rained since yesterday and is still raining – what a summer! Marie had an excellent dinner for us and the unfortunate boîte of the Princesse[4] was not opened — Let me hear how things are going on and what hope there is for a speedy conclusion — The first grafted rose is out this morning an immense pink one —

Always yours
Frederick Delius

I wrote to the P^sse & told her that her caisse was de trop[4] as Marie had prepared us such an excellent dinner. It is useless to say anything more to her as she does not understand these things & means really so well — Telegraph if anything happens & let me give you all the help I can — [5]

Autograph letter, signed and undated, written in English. Jelka later pencilled in 'Spring 1902'.

The original is in the Grainger Museum.

1   Florent Schmitt was preparing a vocal score of *A Village Romeo and Juliet*. Of the four operatic scores by Delius arranged by Schmitt, this was the only one to be published, in Paris about 1906. It was, however, shortly to be supplanted by Otto Lindemann's arrangement, which appeared in Berlin under Harmonie's imprint in 1910.

2   Robert d'Humières: French writer and critic. Among other things, he wrote the scenario for Schmitt's *La tragédie de Salomé* and translated into French the libretto of *A Village Romeo*.

3   The first mention of a work that was to be composed much later. Delius was not to turn to his *Requiem* until 1914, and there is no record of d'Humières having been further concerned with the project.

4   Presumably the Princesse de Cystria presented Delius with a hamper of food that was not needed.

5   Delius and Jelka had spent part of the winter in Paris, Jelka in her mother's apartment at 4, rue Honoré Chevalier, where Frau Rosen was seriously ill. Jelka returned to Grez around the middle of February, Delius following early in March. Here he was evidently offering help in the event of any worsening of Frau Rosen's condition.

(137)
Frederick Delius to Jelka Rosen

Grez sur Loing
Seine & Marne
3 Juin — [1902]

Dearest Jelka —

Of course a "dénouement" must be close at hand now after your description it cannot last long[1] — Your garde malade is a treasure! The Princess is and has always been like that – hence our eternal rows & my rupture complete – She has many excellent points and is a faithful friend – You see she is a "parvenue" herself amongst the *aristos* – her noblesse only dating from Napoleon (Her "mama" I believe was a fille naturelle of somebody or other – So that explains much). If you care to answer her letter in a satirical & common sense way do so, as you are not supposed to know all the "peripeties" that I & she have gone thro' – I never say anything to her now as I have so little to do with her – and she knows what I think au fond – If you care to let her know what you think, do so by all means – I enclose a letter from Albertine,[2] when you have time write me a "Schema" so that I can answer her – Shall I tell her I am off to Norway? or keep it close & let the money and letters be given to you – if you should be obliged to come later – I am thinking of sailing on June the 19th In that case you would have to meet me at Nevlungshavn[3] – We shall have to make up a case of things, eatables, etc for our Hut – None of the new roses are yet out except the big pink one I sent you in the basket yesterday – I am nearly at the end of my Opera and shall have done in 3 or 4 days[4] Keep up your spirits and get as much sleep and air as possible –

always yours
Frederick

Autograph letter, signed and dated, written in English.

The original is in the Grainger Museum.

1   The reference is to Frau Rosen's illness. She died on 11 June.

2   Albertine Krönig's letter, dated Berlin, 31 May 1902, is preserved in the Grainger Museum. She wanted to send Delius's things on before going away for a time, adding, 'You intended, according to what you wrote to me, to get your "Paris" performed in Paris, why did nothing come of it?' Delius asked Jelka to draft a reply.

3   On 3 May, Iver Holter had written to Delius from Christiania. Delius had evidently asked him about accommodation in the Jotunheim and in Nevlunghavn, with the intention of going to Norway at the beginning of June. Holter advised delaying the visit on account of the unseasonably chill weather.

4   He wrote again shortly after: 'My Opera was quite finished on the 6th of June.' The work in question is the one-act *Margot la Rouge*.

(138)
Frederick Delius to Jelka Rosen

[Grez, September 1902]

Dearest Jelka –

Your letter just to hand – Your Berlin brother is a misérable & F. not much better. they are trying to tire you out & make you agree to everything they want

– *Dont give in* – Felix will also want to *be off shortly* & as you are in Paris, you will be maitresse of the situation – I am alright but yesterday I was thinking strongly of your Berlin brother & he was evidently thinking of me. Of course he must be wild against me – knowing probably or thinking that I have spoiled all his little schemes on you – If I ever meet him & he says two words to me – I think he will regret it – I will not boast, but I really think so. Dearest – dont get nervous – Shall I come to Paris so as to be near you? telegraph and I will come at once & live 15 Rue Jacob – If it takes 6 months you must not give in one jot. Let Felix be slow, let him go or stay – but hold your own – Why dont you write me more explicitly I could then know what is going on, what is his share & what is yours – What do you get instead of the silver *I* should have taken the silver – as that is always useful & of worth, whilst old furniture & bric a brac can be bought cheap & are of really little value – Have the diamonds come? Whilst you are settling up *settle up once for all everything* – You surely dont want to begin again with them about the jewels! as for his things here – of course you must send them at his expense *at once to Berlin* – hold out as long as they do – I will come to Paris at a word from you & stay near you until it is all finished – *all* & *not part*. If F in Berlin is not satisfied let him come to Paris – but is not Felix executor? I think it would help matters on if *you* were to threaten to prolong matters, or cast the whole thing on to chancery. You would see what a face they would then make – you see they think you will give in ultimately to their plans. *Or* have the whole thing expertised and then divide it according – What does it matter whether it costs 2 or 300 ^{frs} – I repeat that I would take all the silver I could get & leave them more of the beds & furniture. Telegraph at once if you want me – The weather here is not nice – Cloudy & windy – Should you come out here suddenly dont forget to bring oatmeal – The meal that was left here, turned bitter – Keep up your spirits dearest girl & fight it out bravely to the end – I am thinking about you all the time. Marie sends her love and she also has the feeling that they are cheating you –

always yours
Frederick

Autograph letter, signed and undated, written in English. Jelka later added 'September 1902'.

The original is in the Grainger Museum.

A protracted family squabble over Serena Rosen's will was now under way, and Delius was anxious that Jelka (and no doubt he himself) should not be cheated. In another letter from this period written from Grez, he told Jelka, in Paris at the time: 'We will arrange the house as soon as we can, the dining room will be delightful – I was looking at it yesterday – Oh! for sufficient ready cash!! Write me at once all about things and be as hard as the *"Diamanten"* ma perle!'

The references in this letter to members of Jelka's family are not particularly clear. She had two brothers, Fritz (1856–1935) and Felix (1863–?), and her mother's only surviving brother was another Felix (Moscheles), who lived in London.

(139)
Maurice Ravel to Frederick Delius

St. Jean-de-Luz   *Wednesday 10* [September, 1902]

My dear Delius,

I received your letter after some delay, caused by my own thoughtlessness. I had omitted to leave my address at Angoulême, where your card has remained until today. I hope you will please forgive me.

The transcription is well under way but I must ask you to give me until the end of this month to finish it; I hope however to be able to send it to you before then.

Would you also, in your reply, tell me if it is absolutely necessary to transcribe the prelude for 2 hands. It would have a much better effect with 4 hands.

Very cordially yours
Maurice Ravel

41 *rue Gambetta*
St. Jean-de-Luz
(*Basses Pyrénées*)

Autograph letter, signed and dated 'Mercredi 10', written in French.

The original is in the Delius Trust Archive. It is the first of two letters written by Ravel to Delius that have been preserved (see also Letter 140).

Maurice Ravel (1875–1937): French composer. He studied at the Paris Conservatoire, where Fauré was one of his teachers. Delius would by now have known him for some years, having almost certainly met him in the context of the Molard circle. Ravel was preparing for Delius a vocal score of the one-act opera (or 'lyric drama') *Margot la Rouge*, whose full score Delius had completed in June. This arrangement was actually published, in Paris about 1905.

(140)
Maurice Ravel to Frederick Delius

St. Jean-de-Luz.   *Friday 3/10* [1902]

My dear Delius,

You will receive by the same post the transcription of *Margot*. I am keeping the full score for a few more days to make the changes we agreed upon. I was wrong not to have discussed this matter with you earlier; my transcription was almost finished when I received your card, but I think I can manage. You can now get on with the translation. The alterations ought not to be very important, and besides, the translator will certainly have to make others.

As regards the music, I have corrected the obvious mistakes (forgotten accidentals, etc.). I have transcribed literally certain doubtful passages and will discuss these with you later, except for a few bars (Scene V. *Pourquoi me confier ces choses-là*) which seemed mysterious to me, and which I have left blank.[1] I would also draw your attention to one line without music in the orchestral score (Scene II *La Patronne: Il te pince donc bien, ton nouveau béguin*).

As soon as you get the score, please advise me of its receipt, still at the same address 41, rue Gambetta.

A bientôt, dear friend. If you see Schmitt, please give him my regards.

Cordially yours
Maurice Ravel

Autograph letter, signed and dated, written in French.

The original is in the Delius Trust Archive.

1   In Ravel's manuscript, preserved in the Delius Trust Archive, Delius himself filled in this passage.

Ravel's work on Delius's opera leads inevitably to the question of what kind of an impression it may have made on him. Certainly none of the published material on his life and work hints at any influence on him by the older composer, whom he had known for some time. Nor was Ravel himself ever to acknowledge any debt to Delius. It is conceivable that in 1902 he saw the score of *A Village Romeo and Juliet* while it was being transcribed by Florent Schmitt. He may even have discussed with Schmitt matters connected with his own *Margot la Rouge* commission; after all, Schmitt had by then completed four operatic transcriptions for Delius and would, therefore, have been in a position to give useful advice to the younger composer. It is interesting that not long after finishing his work on Delius's opera, Ravel embarked on a score unlike any he had composed before, the song-cycle *Shéhérazade*. His opening setting, 'Asie', the longest of the cycle of three, in particular marks with its expressive recitative with Delian overtones a new departure for the twenty-seven-year-old composer. At times the effects he achieves with a soaring soprano line set against a glowing, many-stranded orchestral background are startlingly reminiscent of Delius's technique, itself demonstrated in a number of passages in *Margot* where the soprano is dominant or is joined briefly by the baritone.

It may, then, be said that while Ravel later acknowledged Debussy's 'spiritual influence' on the cycle, he seems to have remained unaware of the technical avenues subconsciously opened to him through his absorption, for a time, of some of the music of Delius's maturity.

Delius had actually written *Margot* as an entry for the *Concorso Melodrammatico*, sponsored by the Italian publishing house Sonzogno. The prize, however, was taken by

Lorenzo Filiasi (1878–1963), whose one-acter *Manuel Menendez* was performed in Milan on 15 May 1904.

(141)
Albertine Krönig to Frederick Delius

Berlin 6 Oct. 02.

Dear Fritz,

Having returned from Bielefeld the day before yesterday, I received your letter here today, the contents of which cause me the greatest surprise. It seems to me very ill-advised for you in your position to want to start a family, when you have still no prospects for the future, and you either will not or cannot take on teaching or conducting an orchestra, which would assure you of an income. In any case you must set forth your circumstances to the new family and also to your fiancée *quite honestly*, that everything which you have received from your parents up to now, including the farm in America, is reckoned against your personal inheritance, so that considering that there are 11 brothers and sisters there will hardly be very much over for you. To appeal to the name of Delius & to awaken in your relatives hopes of affluence is as foolish as possible, & can only bring misfortune.

None of your musical works has as yet been performed with decisive success, so as to be a source of revenue to you. So I advise you seriously not to think of marriage until you have won an assured position, or unless your bride has sufficient means for a family to live on without anxiety, and you can cover your expenses by this means. Reciprocal love suffers no harm from a postponement, provided each is attached to the other. For the present I will continue to give you 100 M monthly for another year, but do not let me in for *anything more*. Since Minnie is also in straitened circumstances & no longer gets anything from home, I have also undertaken to help her for the time being. Well, I beg you not to take any ill-considered step, you hardly know what the expenses of a household & the maintenance of a family amount to, your bride's estate would have to be pretty large to cover everything. I felt compelled to write you this immediately. Perhaps you will take great exception to it, but I consider it my duty

With greetings from your Aunt

Albertine.

Autograph letter, signed and dated, written in German.

The original is in the Delius Trust Archive. It is the first of eight letters and postcards, dating from 1902 to 1905, that Delius received from his aunt and that are preserved in the Archive. One further letter, dated 31 May 1902, is in the Grainger Museum.

(142)
Florent Schmitt to Frederick Delius

Ecole Française d'Athènes
1st November 1902

My dear Delius

I'm taking myself off to Germany. Am I likely to come across you in Dresden, Leipzig or Berlin?[1] Could you give me a few tips on these three cities, above all on how to live there in the most economical way. If you can put me in touch with some of your friends I would be very grateful to you. In London I looked for M. Runciman but never actually managed to meet him. I saw Messager[2] there and we talked about you. I went to Covent-Garden a few times. The orchestra is good but the London public seems to me quite indifferent and I don't think that England is a country of the future for music.

Have you seen Ravel? If you get the chance give him my regards, and to Molard too. What are you working on at the moment. Have you sent off to the Sonzogno competition.[3] I'd be very surprised if an Italian didn't get the prize!

I intended to stay in Greece for 2 months. But I must say it's too ancient a country. It would seem that now it is closed to all civilization. I think I'd much prefer Egypt but that will have to be for later on. I'm off tomorrow for Constantinople and from there I'll be making for Vienna.

Hoping to hear from you soon. All the best and my kind regards to Mademoiselle Rosen.

Did you go back to see the female wrestlers again!

Florent Schmitt

Vienna poste restante

Autograph letter, signed and dated, written in French.

The original is in the Delius Trust Archive. Two other letters from Schmitt to Delius, dated 1898 and 1907, are also preserved.

1   No record of a meeting at this period between Schmitt and Delius has been found, but Delius himself was in Berlin on 15 November to hear Busoni conduct *Paris* in the Beethoven-Saal. Of incidental interest, on the subject of this performance Busoni had written to Ida Gerhardi from Berlin as early as 22 July; his letter was a waggish one:

'What are you doing with this miserable score?

What are you doing, peddling it around like this? . . . "I reply to you by return that it is early enough if I have the score on the 1 Sept." but *not later* and with *faultless orchestral parts*. I am a novice at conducting, the work is difficult & unknown, so I must not take too many risks.'

2   André Messager (1853–1929): French composer and conductor. As a friend of
Theodor Delius, he would have been among the first French musicians of distinction
with whom young Fritz became acquainted in his earliest years in Paris. He conducted
frequently at Covent Garden in the early 1900s, when he was Artistic Director there.

3   See Letter 140, note 1.

(143)
Max Schillings to Frederick Delius

Munich (19).
20. Dec. 02.

Dear Sir,

I am very grateful to you for sending me the score of your "Zarathustra". I very
much hope that I shall be successful in recommending it for performance at the
next Tonkünstlerfest in Basel, as the piece is very interesting & *Stimmungsvoll*.
– At last year's festival I was unable to find room for your "Paris", which seemed
to me to be an interesting problem, as it did not have the necessary appeal to
the Committee. – Yours respectfully

M Schillings.

Autograph postcard, signed and dated, written in German. Addressed: Herrn Frederick
Delius / Grez sur Loing / Seine et Marne / *France*.

The original is in the Delius Trust Archive. It is the first of thirty-nine letters and
postcards written by Schillings to Delius between 1902 and 1910 that have been
preserved.

Max (von) Schillings (1868–1933): German composer and conductor. After studying
in Bonn and Munich, he was active at Bayreuth from 1892. He was to conduct at
Stuttgart from 1908 before becoming intendant at the Berlin State Opera from 1919
to 1925.

1903

The year's earliest excursion abroad was to Düsseldorf, where Delius attended on 12 February Buths's performance of *Paris*. Fairly soon after Delius's return to France, Edvard Munch arrived to stay for part of March with Delius and Jelka at Grez. This was to be a year when the two men corresponded and met frequently. A further advance in public awareness of Delius's music came on 12 June, with the *Mitternachtslied Zarathustras* being played, in Delius's presence, at the annual festival of the Allgemeine Deutsche Musikverein, held this year in Basel. Interest in Germany itself was clearly rising, with Haym and Buths in particular now studying his works carefully and planning performances.

Most of the summer seems to have been spent in Grez; but Jelka and he left Paris on 21 August for a holiday in Antwerp, Amsterdam and on the Dutch coast, before returning to Grez, where they at last married.

Actual record of composition this year is slight and rather uncertain. It may well have been that with more opportunities opening up for his music in Germany, Delius's major preoccupation for a time became the revision and preparation of earlier scores, and correspondence and meetings with conductors and possible publishers. At all events, by the end of the year he had succeeded in securing further important performances in Germany for 1904.

Appalachia (RT II/2). Revised work completed?

Sea Drift, for baritone solo, mixed chorus and large orchestra (Whitman) (RT II/3). Begun this year?

(144)
Edvard Munch to Frederick Delius

Hotel Hippodrome Am Knie Charlottenburg [Berlin]
30/ 1 1903

Dear Delius,

Many thanks for the invitation – I long very much for Paris and shall probably be able to come – later – at the end of February – I should like to exhibit at

L'Independants[1] — I would be delighted to stay for a while with you then — it must be very beautiful — But I am afraid of a lady in Paris[2] and expect new bad things — Write and tell me what you know — she herself has so many allies — Unfortunately my finger is still not healed — I don't think I can come to Düsseldorf how long are you going to stay there?[3]

Best wishes to you and Fraulein Rosen

Your friend
E Munch

Autograph letter, signed and dated, written in German.

The original is in the Delius Trust Archive.

1 The annual exhibition of the Société des Artistes Indépendants takes place in Paris in the spring. Founded in 1884 by artists whose paintings had been rejected by the official Salon, it was unique in that no jury selected or rejected an artist's work. More recently, exhibits were limited to two for each artist, but this limit did not obtain at the period when Munch, Jelka and Ida Gerhardi, among other of Delius's friends, were frequent exhibitors.

2 Munch's affair with Tulla Larsen had ended in 1902 in a quarrel that involved an accident with a pistol, causing the artist to lose part of a finger. Munch now developed an almost pathological fear of her. In seeking to evade her, he made his way to Grez, where he spent part of the spring of 1903 with Delius and Jelka. Writing from Leipzig to his aunt, Karen Bjølstad, on 27 February, he mentioned that he would be going to Paris shortly, but would be staying at Delius's and would 'keep myself hidden for understandable reasons'. (Inger Munch, ed. *Edvard Munchs Brev. Familien*, p. 174).

3 Buths was to conduct *Paris* in Düsseldorf on 12 February. Delius travelled first to Elberfeld by rail, spending part of the journey in the company of Isidore de Lara. He visited Hans Haym — hoping to encourage him to perform *Lebenstanz* in the autumn — and Hans Gregor, who as intendant of the Stadttheater in Elberfeld was to produce *Koanga* little more than a year later. He arrived in Düsseldorf on 9 February.

(145)
Déodat de Sévérac to Frederick Delius

[Paris, 7 March 1903]

Dear friend,

I have just sent off (registered post) your score.[1] So you will receive it at your home tomorrow — When are you coming? I should be very happy to shake you by the hand and to have a chat about all the things which interest us — Van Gogh and Gaugin etc!

> Yours
> Sévérac
> 17 rue Brey

Autograph *carte-lettre*, signed and undated, written in French. Addressed: Monsieur Delius / Compositeur de Musique / Grez sur Loing / *Seine et Marne*. Postmark: PARIS 7 –3 03.

The original is in the Delius Trust Archive. It is the only item of correspondence from de Sévérac to Delius that is preserved.

Déodat de Sévérac (1873–1921): French composer. Documentary evidence of his acquaintanceship with Delius has not been found elsewhere than in this one communication. He was, however, a close friend of Daniel de Monfreid and probably therefore occasionally moved in the Molard circle while studying in Paris at the Schola Cantorum.

1   I have been unable to determine the identity of this score.

(146)
Jelka Rosen to Auguste Rodin

> Grez sur Loing
> S. et M
> 12.3.1903

Mon cher Maître,

Yesterday I took my pictures to the "Indépendants" and intended to visit you, but I had to catch my train back and it was impossible. I have therefore to bore you a little in writing.

Monsieur Osthaus,[1] our Maecenas from Hagen will be in Paris in a few days. He then wishes me to take him to visit you and he wants to buy an important work from you. I should so much have liked to see you beforehand to tell you again to be well on your guard with him, and to do business in writing and before witnesses. For I should never forgive myself if he gave you the trouble he gave to Mlle Gerhardi and another friend, then me. He didn't buy my picture (the one he bought by verbal agreement in the autumn) and now he lets me know that if I help him to get a Rodin cheaply he will buy something from me.

You understand, cher maître that I would *never* stoop to this sort of business. I would a thousand times rather he bought nothing at all from me. He is *very* rich and he must pay you the prices you ask. Besides I am convinced that, anxious as he really is to possess a work of yours, he will not dare to treat you like us – unknown and petty women! He is very friendly with Doctor Linde[2] at Lubeck who has eleven of your works. Linde is coming to Paris too. Only I think Linde doesn't know of Monsieur Osthaus's little peculiarities in business matters. Everything that happened to us is also a little the fault of Mlle Gerhardi who made our sales amicably and with complete confidence in him. Young Munk, a very, very interesting Norwegian painter is here too. He is showing at the Indépendants. I send you a card for the Vernissage if this should interest you. As for me I have plucked up courage and sent my big picture, that erotic garden you saw.[3] I believe I have done as well as I can in it; but I have my misgivings. If it is badly lit it will have an atrocious effect; I should like you to see it, while trembling at the idea. I am working hard; but how this giving birth to a work of art is difficult and how eternally unfulfilled I am in my aspirations! Munk has encouraged me, like you. After all, for me the main thing is to be aware of my right to work.

I am overjoyed at the thought of seeing your works again – which express so powerfully what I feel confusedly. Oh dear great friend! What delight, this love of Beauty, of its artistic expression. This no-one could ever tear away from me!

Delius joins me in sending you our devoted and sympathetic wishes!

Yours
Jelka Rosen

The Osthauses will be in Paris about the 17th.

Autograph letter, signed and dated, written in French.

The original is in the Rodin Museum.

1   Karl-Ernst Osthaus (1874–1921): young patron of the arts. At this period he was director of the Folkwang Museum in Hagen, Germany. Jelka, together with Ida Gerhardi, was responsible for introducing him to Rodin, whom he finally met in Paris in April 1903 and from whom he was ultimately to purchase two bronzes and a marble.

2   Dr Max Linde: of Lübeck, an ardent admirer of Rodin's works. He had a lengthy correspondence with the sculptor and collected a considerable number of his statues. Linde was a discriminating collector. He was introduced to Munch in 1902 and became very friendly with the artist, who painted portraits of him and of members of his family.

3   Five works by Jelka are listed in the society's 1903 catalogue: *Un jardin*, *Etude*, *Printemps*, *Esquisse* and *Etude en pastel*. There seems little doubt that it was to the first of these that she referred in this letter (see also Letter 122).

(147)
Frederick Delius to Edvard Munch

Grez sur Loing
Seine & Marne
Monday [23 March, 1903]

Dear Munch —We left yesterday evening at 5 o'clock — Behrend[1] writes to tell me that you can sell some engravings to Dr Robin, a friend of mine & his brother-in-law & suggests that you take your engravings there. He lives at 53 B^d de Courcelles[2] He says that you must tell him the prices. Robin is a splendid fellow & tremendously intelligent. Behrend tells me that the prices of your pictures are much too high & that you will certainly not make much progress in Paris with such prices — I think you would be wiser to set your prices rather less high — For example — The Tree & the melancholy Woman 1000 frs. & the big picture 2500 — & the small pictures 4 & 500 frs[3]

Behrend loves your pictures & would like to help you. But he knows conditions in Paris from A to Z. & knows how things have to be done & how not — Farewell now — Frl Rosen sends her best wishes.

Your friend
Fr. Delius

Dr Robin
53 Boulevard de Courcelles
Mention my name & if Robin is not there ask for his wife —

Autograph letter, signed and undated, written in German.

The original is in the Munch Museum.

1   R. S. Berend: mutual friend of Delius and Munch, and an art connoisseur in Paris.

2   When Munch called at Robin's address soon afterwards, he was, to his chagrin, turned away by a secretary. On hearing of this, Berend wrote to apologize to the artist. He had asked Delius to tell Munch to *send* his engravings to Robin; no one had been expecting the artist to turn up in person. However, Berend was able to add, on a more cheerful note, 'I have learned with pleasure from Monsieur Delius that you have sold one of your pictures at the Indépendants' (undated letter from Berend to Munch in the Munch Museum).

3   For discussion of the identity of the various pictures mentioned in the Munch and Delius letters, see John Boulton Smith's edition of the correspondence.

(148)

Charles Russell & Co. to Frederick Delius

37, NORFOLK STREET, W.C.
LONDON. 1st May 1903.

Dear Sir,

Oscar Wilde deceased.
"Salome"

We write to inform you that we have not in any way forgotten your application, and your proposal is having the careful consideration of our Client's Agent and we expect to hear from him by the end of next week stating the terms on which he would advise our Client to enter into an agreement with you as to the musical rights of Salome.[1]

Our Client has not got a copy of Salome in English, but we think we could obtain one if the matter is proceeded with.

Yours faithfully
Charles Russell & Co

F. Delius Esq,
Grez sur Loing
Seine et Marne

Autograph letter, signed (but signature illegible) on behalf of Charles Russell & Co., dated, written in English on the company's headed notepaper.

The original is in the Delius Trust Archive. It is the only item of correspondence from this company to Delius that has been preserved.

1 An undated letter from Haym, who had recently read a review of Strauss's *Salome*, probably indicates why Delius's interest in the work was to prove abortive: 'What a pity that Strauss took the material away from you! Couldn't you do it nonetheless, and especially now?!'

(149)

Frederick Delius to Edvard Grieg

Grez sur Loing
Seine & Marne
[mid-June 1903]

Dear Grieg –

I have just heard that you have celebrated your 60th birthday.[1] It is such a long time that we have heard nothing from each other which is certainly my fault, but my wishes & greetings for this day are none the less heartfelt. I still think with pleasure of the lovely times we have had together & I hope that life will bring us together again — Unfortunately I was not in France during your stay in Paris otherwise I would have greeted you there. As for me I am quite well, I live in the country near Fontainebleau devoted entirely to my work & am slowly making progress. I have just come back from Basel where my Mitternachtslied from Zarathustra for baritone solo, men's chorus & orchestra was played at the German Tonkünstlerfest[2] — I even think that I have managed to get a publisher thereby!! I should be very glad to hear that you and your dear wife are really well — Once again heartiest greetings to you both —

Yours
Fritz Delius

Autograph letter, signed and undated, written in German.

The original is in the Bergen Public Library.

1   Grieg's birthday, on 15 June, had been celebrated in the style of a national feast. Among the guests visiting Troldhaugen that day had been the Norwegian prime minister and his wife, together with Bjørnstjerne and Karoline Bjørnson. A special train had been laid on from Bergen and festive tables placed outside for the 150 guests who could not be accommodated in the house itself.

2   The Swiss conductor Hermann Suter had given the *Mitternachtslied* at Basel on 12 June. Its performance originally had been recommended by Schillings, and a letter to Delius from the secretary of the Allgemeine Deutsche Musikverein, dated 12.5.03, reads: 'You will already have learned through Herr Rich. Strauss that your composition "Das trunkene Lied" has been put on the programme of the Musikfest at Basel.' (*Das trunkene Lied* was Delius's first title for the *Mitternachtslied Zarathustras*.)

(150)
Hans Haym to Frederick Delius

[Elberfeld, 19 June 1903]

Dear Delius, How did things go in Basel? Your card has just come & answered this question, so that I am able to congratulate you. Must nonetheless still just write to tell you that I am absolutely full of your Piano Concerto. It is really a marvellous, ravishing work! Why have you held it back from me for so long?! For two pins I would play it myself. I really don't need to go into raptures to you about its many beauties, its splendid thematic work etc. etc., but I have already written enthusiastically to Buths. Following his example I have more-over transcribed your Lebenstanz for 2 pianos.[1] He will be visiting me very soon, as we want to revel in it & in Paris and in the Piano Concerto. Please let me always share in everything new that you write!   Yours   H.

Autograph postcard, initialled and undated, written in German. Addressed: Herrn F. Delius / Grez sur Loing / *Frankreich* (Seine et Marne). Postmark: ELBERFELD 19.6.03.

The original is in the Delius Trust Archive.

1   This arrangement has not been traced.

(151)
Hans Haym to Frederick Delius

E[lberfeld]. 10 July 03

Dear Delius,

Many thanks for your kind letter. And a belated apology for my only having laid hands on a postcard to make a declaration of love to you. Without going into too many details under cover of this envelope, I should nonetheless like to tell you that the favourable impression left by your Piano Concerto has continued to hold firm, indeed through repeated playing has only been strengthened. Let us hope that Herr Petri[1] feels the same about it. If he is not merely a piano virtuoso but a real musician, he ought immediately to have a burning desire to awaken this concerto (which has not yet been played in public?) into resounding life. Before I sent it to London – with the help of my wife & after overcoming some postal difficulties – I was in Düsseldorf to get it from Buths. He had only just looked through it quickly and was not ready to join equally in my delight. I persuaded him however to come with me to the Conservatorium, where there are 2 grand pianos next to each other. We then played it together, he the piano part, I the score, & I had the satisfaction of seeing him too set on fire. We consider that you still betray your descent from Grieg quite noticeably in the concerto, although only in occasional turns of harmony. The main thing is that out of the whole speaks an original spirit. Everyone must come from somewhere, after all, but whereas most people keep within the confines of well-worn paths, you are a pathfinder and to be allowed to follow you – thanks to our prophetic little lady friend[2] – is an experience which gives me great joy.

After the discovery of those two pianos in Düsseldorf I telephoned my wife to ask her to send me through our servant Josef the piano manuscripts of Paris & Lebenstanz. Instead of Josef, Franz & Peter[3] came as messengers & we then played both our arrangements in the afternoon. This coming Sunday we intend to do it again at my home. I have invited along Strunck,[4] Neitzel[5] & Steinbach[6] (the High Priest of Brahms!), but have not yet received replies. Buths will be writing to you to say that he wants to perform the Lebenstanz. I am afraid that I shall have to forego it for the time being, we have no money. Hope Petri will take the bait of the concerto. – Your invitation to Grez is tempting indeed. We would both very much like to come. Once again the wretched question of money comes up & I am very much afraid that I must forego this too & stay at home altogether this year. – Can't you send the American Symphony?[7] Please! And best wishes to all three of you from

Yours
Haym

Autograph letter, signed and dated, written in German.

The original is in the Delius Trust Archive.

1   Egon Petri (1881–1962): German pianist. He studied with Carreño, Buchmayer and Busoni. His interest in Delius's work seems on this occasion not to have been awakened: 'A pity that Petri doesn't want to play the concerto,' wrote Haym on 15 September, at the same time reminding Delius that Buths might, however, one day play it.

2   Ida Gerhardi.

3   Two of Haym's sons, both of whom were to die on active service in France in 1918.

4   I have been unable clearly to decipher this name from Haym's script.

5   Otto Neitzel (1852–1920): German pianist, teacher and critic. Writing to Delius on 15 September 1903, on the notepaper of the *Kölnische Zeitung*, he mentioned that he would be 'glad to take on the translation' (perhaps of *Koanga*) for a reduced fee.

6   Fritz Steinbach (1855–1916): German conductor and composer. At this period he was director of the Cologne Conservatorium. He was celebrated for his interpretations of Brahms.

7   *Appalachia.* Not a symphony but a set of orchestral variations. Delius frequently referred to his larger orchestral works as 'symphonies'.

(152)
Julius Buths to Frederick Delius

Düsseldorf 19th July 1903.

Dear Herr Delius,

I still have to thank you very much for your kind letter and friendly invitation to come to Grez. I would certainly be glad to come if I did not have some dutiful scruples. My Musical Director-nerves need thorough relaxation in pure, ozone-full air, and my paternal duties require me to be in Freiburg i.B. at the beginning of September, when my second little daughter is being confirmed. I have only four weeks' leave of absence and to make two long journeys within this period is hardly feasible. If we did come to Grez we would naturally not want to miss seeing Paris, and there would be another duty for me there, in that I should very much like to get to know Frau Jaell-Trautmann,[1] who has written a wonderful analysis of a piano-method.

You see what an agonizing job it is to know what to do.

If you write and tell me once more that it might be "baking" hot in Grez, then I shall finally decide to come after all, if Dr Haym comes with me. It would in that case have to be between the 10th & 24th August or between the 7th & 14th September.

Dr Haym will already have written to tell you how much he & I have been occupied with you recently. Last Friday we played your two works "Paris" and "Lebenstanz" to Strauss in Cologne. The impression made on Strauss was definitely in your favour. Henceforth you will certainly have an advocate in him for the future Tonkünstlerversammlungen. He urgently advises you, as I have also told you before, to get both scores copied legibly, on staves set closer together, each time indicating the instruments at the side of the staves, so that anyone looking at them for the first time can find his way more quickly through your script and arrangement. Time is money[2] too for the musicians who read through novelties, and such apparent superficialities as these make the introduction of a work so much more easy. You should send in both your scores to the Tonkünstlerverein. Since, as you told me, Schillings too has shown himself to be well disposed towards you, you will certainly pull it off.

I hope Haym has not yet given away to you the fact that I intend to perform your "Lebenstanz" on the 14/15 January, but that is the case, and I hope it pleases you. If on top of that your Piano Concerto is played in Elberfeld on the 17th Jan. then that would be really wonderful.

Are there already orchestra parts for the "Lebenstanz", if not, I shall start having them written out for us straight away.

So much for today. Best wishes from me and mine, and kindest regards to the ladies Rosen and Gerhardi.

Yours most sincerely
Buths.

Autograph letter, signed and dated, written in German.

The original is in the Delius Trust Archive. It is the seventh of twenty-one letters and postcards written by Buths to the Deliuses between 1903 and 1907 that are preserved in the Archive.

1   Marie Jaell-Trautmann (1846–1925): Alsace-born pianist and composer.

2   The words *time* and *money* are in English in the original letter.

(153)
Julius Buths to Frederick Delius

Düsseldorf 26th July
1903

Dear Herr Delius,

After your letter, which was so extraordinarily kind and friendly, I really feel under an obligation to come and stay with you, but on more sober consideration I feel I must deny myself this pleasure. The time is too short for me to manage a stay both on the Seine and in the Black Forest, and I feel my brain really does need to relax into general affairs. I feel I must avoid any intensive stimulation for the time being; there are some psychological reasons as well which make it impossible for me to absorb important, new impressions at the present, and which indicate to me that I would not be, even to you, what I should like to be, nor could I offer to you what I should like to be able to offer. I have a kind of feeling that once we were together for any length of time there would be so much to go over between us, between the man who has such exceptional confidence in his artistic instinct and in his initiative, and the man who although, thank God, he has not yet lost his artistic instinct, nevertheless has not found a way to get it to prevail over his theoretical conscience. So it is in the end no wonder if the creative vein in me ran dry, nonetheless with every work of genius which I meet I always feel that I am powerfully attracted as by a magnet and yet that I have to be able to justify, in my own eyes, the love which it kindles in me, in that I have to be able to recognize that which is legitimate in the new creation as an enrichment of legitimacy in art as a whole. I have not yet got to know you fully, that is proved above all else by your new work. It is undoubtedly the most significant and most original work you have written to date, but at the same time it opens up all the more acutely the whole question of your approach to music. If your works up till now have still been in a certain sense programme music, great mood-depictions, impressionistic in the sense that a mood, however it may have originated, has been set to music in terms of motifs, – still, in your new work the impressionistic element is really only secondary, only a formal device; it is the deep, emotional, genuine expression of a melody already completely formed, (in other words not mere melodic flourishes or "never-ending" melody) which binds you under its spell, and which you, with all the means by which you feel, think, create, fully savour, and present your music, wish to refashion in your own way. This is the salient point of difference between a programme music which is the depiction of mood in sound, and absolute music, which it is really only possible to define in terms of music itself, but which in any case is something deeper than what we label as mood. Mood is really only the musical sub-stratum, whilst the expression of music, of real music, is at one and the same time both personal and typical. The real melody, the real motif or theme, call it what you will, has in it this element which is both personal and typical, it is something both created and creative at the same time, something individual and yet universal in music at the same time, it is both nature and precept in a single unit, and something of such generative power that it has taken the intellectual activity of centuries for that which is legitimate in our art to evolve from its simple beginnings and to keep on evolving. This sense of legitimacy is an intrinsic part of art itself, it is artistic consciousness, if I may express it thus. It is our duty to attain to this consciousness; the acquisition of this consciousness is what I call education, whether it be self-education or that acquired under the guidance of another. To come to a halt in one's education is naturally just as wrong as to fight shy of education altogether. But I must go back again. I called the sense of legitimacy in art consciousness, or vice versa, consciousness the standard of legitimacy in art. As Schopenhauer would have put it: the artistic intellect as opposed to the creative instinct or artistic will, and just as in man intellect and will are bound up together, so nature and precept form a unity in art. The intellect which has already been projected a thousand times by the will into production of a work of art can, however, be recovered by our own intellect and turned to good account as an intensifying factor in ourselves. In art in the way in which we first accept it as a precept, turn it to good account as a precept and then dispense with it again when we recognize that it no longer has any legitimate force.

And now, finally, the application of all this to your approach to music. Your new work demonstrates to me that for you everything in the world which you have seen and experienced with emotion is capable of becoming music, that the world surrounds you in terms of "sound" and that these sounds you carry in your very being. You "hear away into distances" which others have not yet heard; I might say you lay bare every sinew of sound to our astonished ear. As the air surrounds a physical body so your sound surrounds your themes. In that sense I say you are endowed with a natural impressionism. "Paris" and "Lebenstanz" are elaborations of moods in accordance with the expressive import of each.[1] In "Apalachia" there is in addition a new impetus, not so much in the psychic and sound element in the music as in the formal — and contrapuntal nature of it. I should like to call this the intellectual side of music, and it follows from this designation, as I have already said above, that I find the intensification of the mode of expression all the greater an advance. It also follows that the internal sense of what is legitimate should appear all the more clearly. Instinct guides us, leads us, carries us away, inspires us, intellect must convince us.

All this I am writing down more for my sake, (and so I ask your forgiveness) in order to become clearer in my mind about a puzzling effect of your work. You see, when I went through your work for the first time, I was overwhelmed by the "fullness of the vision". On a second examination I was no longer impressed on the same level, I lost the sense of the necessity of many turns of expression, the detail was beyond me and I could not consider that the structure of the piece was sufficiently regular. In parts I find the piece quite outstanding, as outstanding as anything anywhere in music, but this absolute non-acknowledgement of rules and laws –

But I will not tire you, dear Herr Delius, and only ask you to have forbearance with me, if on your part you assume that I am still too much behind the times in my views on art, because I always end up talking about rules and laws, but I also ask you to believe that all I have said to you really comes from my respect for your outstanding creative talent.

I shall of course continue to work on your piece and make it my own. Only for the moment I must call a halt, and just relax. Dʳ Haym also thinks that we should call off the idea of Paris in midsummer. Our plan is to follow up your kind invitation to Grez about Easter next year.

I shall still be here for the next fortnight; if you can send the "Lebenstanz" parts direct, I can look and see whether they will do, or whether we ought to get a copy made for ourselves.

In cordial friendship

Yours
Buths.

Autograph letter, signed and dated, written in German.

The original is in the Delius Trust Archive.

1   The correspondence shows that Buths and Haym had been much occupied with these two works. Buths confirmed to Delius on 24 June that he had completed his own arrangement of *Paris*, and that Haym was well under way with *Lebenstanz*.

(154)
Edvard Grieg to Frederick Delius

Troldhaugen near Bergen
1/9/03

Dear Delius,

Many thanks for your birthday greetings to the 60-year old! It is true that these thanks come late. But I am afraid that I have only too good an excuse. Since the end of June I have been seriously ill and am not really allowed to write letters yet. The festival (a whole week) with concerts and banquets was beyond my strength. I was allright¹ as long as the business lasted, but afterwards came the reaction. You would however have loved the festival. The concerts were a tremendous success under Halvorsen² and his National Theatre orchestra. And Björnson's speech was something special.

And now, dear Delius, how are you? I missed you *very* much during my stay in Paris. I am very pleased to learn from your letter that you are in a position to work completely peacefully on your own. I hope you have been cultivating your patience assiduously. For an operatic composer must have 50 times more of it than any other musician. He must, too, be an optimist by nature, or else he will worry himself to death or at least make himself ill. Congratulations on Basel! Do send me the piece when it comes out. What a pity it is from "Zarathustra". I have to think of Strauss, and I have no stomach for Strauss! That is to say, I am a great admirer of "Tod und Verklärung". But afterwards he just becomes insolent and beauty, I mean inventiveness, fantasy, bears no relationship at all to insolence. But of course, German musicians must always have a German beast on the pedestal, which they can worship. Wagner is dead. They must have something to satisfy their national pride. Better then a substitute than nothing at all. It is really too funny for words.

Now, please write again soon. For there will be no further opportunity on the 70th birthday!

Kindest regards, also from my wife.

Yours
Edvard Grieg

Autograph letter, signed and dated, written in German.

The original is in the Delius Trust Archive.

1   In English in the original letter.

2   Halvorsen was now conductor of the National Theatre's orchestra. This had succeeded the orchestra of the old Christiania Theatre, whose doors were closed in 1899 and whose company had transferred to the newly founded National Theatre.

(155)
Jelka Rosen to Auguste Rodin

Grez sur Loing
S. et M
14.9.1903

Cher maître

It is a long time since I last saw you and I meant to come to see you the other day in Paris, but didn't have the time. I wanted to tell you that I passed through Calais and stopped to have a look at your superb Bourgeois there. I cannot describe to you the immense impression that this work made on me. I had one of those rare and sublime moments when one is completely imbued with the beauty of a work of art and I thank you for this!

I spent a few weeks in Holland mostly by the sea; this beautiful monster always attracts me; I was with my friend Delius; and now we are to be married on the 23rd of this month. I am a little apprehensive of this ceremony at the mairie at Grez; but no doubt one must learn to be ridiculous with grace![1]

My friend, Mlle Gerhardi has spent part of the summer here with us – she is now in Paris where she has work to do and she is sure to come to see you.

I should love to see you again, cher maître and learn what you are doing and how you are. We shall have a little pied-à-terre in Paris for the coming winter, so I hope to be in town a little more often.

Delius sends you his best regards

Your devoted
Jelka Rosen

Autograph letter, signed and dated, written in French.

The original is in the Rodin Museum.

1   Rodin sent a congratulatory (undated) note on the marriage: 'It is the ancient custom and there must be a consecration of your union

'I congratulate Monsieur Délius and beg him to accept my kindest regards.'

Meanwhile, Ida had written, from 12, rue de la Grande Chaumière in Paris, to her sister Lilli on 21 August: 'she has earned it for everything she does for Delius & I hope Delius will remain as peaceful & calm as he is now; he was very kind & affectionate with Jelka & that was her best consolation during this time [Jelka had been suffering with eye trouble] & by marrying, her home now really is a home at last, as she is completely separated from her family' (Gerhardi/Steinweg collection).

(156)
Frederick Delius to Edvard Grieg

Grez sur Loing
Seine & Marne
28 Sept 1903

Dear Grieg –

It was really a pleasure to me to receive your kind letter & to hear something in more detail about you again – On the 25th[1] I married my friend Jelka Rosen here in Grez. (Civilement of course) have got even further away from God & Jesus. We lived together for 6 years, but we found it really more practical to legalise our relationship – One gets everything cheaper & one receives free &

without further ado a certificate of honesty & good manners — If you go to
Germany next winter let me know for I have several performances & I should
very much like to introduce my wife to you & Frau Grieg — She is a painter &
very gifted — & then I should so much like you to hear my music — You only
know my very first attempts — Unfortunately I can't send you anything either
for I have not yet found a publisher although I must say that I haven't tried very
much either[2] & am writing orchestral music exclusively. Every year I have 3 or
4 performances in Germany — Buths in Düsseldorf & Dr Haym in Elberfeld
give my latest scores every year — Buths has arranged "Paris" The song of a
great city — a symphonic work of mine for two pianos & Dr Haym has done the
same for "Lebenstanz". I shall try to send you these arrangements if I get the
chance. I don't need to tell you that *my* Mitternachtslied has absolutely no
relationship with the Strauss Zarathustra, which I consider a complete failure:
Yet I find that "Till Eulenspiegel" & Heldenleben especially are splendid works.
Tod & Verklärung I find not so significant although there is much that is
beautiful in it. There is still too much Liszt & *Berlioz* about it — I think he will
do his best work in humorous things. His tragedy is "Dick & Deutsch". Do
write to me about your winter plans so that we can perhaps see each other again
this winter & spend a few splendid days together & experience old & new moods
— I send you & your dear wife my very best wishes & remain

    affectionately as ever
    Yours
    Frederick Delius
    (new name!)

Autograph letter, signed and dated, written in German.

The original is in the Bergen Public Library.

1   The original marriage certificate clearly has 23 September.

2   Not quite true, as Delius had been in touch with a good many publishers over the
years, most recently with Aibl in Munich and with Breitkopf & Härtel in Leipzig. The
latter firm, at least, had not turned him down completely, but had informed him that
for the present they had too much on their hands to devote much time to new works.

(157)
William Shaw to Frederick Delius

DELIUS & CO.

Bradford 28 Sept 1903

Dear Mr Fritz,

I received yours of the 23rd. & have been unable to reply until now. The scheme
of floating the business as a limited Co. has been abandoned & the people have

bought the business from us as a going concern for £2000 stg goodwill, *paying off everything and everybody*. To-day we are all out of work and have to interview the new proprietors in turn to see whom they will employ I am afraid that some of us will be left out in the cold as their intention is to reduce the staff and supply the management from amongst themselves. Your Ma has written to me to send you £25 stg as a wedding present and I hope to send you the money in a post or two. For the present we are barred from withdrawing from the bank or handling monies. We had been trying for months to find a purchaser, but no one would listen to giving a penny for goodwill. As you will see someday nearly all the splendid profits made since your father died have had to be written off for bad debts, contracted in his time or since.

The business will be continued as Delius & Co — , without any public notice. Your Ma's money will be paid out as they will not have any partner.

I shall be pleased to give you any further information. I tender you my sincere good wishes to you and yours and trust you may both live a long and happy life

I remain.

Yours truly
W. Shaw

You can write to me % of Delius & Co as I am privledged to stand by the books and accounts to see that the Trustees interests do not suffer.

Autograph letter, signed and dated, written in English on headed notepaper.

The original is in the Delius Trust Archive. It is the fifth of six letters written by Shaw to Delius between 1891 and 1903 that have been preserved. One further (and incomplete) letter from Shaw, dated Oct 16th 1903, begins 'Mrs Delius', and is also preserved in the Archive.

William Shaw: secretary of the Delius family business at Bradford (see Letter 116). The collapse of the firm and Delius's almost simultaneous marriage to Jelka may be seen as an ironic twist to the composer's fortunes. The hope of any further support from the family had evaporated, and for a time Jelka was clearly to be his financial mainstay.

(158)
Frederick and Jelka Delius to Edvard Munch

[Paris, 3 October 1903]

Dear Munch. How are you? & when are you coming here again? I have just rented a studio at Avenue d'Orleans 110 & shall be in Paris rather more often this winter. Frl R & I have just legalized our relationship as we consider it more practical — We have been in Holland but the weather was awful — Do let us hear from you & fare well

Yours
Fr. D.

Grez sur Loing
S & M.

1000 greetings & good wishes for your beautiful art
Jelka Delius

Autograph postcard, signed and undated, written in German. Addressed to Munch at Aasgaardstrand, readdressed to Lübeck and again readdressed to Berlin. Postmark: PARIS 3 -10 03.

The original is in the Munch Museum.

(159)
Edvard Grieg to Frederick Delius

Kristiania 23/10/03
Hotel Westminster.

Dear Delius,

Many years ago I got to know and became very fond of a certain *Fritz* Delius. Whether that will be the same with *Frederick* Delius, I really don't know. Where did "der alte Fritz" go wrong then? Both my wife and I ask: Are we never again to see the selfsame man? We had got to like him very much.

Well now, my dear friend, we are of course looking forward very much to making the acquaintance of the newly-wed Mr. Frederick. Likewise his esteemed wife. Our heartiest congratulations and best wishes to you both! You know me well enough to realize that preachers viewed as a tribe are anathema to me. A marriage without preachers has something much more idealistic about it than a church marriage. But as you say: It is cheaper! (Very good!) And for the masses, more moral! (Just as good!)

You have now reached the zenith of your life, I mean that point in life when the artist does his best work. I should love to have the opportunity to become aquainted with the present products of your muse. Well, we shall be coming to Germany again one day. Perhaps even next year. Unfortunately my uncertain state of health does not allow me a longer stay in damp and unhealthy Leipzig. You see, I have arrived at that stage in life when I could no more write "A Dance of Life". Rather "Weariness of Life", also a subject for a symphonic poem! And herewith enough for today. We are staying here for the time being and spending Christmas with the Björnsons at Aulestad. The old man is splendid! Strength and gentleness in one!

Our heartiest greetings, also to your wife!

Yours
Edvard Grieg.

Autograph letter, signed and dated, written in German.

The original is in the Delius Trust Archive.

(160)
Halfdan Jebe to Frederick Delius

Colombo November 1903.

Dear Delius,

It is already some time since I received your kind letter, and I want you to know that only rarely in my life have I been so happy over a letter. Well, to understand this you would have had to have experienced what it is to smell land again after an eternal voyage. I do not intend to write a long letter to you today, it is not comfortable enough here to handle pen and ink, my revolver fits my hand much better, and I only wish I could use it freely and that I could send you a couple of tasty human hams – damned rabble! – I bet you would eat it with relish even if it were as hard as wood. – But, the long adventure story which I have now finished, not on paper but with bleeding footsteps across the world, through still-untouched pits of Bohemian living conditions, this wonderful adventure I bring home alive, – not for the children and not for the grown-ups, only for the few who could never get tired of the game. I have travelled very far, much further than China and Japan. I have simply gone out into the world; I have carried an idea to its logical conclusion, I have brought a life to an end, I have died, finished with it – this is the transmigration of the soul. You ask me to tell you something, and I should very much like to, but where to begin and – the time when I made interesting journeys and sought beautiful experiences is long since past, I have tried much harder to avoid seeing the damned sights and to get away from them, to soar away freely through the atmosphere, as it were. Alas, how often have I fallen to the ground again with broken wings.

I was in Ceylon for over a month, came here from Calcutta on an Austrian ship where I had stowed away – it costs nothing and is very exciting.

I have been alone, quite alone, for a long time now, for three, four months, and obviously this is the only good way of going to foreign countries and people.

In order to live I give a concert now and then, gave two here in Colombo and one at Kandy – the papers write that I am the first violinist who has ever come here, compare me with Sarasate and Madame Neruda, etc. but in spite of this my concerts don't bring in any more than is necessary for living. The people here are extraordinarily poor, here in one of the richest countries in the world. On the other hand one needs very little to live if one is not extravagant. I live among the natives, eat curry and rice twice a day and am very healthy. In all countries I have lived among the natives. These (in Ceylon) have become utterly English, and therefore unbearable. What's worse than the English? (Rotten, rotten, by Jove !)[1] You say I should have written you a letter from China instead of from parvenu-Japan. Quite right. But you see, he who understands China does not write any letters from there. No words can describe China. I went to Canton, the town many millenniums old, and it is from there that I have my most beautiful impressions even though I know Shanghai much better. Few Europeans were in Canton, and those who were there saw little out of fear. Well, I admit my life was threatened violently, but of course that can happen elsewhere as well and is therefore not worth the telling. What is of worth is a glimpse into and for a few days getting into the spirit of one of the most glittering cities in China, where nothing, absolutely nothing foreign has yet penetrated. I spent a month in Shanghai, not too much for this city of pleasure, where the marvellous tea gardens and opium houses are to a certain extent open to Europeans. I shall tell you about it later. You ask if people in these countries are just as moral as in Europe. My dear friend, here, or in India the women are burned alive with their dead husbands, and, I give the word to one of my acquaintances, a very "well educated and intelligent" man:

Morals in India are therefore higher than in any other country in the world.

In Japan only can you buy young girls very cheaply. But what the devil do you want with young girls. Give me refined old whores. I don't mean fucked out old cows, but faded roses with delicate perfumes. These are not to be found in particular nations or societies, but grow singly and hide themselves away because only so few have any notion of their wonderful beauty. As for the Japanese they have many fine traits. I lived out in the country with them, where they are genuine and unspoiled. I wore Japanese clothing, spoke Japanese and joined in their simple idyllic life, and I became fond of them. But nothing in the world (while we are talking about women) can be compared with that willowy little peppered creature called a Kongai, the Annam woman, as a young girl she is by nature already so spicy that she can be enjoyed without disgust, even if she is only in bud.

Yes, in this land of "Annam" I stayed for eight months, this land, where there is nothing to see, but whose subtleties cannot be described, gliding past as they do so wonderfully softly and still so piquant, this land I have learned to love.

Yes, I have been a bit everywhere, in the Dutch countries too, but not as far as Java.

Over a year away from Europe, I must go back soon, it is glorious here, in Ceylon, but I am longing for home now. I should like to spend a couple of years quietly at home, and some time later perhaps you will come with me to visit a few beautiful places, and to lead for a year a life just as idyllic, just as ideal as your peaceful life at Grez. More about this later, I know you are going to want, when I tell you about it all some time or other, you are going to want to trot around the globe a little, even if not so far as the Pacific islands. Believe me, Annam is the only country in the world where you would feel completely at home. But I must not write more about this, or I may be likely to take the wrong steamer. But I must be off to Europe now, perhaps I shall stop in Egypt for a few days to get used to the cold, and perhaps I'll travel via Paris and shall see you. Yes, it will be strange to be in Paris again, and meet those good old Bohemians. Oh! what a life-lie – I have carried bohemianism to its logical conclusion, to super-bohemianism (in your parlance) We humans need a belief, – whether the initiator is called Buddha or Darwin is of no consequence – to carry an idea to the end, until death, is in any case a great moral victory, the only road to a rebirth in a higher form. –

I went twice to Kandy, the old city of the Singhalese kings. It is very small and very beautiful, the surroundings are wonderful, the little lake with the Buddhist temple very stylish, he who knows the temples of China and Japan will have a feeling similar to those who come from the most splendid European cathedrals to the modest churches in Jerusalem.

Well, fare *well*, dear friend, many thanks for writing to me, for so long, so long I had heard from nobody, it was as if I would find them all dead – how beautiful, how fantastically multi-coloured Europe looks from a distance –

Till we meet again

Yours
Halfdan Jebe.

Autograph letter, signed and dated 'November 1903', written in German.

The original is in the Delius Trust Archive. A total of twelve letters written by Jebe to Delius, dating from c. 1898 to 1905, are preserved in the Archive.

None of Delius's side of the correspondence with Halfdan Jebe has been found, and in the light of Dr John Bergsagel's recent intensive researches into Jebe's life and work, it may be assumed that such correspondence has long been lost. The probability is that Jebe, ever on the move, rarely kept his incoming correspondence. At all events, the series of letters that he wrote to Delius bears witness to the warm friendship between the two men, and indeed to its Rabelaisian overtones. Some years later, Delius was to write to Adey Brunel: 'Jebe is the only man I have loved in all my life', and Dr Bergsagel writes in fresher perspective: 'I do hope it may yet be possible to bring poor Jebe in out of the cold . . . perhaps with emphasis on the musician, the man Delius loved, rather than the dissolute companion in vice. . . . is it not more likely that Delius, the older man, the greater artist, the stronger personality, "rich" and aristocratic, was the one who exerted influence on the footloose lad — presumably in his early 20's when they met?' (letter to the author, 29 January 1979).

1   In English in the original letter.

(161)
Edvard Munch to Frederick Delius
[Draft]

Lützowstr 82 [Berlin]
[December? 1903]

Dear Delius,

I still have my studio in Paris — Can you do anything — or advise me how I should make the best use of my things — An exhibition at Bing's perhaps? — I shall probably come to Paris in February — Perhaps something could be done in the meantime —

Do you know of a big place where I could exhibit my frieze[1] — ? Perhaps it could be arranged through Lugné Poé[2] in a theatre — I have large exhibitions here in Berlin and Vienna — and am working hard in my studio — But it's not practicable to have two studios —

So you are tied up and I am still a free journeyman

But I always have feelings towards the enemy — Woman I think you know Eva Mudocci[3] and B. Edvards — They are here — Fraulein Mudocci is wonderfully beautiful and I almost fear I have taken a fancy (one of thousands) to her — What do you think? After the last affair with T I am madly apprehensive — Write to me but don't send me "the white cat"[4] again At any rate don't tell me anything about it

Best wishes to you and your wife

Are you coming to Berlin and when?

Autograph draft letter, unsigned and undated, written in German. It was never sent, and is obviously a first draft of Letter 162.

The original is in the Munch Museum.

1   Munch's *Frieze of Life* series of paintings occupied him for many years.

2   Aurélien Marie Lugné-Poe (1870–1940): French actor-manager and founder of the celebrated Théâtre de l'Oeuvre.

3   Eva Mudocci (1883–1952): English violinist, born Evangeline Muddock. She met Munch in Paris in March 1903, and their relationship lasted for several years. She is

depicted in three well-known lithographs by Munch: *Madonna*, *Salome* and *The Violin Concert*, where she is shown with her regular pianist partner, Bella Edwards.

4   The reference is obscure. John Boulton Smith thinks that it may be to Tulla Larsen, rather than to Judith Ericson Molard, as has hitherto been thought.

(162)
Edvard Munch to Frederick Delius

[Hamburg, December 1903]

Dear Delius,

I should like to exhibit my large frieze in Paris (a part of it was already exhibited at L'independants 7 years ago) –
    Do you know of a place? I had thought of getting one through Lugné Poe – Perhaps in his theatre? Could you speak to him – and how would you advise me on making accessible to the public – or selling – the pictures which are left in my studio at Boulevard Arago 65 –
    I shall exhibit some of them at L'independants in any case – But what do you think? Otherwise – Perhaps L'Art Nouveau – I have had two big exhibitions here with the Secession and at Cassirers[1] – with artistic success –
    I am going to Weimar in January to paint Count Kessler Perhaps will go on from there to Paris –
    The Vienna Secession is now arranging an exhibition of my collected paintings – So all is going well in Germany – but I should like to do something in Paris –
    How are you and your wife? I am looking forward to seeing both of you and your lovely house again – I am in Hamburg now and am going to Lübeck –
    Best wishes to you and your wife

Yours   E Munch

Temporary address
    Dr. Max Linde
    Lübeck
The frieze needs a lot of space

Autograph letter, signed and undated, written in German.

The original is in the Delius Trust Archive.

1   The Paul and Bruno Cassirer Galleries were on the Unter den Linden in Berlin. Paul was cousin and Bruno brother of Delius's friend the conductor Fritz Cassirer (see

Letter 167). At the beginning of 1904 the Cassirers obtained sole rights to the sale of Munch's graphics in Germany.

(163)
Frederick Delius to Edvard Munch

Grez sur Loing
Seine & Marne
31 Jan 1903
[i.e. 31 December 1903]

Dear friend –

I have just received your letter & am very glad that things are going so well for you in Germany – I would advise you firstly to exhibit some (5–6) of your best pictures at the *"Independants"*. I will then try to send as many people there as possible *Afterwards* to exhibit your frieze (in May-June) perhaps at Georges Petit's – L'art Nouveau is no good for you – You must send me the dimensions as quickly as possible & then I can look around in Paris for a suitable place – Nouveau Theatre is no good either. It is rather dark & Lugné Poë will (if I know him well) not do anything for art. I am going to Paris in the middle of January &, as soon as I have the measurements of your frieze, will make careful enquiries – I have a concert in Düsseldorf on the 21ˢᵗ January.[1] Perhaps, on your way to Paris you could pick me up & we could then travel back together. In any case send the measurements at once –

Farewell. My wife & I send our heartiest New Year wishes & greetings –

Yours
Fr Delius

P.S
Karsten[2] decamped from here *in the night* without paying of course –

Autograph letter, signed and dated, written in German. Delius mistakenly wrote 'January' for December.

The original is in the Munch Museum.

1 *Lebenstanz* was to be given in Düsseldorf by Buths, who wrote to Delius on 13 December: 'I am looking forward to the German premiere of this piece.' Among other things, he told Delius that he was busy translating the text of Elgar's *Apostles*.

2 Ludvig Karsten (1876–1926): Norwegian painter. He studied under Carrière in Paris in 1901 and was often to return to that city. He was influenced technically by Munch, and his relationship with the older painter was characterized by mutual distrust; they were to come to blows after a violent quarrel in Aasgaardstrand in little

more than a year's time. The event is recalled in a number of Munch's subsequent
pictures.

An ironic postscript to the episode in Karsten's generally garrulous life mentioned
in this letter is furnished by a letter he wrote to Munch from Paris shortly afterwards.
He offered to send Munch's pictures to the Indépendants for him (the exhibition was to
open a month later), but asked Munch for the fee in advance, as he had barely enough
to manage on. He added, 'Do you know moreover that Delius has got married to Melle
Rosen!' (original in the Munch Museum).

1904

In mid-January Delius left Grez for a stay of some three months in Germany. Buths gave the first performance of *Lebenstanz* on 21 January in Düsseldorf, and a performance of *Paris* followed on 12 February. More important, one of Delius's operas was at last to be staged. This was *Koanga*, in three performances, the first on 30 March, conducted at Elberfeld by Fritz Cassirer. The work of revision, adaptation and rehearsal occupied the Deliuses there for several weeks beforehand. Widely reported and reviewed in Germany, the three works now earned Delius on the one hand ardent admirers and on the other critics who were to be persistent in their rejection of his music over the years. After Delius had returned to Grez, the first significant sign of a renewed interest in his work in England came in the form of a letter from Henry Wood, who enquired after *Lebenstanz*. The major new compositional project was *A Mass of Life*, at least one of whose movements, a self-contained 'Dance Song', was completed by May and soon in the hands of Buths and Haym. Haym, in the meantime, had shown that he was prepared to risk his reputation by programming several of Delius's larger works for his autumn season.

An August and September holiday was spent, in part at least with Cassirer, in Brittany. It was about this time that together with Cassirer Delius selected the Nietzsche texts for the larger part of the *Mass* and sketched out the grand design of the piece.

The Elberfeld concerts in October were another step forward. *Appalachia* was given its first performance by Haym on 15 October; and the second concert on 24 October took the form of a 'Delius-Abend' consisting of *Paris*, *Lebenstanz* and the Piano Concerto. The latter was also a first performance, with Buths as soloist and Haym conducting. Returning to Grez, Delius settled down to work once more. The centrepiece, above all other works, of his compositional endeavour was now the *Mass of Life*.

Sea Drift (RT II/3). Completed this year?

A Mass of Life, for soloists, mixed double chorus and large orchestra (Nietzsche) (RT II/ 4). Begun (one 'Dance Song' completed by May).

(164)
Edvard Munch to Frederick Delius

[Lübeck, early January 1904]

Dear friend,

My frieze should really have a space of 14 × 14^m – could however be reduced if necessary –

Would it not be possible to have an exhibition at Duran Ruel's?[1] (But not the frieze) My work would show to great advantage there –

At L'Independants the people gave me such a bad hanging position before and if they do it this time too it will be unpleasant –

When you come to Paris what is your address? I won't be arriving in Paris until February as I have to paint Count Kessler in Weimar –

It is very unpleasant having these Norwegians going around and running up debts – They harm others who have less money but cannot live in this way –

Gunnar Heiberg will probably completely ruin my old hotel in the rue de Seine –

Best wishes to you and your wife –

Yours   Edv. Munch

Temporary addr.
    Dr Max Linde
    Lubeck

Autograph letter, signed and undated, written in German on the headed notepaper of the Hansa Café, Lübeck.

The original is in the Delius Trust Archive.

1   Properly Durand Ruel, a well-known Paris gallery.

(165)
Jelka Delius to Auguste Rodin

Elberfeld 27.2.1904
Hotel Bristol

Cher maître,

I have been meaning to write to you for a long, long time, but an enormous amount of work has prevented me from doing so. First of all please accept my best wishes for the 10 months of this year which are left to us! And may these ten months be filled with every joy for you.

I must tell you that we have been here since January because they are presenting an opera by my husband, the libretto of which I have translated from the English.[1] The production here has given rise to so many difficulties that we have had to adapt parts of the libretto. – My husband does not know German well enough, so it was mostly I who had to do this. The whole thing being awfully urgent we really worked day and night. But now everything is well under way; the singers and the conductor, somewhat recalcitrant at first are now growing more and more enthusiastic about it. The music of Delius is not the sort that one can like superficially – it is rather like your sculpture – one either finds it abominable, or one loves it with one's whole being. I want you to know that here in this dismal town, full of black smoke, modern industry, machines, rich and very ugly people – here I love your works better than anywhere. I should love always to talk about them to these people who do not recognize Beauty, who look for it in ugly painted and sculpted confections.

When we last visited you we saw the two creatures who love each other so passionately, "The Sparrow-hawk and the Dove"[2] you call them, I believe. I cannot forget them and what joy to see them always – I should so much love to possess them and since you had the extreme kindness to promise me a bronze, I dare to ask for this group.

I fear that you are shaking your head – and that you are thinking that I am forward indeed. But, Dear one, I know it but I swear to you that I love it *so much, so much*, that in this lies my excuse. We lead a unique life, in that we only receive in our home people who are capable of understanding a thing of artistic beauty who will see nothing wrong in a very erotic work. And if this work were in my home, it would give the most exquisite joy to my friends, to many people who now never have the opportunity to see such a thing. And I would be your prophet, I would make them understand and admire the beauty of life, of creation in this sublime group. The more I walk through life the more I see that the people who understand love as an expression, the finest expression of Beauty are rare. And this is so sad. Ought they not to bring into the world children ugly in mind and body if they conceive them while believing that they are doing something dirty? It is a dismal thing to have been conceived like that. – – – I like to believe that people with sensitive and impressionable hearts and souls have been created with joyful pride.

And so, cher maître allow me this hope of possessing and caressing a thousand times with my worshipping gaze this beloved group!!![3]

Artistically here there is nothing but imitations of Boecklin[4] He himself had talent but he always remained romantic and literary and these imitators must logically be base creatures – and they are. The Germans still have too much of the thinker about them and not enough of the naïve visual sensualist. They only unaffectedly understand music. They are trying to understand the visual arts and I believe that one day they will perhaps succeed. Just now there are only rare exceptions.

I am ashamed, this is my third sheet, but I feel so far away – so exiled from France that I must allow myself this pleasure of chatting to you. We shall be staying here until the middle of April. The Opera is called "Koanga"; it will be performed in the middle of March and then they are furthermore going to perform a concerto for piano and orchestra, a Symphony "Ronde de la Vie" and a cycle of songs for voice and orchestra, all by Delius, at a concert here[5] Delius is very impatient to return to France – as for me I love to be wherever he is and I find it great fun when he alarms the worthy Germans with his ultra-modern ideas! He joins me in expressing his devoted admiration for you! I dare not ask you to write to me, knowing how precious your time is, but needless to tell you what happiness it would give me to receive a line from you.

Your devoted
Jelka Delius

Autograph letter, signed and dated, written in French.

The original is in the Rodin Museum.

1   *Koanga* was to be given on 30 March (followed by two further performances) at the Stadttheater, Elberfeld, under Fritz Cassirer's baton.

2   *L'épervier et la colombe.*

3   Rodin was to keep his promise, although it was not *L'épervier* but a small bronze of Pierre de Wissant, one of the *Bourgeois de Calais*, that he gave to Jelka in November 1904.

4   Arnold Boecklin (1827–1901): Swiss painter. His individual treatment of ancient mythology was the basis of his reputation, and he was much admired in his time.

5   The works actually performed were *Appalachia* on 15 October, and the Piano Concerto (soloist Buths), *Lebenstanz* and *Paris* on 24 October. The conductor at both concerts in Elberfeld's Stadthalle was Hans Haym.

(166)
Georges-Daniel de Monfreid to Frederick Delius

Sᵗ Clément 4 May 1904

My dear Delius

Believe me, we, too, are longing to see you again & to have a chat about the time – already a good way back, isn't it? – when you used to have us up to your little apartment at Montrouge, round the table for a cup of your good old steaming "Tara Tea". What a lot of water has flowed under the bridges, as they say, since those faraway days! . . . Both my wife and I are very touched by the kind memories which you keep of us, in spite of the circumstances that have separated us for several years – We too, my dear friend, keep the same warm feelings for you, just as keen & just as sincere, because they come from a community of ideas & of feelings, a similarity of tastes & of appreciation of art & the things of life. At my age one has eliminated many useless comradeships, many idle or embarrassing acquaintances: all that remains are the *true* sympathies, the friendships with ties that are deep & intimate. And these one values just like a very precious possession.

Yes, we shall try to pay you a short visit in Grez when we are down there; for we are packing up and expect to be in Paris in a few days – about the 15th, probably – I'll write to you as soon as we have arrived at rue Liancourt.

So I look forward, my dear Delius, to the great pleasure of seeing you, of talking together about art, about friends, about poor Gauguin, gone now, but not *dead* for us, because the memory of him will enliven our thoughts and our conversations for a long time to come.[1]

In the meantime my wife sends many good wishes, to which I add my own, asking you to give our kindest regards to Mrs Delius.

Yours sincerely

G. Daniel De Monfreid

Autograph letter, signed and dated, written in French.

The original is in the Delius Trust Archive. It is the second of six letters written by Monfreid to Delius between April 1904 and June 1910 that have been preserved.

1   Gauguin had died on 8 May 1903, Monfreid first learning of the event on 23 August. Writing to Delius on 17 April 1904, he enquired, 'Did you know about Gauguin's death? I wanted to send you a notification; but I did not have your address. His end must have been very sad; from the details I have been able to glean it seems that his death, almost sudden, took place in conditions of deplorable neglect. His works have for the most part been dispersed or spirited away by the wretched band of Tahitian settlers or officials.'

(167)
Fritz Cassirer to Frederick Delius

Elberfeld
13. V. 1904.

Dear Herr Delius,

Many thanks for your letter. It finally wrung a reply out of my lazy attitude to writing. Actually I was just going to write to you anyway – without your needing to wring blood from this particular stone! Korten[1] told us yesterday that "Paris" is not to be performed in Frankfurt.[2] We therefore decided not to go there at all and wished to inform you accordingly. Did this come about naturally? Or did some mysterious theatre official à la Elberfeld act as diabolus ex machina here too? We were very annoyed about it and have outlawed and excommunicated the whole Frankfurt gang of musicians.

Well, fortunately you are one of those who can wait, who perhaps are meant to wait! Just let "whirlwind and dry dust twist and fly about" with equanimity. I tell you, some day you will not know yourself how it happened that you became really – famous. I did not get the chance for a long time to look at "Romeo & Juliet". It took very long for us to settle down completely. And when I had played the whole work through and was intending to write to you with it fresh in my mind, sad news called me to Berlin. There I witnessed a second death, which affected me greatly, and this agitation which still leaves me trembling has rather blurred my feeling for your still, sublime work, so softly restrained and so fragile. In the meantime there was my necessary work on the "Sängerweihe" in which the scent and savour of the whole of Wagnerianism, in the bad sense, is as it were condensed – it's difficult to avoid getting indigestion.

"Romeo and Juliet" is very beautiful, just like my idea of your development. If I have to make one reservation, then it is to the effect that the romantic nature of the subject has not allowed your musical language to remain on the *absolutely* original level of "Koanga". I am so spoiled by Koanga that I would not permit anything of that kind to you, of all people. Among the works of your latest, completely free manner, apart from Palmyra's *"Aria"* I also know the *"Tanz-lied"*.[3] So I have some idea where your road has led you, and I will not worry myself – or you – unduly if you do not seem to me to be quite as original here and there in your *sensibilities* in "Romeo and Juliet" as in "Koanga".

Still, these are minor matters. It's only because it concerns you that I did not wish to let anything pass without mention! We have come to such an understanding of each other that it almost seems out of place to me to tell you something good about the work as well. Of course it is very beautiful, there is no dought![4] And I am very *grateful* to you for having done it! And for having dared to be so quiet, so simple, so sincere in an opera! And for having forgotten the *"Gallery"*! One of the finest things is the beginning, which contains so much sunshine and heat, so much "air"! After that, the level drops slightly and then rises right until the end! The third act is the best. In the "Vision" of act II I feel something more striking, more significant ought to take place – however that is a minor detail. I think the first act drags a bit after the prelude. Still, it is a good thing that it is the first. All in all – this repressed ardour, this near-chaste anxiety of the modern soul, this deep, passionate stillness – you are the first who has dared on the operatic stage to speak so softly, to be so – "aristocratic". I say nothing about your music, since it is by – Delius! That prohibits me from – praising it. – –

You ask me if I am willing to write a libretto for you. I like the idea very much. Perhaps it can be done. But it will be difficult for me to find a subject to suit me. And I have no mind to invent new subjects. Still, I am thinking it over. If you should have an idea, write to me about it. Perhaps together we shall succeed. It would be a joy to me.

Our excursion to the Atlantic is on. We shall be writing to you with further details, but I don't think that we shall be at Grez before the 1st August. We are still undecided as to whether we shall go to Paris before or after Grez. We could perhaps first stay a few days with you, then go to the seaside by a roundabout route, stay there for 3 weeks and go to Paris on the 1st September for the opening of the opéra comique until about 8th September. We are looking forward very much indeed to France and to seeing both of you. We shall bring Evchen with us.

Here it is very lovely just now. We are very happy in our little house and have no real feeling that in fact we are living in Elberfeld. It is a pity that you cannot come to see us. And now perhaps not even next winter. The Gregor[5] affair is still unsettled, and I can now well understand your reluctance to have "Romeo and Juliet" performed here. I personally am thereby missing a great pleasure. I also regretted very much that you did not send me any of your works. I might perhaps have made use of my summer muse to write something about you. There are some anti-Wagnerian things as well which I would like to get off my chest. Perhaps it can still be done. Your scores are in safe custody here, including our child of sorrow, our "comedy success" – "Koanga".

Wedekind[6] has written very much. He is no doubt the best of all of them. Here are a few titles:

"Der Kammersänger" (1 Act)	Munich,	Langen, Verlag.
"So ist das Leben"	"	"	"
"Der Erdgeist"	"	"	"
"Der Liebestrank"	"	"	"

He is a genius. Such coldness of vision is truly a miracle in Germany. I am glad to hear that you like it.

So there. In view of my laziness, that should be enough. The End!

Our kind regards to you both. We are very much looking forward to seeing you again.

Yours
Fritz Cassirer

Autograph letter, signed and dated, written in German. Envelope addressed: Herrn / Fredrick Delius / *Grez sur Loing* / Dep. Marne & Seine / FRANKREICH.

The original is in the Delius Trust Archive. Some forty letters and postcards written by Cassirer to Delius between 1904 and 1910 are preserved in the Archive.

Fritz Cassirer (1871–1926): German conductor and writer. He studied in Munich and Berlin and held posts as opera conductor at Lübeck, Posen, Saarbrücken, Elberfeld and Berlin for a few years before retiring early to devote time to writing. In 1904 he was to help Delius in selecting the passages from Nietzsche's *Also sprach Zarathustra* which were to make up *A Mass of Life*.

1 Ernst Korten: German composer, notably of operas in the 1890s and early 1900s.

2 'One of your works will definitely be performed in Frankfurt,' wrote Schillings from Munich on 10 February 1904. 'R. Strauss favours the "Lebenslied" [*Lebenstanz*] most. And you?' However, writing again on 19 March, he confirmed that it was *Paris* that was on the programme for the Tonkünstlerfest to be held at Frankfurt at the end of May, although Delius himself had proposed *Appalachia*. Despite Schillings's support, everything fell through, and Delius was not represented. 'Frankfurt was a *great* fiasco. Thank God you were not there!' wrote Cassirer on 14 June.

3 One of the two *Dance Songs* from *A Mass of Life*.

4 *there is no dought*. In English in the original letter.

5 Hans Gregor: intendant at the Elberfeld Stadttheater. He was now planning to establish a Comic Opera in Berlin.

6 Frank Wedekind (1864–1918): German author. Best known as a dramatist, especially for his early play *Spring Awakening* (1891), he also wrote novels and poetry. His treatment of sexual matters was considered advanced for its time.

(168)
Henry Wood to Frederick Delius

25^A, NORFOLK CRESCENT,
HYDE PARK. W.

May 25.1904

Dear Mr Delius,

Will you be kind enough to send me the score and parts of your new work called "Lebentanz"[1] I am anxious to produce it at our concerts which begin in August –
With kind regards

Sincerely yours
Henry J Wood
PP

Autograph letter in the hand of Olga Wood, dated, written in English on headed notepaper. Signed *per pro* Wood.

The original is in the Delius Trust Archive. It is the first of some forty communications sent by or on behalf of Wood to Delius between 1904 and 1921 that have been preserved.

Wood was to be the first English conductor to give a major work by Delius in London: the Piano Concerto, soloist Théodor Szántó, on 22 October 1907. He had married the singer Princess Olga Ouroussof in July 1898, who in 1909 (the year of her death) performed some of Delius's songs. No letters from Delius to Wood have been found.

1   Delius sent Wood the scores of both *Lebenstanz* and *Paris* in 1904. *Paris* was actually rehearsed, with a view to a performance during the 1905 Promenade season; but Wood later clearly saw that he would have to devote a great deal of rehearsal time to such a complex 'novelty': 'rather than give a bad performance of your work I did not give it at all' (see Letter 184).

(169)

Julius Buths to Frederick Delius

Ddf. 30/5 04.

Dear Herr Delius.

Haym has left me in doubt myself as to whether he can give the Elberfeld concert in June or not; but it appears that in view of his cure treatment & also in accordance with your wishes he is saving things until the autumn. He is still in Maria i. Schnee near Bozen.[1] He has the musical material of "Lebenstanz" in Elberfeld. I have not exerted any direct influence on Wood, perhaps Wood was influenced by Mr. A.J. Jaeger of Novello & Co., with whom I have frequently spoken about you, or by a short article of Neitzel's in Signale,[2] in which he talks about Düsseldorf & also about you. In any case I am pleased to hear that people are beginning to think about you elsewhere too. Can you send me my copy of your Zarathustra-Nachtlied?

Best wishes
Yours   Buths

Autograph postcard, signed and dated, written in German. Addressed: Herrn Frederick Delius / Grez sur Loing / Dép. Seine et Marne / *La France*.

The original is in the Delius Trust Archive.

1   Haym was recuperating in the south Tyrolean mountain resort of Maria im Schnee from a recent illness.

2   *Signale für die Musikalische Welt*, a musical journal published in Berlin.

(170)
Halfdan Jebe to Frederick Delius

Slemdal near Kristiania
[21] June 1904.

Dear friend,

I think you are back from Germany now, perhaps since some time ago, and I ought to have written to you before. It's terrifying how quickly time passes. It's now more than four months since I've been here − incognito − well almost, I haven't seen anybody apart from my wife and one or two idiots who come to see us. Otherwise, life and especially work would have been impossible here where *nobody works*. So I am ever a foreigner here and am considered as such. I'm living in the country not far from Holmenkollen where my wife has an apartment. It's charming. What have you been doing in Germany? That's right, I didn't get the time in Paris to go and see that so-and-so of a cellist. Did you get a letter from me sent to his address? It was sent by registered post and if you didn't receive it, a complaint should be made. I had thought of going to Paris this summer but first of all I'm rather badly off and anyway during the summer we are as well off as possible here, my wife has been given leave from the theatre because of my coming back and she is very glad to be free. We are now living on whatever is given to us and if it is not given we take it. I know that you don't approve of this system, but I'm telling you that it is most noble. You, who are fond of changing like a chameleon, you'll become a thief one fine day, you'll see!

Now thanks to this fine system I have all but finished a great musical work which is sure to be played on every stage of Europe and America, and should it not be played I don't care a damn because it's an unparalleled masterpiece.[1] And I want to plunge myself into vices which have not yet been imagined as soon as the job is done.

Yes sir! *Vice is the well-spring*. Now, what do you intend to do, what are you doing, what are your plans? Are you still a fancier of Annamites, Japanese, Siamese girls etc. or do you prefer le tabac de la régie? Sometimes I burn with a feverish desire once more to see the countries where I felt like a new-born child! But I've no time to think about anything, anything like this before the autumn. I have had news from Ceylon, but nothing yet from Cochin-China. − How is your wife? I deeply regret annoying her when I was in Grez.[2] I've thought about it a great deal and I've discovered the reason, which, as a matter of fact, was serious, though that doesn't concern you. What are the two of you doing this summer? If you come to Norway you now know where to find me = *Slemdal*.

With kind regards to your wife from mine and from myself.

your old
"Rotten"[3]

Autograph letter, dated 'Juin 1904', written in French. Envelope addressed: Frederic Delius Esq. / Proprietaire / Grez sur Loing / Seine & Marne / *Frankrige*. Postmark: SLEMDAL 21 VI 04.

The original is in the Delius Trust Archive.

1   The opera *Vesle Kari Rud* was composed in 1904 and 1905, in collaboration with the writers Peter Egge and Christian Krohg. Jebe returned to the subject in a letter written to Delius on 23 April 1905: 'My great lyric-dramatic-symphonic-chromatic opera has fallen like a bomb on the peaceful family camp of our National Theatre.

    'I know this much and no more I have been offered a performance of the major part of the music at a concert. This I have rejected. Perhaps that will be the end of it all, but I still consider it possible that the work will be taken into the repertoire next winter.'

2   It has not been discovered what offence was given to Jelka.

3   In English in the original letter. Alternatively, in Norwegian it means *The Rat*.

(171)
Hans Haym to Frederick Delius

Dear friend,

I am still completely unable to come to terms with your "Tanz-Lied", therefore have given up my intention to rehearse it with a few ladies, at least for this summer.

On the other hand Appalachia has grown very dear to me. I have had two orchestral rehearsals of it & am delighted to be performing it. There are some damned high violin passages in it, and the high celli in the Giocoso variation are difficult too. But as I said, I find the whole thing superb and as rich as an entire life. We shall yet live to see Buths agreeing with enthusiasm, just as in the meantime he has become converted to Zarathustra. His critical remarks derive for the most part straight from the schoolroom, e.g. re the repeated theme in Appalachia, first in C then in F, which I find particularly beautiful, it is just as if the tragic moment were already being foreshadowed in it, as if the theme wanted to say: I am not as harmless as may at first appear.

How there can be any doubts about the choice between Appal. & Sinf. dom.[1] I do not understand. What a watery concoction from Strauss this time! I have already had a rehearsal of it too & found the impression gained by my initial reading fully confirmed. Absolutely nothing new, no humour, no depth, really a terrible void. I had an argument with Buths over this too, of course he can't bring himself to drop Strauss so easily & is too much under the spell of the leges tabulaturae for this new "masterpiece" not to impress him highly. Next Sunday I hope to play the Appal. on 2 pianos with him. The Mysterioso with the viola solo sounded wonderful. Altogether everything sounds good. Your sounds often require a soft pp. It makes many things intelligible & poetically effective, which in mf seemed to be ugly. Appalachia will be done in the 1st concert on the 15th October. I then hope to be able to do Lebenstanz & Piano Concerto about the same time (best of all with "Paris" as well). Date not quite fixed yet.

I am very well. I have certainly not travelled around very much, as you seem to assume. The 5 weeks in Maria im Schnee were the main thing, afterwards I wanted to go a few 100 metres higher still.

Indeed this summer has been quite heavenly. But it must have been nice and hot for you in Grez! Just the thing for plein air models.[2] Here too there hasn't been a drop of rain & our children run about on the lawn & climb the trees in their birthday suits. But of course they are looking forward to the holidays, which we all (only Susanne will be put up elsewhere) intend to spend together in Switzerland, 1700m. up, in a place which has been recommended to me. Charges: 24 frcs a day for 2 adults & 4 children. It seems you're going to the seaside? Mountain air always does me much more good. But I am very much looking forward to the Loire tour, we will be keeping it in mind for next spring.

As soon as your choral work is ready, I'll get it to look at, won't I? Can you tell me why the "Tanzlied" just doesn't appeal to me? It seems quite different from your other things. I just don't know how to grasp it, however much I would like to do so. Thanks for your letter & best wishes to your dear wife.

Yours   Haym

E[lberfeld]. 25.7.04

Autograph letter, signed and dated, written in German.

The original is in the Delius Trust Archive.

1   Strauss's tone-poem *Symphonia Domestica*, op. 53 (1902–3).

2   The reference is to Jelka's nudes.

(172)

Hans Haym to Frederick Delius

[Elberfeld, 6 August 1904]

Dear friend, Just about to leave for Switzerland (Seewenalp near Schüpfheim, Canton of Lucerne), I am instructing the Orchestra Librarian to send the music to London. Yesterday was a Delius festival for us. In the morning I played Appalachia with Buths, in the aft. the Piano Concerto. He has a splendid command of it & will play it magnificently. For the time being we propose to do it on the 21st Oct. He was also quite enchanted by Appalachia, admittedly not without expressions of dogmatic pangs of conscience ("after all we cannot completely renounce our education"), but I confidently believe that he will do it at the 1905 Musikfest. At first we went deeply into each single section, with several repeats, afterwards we played the whole thing right through again from A–Z. It sounds pretty good even on 2 pianos. During the concerto one rather misses the distinction between the timbres, I am very curious to hear it. But the 5/4 time will not be exactly easy for the orchestra. Item – we admire & love your truly original genius! Salem Aleikum!

Autograph postcard, unsigned and undated, written in German. Addressed: Mr Frederick Delius / Grez sur Loing / Frankreich / (Seine et Marne). Readdressed: Loctudy par Pont l'Abbé / Finistère. Postmark: ELBERFELD 6.8.04. Final receiving postmark: LOCTUDY 11 AOUT 04.

The original is in the Delius Trust Archive.

(173)

Edvard Grieg to Frederick Delius

[Troldhaugen] 23/8/04.

2 Norwegian peasants send their most hearty greetings to the Breton ditto!

Yours
Edvard Grieg

Picture postcard: *Bjørnson og Grieg paa Villa Troldhaugen* [Bjørnson and Grieg at Troldhaugen], signed and dated, written in German. Addressed: M. Fr. Delius / Loctudy / Finistère. / Bretagne, France. Postmark: HOP 23 VIII 04.

The original is in the Delius Trust Archive.

This communication, together with two postcards from Haym similarly addressed (or readdressed) and postmarked 23 August and 6 September, are almost the only first-hand clues to the Deliuses' summer whereabouts. Fritz Cassirer had, however, written on 14 June: 'I shall arrive *with* wife and child at Grez on 23 July, then we shall still reach Loctudy early enough.'

(174)
Henry Wood to Frederick Delius

25ᴬ, NORFOLK CRESCENT,
HYDE PARK. W.

Oct. 7. 1904

Dear Mʳ Delius,

I have already sent the parts of "Lebenstanz" off to Elberfeld[1] and I regret very much it will be impossible for me to perform it this season at the "Proms" owing to the great difficulties[2] I will attempt another year I hope —

With many regrets

Sincerely yours
Henry J Wood
PP

Autograph letter in the hand of Olga Wood, dated, written in English on headed notepaper.

The original is in the Delius Trust Archive.

1   Haym was to give *Lebenstanz* at Elberfeld on 24 October. Wood also had the score of *Paris*, having asked on 4 September: 'may I keep it a little longer as I may be able to produce it next season for you.'

2   There were to be further disappointments for Delius towards the end of the year, with refusals in November from the firms of Max Brockhaus, Leipzig, and Bote & Bock, Berlin, to publish *A Village Romeo and Juliet*. In the middle of October, however, Siegel of Leipzig had at least expressed to Haym an interest in Delius's works. The good news was that Cassirer was able to confirm on 9 October that *A Village Romeo* and *Margot la Rouge* were on the list for the new Komische Oper in Berlin.

1905

Delius spent the early part of the year in Grez. Again, he was ready to give a helping hand to Edvard Munch during preparations for the Salon des Indépendants, where, not for the first time, Jelka too was exhibiting. Germany continued to take up his works, *Paris*, for example, being given under Siegmund von Hausegger in Frankfurt (towards the end of the year it was also to be given in Brussels). A newer work was in the hands first of Schillings, then of Haym, although it had to wait until 1906 for its first performance: this was *Sea Drift*. *Appalachia* was confided to Buths for performance in June, with the Deliuses present, at the Lower Rhine Festival, Düsseldorf. And *A Village Romeo and Juliet* was now provisionally scheduled for Hans Gregor's new Komische Oper in Berlin.

Summer visitors to Paris and Grez included Fritz Cassirer and the conductor Oskar Fried, and they would have watched with considerable interest the development of *A Mass of Life*, again much the major preoccupation of Delius's year. By the beginning of November, the final bars of the work had at last been penned.

A Mass of Life (RT II/4). Completed.

Sonata No. 1, for violin and piano (RT VIII/6). Sketched in part.

(175)
Halfdan Jebe to Frederick Delius

Norway
[24?] January
1905.

My dear Delius,

It is a very long time since I heard from you, are you perhaps ill?

I received this summer your marvellously amusing letters, and an idyllic card from Finisterre, which told me that you were content but still a little melancholic (the swans which swam on the water there told me this) and I thought very calmly: this is the Delius from Rue Ducouëdic, and on that day I visited the most beautiful flowers in the woods, didn't pick them, didn't touch them, — Peace on Earth and in the Woods — Oh, what a beautiful feeling!

Did I say "feeling"? Where are my feelings? — There at the piano — What, Nonsense, they're only the photographs of Beethoven and Wagner, it's washerwomen who have feelings —

Washerwomen, how vulgar! not even a Chinese. —

Oh, and I recently received your letter in French. Bravo Fritz, you are making progress, the whole letter from beginning to end in *one* language is something that's against your principles — But where are your principles are they too perhaps with washerwomen?

I did enjoy your letter. I see that you are in Grez again and that you are looking forward to Christmas, you old cochon, you ate oysters and supped white wine. You went to Paris, just for a few days, but what days! How immoral! You suppose in your letter that I shall go to Paris for Christmas "*as always*".

Woe betide you! how dare you presume that I do something *always*.

The only thing that can justify such a presumption of yours would be that it may look unnatural for me to exhibit my snow-white innocence here for so long. But who tells you anyhow that I didn't spend the whole summer in Paris. I shall not mystify you, I wasn't in Paris, but I wasn't here either. I was in my Innocence, in my brightest snow-white Innocence.

From there I wrote many letters to you perhaps they were snapped up by the censor.

But now I am here — passing through — will stay a little longer one month, two months. A beggar has plenty of time, plenty of lovely happy time and Innocence never gets bored. How they shine, night and day, how my wholesomeness defies the attacks from front and from behind without hatred, attacks which come from miserable people. How short the reach of power, how blind is pomp, what difference does a "coup de pied" make to a beggar, it does you good right to the tip of your prick.

Yes, my oriental-tropical healthiness resists everything — wicked, harsh, cold, dirty, stupid and false, nothing hurts; as long as I have something left of this universal medicine, a squirt of which I've had every day since I became an Oriental, mouth eyes nose ears and arsehole. Yes, the whole of my soul is permeated by innocence, and my body knows only sublime pains.

Apart from this interesting condition of mine, I have not much news to tell. That is, I see nobody. I live in a studio, and my wife has another studio in the same house. We see each other every day and enjoy the central heating a truly poetical contrivance. Since this central heating appeared the question is: Equator or Norway. One puts a different shirt on, one's red, the other white, but both hot. —

Of interest here there's only: Heiberg's new play has had a tremendous success and he is said to be very delighted about this. Furthermore it is a masterpiece technically, the idea is obviously inspired by *you*, Herr Idealist and Proprietaire![1]

Your old friend Charlotte-Bödker-Näser[2] – now Winter-Hjelm, hence married again, I've met from time to time. She is now quite ripe for the job of brothel keeper but as she remains ever a dilettante, all she has done has been to found a society where for the time being she can work as a procuress. At first I thought she would be just the one to take on a world tour.[3] But . . .[4]

Autograph letter, dated 'Januar 1905', written in German. Owing to a missing page or pages, the text is not complete and lacks a signature. The reference to 'Heiberg's new play' dates the letter as some time after the first performance on 16 January, and in fact a receiving postmark on the envelope is just decipherable as GREZ 27 JANV 05. I have therefore proposed 24 January as a notional date of writing. The envelope, partly torn, is addressed: Monsieur Frederik D[elius] / Grez sur Loing / Seine et Marn[e] / France. The reverse of the envelope bears the legend Afsender: Halfdan Jebe./ Alfheim, Kristiania / Norvège./ (Première partie). This latter parenthesis may indicate that the continuation of this letter was sent afterwards. If so, it has not survived.

The original is in the Delius Trust Archive.

1   *Kjaerlighedens tragedie* (*Love's Tragedy*): begun as long ago as the summer of 1901, this play, generally considered to be Heiberg's finest, was completed in the summer of 1904. Directed by the author, it opened at Christiania's National Theatre on 16 January 1905. A piece of realist drama, partly inspired by Ibsen's *When We Dead Awaken*, its first production enjoyed a considerable success. Delius was clearly alluding to *Love's Tragedy* in an undated letter he wrote to Heiberg from 30, avenue de l'Observatoire: 'The play is brilliant! You have never written anything better – not so good! – but I don't feel she should kill herself – it isn't necessary and it is only for dramatic effect. All the same, it's a strong play and a masterpiece.' (The original letter, written in Norwegian, is in the Oslo University Library.) It is of incidental interest that Karen, the leading female role, was played by Johanne Dybwad, now Norway's first actress, who had played Ella in *Folkeraadet* a little more than seven years earlier. Jebe's remark in this letter has, I think, a tongue-in-cheek element, since there is little in the play or in its leading male character that seems likely to have been inspired by Delius.

2   Christiane Charlotte Bødtker (1868–1920): Norwegian pianist. She studied in Berlin and then travelled to the United States, where she married Wilhelm Naeser in 1892. They later lived in Chile. After her husband's death she returned to Norway and married in 1904 Louis Pignol Winter-Hjelm, son of the doyen of Norwegian music critics, Otto Winter-Hjelm.

3   Two further letters from Jebe, written in the spring of 1905, take up the theme of the 'world tour'. In the first he asked, 'what about our world tour at last.' Although he had in mind some women singers to take along, he now harboured serious reservations concerning Delius's stated intention to join him. In the second he reiterated, 'I very

much hope that we can again seriously consider the great Pacific-journey. *I* have never given it up.'

4   The last sentence on the page begins: *Aber nur möglich, Amateur* . . .

(176)
Edvard Munch to Frederick Delius

c/o Hotel Janson
Mittelstrasse
Berlin
[8? February 1905]

Dear friend,

Please be so kind as to pay my membership subscription for L'Independants[1] — I shall send it to you at once — I have just come back from Prague — where I arranged a large exhibition — and am waiting for money —

I shall perhaps send a larger picture as well — my best things are now in Prague — It was splendid in Prague — I was the guest of the artists — and there were many parties — The mayor put his carriage at my disposal —

I long very much for Paris — I should also like to visit you both in your very beautiful house but don't know if I shall get the time —

Do come to Aasgaardstrand some time!

Well, I shall write again soon — In a few days I shall send the money — but please make sure that I remain a member and lay out the money — Death to my enemies and greetings to my friends —

Your old
Edv. Munch

Please tell me how Fraulein Eva Mudocci[2] is getting on — have you run into her

---

Autograph letter, signed and undated, written in German.

The original is in the Delius Trust Archive.

1   Delius had written from Grez on 3 February to ask if Munch wanted him to do just this. Jelka was also to exhibit — and indeed to sell — two pictures at the same exhibition.

2   See Letter 161, note 3. The Deliuses visited the Eva Mudocci–Bella Edwards duo in Paris at least twice in 1905. On their second visit in the autumn, one of Delius's works was played to them, although Eva Mudocci, who recorded the event in a letter to Munch, did not specify which piece.

(177)
Frederick Delius to Edvard Munch

Grez sur Loing
Seine & Marne
11 Febr 1905

Dear friend

I have today sent 25 frcs to the Independants that is everything as you will see from the enclosed letter. I was very glad to hear that you were so successful in Prague & I hope you will be successful here too. But one day you must put on a very big exhibition with all your best things.

There will always be a room for you here at our home & we should be delighted to see you here — We could then all go to Paris together for the exhibition. Frl Eva Mudocci is in Paris, I know, but I have not seen her for a long time. She is charming.

Best wishes from us both

Yours
Fr. Delius

Autograph letter, signed and dated, written in German.

The original is in the Munch Museum.

(178)
Ada Crossley to Frederick Delius

6ᵛ BICKENHALL MANSIONS,
GLOUCESTER PLACE, W.

19.2.'05

Dear Mr. Delius

— It was through the kindness of Madame Minna Fischer,[1] that I was fortunate enough to re-introduce your Song "Irmeline Rose" on Monday night last. —

— I also have a copy of the beautiful "In the Seraglio Garden". — I had them both transposed lower, — as they were too high for me. — — (My voice is quite Contralto — & not a mezzo range!) — I thank you so much for your kind suggestion that I should see the Cyclus[2] — with your score & parts. — There is nothing I should like better than doing them at either the Norwich or Sheffield Festival in October next, — if it can be arranged. —

– I should be so happy to see any MSS. that you might kindly send me! – I got your address a short time ago from Mr. Runciman in the hope of getting direct from you – more of your quaint & beautiful compositions. –

("Irmeline Rose" was very much liked.)

– Believe me –
Very truly yours
Ada Crossley

Autograph letter, signed and dated, written in English on headed notepaper.

The original is in the Delius Trust Archive. It is the only item of correspondence preserved from Ada Crossley to Delius.

Ada Crossley (1874–1929): Australian contralto. She lived in London after 1894, studying with Santley and, later, with Marchesi, and toured widely in Australia and the United States. Her letter is evidence that even if Delius's larger works had still not been taken up in England, his songs were occasionally performed.

1   See Letter 90, note 2.

2   The *Seven Danish Songs*.

(179)
Max Schillings to Frederick Delius

MÜNCHEN (19) 28 II.05
Aiblingerstrasse 4.

Dear Herr Delius,

Excuse pencil – I am writing on the journey to Leipzig. Shortly before I left I received your letter & do wish to tell you right away that although I understand your decision to withdraw "Appalachia" from Graz out of consideration for Buths, nonetheless I cannot adequately express my regret for that decision! The performance in Graz would have opened up completely *new* circles to you and the interests of the Musikverein itself would also have been well served by your splendid piece. I would gladly propose that we now put "Seadrift" on the programme; but, as I have already written to tell you: we have already made provision for so many vocal works. What about "Paris" or "Lebenstanz" then? Please write and let me know *at once*. I am writing to Rich. Strauss at the same time and asking for his opinion. By the way I do *not* understand Buths' apprehensions. If he is convinced of the merits of "Appalachia" – why should he be bothered about any stupid criticisms there might be?? The truth of the matter is that he wants to be the first to bring you before the listening public in

PLATE 33   Fritz Delius in London, 1899. (*Coll. Christopher Brunel.*)

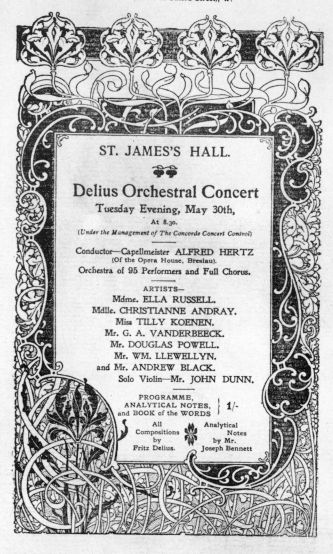

ST. JAMES'S HALL.

Delius Orchestral Concert
Tuesday Evening, May 30th,
At 8.30.
(Under the Management of The Concorde Concert Control)

Conductor—Capellmeister ALFRED HERTZ
(Of the Opera House, Breslau).
Orchestra of 95 Performers and Full Chorus.

ARTISTS—
Mdme. ELLA RUSSELL.
Mdlle. CHRISTIANNE ANDRAY.
Miss TILLY KOENEN.
Mr. G. A. VANDERBEECK.
Mr. DOUGLAS POWELL.
Mr. WM. LLEWELLYN.
and Mr. ANDREW BLACK.
Solo Violin—Mr. JOHN DUNN.

PROGRAMME,
ANALYTICAL NOTES, } 1/-
and BOOK of the WORDS

All
Compositions
by
Fritz Delius.

Analytical
Notes
by Mr.
Joseph Bennett

PLATE 34   Delius Orchestral Concert programme cover.
(Coll. Manuel Tarshish.)

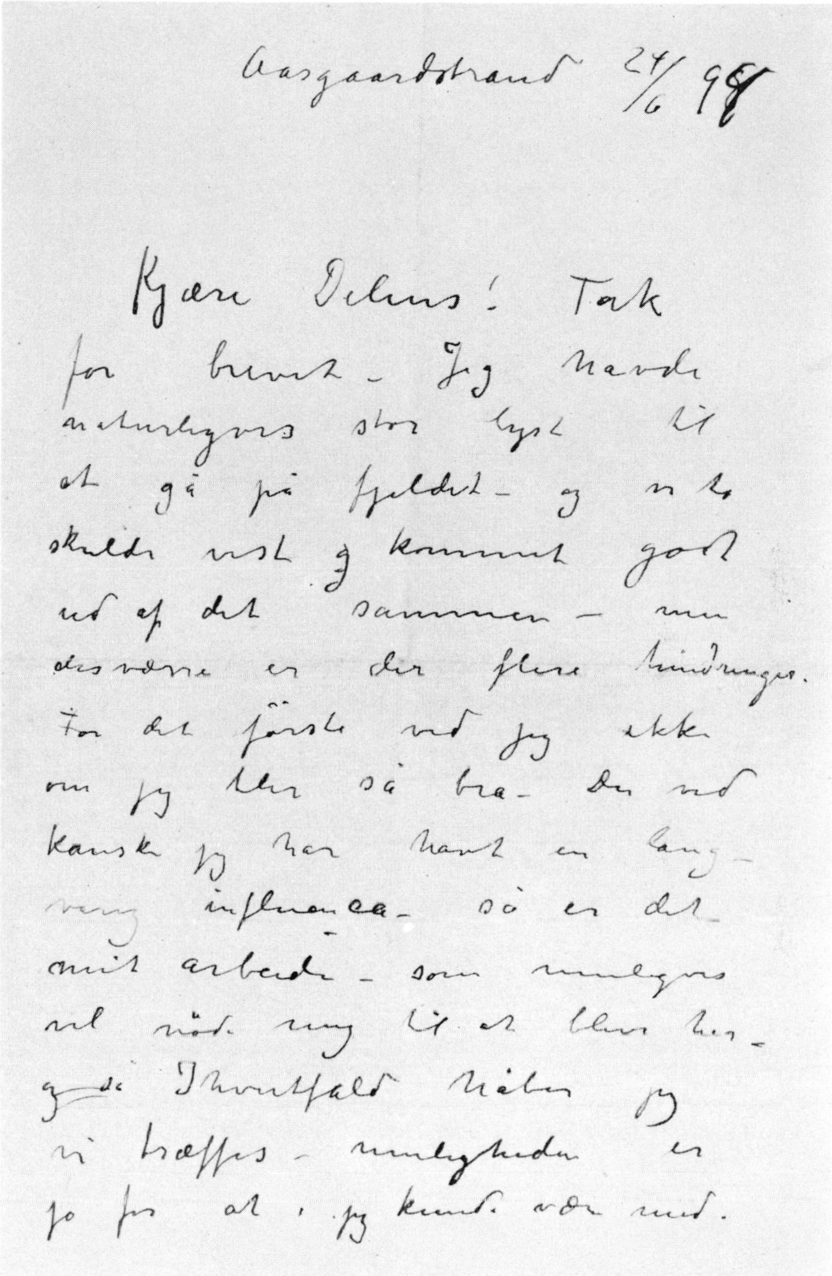

Aasgaardstrand 24/6 99

Kjære Delius! Tak for brev. — Jeg havde naturligvis stor lyst til at gå på fjeldet — og vi to skulde nok jeg komme godt ud af det sammen — men desværre er der flere hindringer. For det første ved jeg ikke om jeg bliver så bra — da jeg nu kanske jeg har havt en lang-varig influenca — så er det mit arbeide — som muligens vil nøde mig til at blive her — i tilfald tror jeg vi træffes — muligheden er jo for at jeg kunde være med.

PLATE 35　　Letter from Edvard Munch to Delius, 24 June 1899 (see p. 159).

PLATE 36   Elise Delius. (*Coll. Delius Family Archive, Bielefeld.*)

PLATE 37   (a) Karl-August Gerhardi, by Ida Gerhardi
(*Gerhardi/Steinweg Collection*); (b) Ferruccio Busoni, 1903, by Ida
Gerhardi (*Gerhardi/Steinweg Collection*); (c) Auguste Rodin.

PLATE 38   Letter from Auguste Rodin to Jelka Rosen, 10 July 1901
(see pp. 192–3).

PLATE 39   Jelka Rosen, 1901, by Ida Gerhardi.
(Gerhardi/Steinweg Collection.)

PLATE 40   Hans Haym.

PLATE 41   (a) Florent Schmitt; (b) Maurice Ravel, 1898;
(c) Gabriel Fauré, c. 1900; (d) Déodat de Sévérac.

PLATE 42 (a) Max Schillings: a contemporary caricature; (b) Arthur Nikisch, by Ida Gerhardi (*Gerhardi/Steinweg Collection*); (c) Richard Strauss; (d) Julius Buths (*coll. Elgar Birthplace Trust*).

PLATE 43   'Salome' (Eva Mudocci and Edvard Munch),
by Edvard Munch. (*Coll. Munch Museum.*)

PLATE 44   Frederick Delius, 1903, by Ida Gerhardi.
(*Gerhardi/Steinweg Collection.*)

PLATE 45   (a) Percy Pitt; (b) Harold Bauer; (c) Olga and Henry Wood;
(d) Ada Crossley.

Bjørnson og Grieg paa Villa Troldhaugen

PLATE 46   Bjørnson and Grieg at Troldhaugen (see p. 247).

PLATE 47   At the Lower Rhine Festival, Düsseldorf, Whitsun 1905:
Oskar Fried, Erich von Hornbostel, Delius, Hans Haym, Jelka Delius.

PLATE 48   (a) Karl Walser: The Paradise Garden. Original design for the
Berlin production of *A Village Romeo and Juliet* (*Swiss Theatre
Collection, Berne*); (b) Costume design for Marti (*Swiss Theatre
Collection, Berne*).

a music festival programme – But *you* have made the decision, so that is an end to it. A pity! –

With most cordial greetings   Yours

M Schillings.

Autograph letter, signed and dated, written in German on headed notepaper.

The original is in the Delius Trust Archive.

The 1905 Tonkünstlerfest (the festival of the Allgemeine Deutsche Musikverein) was to be held at Graz in Austria. Delius initially had agreed to *Appalachia* being performed there, but following its first performance in Elberfeld on 15 October 1904, he now had promised it to Buths for the Lower Rhine Festival in June. A postcard from Buths on 27 February gently reminded him that *Appalachia* 'will above all be safer with us than with the "Tonkünstlers" '. With the organizers of the Graz festival having already announced that this work was to be performed, Delius's difficulties were compounded: letters arrived from the *Neue Zeitschrift für Musik* asking for details of the piece for the 'Festival Number', and from the composer August Reuss congratulating Delius on being on the Festival's programme once again after the 'unpleasant incidents' of last year. 'Der Buths der tut's' ('It's Buths's doing'), wrote Schillings laconically on 8 March.

(180)

Edvard Munch to Frederick Delius

c/o Giebfrieds Hotel
Kobbel 9 – Hamburg
[early March 1905]

Dear friend,

Please complete the list   Cassirer[1] has probably enclosed titles and prices – The titles are probably on the back – You are sure to sort it all out –

– 1) Vampire 2) Madonna or loving woman 3) Strindberg 4) The Wave (Litho) 5) Le Soir Bois en 3 Couleurs Claire de Lune Bois en 3 Couleurs and so on.

The Wave (la vogue?) Litho and Number 8 is not labelled I don't remember what it is. Write a name in. If there are no price lists, then please fix the prices between 50–80 Frcs –

I should like to come and see you next winter perhaps and paint something – Best wishes to you and your wife

Yours   Edvard Munch

Did you get the card – where I ask you to have the engravings framed and glazed cheaply – ?

Please give my regards to Fraulein Mudocci do you know her address

Autograph letter, signed and undated, written in German on the headed notepaper of Giebfried's Hôtel, Hamburg. Munch in the address wrote 'Kobbel' for 'Koppel'.

The original is in the Delius Trust Archive.

1   Probably Bruno Cassirer. See Letter 161, note 2.

(181)
Fritz Cassirer to Frederick Delius

FRITZ CASSIRER   ELBERFELD, 30.III.1905.
                                                        BISMARCKSTR.15.

Herrn Frederick Delius,
Grez sur Loing

Dear Delius,

Many thanks for your letter. At the beginning of May we shall be in Paris, where we hope we shall be able to see you.

The purpose of this letter is to draw your attention to Herr Bolten-Bäckers, Köln a.Rh., Herwarthstr.17. This gentleman has translated many operas already and is perhaps the right translator for "A Night in Paris".[1] (The title has been suggested by Gregor.)

I have now gone through "R. & J." again. The thing is quite simply magnificent. If this does not find favour with the public, I will resign from the Theatre!

How I would love to stage it myself!

Dr. Haym has been fiercely attacked at a meeting of the Town Council, on account of – Delius. One man recommended his dismissal.

We are looking forward to talking to you both in Paris.

With kind regards

Yours
Fritz Cassirer.

Autograph letter, signed and dated, written in German on headed notepaper.

The original is in the Delius Trust Archive.

1   *Margot la Rouge*. Delius's one-act opera was gradually to recede from the Komische Oper's sights. 'I personally am not very keen on it,' wrote Cassirer to Delius on 28 July 1905, returning to the subject on 5 August. He was not very interested in it 'on account of the tearful ending and the violettes blanches'.

(182)
Hans Gregor to Frederick Delius

"Komische Oper"
Direktion: Hans Gregor.

Berlin, 23 June 1905

Herrn Frederik Delius
Grez sur Loing

Dear Sir,

Will you please send to the address of frl. Lola de Padilla[1] in Baden-Baden, Hotel Schirmhof *by return* a piano arrangement of your opera "Romeo & Julia auf dem Dorfe", furthermore please send on to me as soon as possible the complete material.

With best wishes, to your wife also,

Yours sincerely
Hans Gregor.

P.S. How are things in Grez? Unfortunately my stay in Paris was very brief this time. That is why I was unable to spend a pleasant day in the Forest of Fontainebleau. Les affaires sont les affaires, aren't they? When shall we be seeing you here?

Yours sincerely
H G.

Autograph letter, signed and dated, written in German on headed notepaper. The first part of the letter is not in Gregor's hand, but presumably that of a secretary. Gregor's autograph follows from his full signature.

The original is in the Delius Trust Archive. It is the last of eight communications written by Gregor to Delius between 1903 and 1905 that have been preserved.

1   Lola Artôt de Padilla (1876–1933): French operatic soprano. She was to create the role of Vreli in the Berlin production of *A Village Romeo and Juliet*.

(183)
Lola Artôt de Padilla to Frederick Delius

Wednesday   9. Boulevard d'Argenson.
9 August 1905   *Neuilly s/ Seine*

Monsieur!

Thank you for the 2nd act of Romeo und Julia, and if I didn't tell you earlier that I had received it, this is because I was counting at the same time on telling you the outcome when I had seen the last acts.

I am likely to leave any day now for Norway, but my departure might well be a little delayed! –

As I was not sure, I did not wish to leave Mr Gregor waiting for my reply any longer, and since you tell me that there are no vocal surprises in the last acts, I have just written to tell him that the role of "Vrenchen" suits me, and that I can sing it! –

I have seen the 2 acts, and believe that it will all be within my range! –

As soon as you have received the last acts write me a line. I will then give you my address in Norway – For the moment you can still send everything *here*. –

When I am *sure* of my day of departure I will send you *a line* and let you know. In the mean time I send you my kind regards

Lola Artôt de Padilla – .

Autograph letter, signed and dated, written in French.

The original is in the Delius Trust Archive. It is the only item of correspondence from Lola Artôt de Padilla to Delius that has been preserved. See also Letter 182, note 1.

(184)
Henry Wood to Frederick Delius

4, Elsworthy Rd.
LONDON, N.W.
6. November, 1905

Dear Mr. Delius,

I regret very much that I was not able to do your work "Paris" we rehearsed it but I was unable to do it after all as during the Promenades I have not sufficient time to give works as much rehearsal as I should wish so rather than give a bad performance of your work I did not give it at all.[1] I have now sent the score and parts off to Mons. Sylvan Dupius,[2] 134 rue Pottagère, Brussels.

With kind regards,

Yours sincerely
Henry J. Wood
pp

Typed letter, signed pp Henry J. Wood, dated, written in English on headed notepaper. The original letter-heading, 25A, NORFOLK CRESCENT,/ HYDE PARK,/ LON-DON, W., has been crossed out, except for the word LONDON.

The original is in the Delius Trust Archive.

1 This was disappointing news indeed for Delius, and it meant that almost two more years were to go by before a major work of his was given in London. There was, however, the minor consolation of the occasional song recital, such as that given by Susan Strong at the Bechstein Hall in London on 8 April 1905, when Delius was represented in a programme of mainly modern composers.

2 Sylvain Dupuis (1856–1931): Belgian conductor, composer and teacher. He was conductor in Brussels at the Théâtre de la Monnaie and the Concerts Populaires from 1900 to 1911. *Paris* was given under his baton on 3 December.

(185)

Sylvain Dupuis to Frederick Delius

Bruxelles, le 20 Déc. 1905.

Concerts Populaires
Sylvain Dupuis

Dear Monsieur,

By the same post I return to you your large orchestral score as well as the reduction for 2 pianos of "Paris", and thank you very much for having entrusted to me your beautiful work, which I took great pleasure in bringing to the attention of a Brussels audience.

I am afraid that not all of them understood its finesse but everyone acknowledged that it had come from the pen of a composer of real talent.

The main criticism was on the broad development of your impressions of night, and it was regretted that your intentions on this subject were not known. It would have been preferable to have, so it ran, an explanatory text. I congratulate you nonetheless, and am delighted to have had the opportunity of performing your work under excellent conditions.

With kindest regards,

Sylv. Dupuis

Autograph letter, signed and dated, written in French on headed notepaper.

The original is in the Delius Trust Archive. It is the last of four items of correspondence written by Dupuis to Delius between September and December 1905 that have been preserved.

Sylvain Dupuis: see Letter 184, note 2.

1906

In January Delius left Grez for Berlin to help Oskar Fried prepare *Appalachia* for performance on 5 February with the Berlin Philharmonic. He stayed for most of what turned out to be a busy February and furthermore entered into contractual arrangements with Harmonie Verlag to publish his works. Yet again, on his return to Grez, he found himself acting as Munch's unpaid but willing agent in respect of the Indépendants exhibition in March. Harmonie were now already at work preparing *Sea Drift* and *Appalachia* for publication. The first performance of the former came at the annual festival of the Allgemeine Deutsche Musikverein, given this year in Essen in May, with Delius present. Hans Haym and the young conductor Carl Schuricht were there too, among others. A few weeks earlier Haym had made a visit to Grez.

Late in June, after a break of seven years, Delius was back in Norway, staying for a time at Aasgaardstrand and making an excursion into the mountains, before leaving for home at the end of August.

In the meantime, the score of *A Mass of Life* was making its round of conductors, and Schillings, Haym and Cassirer all showed signs of being daunted by the scale of the work. One of the tasks undertaken in the autumn was some revision of the Piano Concerto with the pianist Theodor Szántó. And the year ended with indications that England, notably in the person of Henry Wood, was again tentatively renewing interest in his work. Delius was still waiting for a real breakthrough in the country of his birth and had by now good reason to feel puzzled, if not worried, by the continuing neglect of his music there.

Piano Concerto in C minor (RT VII/4). Further revision.

Songs of Sunset, for soprano and baritone solo, mixed chorus and orchestra (Ernest Dowson) (RT II/5). Begun.

(186)

Harmonie Verlag to Frederick Delius

BERLIN W.[35],
Schöneberger Ufer 32.
[early 1906]

Herrn Fr. Delius,
Grez sur Loins near Paris

Herr Kassierer, the conductor of the orchestra of the "Komische Oper" here, tells us that your works, in particular "A Village Romeo and Juliet", are shortly to be performed here.

We take the liberty of bringing our publishing house to your notice and of asking you to consider our publishing and distributing your works.

In commending our services to you, we shall be pleased to give you any further information

Yours faithfully
Harmonie

Typed letter, unsigned and undated, written in German on the headed notepaper of "HARMONIE"/Verlagsgesellschaft für Literatur und Kunst.

The original is in the Delius Trust Archive. It is the first of nearly 150 letters and postcards from the firm of Harmonie to Delius, dating from 1906 to 1910, that have been preserved.

(187)

Oskar Fried to Frederick Delius

Nikolassee/Wannseebahn 5.1.06.

Dear Delius;

Come to Berlin *at once*! The orchestral parts of Apalachia really are in an incredible state! I have not enough time to put it in order, and we have certainly not got enough rehearsals to put up a good performance with the music as it is.

No signatures! No dynamic markings — or very deficient ones! Whether flute or piccolo is not clear! With the two bassoons one never knows whether tenor or bass clef!

The material must be put right before the first orchestral rehearsal, otherwise I cannot perform it.

You must realise that we have no time here in Berlin for reading-rehearsals!

The material must be clear and distinct, otherwise the musicians will certainly approach this new and difficult work with reluctance. So please set out as soon as you receive my letter and help me to put the orchestra music in order, otherwise the performance will come to nothing.

Telegraph me as to when and whether you are coming
Great haste is essential.
Oskar Fried.

Autograph letter, signed and dated, written in German.

The original is in the Delius Trust Archive. It is the eighth of thirteen letters and postcards written by Fried to Delius between June 1905 and March 1910 that have been preserved.

Oskar Fried (1871–1941): German conductor and composer. A pupil of Humperdinck, he had become director of the Stern Gesangverein in Berlin in 1904, and was to conduct *Appalachia* there on 5 February. His acquaintanceship with Delius is first documented in 1905, when the Deliuses invited Fried and his wife to spend a holiday with them at Grez in the summer, and in spite of very evident financial difficulties they had done so. 'I have hardly ever in my life looked forward to a journey so much as now,' wrote Fried on 25 June; and the holiday indeed lived up to his expectations. Like Delius, Fried was attracted to Nietzsche's writings and composed in 1904 *Das trunkene Lied* (op. 11), using the same source, *Also sprach Zarathustra*, as Delius was using for *A Mass of Life*.

(188)
Frederick Delius to Edvard Munch

Kleist Str 38[II] [Berlin]
23 Feb [1906]

Dear friend –

I have been here in Berlin since 8 January.[1] A symphony of mine was performed on the 5th February & everything went off very well. I am returning to Paris on Monday & will attend to the matter. You must send your pictures to the Independants at once. Grandes Serres. Cour la Reine. Acceptance days are 9. 10. 11 March: so you have still got time. I will pay for you –

Farewell – My wife sends her best wishes.

Your friend
Fr. Delius

Autograph letter, signed and dated, written in German.

The original is in the Munch Museum.

1   Following the performance of *Appalachia*, Delius set about promoting his music in Berlin, staying on there with Jelka. He entered into negotiations with the publishing

house of Harmonie, which sent him a draft contract on 17 February and agreed to publish *Appalachia*. He also called on the secretary of the Allgemeine Deutsche Musikverein and learned of the acceptance of *Sea Drift* for the next Tonkünstlerfest, at Essen. He would certainly too have visited the Komische Oper to discuss the plans for the production of *A Village Romeo and Juliet* with Gregor and Cassirer.

(189)

Edvard Munch to Frederick Delius

[Weimar, 2 March 1906]

Dear friend, I have sent off 3 paintings and 3 engravings –

The paintings are called – Les buveurs – Paysages de Thüringerwald 2 pieces – Price for each picture 1000 Frcs. –

3 Lithos – Mr. K¹ – Mr. Henry van de Velde and Nietzsche – I leave it to you to reject the latter if you find it bad –

The works have been sent by express goods, and will be there soon

Yours   E M

Price of the lithos 60 Marks each

Autograph postcard, initialled and undated, written in German. Addressed (rather chaotically): Monsieur Fritz Delius / Componist / Par Paris / Grez sur Marne / Seine et Oise / Marlotte. A postal official added the correction: bon pour Gretz sur Loing / Seine et Marne. Postmark: WEIMAR 2.3.06.

The original is in the Delius Trust Archive.

1   The reference is to the 1906 lithograph of Albert Kollmann.

(190)

Edvard Munch to Frederick Delius

[Berlin, 15 April 1906]

Dear friend. Please tell the forwarding agent to collect my works – and to store them until I give him instructions –

Please let me have a card and tell me whether this has been done. Will you and your wife not visit me in Weimar some time?

Your friend   E M –

c/o Hotel Sanssouci, Linkstr

Autograph postcard, initialled and undated, written in German. It bears the printed stamp of the Hôtel Sanssouci, Link-Strasse 37, Berlin. Addressed: Herrn Fritz Delius / Compositeur / *Grez sur Marne (Marlotte)* / Seine et Oise / *Paris*. (The exasperated tone of Delius's postcard reply of 19 April, 'You always write my address wrong!', is understandable.) Postmark: BERLIN N.W. 15.4.06.

The original is in the Delius Trust Archive.

(191)
Edvard Munch to Frederick Delius
[Draft]

[April/May 1906]

Dear Delius,

I have no forwarding agent but I thought you had engaged someone −[1]
− I have lost the papers − Will you tell me what is to be done −
Perhaps you could write to someone about this matter − I have written to
Mitchell & Kimbell
Marche St Honere[2]
but I don't know if it is alright without papers − Perhaps it has to go through the forwarding agent of L'independants − (There's a forwarding agent Delibes)
Pecuniarily and artistically and also physically I'm alright − Unfortunately that dirty business with Fräulein L − 3 years ago gave me such a nervous shock that my nerves are still not in a fit state[3] − I can hardly associate with people at all − and it's bad because I have so many friends in Weimar now − I have a lot of friends in Jena too − Won't you come over there sometime −
Here I am having great successes but would like to exhibit in Paris sometime − Perhaps it might be possible to find some premises −
I am now looking for a place where I can work in peace and quiet −
These 4 years of torture with Fr. L and the splendid final result[4] have inflicted a hellish wound on me −
It has very much amused the other dear friends −

Autograph draft letter, unsigned and undated, written in German. It was never sent.

The original is in the Munch Museum.

1   Delius had reminded Munch on 19 April: 'You never told me who your forwarding agent is!'

2   Marché St. Honoré.

3   Munch's nerves, already affected when he took refuge with the Deliuses in the spring of 1903, still had not recovered from the aftermath of his affair with Tulla Larsen.

4   An ironic reference to his accident with a revolver in 1902, for which he blamed
Tulla Larsen.

(192)
Edvard Munch to Frederick Delius
[Draft]

[May? 1906]

Dear friend, Many thanks for your efforts. The French are probably angry with
my pictures again — But I do really feel that the most daring works must be
exhibited at L'independants — Do you think it would be possible to arrange a
large exhibition in Paris — Do you think the premises of L'Independants are
available for renting in the autumn? — I give you two of my engravings —
Which will you have? — [1]

Greetings   Yours
Edvard Munch

Bad Koesen Saxen–Weimar

Autograph draft letter, signed and undated, written in German. It was never sent.

The original is in the Munch Museum.

1   Delius's response to this question is not recorded. Munch's letter was a draft, and if
a final version was indeed sent to Delius, it has not been preserved. What is known is
that Delius did possess a number of Munch's works, all of which were dispersed after
Jelka's death. (The works are listed in Appendix B of John Boulton Smith's edition of
the Delius–Munch correspondence.)

(193)
Harmonie Verlag to Frederick Delius

BERLIN W. 35, 8 May 1906
Schöneberger Ufer 32.

Herrn Frederick Delius,
Grez sur Loins

Dear Sir,

In reply to your card and your letter we must first inform you that Herr Rösch[1]
has just telephoned to let us know that Spiess of Brunswick, the Court Opera

singer, who was to have taken the baritone part, is now not going to do so presumably owing to other engagements, and in 2 days we shall be told who is taking his place in Essen, we shall then immediately send this gentleman a vocal score. Herr Witte,[2] the orchestra conductor in Essen, received a fully corrected proof, together with the good full score of "Sea-Drift" in the middle of last week, which is in good time. "Appalachia" has also been sent to the music engraver in Leipzig for copying, and we feel we should be able (within about a week) to send you the proofs. The first finished copies of the piano score of "Sea-Drift" will be forwarded to you in 6 days. We have not yet received the final proofs of the songs back from you, but hope to have them soon, so that the songs will be ready in good time before the performance in Essen. We are returning herewith Herr Suter's[3] card with best thanks.

Yours faithfully,
Harmonie

I regret to say that Herr Fall has not finished the analysis ordered from him & for no reason we can understand only told us the position when it was too late to order it from anyone else. We are extremely sorry about this!

Typed letter, signed 'Harmonie' and dated, written in German on the headed notepaper of HARMONIE/ VERLAGSGESELLSCHAFT FÜR LITERATUR UND KUNST. The unsigned postscript in in longhand.

The original is in the Delius Trust Archive.

1   Friedrich Rösch (1862–1925): German lawyer and composer, and secretary of the Allgemeine Deutsche Musikverein. He studied music under Rheinberger in Munich, and founded, together with Richard Strauss and H. Sommer, the Genossenschaft Deutscher Tonsetzer in 1898.

2   Georg Witte (1843–1929): Dutch conductor and composer. He studied at The Hague and Leipzig, subsequently teaching music in Leipzig and Alsace, and becoming conductor at Essen in 1882. *Sea Drift* was given under his baton at the Tonkünstlerfest on 24 May 1906, with Josef Loritz singing the baritone role.

3   Hermann Suter (1870–1926): Swiss conductor, composer and teacher. He studied at Laufenberg, Basel, Stuttgart and Leipzig, then conducted and taught at Zurich until moving to Basel as musical director in 1902.

(194)
Edvard Grieg to Frederick Delius

Troldhaugen 30/6/06.

Dear friend, An old man, so exhausted by physical suffering that he is fit for nothing more, bids you heartily welcome to Norway. Are you not coming to the Westland? Do try to! It would probably be the only chance for us to see each other again. We recently heard some very nice things about your wife from Felix Moscheles in London. Is she with you? Best wishes to you both from Nina and from your

Edvard Grieg

Autograph picture postcard, signed and dated, written in German. The view is of the fjord at Troldhaugen, *Nordåsvannet*. Addressed: Komponisten Hr. Fritz Delius. / Fredriksvaern/ (*Bedes eftersendt*) [Please forward].

The original is in the Delius Trust Archive.

(195)
Frederick Delius to Edvard Munch

[7 July 1906]

Aasgaardstrand.   Dear friend

I am very disappointed that you are not here. It is splendid here & fine weather. I am going into the mountains for a few weeks & then I shall return here for a few weeks & hope then to see you.[1] Yesterday I greeted your sister and aunt in your lovely little house. The garden is very fine, the flower bed too! My wife is also here & we both greet you heartily.

Your friend
Fr. Delius

Autograph postcard, signed and undated, written in German. Addressed: Herrn Edvard Munch / Russischer Hof / Weimar / Tyskland. Postmark: AASGAARD-STRAND 7 VII 06.

The original is in the Munch Museum.

1   A second disappointment came on Delius's return to Aasgaardstrand: 'I am very sorry,' wrote the composer to Munch (still in Weimar) on 2 August, 'that you are not coming here this summer.'

(196)
Edvard Grieg to Frederick Delius

Troldhaugen
Hop near Bergen
21/7/06

Dear Delius,

I am very poorly and cannot meet you anywhere, unfortunately, much as I should like to. I have, it is true, always had frail health. But now, with old age as well, life has become more and more of a burden to me. Through physical suffering I am unable to work, although I feel that I still have it in me. That is what makes existence so unbearable for me. That is of course not the right frame of mind for "Storfjeldsaeter". Forgive me. But I did not want to put you off with empty phrases. I really am delighted that you are so active; I still have the good fortune to be able to admire and love other artists and other art and so it would be an event for me to be able to be present at a performance of your opera in Berlin.[1] But whether I shall be allowed to travel to Berlin next winter is very doubtful indeed. It is not entirely out of the question however and Berlin particularly attracts me. In later years I always felt better there than in Leipzig and Copenhagen. It looks from your card as if you are not coming to the Westland. But if you should, I know that you will not pass by my door.

My wife sends her greetings to you and to your wife. Likewise does

Your
Edvard Grieg

Autograph letter, signed and dated, written in German.

The original is in the Delius Trust Archive. It is the last extant letter to Delius from Grieg, who died on 4 September 1907.

Delius appears to have visited Fredriksvaern some time late in June, leaving Jelka to paint in Aasgaardstrand. He returned to Aasgaardstrand early in July, leaving for Christiania about 8 July, and then for the Storfjeldsaeter in the Rondane region of Norway on 9 July. While he was away, Jelka suffered some depression, but Delius appears not to have been in the least anxious for her to join him in the mountains. He returned again to Aasgaardstrand on 25 July, where it seems they both stayed for most of August. Max Schillings had hoped to join them there, but ultimately convalescence from an illness prevented him from doing so. By early September, the Deliuses were back in Grez.

1   A Village Romeo and Juliet.

(197)
Hermann Suter to Frederick Delius

Lauenen near Gstaad
Kt Bern.
18 Aug. 1906.

Dear Sir,

I have today returned to the "Harmonie" Press in Berlin your "Messe des Lebens". For this winter it seems to me that it would be wiser for me if at a time when I am making some major demands on my choir (Berlioz Requiem, Bach B minor Mass) I could also make some lesser demands on them. In this way my *whole* Society, which as such has not yet sung anything of yours, might become acquainted with your style and won over for you by means of a smaller work: I have "Seadrift" in mind, which enchants me more each time I play it. I feel that if I can get Messchaert for the baritone solo the work will be interpreted ideally. Who, by the way, sang it in Essen?

The "Messe" is a very difficult proposition, particularly for soloists and choir. Nevertheless I found that there is already a definite inclination on the part of the gentlemen of the Committee to make an approach to you; this will grow still stronger once the choir knows and has mastered your "Seadrift" and if the members of the choir may be told that you had so to speak intended and expressly written the work for them. I have of course revived my own enthusiasm first and foremost for the deep poetry of the "Trunkene Lied";[1] I was particularly captivated by No III of the 1st Part "In dein Antlitz sah ich jüngst"; in fact the wonderful poetry revealed by your music was a continual delight to me. I have a slight misgiving over the fact that so many adagios follow on from each other; I wonder whether they do not work to the detriment of each other and in particular spoil the effect of that incomparable final piece? –

With most cordial greetings to you and kindest regards to your wife, I am, in sincere admiration

Yours
Hermann Suter.

Autograph letter, signed and dated, written in German.

The original is in the Delius Trust Archive.

Hermann Suter: See Letter 193, note 3.

1   Suter had performed this work, subsequently retitled *Mitternachtslied Zarathustras*, at the Tonkünstlerfest in Basel on 12 June 1903.

(198)
Frederick Delius to Theodor Szántó

Gare de   Grez sur Loing
Bourron   (Seine & Marne)
                                                                        [20 September 1906]

Dear Herr Szanto – I hear from Klemperer[1] that you are in Paris. I should very much like to talk with you about the piano part of my Piano Concerto. Would you not like to come out here for a couple of days? You could stay at our home

& we would be very pleased to have you. The weather is lovely. Saturday perhaps & bring the score with you.[2] With best wishes

Yours
Frederick Delius

Autograph *carte-lettre*, signed and undated, written in German. Addressed: Monsieur Th. Szanto / 23bis Aven. de la Motte Piquet / Ier / Paris. Postmark: PARIS 20 SEPT 06.

The original is in the Library of Congress, Washington, D.C. The full correspondence between Delius and Szántó in this collection numbers about ninety items, some of which are from Jelka Delius.

Theodor Szántó (1877–1934): Hungarian pianist and composer. He studied in Vienna and Budapest and then with Busoni in Berlin, subsequently living much in Paris. He was to be the soloist in the first performance in England of Delius's Piano Concerto.

1   The reference is to a mutual friend, Oscar Klemperer, and not to the young conductor Otto Klemperer.

2   In the event, Szántó was unable to go to Grez, and Delius made arrangements to see him instead in Paris on 17 October.

(199)
Carl Schuricht to Frederick Delius

Wiesbaden, Biebricherstr: 3, II.
3.10.06.

Dear Maestro,

Much as I wished to write to you after leaving you in Essen, my subsequent life did not allow me to get down to it: I took up my post as conductor of the Dortmund Philharmonic Orchestra – substituting for Georg Hüttner – straight afterwards, and only now that all that activity is over do I find a little time here in Wiesbaden.

How much inspiration, pure delight and joy "Sea-drift" awakened in me and left imprinted on me, I will not describe to you in more detail, but will just tell you that the mere knowledge of your physical existence has given me a source of inner warmth and joy in activity that enriches me in all my artistic undertakings.

My job in Dortmund was difficult: – as a young conductor, who had completely abandoned his career because of two years' interruption through sickness, suddenly to be put in so responsible a post (Hüttner handed the post over to me when I visited him with my compositions), a post which might easily have overtaxed my strength, it was up to me to sacrifice all consideration for my personal welfare and above all to justify by deeds the colossal confidence placed in me. It came off. I got on really marvellously with the orchestra, and also with Hüttner, the critics, the public. – It was a splendid opportunity to put matters to the test, – that is, to see whether I was any good as an orchestra conductor (that can only be found out on the rostrum) – and in consequence to set a different course for the future! Thank God it turned out so splendidly; so my childhood dream has not deceived me – as a boy of 3 I already used to stand for hours (at concerts and at home) humming and conducting with stubborn persistence; – the orchestra governed my imagination, my games; – only during my illness did I lose hope of realising my dream; and now it has *come true after all*, I didn't *stick it out* alone, no – it's the *basis* of my *life* without which I cannot survive, and through it my spirit and body are as fresh and active as ever!

Now (and that is why I have told you quite so much about it) I can at last *do* what I longed to: perform new works and good older ones; devote my energies to the service of the (terribly few) *real* composers. And so I am asking *you*, dear Maestro, who have so wonderfully revived my hopes for a new flowering of the purest, *most spiritual* and most perfect art, firstly: So long as I have no orchestra of my own, let me get *your* works better known privately: I meet all sorts of people, perhaps some conductor (for instance, Hüttner – Dortmund, or Theil – Danzig) will let me perform something of yours; I also have it in mind to perform something of yours here (Wiesbaden) off my own bat – only I haven't got enough money, and yet I would take the risk if necessary, provided I could get the music for nothing; we must talk about this; but in any case I will devote all my energies to interesting whoever I meet in your works. – To this end I should be very grateful if you could send me on loan, chiefly for detailed study, the score of your *"Sea-drift"*, and perhaps some other not too large a work for orchestra alone (a symph. poem or something similar), because at the moment I cannot buy anything I am afraid; it would be very good if you could send me these works as soon as possible, preferably by return – On 6. 10. I am going to Danzig (where I am doing something of mine) and have high hopes that I might work something good for you there. – – – [1]

And, as soon as I once have a position of my own, *then*, with my modest powers and according to my heart's desire, I can see to it that living, *real* composers *no* longer have to hide their light under a bushel, but can let it shine out brightly, and that after this period of nauseating cliquishness pure beauty and living art at last return to favour.

Please excuse this long letter of mine; I am not a man of words. – As soon as I have your scores I can do a lot – a single individual can do so much, even if he is almost unknown and a beginner with few connections. I will close now, I don't want to *talk* about how much I love your art and how loyal I am to you, I want to show it to you.

Attached are some reviews from Dortmund by way of example; as some sort of example of my other musical attributes I shall venture to send you shortly my work — *only* as a kind of example, you do understand? I shall not lay claim to the title of "composer" until I have done something big.

With kindest regards to your wife and yourself and with my warmest devotion

> Your happy, loyal and sincere admirer
> Carl Schuricht

My fiancée sends her greetings

> In admiration, my best wishes to you and your dear wife,
> Yours sincerely,
> Friedel Heinemann.

Autograph letter, signed and dated, written in German. A short signed postscript is in the hand of Friedel Heinemann, Schuricht's fiancée.

The original is in the Delius Trust Archive. It is the first of five letters and postcards written by Schuricht to Delius (and also one to Jelka Delius) between 1906 and 1910 that are preserved in the Archive.

Carl Schuricht (1880–1967): German conductor and composer. Born in Danzig, he studied in Berlin and conducted at Zwickau, Dortmund, Frankfurt, Wiesbaden and internationally. Delius's larger works were to remain in his repertoire until the end of his life.

1   In a postcard from Danzig, dated 10 October 1906, Schuricht was to acknowledge receipt of a score (*Paris*) and to express the hope of performing it in Dortmund during the coming season.

(200)
Fritz Cassirer to Frederick Delius

FRITZ CASSIRER   BERLIN N.W. 6.X.*1906*
                                                      FLENSBURGERSTRASSE. 1.

Dear Delius,

To my surprise Herr Max Chop,[1] to whom I played through the whole of your opera "R. & J.", brought me your songs and Seadrift in piano score. I had no idea that the things were already out. I have now got to know Sea-drift today! – – – What am I to write? I could have almost howled with delight. I will say no more. I am quite beside myself and wanted just to let you know briefly. Does Zarathustra have nothing but this sort of stuff too? I hope that I shall soon come into possession of the score. You are now so glorious in your maturity. Sitting comfortably and plucking the fruits from the tree! Round and ripe and sweet, it says everything that one simply forgets the artist.

Yours
Fritz Cassirer

I got Herr Chop utterly intoxicated! —

Autograph letter card, signed and dated, written in German. The card has a printed heading.

The original is in the Delius Trust Archive.

1   Max Chop (1862–1929): German music writer, critic and composer, was married to the pianist Céleste Groenevelt. His *Frederick Delius*, the first book on the composer, was to be published in Berlin in 1907. He also wrote a number of articles on Delius (see Letter 235).

(201)
Frederick Delius to Edvard Grieg

Grez sur Loing
Seine & Marne
11/10/1906

Dear friend

I send you today the piano score of "Sea-drift": It is the work which was performed at the Tonkünstler Fest in Essen this summer. The full score, like that of "Appalachia" too is still not yet ready.[1] I hope you will soon hear it in Germany, it gets performed from time to time & my music does not sound well on the piano. When are you coming to Berlin? My opera will probably not be performed before December (Christmas perhaps). I have read that you are giving a concert in Berlin on the 12th April & look forward to it & hope however that you will come to Berlin much earlier. We stayed in Aasgaardstrand until the end of August & then went from Drammen to Rouen by sea & had a splendid journey; utterly peaceful & only sunshine. Here we still have the most lovely summer, no rain & autumn weather yet set in. We are now harvesting our delicious grapes, apples & pears. The poem of Sea-drift was translated by my wife. I hope this letter finds you reasonably well & cheerful & perhaps working on something new. Give your dear wife my best wishes & here's to seeing you again soon in Berlin to which my wife too looks forward

Yours
Fritz Delius

Autograph letter, signed and dated, written in German.

The original is in the Bergen Public Library.

1   Harmonie were shortly to publish both works; and in a letter dated 3 November 1906 the company informed Delius that copies of *Appalachia* were being sent to Mottl, Richter, Wood, Suter, Mengelberg, Hutschenruijter, Dupuis and Busoni.

(202)
Max Schillings to Frederick Delius

Dear Herr Delius,

Die Lebensmesse has arrived. At the moment I am still standing in awe before your gigantic score, whose secrets do not reveal themselves at the first glance. I am shortly going to Dresden where my Moloch[1] is to be performed at the beginning of Dec. & shall see whether there is a choir there which can be entrusted with the task. Is there a piano arrangement?? That is *very* important! I hope we shall see each other when you are in Berlin. Let me hear from you!

Yours sincerely
Max Schillings

M[unich]. 16.Nov. 06.

Autograph postcard, signed and dated, written in German. Addressed: Herrn Frédérick Delius / Grez-sur-Loing / Seine et Marne / *France*. Postmark: MUENCHEN 16 NOV 06.

The original is in the Delius Trust Archive.

1   *Moloch*: Schillings's opera (op. 20), to a libretto by Emil Gerhäuser, after Hebbel, was produced in Dresden on 8 December 1906.

(203)
Fritz Cassirer to Frederick Delius

BERLIN N.W. 26.XI.*1906*
FLENSBURGERSTR. 1.

Dear Delius,

There was no end of trouble here — what with all the debating and discussing. And I could not write to you, as time and time again the following day might have brought the decision.

Gregor became very indecisive after I had got him to read the Keller story. This had an unexpected result in that he announced to me that your libretto was a bowdlerization – he could not perform an opera with a text like that. In addition there were pecuniary misgivings.

Under public pressure our Komische Oper has, in fact, developed in a manner very different to what we had imagined. In particular, like all private theatres in Berlin, we find it necessary to make the most of our successes by innumerable repeat performances. This American feature is so deeply rooted in general conditions here that any opposition would be purely quixotic. –

Then, there is the *quality* of our repertoire. Our greatest success was – "*Lakmé*"![1]

I had absolutely to agree with Gregor's practical objections. Am also convinced that "*Rom. & Juliet*" will not be a box-office success.

I endeavoured to meet his artistic objections (which were always directed against the *libretto* only) by carrying out a partial rewriting of the text (for which I did not have time to obtain your advice if I was not to give up the whole thing for lost). – It was finally decided that I was to play the opera to *Morris*,[2] the Chief Producer, who does *not* know Keller's story. He was to decide whether the work was fit for the stage. – At the same time I had discussed the stage decor with my brother[3] and with Walser.[4] You see Gregor had told me: since he was now convinced that a stage success was out of the question, he would be prepared to perform "Romeo and Juliet" as an Oratorio. Thereupon I suggested to him that we do it with simplified decorations (back-cloth only), which would make a certain stylized effect possible. After all, stage decoration at present definitely tends to artistic simplification. Gregor declared this compromise – as it was less expensive – to be worth discussing, and Walser was of the opinion that it would even be more artisitc, for the very reason that it rises above the level of simple illusion. – In order to decide all these questions, on Thursday the 15th November (that is, a date most remarkable in the history of Delius!) a soirée took place in my house, which was to decide on the life and death of your work. After a small supper, I played from 11 to 1 o'clock at night the entire opera to the following judges: Gregor, Mertens,[5] Morris, Chop, Walser, Bruno Cassirer and his wife. – My struggles over, I disappeared and left the matter to further fermentation. Then the remarkable thing happened that Mertens ran after me and declared that he did not now object any more (he had exerted the greatest influence on Gregor through financial considerations), and that he was deeply moved. The next day he told the Director that he would have liked to have heard the whole thing all over again right away! All, *without* exception, were of the opinion:

1) that the music is magnificent.
2) that the libretto is quite impossible.
3) that a success could only be expected with *rich* and luxurious scenic arrangements. –

There I now stood with my "simplified" decorations, and our stock, dear Delius, was very low. – No decision was reached. We were sitting there till half past two in the night, thinking, drinking, chatting and eating, Walser and Bruno had just woken up again after a refreshing nap, the women could not keep their eyes open, I stayed resolutely silent and fetched bottle after bottle, but Gregor sat together with Chop and established the points where in any event, the libretto would have to be altered. Then they all left, Chop accompanied Gregor through the Tiergarten, talking and talking. For a change he would rave over his sweet angel, his wife, and then Delius would become the subject again. – – –

Last Act. The next morning – as usually happens – they all realized that they had heard a magnificent work. You know. The real deep instinctive success – the only genuine one! – Gregor told me that he was really none the wiser than before, but that he would now find out how much the thing might cost, in order not to neglect anything out of consideration for you and myself. As costumes played no part in it, perhaps it would not be so dear. This last meeting took place on Saturday. Taking part: Gregor, Walser, Bruno Cassirer, myself, Hartwig (the scenery manufacturer), Stage Manager Schmidt. All the details of the decor were thoroughly discussed and things turned out to be not as bad as all that. I will tell you the particulars some other time. Briefly: the performance was agreed, and as Sali and Vreli do already know their parts and can sing them, the choir as well, and Herr Fritz Cassirer as well, it should be possible to put it on at the end of January.

All the details some other time. For today I will only say: that not one note of the music will be altered, that there will however have to be textual (*not* scenic) alterations, that we want to have a *Prologue* – to music – spoken before the first act. – I shall now have to discuss with you a great number of questions of detail, and we shall soon of course be able to work together on them in person. I would only ask you to wait before making your travelling arrangements until you receive further news from me. It is possible that Gregor might be in Paris very soon. He would then explain our ideas to you, so that we do not act without your agreement.[6] If his journey should be postponed, I will notify you at once and then expect you and Frau Jelka in Berlin very soon. We must make many – if only minor – alterations. – So, dear Delius, – have patience for one more week, and then pack your bags.

With regards to both of you from both of us

Yours   Fritz Cassirer

Autograph letter, signed and dated, written in German on headed notepaper. Envelope addressed: M./ Fredr. Delius / *Grez sur Loing* / Dep. S. et M./ *Frankreich*.

The original is in the Delius Trust Archive.

1   Some of Cassirer's misgivings about the newly founded Opera were shared by
Haym, who wrote to Delius on 2 November: 'Gregor does seem to be rather on the
wrong tack with his Kom. Oper. Kills the finest operas with his clever production
tricks. Recently he is supposed to have expressed his intention to give the Walküre as
"intimate" opera! Cassirer doesn't seem to be right for it either.'

2   Maximilian Moris: director, with Gregor, at the Komische Oper.

3   Paul Cassirer.

4   Karl Walser (1877–1943): Swiss artist, illustrator and designer. Brother of the
poet Robert Walser. He moved to Berlin in 1899, and in 1904 became associated with
Max Reinhardt as a theatre designer. He worked with Gregor in the operatic field from
the inauguration of the Komische Oper late in 1905 until his last design commission
for this house: *Romeo und Julia auf dem Dorfe*.

5   Otto Mertens: associate of Gregor and Cassirer at the Stadttheater in Elberfeld.

6   Gregor and Delius met in Paris at the beginning of December.

1907

Before long Delius was once again in Germany, this time with Jelka, to attend rehearsals of *A Village Romeo and Juliet*. The opera opened at the Komische Oper in Berlin on 21 February with Cassirer conducting. Shortly afterwards the composer heard his *Sea Drift* performed at Basel before returning to Paris on 3 March. Little more than a month later he was in London, arranging with Henry Wood for a performance in the autumn of his Piano Concerto. This was an important visit for Delius: he now made the acquaintance of a number of the younger hopefuls on the English musical scene, finding that his reputation abroad had made him a figure of particular interest at home. By the time he returned to France at the end of April, the groundwork had been done that was to assure a revival of his work in England. When he returned to London five months later, it was to help prepare for and then to attend the two concerts which were at last to lift him to the front rank of English composers. On 22 October, Szántó played the Piano Concerto with the Queen's Hall Orchestra conducted by Wood, and exactly one month later Cassirer conducted a Queen's Hall performance of *Appalachia* with the New Symphony Orchestra. Thomas Beecham attended the latter concert, hearing Delius for the first time and becoming an instant convert – after Haym, the most important one yet – to his music.

In the meantime, another influential figure had come into Delius's orbit. This was the gifted conductor and composer Granville Bantock, who now joined forces with Delius to try to bring about the establishment of an English version of the Allgemeine Deutsche Musikverein, a project that was to occupy rather too much of Delius's time for the next year or two. The year ended on an optimistic note. A new friend, Norman O'Neill, spent a few days in Grez, and in England both Beecham and Bantock were planning performances of a number of the rediscovered composer's works.

Piano Concerto in C minor (RT VII/4). Further revision, January and February.

Songs of Sunset (RT II/5). Completed.

Brigg Fair, An English Rhapsody, for orchestra (RT VI/16).

'On Craig Ddu', part-song for unaccompanied chorus (Symons) (RT IV/2). December.

Cynara, for baritone solo and orchestra (Dowson) (RT III/5). Draft full score.

(204)
Henry Wood to Frederick Delius

4, ELSWORTHY ROAD,
LONDON, N.W.
January 3rd 1907.

Dear Mr. Delius,

It is very kind indeed of you to send me the score of "Appalachia" and "Sea-Drift". The latter work I am pushing very strongly with the Sheffield Festival Committee,[1] and I hope it will be included in our scheme.

I trust that your opera will have a big success in Berlin, and if published do send me a vocal score.

For the first time in the history of our Musical Festivals, I have persuaded the Norwich Festival Committee to offer a prize for the best Cantata to last not more than 30 minutes in performance; and I wonder if, as a very great personal favour, you would act as one of the adjudicators? Your colleagues would be Sir Edward Elgar[2] and Granville Bantock.[3] I enclose you the rules for the librettists, which may interest you, and the rules for the composers I will submit for your approval, should you see your way to offering us your valuable services, in the course of the next few weeks.[4]

Do let me know of your arrival in London, as I should like you to come up and have lunch with us, when we can chat over many things.

Sincerely yours,
Henry J. Wood

Typed letter, signed and dated, written in English on headed notepaper.

The original is in the Delius Trust Archive.

1 Wood's efforts were to prove successful, although the performance under his baton did not take place until 7 October 1908, with Frederic Austin, baritone (see Letter 213, note 4), the Queen's Hall Orchestra and the Sheffield Festival Chorus.

2 Sir Edward Elgar (1857–1934): English composer, teacher and conductor. He was educated largely in his native Worcestershire, but had no formal conservatory training. In London he only really came into prominence in 1899, when his *Variations on an Original Theme (Enigma)* was first performed. The first performance of *The Dream of*

Gerontius in Birmingham in 1900 led to two performances in Düsseldorf in 1901 and 1902 under Julius Buths. These established Elgar's reputation on the Continent and started a vogue for his music. He was knighted in 1904.

3   Granville Bantock (1868–1946): English composer, teacher and conductor. He studied at the Royal Academy of Music. Bantock was now principal of the Birmingham and Midland Institute School of Music, succeeding Elgar in 1908 to the Peyton Chair of Music at Birmingham University. Delius was to make his acquaintance in the autumn of 1907, and the two men quickly became firm friends. He was knighted in 1930.

4   Delius agreed to become an adjudicator. The libretto for the prize cantata *The Vision of Cleopatra* had been written by Gerald Cumberland, and the winner's setting would be performed at the 1908 Festival.

(205)

Hermann Bischoff to Frederick Delius

[Berlin, 21 February 1907]

Dear Herr Delius,

Excuse this boarding-house ink, I'm getting another kind shortly. I spent the whole day today at Strauss's, and I told him a great deal about your opera. And what a pity: Strauss would have had time to come to the final rehearsal yesterday. He is interested in your work and intends to come to one of the next performances. This evening he has "Salome" and he has something on on Saturday too. I don't know whether you want to get in touch with him in order to arrange something, or whether you prefer to bide your time. In any case I wanted to let you know.

Well, the best of luck for this evening and hoping to see you again somewhere. Your melodies are with me today wherever I go, especially a certain violin solo on the G-string with a hobbling bassoon accompaniment.[1]

With many kind regards to you both

Yours very sincerely
Hermann Bischoff

Autograph letter, signed and undated, written in German.

The original is in the Delius Trust Archive. Two further items of correspondence preserved from Bischoff to Delius are dated May 1909.

Hermann Bischoff (1868–1936): German composer. He was a pupil of Jadassohn at the Leipzig Conservatorium, and lived for a time at Munich, where he was associated with Richard Strauss.

1   The Dark Fiddler's theme in *A Village Romeo and Juliet*, opening that evening.

(206)
Engelbert Humperdinck to Frederick Delius

E. Humperdinck   [Berlin] 7 12/3

Dear Herr Delius,

I learn from the management of the Komische Oper, whom I asked for your address, that you are no longer here.[1] I regret this very much as I should so much have liked to talk to you before you left. Unfortunately I was down with a cold again for a time, directly after the performance of your work, as a matter of fact, and I was therefore unable to see you again.

"A Village Romeo and Juliet" made an excellent impression on me, particularly the last two acts, which I find most original; as far as the first two acts are concerned I have certain doubts which I would very much like to have discussed with you, but which I think can easily be put right as they are only of a *technical* nature. In any case I hope to renew my acquaintance with your attractive work soon, and, incidentally, I hope with a better orchestra!

Hoping to see you again soon, dear Herr Delius; remember me to your kind wife and best wishes to you both from my wife and myself

Yours most sincerely
E Humperdinck

Autograph letter, signed and dated, written in German on headed notepaper.

The original is in the Delius Trust Archive. One further communication from Humperdinck to Delius is preserved (see Letter 208).

Engelbert Humperdinck (1854–1921): German composer, notably of stage works, of which *Hänsel und Gretel* is the best known. He studied at Cologne, Frankfurt and Munich, and was a special protégé of Wagner at Bayreuth in 1881 and 1882. Humperdinck spent some years in Frankfurt as a teacher and critic, but returned in 1900 to Berlin, where he became a teacher of distinction.

1   Delius had travelled on to Basel at the end of February for the final rehearsal of *Sea Drift* on 1 March, attending the performance conducted by Suter the following day. The composer returned to Paris on 3 March.

(207)
Cyril Scott to Frederick Delius

274 Kings Rd.
Chelsea. SW.
March 16.07.

My dear Friend.

I have seen two exellent rooms at 88 Oakley St. (Mrs Petley) here in Chelsea
which will be free first week in April. They are 30/– the week on the ground
floor and they are next to each other – sitting room in front bedroom at the
back – very nice clean quiet house. If you decide to take them will you write
direct to the said Mrs Petley as I am leaving town & can not arrange further
about them. If you do not want to take those then I think you would have to
put up at an Hotel & look round – There were a good many to let in the
neihbourhood but as I happen to know about these being very respectable &
can not tell you about the others – perhaps it is better to take those one knows
something about in case one may have to deal with dishonesty. So glad about
the opera & am delighted you are coming. No 88 Oakley is only three minutes
from me. I go out of town now as I said before but shall return 2nd week in
April. Best greetings.

        ever yrs sincerely
        Cyril Scott.

Autograph letter, signed and dated, written in English. Envelope addressed: Monsieur.
F. Delius / Grez sur Loing./ Seine & Marm / France.

The original is in the Delius Trust Archive. One further communication from Scott to
Delius is preserved (see Letter 240).

Cyril Scott (1879–1970): English composer and writer, whose greatest popularity was
to be achieved for his piano pieces. He studied in Frankfurt, where he was a contemporary of Balfour Gardiner, Percy Grainger, Norman O'Neill and Roger Quilter.

(208)
Engelbert Humperdinck to Frederick Delius

7 23/3   [Berlin]

Dear Herr Delius,

On the point of leaving for Italy, I have just received your esteemed lines. My
doubts were of a purely technical nature and they cannot be discussed without

having the music to hand. I remember, for instance, that the songs behind the scenes were just as heavily scored as if they had been sung on the stage, whereas one ought to make a distinction. But these are trifles, of course, which you have probably long ago found out for yourself.

With best wishes

Yours
E Humperdinck

Autograph postcard, signed and dated, written in German. Addressed: Monsieur Frederick Delius / Grez sur Loing / Seine et Marne / Frankreich. Postmark: GRÜNE-WALD [Berlin] 23.3.07.

The original is in the Delius Trust Archive.

(209)
Henry Wood to Frederick Delius

4, ELSWORTHY ROAD,
LONDON, N.W.
April 13th 1907.

Dear Mr. Delius,

I have looked through your Pianoforte Concerto this morning before breakfast, and it is just the work I should love to do at my popular concerts. So, will you give me the name of your pianist (and address) in order that I can communicate with him at once, and fix an approximate date in August, September or October. I am returning your score, registered, this morning. If you will let me have it again by August 16th, with the parts (strings 76443) I shall be very grateful. In haste, with kindest regards,

Sincerely yours,
Henry J. Wood
pp A.E.D.

F. Delius Esq.

Typed letter, initialled 'A.E.D.' pp Henry J. Wood, and dated, written in English on headed notepaper.

The original is in the Delius Trust Archive.

Delius had left Grez on 6 April for Paris. Camille Chevillard had agreed that Szántó should visit him at home there on 7 April to play through Delius's Piano Concerto. The

composer continued his journey to London the following day, and lunched with Wood
on 12 April.

(210)
Frederick Delius to Jelka Delius

90 Oakley Str
Chelsea SW
14th/4/07

Dearest Jelka!

Enclosed a letter from Wood as you see he likes the Concerto. They only pay
solists 5 guineas for the promenade Concerts I hope Szanto will play it in spite
of the small fee. It is an opening & Wood says it is the best public in London &
if he is a success he gets other engagements. I wrote to Rösch to accept the
Tonkünstler affair.[1] I think it wise not to let an opportunity go by. Wood was
nice & I think will play my music now. London is a splendid field. Did you get
the bulbs & the paper − It does not pay to send parcels with so few things. The
bulbs cost 1^s/7^P & the parcel post 1^s/4^P. I told Rösch to send you the 60 marks
− I shall soon want more money I have only £5 left & have to pay my rooms
tomorrow. If only Sobernheim[2] would tip up. Otherwise I shall write Arons for
more bank notes.[3] I paid all my things Suits £11-5-0. I shall also have to buy
another pair of boots. My black ones are cracking. I went today, Sunday, to
Hampton Court with Keary It was lovely out there & you have no idea how
beautiful the Hyacinths were & all sorts of other flowers, planted in masses in a
long allée; And then an old garden with yew trees & wonderful old bushes of
red & yellow flowers. The fruit trees in the gardens about Chiswick & Twick-
enham were all in full bloom. We had lunch at an old Inn near the Thames. I
dine tomorrow night with Balfour Gardiner[4] & shall meet some musicians. I
lunch with Percy Pitt tomorrow also. When you come you can either sleep in
my bed which is very wide, or have another room. Try to get someone to catch
the moles! Dont let Charles[5] be lazy it will spoil him entirely. With lots of love
to you. I am yrs always.

Fred

Is the wine bottled?

Autograph letter, signed and dated, written in English.

The original is in the Grainger Museum.

1 See Letter 193, note 1. Rösch now had Delius's Piano Concerto scheduled for the
1907 Tonkünstlerfest in Dresden.

2   I am not sure to which member of the Sobernheim family Delius was referring. Jelka's uncle, Felix Moscheles, had married Grete Sobernheim in 1875.

3   The firm of Gebrüder Arons, of Mauerstrasse 34, Berlin, held at this time some 10,000 dollars' worth of bonds in Delius's name.

4   H. Balfour Gardiner (1877–1950): English composer. Like Grainger, he was a pupil of Ivan Knorr at Frankfurt. After short spells at Oxford and as a music teacher at Winchester College, he devoted himself to composition and then to financing concerts and supporting his musician friends, putting to enlightened use his considerable personal fortune. Delius, particularly in his difficult later years, was to be a grateful beneficiary of Gardiner's generosity.

5   Charles was evidently the gardener at Grez at this time.

(211)

Frederick Delius to Jelka Delius

[London, 16? April 1907]

I have no news of Cassirers.[1] I wrote to the Adelphi Theatre but received no answer. Qu'est-ce? Your Aunt[2] also I have not seen. They were in Paris when I called last. It would be worth while to come over here only to see the Turners in the Tate Gallery – Some are quite remarkable & one sees where Monet got his Thames bridge from – I wrote to Arons for more money. I dined with Balfour Gardiner last night & they played Appalachia thro (a few musicians were there) all were tremendously taken with it. This really is my field.[3]

yrs ever   Fred

Autograph postcard, signed and undated, written in English. Addressed: Madame / Jelka Delius / Grez sur Loing / Seine & Marne / France. Postmark: CHELSEA S W 16[?] AP 07.

The original is in the Grainger Museum.

1   Fritz Cassirer and his wife were due in London during the course of a British tour. Cassirer and Delius were now planning a performance of *Appalachia* in London for some time later in the year.

2   Felix Moscheles's wife.

3   In a further letter to Jelka, dated 18 April, Delius wrote, 'I lunch with the critic of the daily telegraph [Robin Legge] tomorrow. Everybody seems very keen on me here. Especially all the young lot. Cyril Scott I have also seen & he is really very nice.'

(212)

Henry Wood to Frederick Delius

4, ELSWORTHY ROAD,
LONDON, N.W.
April 20th 1907.

Dear Mr. Delius,

I am glad you liked the concert on Thursday. Unfortunately we only had one full rehearsal of Pitt's Sinfonietta, and it did not go as well as it otherwise would have done, had I had more time.

I shall be delighted to see you, and look through the score of your latest work, and will fix up an appointment next week, without fail.[1]

Could you do me a very great personal favour, and accept, with Mr. Granville Bantock, the adjudicatorship of the little Cantata for the next Norwich Festival? As the composers will all be setting the same libretto, it lightens the work considerably, and I do not expect more than 10 or 15 of these short works. As there is nearly two months time in which to perform the work of adjudication, the manuscripts could be sent to you in any part of the world. I hope you will see your way to oblige me. We have received 51 libretti, so there is a chance of getting a decent one I hope.

I enclose you the scheme for the Sheffield Festival (which kindly return) in order that you may see what your work is associated with; but please keep this strictly private and don't give any information about it to the Press.

Sincerely yours,
Henry J. Wood

Typed letter, signed and dated, written in English on headed notepaper.

The original is in the Delius Trust Archive.

1   'I lunch with Wood to morrow', wrote Delius to Jelka on 24 April, '& shall show him the "Messe".'

(213)

Frederick Delius to Jelka Delius

90 Oakley Str
Chelsea
21/4 07

Dearest

I received your two letters this morning. Perhaps it is just as well to postpone your visit until the autumn, as I want to get back as quick as I can to do a little work before Dresden & it would be a pity for you to stay only 3 days. Meet me then in Paris on Monday evening. My stay has been most successful & I should have no difficulty here to take the first place. Everyone wants me to come and live in London. I also met Percy Grainger,[1] a most charming young man & more gifted than Scott & less affected. An Australien — you would like him immensely. We all meet at his house on Thursday for music. My Concerto & Appalachia. I have become acquainted with the musical critic of the daily Telegraph — Robin Legge.[2] He has a very charming wife & daughter & they have invited me already several times. He is all fire & flame. I left him the score of Appalachia & he & Percy Grainger are quite enthusiastic about it. Enclosed a little note Grainger left at my house after he had seen & played the score.[3] He is impulsive & nice. There is a splendid Baritone here a Mr Austin,[4] *very musical* & I hope he will sing Sea-drift at Sheffield & later the "Messe". I take the score of the "Messe" to Mr Kalisch[5] this morning. He has just written me for my songs as some singer[6] wants them for her recital I shall have to buy a copy I suppose — 3 shillings is très dur — I shall try to get the curtains & muslin & shall ask your Aunt where to go. I go with them to the Theater tonight. My clothes are splendid & my shirts [?] also. In Paris they would have cost just the double. Labels to tie I have bought & will buy sticking labels. Did you have your tooth out? I cannot correct the voices of S.d. here. I am too hurried & busy & shall wait until Grez. I have also not quite finished the Concerto. We must be in no hurry for an Editor. If it is a success I might get a lot of money for it — The voices will cost very little.

> With love
> your loving
> Fred

Autograph letter, signed and dated, written in English.

The original is in the Grainger Museum.

1   Percy Aldridge Grainger (1882–1961): Australian composer and pianist. As a pianist he was a prodigy, studying with Pabst in Melbourne and Kwast and Knorr in Frankfurt, where he came together, as a member of the 'Frankfurt gang', with some of the younger and brighter English musicians at the Conservatorium. By now, he had toured widely, notably in Europe. Together with Rose Grainger, his mother, he was now staying in London, where he was much in demand in musical salons and the society which frequented them. He was to become one of Delius's most devoted admirers.

2   Legge had been a contemporary of Delius at the Leipzig Conservatorium.

3   This undated note, here quoted in full, is preserved in the Delius Trust Archive:

Excuse my writing, but I do think the harmonies & all I can make out of the score just *too* moving & lovely.

Longing to hear it

Till Thursday

Yrs

Percy Grainger

4 Frederic Austin (1872–1952): English baritone. He also composed and was an organist and a teacher, Delius's initial judgement *'very musical'* being a fitting description of the whole man. He was to sing *Sea Drift* at the 1908 Sheffield Festival.

5 Alfred Kalisch (1863–1933): English writer and critic who had been greatly impressed by Delius's 1899 concert. Delius was hoping that Kalisch would translate the *Mass of Life* text into English (Kalisch was, for example, later to be responsible for the English libretti of *Der Rosenkavalier* and other Strauss operas). Harmonie, however, were to turn him down on the grounds of expense and to propose their own translator, John Bernhoff.

6 The renowned Mrs Kirkby Lunn.

(214)

Frederick Delius to Percy Grainger

90 Oakley Str

Chelsea SW

22/4/07

Dear Grainger!

Thank you so much for your kind words about "Appalachia" which pleased me exceedingly[1] I hope you will hear it once in London as it sounds better on the Orckestra than on the piano. I will bring the piano score on Thursday & also the Concerto & am looking forward to meeting you again.

Sincerely yours

Frederick Delius

Autograph letter, signed and dated, written in English.

The original is in the Grainger Museum. It is the first letter from Delius to Grainger in an extensive correspondence that was to be maintained almost until Delius's death.

1 See Letter 213, note 3.

(215)

John Coates to Frederick Delius

9^M HYDE PARK MANSIONS,
LONDON, N.W.
Apl 25 1907

My dear Delius

Welcome to England! I have been wanting to get into touch with you for the last 2 or 3 years. Buths of Düsseldorf gave me your address & I lost it. I want to get hold of your songs. I should be delighted if you would help me by putting me on to those which are suitable for tenor — it was quite an accident that I heard from Frederic Austin the other day that you were in London. Will you come to the annual dinner of our old Bradfordian club at the *New Gaiety tomorrow Friday at 7.30 for 8.* as my guest? Do, it would be delightful There are not many of us — we are all old Bfd Grammar School boys You are sure to know all of them — I shall sing a few songs afterwards — that is all — so you will have nothing to do but to sit & smoke & think of old times.

I sincerely hope you will be able to come — then we could have a chat about your music

Yours sincerely
John Coates

Autograph letter, signed and dated, written in English on headed notepaper.

The original is in the Delius Trust Archive. It is the first of five letters written by Coates to Delius between 1907 and 1910 that have been preserved.

John Coates (1865–1941): English tenor (although he sang baritone roles until the turn of the century). A pupil of Burton and Bridge and later of Shakespeare, his breakthrough as a tenor came as Elgar's Gerontius at the Three Choirs Festival of 1902. Like Delius, he had attended Bradford Grammar School, and later remembered the composer as a boy with some affection. His repertory was to include a number of Delius's songs.

(216)

Robin Legge to Frederick Delius

21. May 07
33, OAKLEY STREET,
CHELSEA, S.W.

My dear F.D.

Many thanks for your letter. I will come over to Grez if ever a chance offers — you bet! The day you left town[1] I was appointed chief critic of the *Daily*

Telegraph, so that now I have the most responsible & authoritative position in the press. I saw Henry Wood the other day, who it seems has by no means let the grass grow under his feet on the subject we spoke so much of. He told me [he] had typewritten the sketch of a great scheme – but I have not yet seen it.[2] When I see it I will write to you. I have been booming the "Ring" in English like blazes in the *D.T.* & absolutely the only people who have damned me for a Philistine are – English! Truly the most antiBritisher is a Britisher. Richter said last week that never had he conducted the Ring in which so much beautiful *singing* – not barking – was to be heard as the 2 cycles he directed here this month. I have been every night to the opera.

Cassirer lunched with me a few days ago on his way to see Sharpe, the agent. But I have not yet heard the result of the interview. He said he would let me know. A delightful fellow. We spoke German for 3½ hours!

Cyril Scott has written a violin sonata. I've not heard it but Percy Grainger says he does not care for it. At Covent Garden last night I met your London conductor Herz – a genial old fellow who spoke so nicely of you. Also I have seen a good deal of Whitehill[3] who says the same. He is a very pleasant fellow, full of artistic ideas who doesn't always put them into use on the stage. He sang Wolfram very beautifully yesterday. He is to be Wotan in the English "Ring" under Richter next January. It will be a fine blow to the anti-English lot, Hans Richter being so keen. I am to be the guest of the evening at the annual dinner of the London Symphony orchestra next Sunday evening. May get a chance for a talk to one or two. The world is wagging very pleasantly, & though doing prodigies of work I am very cheery. Greetings of the most cordial character to you from us all.

Y[rs] ever
Robin H. Legge.

Send me your photo: & tell me all about the Tonk. Versammlung.[4] & all your news.

Autograph letter, signed and dated, written in English on headed notepaper.

The original is in the Delius Trust Archive. It is the first dated item of seventeen letters and postcards written by Legge to Delius between 1907 and 1910 that have been preserved.

1   Delius returned to Paris on 29 April.

2   Evidently the embryonic Musical League had been discussed. It was a project which was to occupy Delius considerably for some time.

3   Clarence Whitehill (1871–1932): American baritone. He had sung in Brussels (making his début there in 1898), Paris, Bayreuth and New York by the time he took on the role of Koanga when Delius's opera had its première in Elberfeld in March 1904.

4   Other correspondence points to Delius not attending the 1907 Tonkünstlerfest in Dresden.

(217)
Frederick Delius to Percy Grainger

[Grez, 31 May 1907]

Dear Grainger!

I sent you "Appalachia" which *please take with* you to Grieg[1] when you go as he knows nothing of my music & it will put us in touch again as I really like him so much. I am working at something new — So you need not be in a hurry to send *G. Bushes*.[2] Give it me when I come to London. The score of A is of course for *you*, only shew it to Grieg.

  Affectionately yr friend
  Fr Delius

Autograph picture postcard, GREZ-SUR-LOING — *Le Pont*, signed and undated, written in English. Addressed: Percy Grainger Esqre / 5 Harrington Rd / South Kensington / Londres S W / *Angleterre*. Postmark: GREZ 31 -5 07.

The original is in the Grainger Museum.

1   Grainger was about to leave for Bergen, where he was to stay for the first time with the Griegs. 'I have never met anyone who *understands* me as he does,' Grieg was to write of him in his diary.

2   'Green Bushes (Passacaglia on an English Folksong)', nos. 12 and 25 of Grainger's *British Folk Music Settings*, was composed in 1905–6. It was rescored for two pianos (six hands) and as such first published by Schott in 1921, the full score following in 1931.

(218)
Henry Wood to Frederick Delius

4, ELSWORTHY ROAD,
LONDON, N.W.
June 5th 1907.

My dear Mr. Delius,

I am delighted to hear that your Piano Concerto is in the hands of the editor, and if I receive it by August 15 or 20 it will do nicely, provided you promise to correct all the parts and duplicates yourself.

I am sending on your Messe to-day to Harmonie. I believe that John Bernhoff is a very clever man, and hope he will make a great success of the translation of your work into English.[1] I need not say I have looked through your score several times with the keenest interest, and I have lent your "Appalachia" to Mr. Arthur Fagge, the Conductor of the London Choral Society, and think it is not unlikely he will produce it in London next season, but of this more later.

I fear Mr. Legge's scheme[2] has fizzled out altogether, as I have heard nothing more about it. I quite agree with you that it is high time something was done in London for a proper series of orchestral concerts which will not depend upon door money, and which will be entirely subscribed for before the doors open, but so far I have failed utterly to bring this about.

When you are over here, we will try and go into the matter, and I shall probably ask you to call upon some people with me, as it can only be done by talking to them personally, and unfortunately I have so little time for interviews. I hope by then to have the whole idea typed out, with the number of concerts, expenses, and all details on paper. I will also plank down £100 myself to start the subscription and guarantee, as I am never going to rest until I bring off this scheme.

My Directors are funky about it, because they think it may interfere with their regular season of 12 concerts, and affect the receipts, which Heaven knows are bad enough as it is.

Please do not suggest an English Ton-Kinstler as if you heard the local orchestras, even in places like Liverpool and Birmingham, you would have a fit. They have improved a good deal in recent years, but are still incapable of playing a modern work by Strauss or yourself: why they cannot even accompany "Elijah" decently! But, pray don't breathe a word of this opinion to anyone.

The provincial orchestra player, with very few exceptions, through playing so many years in Music-halls and Theatres is quite unfit technically to tackle even a Beethoven Symphony. I am constantly conducting in important centres like Birmingham, Manchester and Liverpool, and even the Scottish Orchestra, and know the class of material.

Richter's idea of giving the "Ring" at Covent Garden is undoubtedly proposed with the idea of giving himself a nice operatic engagement in January, and to put money into the pockets of the Opera Syndicate, who have the theatre on their hands. In future they are going to ruin the concert business in London by running a season of Italian opera in the Autumn, and then after Christmas another with a very doubtful English cast for January, February and March, to be followed by the grand Society season in April, May, June and July. As it is directly the season starts at Covent Garden our receipts at the Promenades drop £40 or £50 per night.

England has had no opera for many years, and now we are getting it, the public flock in their thousands, but in five or six years time they will get tired, because they really only go to hear the tenor or the soprano, and not to hear author or composer.

We shall be in Paris for ten days from July 1st, and must arrange a meeting, though I am not quite sure at the present moment where we shall stay, but will let you know later.[3]

Many thanks for so kindly sending my wife your songs, which she will look through and write to you about personally.

With our kindest regards,

Sincerely yours,
Henry J. Wood

F. Delius Esq.

Typed letter, signed and dated, written in English on headed notepaper.

The original is in the Delius Trust Archive.

1   Bernhoff made the original English translation of the text of *A Mass of Life*. It appears in the first publication of the work, later in 1907, by Harmonie Verlag. In spite of Wood's hopes, it can by no means be said that the translation was either satisfactory or successful.

2   The Musical League.

3   Wood was to pay a day's visit to Grez on 9 July.

(219)
Frederick Delius to Percy Grainger

Grez sur Loing
Seine & Marne
10th June 1907

Dear Grainger!

I just received your card and am very glad you like "Appalachia".[1] In a week or so I shall send you "Paris" which is shortly going to be published & which will have to be arranged for piano. I have proposed you to my Editors & if the work interests you, perhaps you might undertake it.[2] I believe they pay fairly well. Otto Singer did "Appalachia". Professor Buths of Düsseldorf arranged Paris for 2 pianos – I will also send you his arrangement with my full score.

Perhaps when I come to England you will be able to let me have the score of Green Bushes which I should just love to have. In the summer I have always a great longing to go to Norway & live among the Mountains. I love the light nights so. Which way will you go? Let me know also when. The feeling of nature I think is what I like so much in Griegs best things You have it too & I think we all 3 have something in common. I wont swear that I shant turn up on the steamer when you go to Bergen. If Grieg were only young & well enough to go into the hills we might have a lovely time. Give my kindest regards to your mother & believe me

ever your friend
Frederick Delius

I wish you a tremendous success for your concert & shall think of you on the 15th.

———————————

Autograph letter, signed and dated, written in English.

The original forms part of the estate of the late Ella Grainger, White Plains, New York.

1   Grainger had written from London on 8 June: 'A thousand thanks for the Appalachia score. *how* interesting it is. Of course I shall just love to show it to Grieg & bear him your messages.'

2   There is no evidence to suggest that Grainger ever arranged *Paris*. Much later – in 1922 – he was to arrange *A Dance Rhapsody* No. 1 for two pianos (four hands), which was published by Universal Edition the following year.

(220)   •
Balfour Gardiner to Frederick Delius

Sea Bank Farm
Chapel St Leonards
Alford. Lincolnshire

17.6.07

My dear Delius,

Forgive my long delay in answering your letter & very kind invitation, which I shall accept with the greatest pleasure.

The time which would suit me best to visit you would be in the beginning of August:¹ but if that were not convenient to you, I could come any time that month – in September I am engaged. I am already expecting to enjoy that visit immensely: nothing pleases me better than the peaceful life of the country; & I hope you will not feel under the obligation to arrange any excursions, or do anything different to your ordinary occupations.

And if you would leave me some hours for work, I should be completely happy.

We will discuss the S.B.C.² when we meet.

Give my kind regards to your wife & believe me

Very sincerely yours
H. Balfour Gardiner

Autograph letter, signed and dated, written in English.

The original is in the Delius Trust Archive. It is the first of twenty-four letters written by Gardiner to Delius between 1907 and 1910. A further three letters preserved in the Archive are dated 1929 and 1934.

1   On 23 July, Robin Legge wrote to Delius: 'Balfour Gardiner tells me he is going over to see you – also Cyril Scott. The latter is devoted now only to "occultism" – & is seen everywhere with a black Yogi who is supposed to hold in his head all the Secrets of the Universe. Scott is a whole-hogger in the matter.'

2   Society of British Composers. Founded in 1905 under the aegis of Frederick Corder and Tobias Matthay, 'with the intention of doing for England what Belaieff had done for Russia', the society published over the imprint 'Charles Avison Ltd.'.

(221)
Richard Dehmel to Frederick Delius

5.7.7.
BLANKENESE BEI HAMBURG PARKSTRASSE 22

Dear Sir,

I have noted from the newspaper enclosed that you intend to bring out a choral work under the title "Lebensmesse". Presumably you do not know that I have published a choral poem under the same title, and that this title was invented by me personally; the word "Lebensmesse" did not exist in the German language before. My poem has also been set to music several times; admittedly none of these compositions has yet been performed, but negotiations are in progress. So it is as much in your interest as in mine that you should choose another title for your work. I am very sorry that I must ask this of you; but you will realize that I cannot waive my copyright. Moreover you will easily find in Nietzsche himself a title which fits your Zarathustra choral work as well, or even better. In any case I hope that, as an artist whom I highly esteem, you will sympathize with the embarrassing position I am forced to take up, and not take my request amiss.

Yours very sincerely
Richard Dehmel.

N.B. I should like a reply as soon as possible.

Autograph letter, signed and dated, written in German on headed notepaper.

The original is in the Delius Trust Archive. It is the first of three communications from Dehmel to Delius, all dated 1907, that have been preserved.

Richard Dehmel (1863–1920): German poet, influenced by Nietzsche's philosophy. He was one of the group of artists and writers that included Munch, Strindberg, Heiberg, Knut Hamsun and Christian Krohg who frequented the Zum schwarzen Ferkel café in Berlin in the 1890s and who in a number of cases were also individually associated with Delius.

(222)
Arve Arvesen to Frederick Delius

Eidsvold 2/8 1907

Thank you very much for your letter. As far as I know 4,500 francs is not much for the violin, but in any case it is too much money for me to be able to buy it without more ado. I am sure you will agree with me in this.

On the 19th of this month, I am going on a two months tour with *Karl Nissen* (Norw. pianist) and I shall not be back in Kristiania until about the 25th–30th October. If you have still not sold the violin by that time, perhaps we can write about it again then.

My brother and his wife send you many kind regards.

Yours
Arve Arvesen

Autograph letter, signed and dated, written in German on the headed notepaper of William Arvesen, Lawyer.

The original is in the Delius Trust Archive. It is the only letter from Arvesen that is preserved in the Archive.

An earlier note sketches Arvesen's career (see Letter 13, note 4). It may, however, be useful to round out the picture of this close friend of Delius from the Leipzig and earlier Paris days. As a boy Arvesen had studied violin under Gudbrand Bøhn (who, incidentally, was to lead in 1897 the orchestra at the Christiania Theatre when *Folkeraadet* was performed). He went to the Leipzig Conservatorium as a sixteen-year-old, studying there under Sitt from 1885 to 1888. It was during this period that Adolph Brodsky's celebrated chamber concerts exerted a strong influence on him, attracting him henceforth to chamber music above all other forms. From 1889 to 1892 he studied with Marsick in Paris (where his début as a performer came in 1891), and from 1892 to 1895 with Ysaÿe in Brussels. He was then active as *konsertmester* in Finland until the turn of the century, returning in 1900 to Norway. After a spell in Bergen, he taught and performed in Gothenburg from 1903 to 1905, moving then to Christiania, where he taught until 1928 before finally settling in Bergen as principal of the Conservatorium there. He founded the Arvesen Quartet in 1916; this was succeeded in 1921 by the Arvesen Trio, noted for its performances of newer music.

No record of any meetings between Arvesen and Delius after Delius's early Paris period has yet come to light. Useful sources of documentation on Arvesen are *Tonekunst*, Årg. 1929, Nr 18, pp. 246–7, and *Nordisk Musikerblad*, Årg. 1951, Nr 2, p. 9.

(223)

Breitkopf & Härtel to Frederick Delius

BREITKOPF & HÄRTEL, LONDON.

LONDON, W. September 3rd. 1907.
54, Great Marlborough Street.

Frederick Delius, Esq.,
  Grez sur Loing, Seine et Marne.

Dear Sir,

We take the liberty of writing to ask whether you would have any objection to our reproducing a portrait of yourself in our fine series of postcards of celebrated musicians, and in this case we would esteem it a favour if you could kindly let us have a portrait for this purpose.[1]

You will no doubt be pleased to hear that we have recently made arrangements with "Harmonie" of Berlin whereby we have acquired the sole selling rights for your works in England.

Thanking you very much in anticipation.

We beg to remain, Dear Sir,
Yours faithfully,
for Breitkopf & Haertel.
Ott Kling

Typed letter, signed and dated, written in English on headed notepaper.

The original is in the Delius Trust Archive. It is one of the first of forty-five letters sent by Breitkopf & Härtel, London, to Delius between 1907 and 1910 that have been preserved.

Otto Marius Kling: manager of Breitkopf & Härtel, London, and from 1915 until his death in 1924, proprietor of J. & W. Chester.

[1] Delius was sent 'a dozen of the finished portrait cards' by Breitkopf on 23 September.

(224)
Percy Grainger to Frederick Delius

Svinkløv. Jutland.
9.9.07.

My dear Delius

Warmest thanks for your kind sympathetic card. Isn't it too sad, darling sweet little Grieg's death?[1]

I had such an unspeakably happy & uplifting time with them. I left them about a month ago.

He was always talking of you, affectionately & admiringly, & told me lots of jolly anecdotes of your trips together in the High Hills.

I showed him Appalachia & played him bits & he studied often in the score, & was *keenly interested.*

On the very day I got M[rs] Grieg's wire telling me of his death I was planning to write you & convey to you Grieg's delight when I proposed to him that I'd ask you to send him a score of Appalachia.

3 Cheers re your Brigg Fair work.[2]

Longing see it & you.

In frantic haste, & warm thanks for your friendly sympathy

Yrs ever
Percy Grainger

% E.L. Robinson – 7 Wigmore St. Lond. W.
Am playing at the 1st Grieg Memorial concert in Denmark Friday next

---

Autograph letter, signed and dated, written in English.

The original is in the Delius Trust Archive. Grainger's many letters, either as originals or in copy form, are widely distributed: principal owners are the Library of Congress, the Grainger Museum and the Delius Trust.

1   Less than two weeks before his death on 4 September, Grieg had written to his friend Julius Röntgen: 'Grainger was a splendid fellow! *How* he played and *how* dear and kind he was!' (letter dated 23 August 1907, quoted in Julius Röntgen, *Edvard Grieg* ('Beroemde Musici', Vol. 19, 2nd ed. {Den Haag: Kruseman, 1954.}). Delius, having learned of the event from newspaper reports, wrote on 6 September to ask Grainger for particulars.

2   Grainger had set the folk song 'Unto Brigg Fair' for unaccompanied chorus, and the work had been published by Forsyth in 1906. Inspired by this setting, Delius composed his orchestral work, subtitled 'An English Rhapsody', in 1907 (he had 'finished an English Rhapsody', as he wrote to Szántó on 11 July), and subsequently dedicated it to Grainger.

(225)
Nina Grieg to Frederick Delius

Troldhaugen 16–9–07.

Dear Delius,

Thank you for having written to me. I am sure I need not tell you "how and where the misfortune happened", you will have read it everywhere. You will also know without my needing to tell you that I am sad and lonely. Until the day before his death he still hoped to go to England, to fulfil his obligations.[1] He rallied so marvellously and gathered the rest of his energy just so as to be able to live long enough for this. Only the fact that he had to suffer so indescribably during the last months can reconcile me to the thought of his death. I have to return again and again to this thought in order to overcome my own disgust with life. Well, I won't distress you, I think you will understand.

I intend to return to Troldhaugen each spring, as long as I survive. But next week I am going to stay with some friends in the country in Denmark, and perhaps in the New Year with friends in England. I would like to meet you again, dear Delius, and get to know your wife.

In old friendship
Yours
Nina Grieg.

Autograph letter, signed and dated, written in German.

The original is in the Delius Trust Archive.

1   The principal obligation was a visit to the Leeds Festival in October, when Grieg was to have conducted three *Scenes from Olav Trygvason*, together with the A minor Concerto with Grainger as soloist. In the event, Stanford took over the baton for this memorial concert.

(226)
Frederick Delius to Granville Bantock

Grez sur Loing
Seine & Marne
19th Sept. 1907

Dear Mr Bantock –

Mrs Olga Wood wrote to me and asked if I had anything for Soprano & Orchestra for her to sing at your concert in Birmingham March 25th 1908. I was very pleased that you had expressed a desire to have something of mine played & thank you very much indeed. I have just finished a cyclus of songs by Ernest Dowson, for Soprano, Baritone, small chorus & Orchestra.[1] Would it be possible to have this done? Mr Austin, I am sure, would sing the Baritone part splendidly. The chorus is not difficult. Otherwise I only have my 7 danish Songs. Of course I should prefer my later work to be given. If it would interest you I would send you the orchestral score of "Paris" which has not yet been given in England. I come to London on October 1st for a few months and should so much like to make your acquaintance. I should have loved to come up to Stoke on Trent for the performance of your "Omar Khayyam" together with Austin, but I had an engagement for that day: Austin having told me of the Concert only 2 days before.

With kindest regards

I remain
Sincerely yours
Frederick Delius

I hope I shall hear something of yours this winter!! Wood plays a piano Concerto of mine on Oct 22nd.

———————

Autograph letter, signed and dated, written in English.

The original is in the Delius Trust Archive. It is the first of seventy-four letters and postcards written by the Deliuses to Bantock between 1907 and 1930 that have been preserved. A final item, dated 30 July 1934, is from Jelka to Lady Bantock.

1 *Songs of Sunset*. Delius had turned to the works of the English poet Ernest Dowson (1867–1900) for the text of his latest composition.

(227)
Fritz Cassirer to Frederick Delius

Charlottenburg Fasanenstr. 84
9.X.07.

Dear Delius,

I now hear from Sharpe that he is not in a position to obtain a choir for me. I will therefore give a concert without a choir, which with regard to "Appalachia" and "Seadrift" I very much regret. The choir from Leeds – so Sharpe told me – would entail the expense of the railway journey. This would make it particularly dear. If you or one of your friends are in a position to obtain a good choir for me approximately from the 15 October, then I am willing to revert to my original idea for a programme.

i.e.   1) Undecided. Perhaps an Engl. overt. or suchlike.
  2) Seadrift.
  3) Appalachia.
  4) Heldenleben.

If not, I would give Paris and Briggfair, which would certainly be awkward inasmuch as one of these works is not known to me at all, the other only superficially, and I would have to study them first. I sent you a telegram today so as to get the music as soon as possible.

I shall not be in London until the 1 November, and have today written to Sharpe that I shall definitely take the Hall for the 22 November. As regards the orchestra, I am insisting on *two* extra rehearsals, i.e. *three* in all. These must be conceded by the orchestra. As this point is still not settled, I am now committed to "Queen's Hall" and to the 22nd November, but not yet to the "London Symphony Orchestra".

If *you* could now send me within the next few days some accurate particulars about the "Beecham-Orchestra", it would still be possible that I might decide in favour of *these* people, because of the money it would save and because of the better opportunities for rehearsal. I read in the "Daily Telegraph" that they are going to give a concert in a few days' time. Perhaps you might go and listen to them? I suspect they will not be mature enough yet. The London Symphony Orchestra has the advantage of having performed "Heldenleben" under Richter last year. So they have perfected it and I would save a lot of time, which I could devote to the new works. Nevertheless, I will first await your further news. Just imagine, the London Symphony Orchestra asks *1000* M. per rehearsal! The concert would cost 7000 M. *without* a choir, without a baritone. Horrendous!

I received from "Harmonie" the piano scores and full scores of "Seadrift" and "Appalachia". I have not got the "Mass" yet, but they have advised me from Leipzig of its dispatch.

I have yet another idea. "Seadrift" requires a large choir, but "Appalachia" does not. What if I had the choral part performed by about 20 *professional* soloist singers. Perhaps young music students who are studying singing? Would this not be possible in London? Should not an attempt be made to find such people by advertising? What do you think? I would so much like to perform "Appalachia" or "Sea-drift". Such people would be able to learn the "Appalachia-chorus" within a week. −

Could you give me some good advice as to who can see to the appropriate publicity? Can Sharpe do that? Who manages that sort of thing in London?

I am carrying on correspondence with Sharpe, but I am greatly handicapped by my imperfect English. Would you not think it advisable for you to have a talk with him some time?

In any event I await your reply regarding the "Beecham Orchestra".
With kind regards also from my wife to both of you

Yours
Fritz Cassirer

Autograph letter, signed and dated, written in German.

The original is in the Delius Trust Archive.

The Deliuses had been in London since the beginning of the month, staying at Balfour
Gardiner's house, 7 Pembroke Villas, in Kensington.

(228)
Havergal Brian to Frederick Delius

Gordon Street
Hartshill
Stoke-on-Trent

1907
Oct 12th.

Dear Mr Delius

I hope I shall not be too late with my Suite. I have asked B & H of Gt
Marlborough St to hurry up. I send you one of their lists with critiques on the
Suite. It is *not* a big work but it is the last thing I scored.

I have a Symphonic Poem here called "Hero" after Lord Leighton's painting
but it is a morose subjective subject & I'm a bit suspicious of audiences after
recent experiences.

Heartiest wishes & with all respects & cordiality

from
Havergal Brian

Autograph letter, signed and dated, written in English.

The original is in the Delius Trust Archive. It is the first of ten letters written by Brian
to Delius in 1907 and 1908 that have been preserved.

Havergal Brian (1876–1972): English composer. In spite of having to earn a living
from a variety of jobs often unrelated to music, Brian proved to be a prolific composer.
His *English Suite* No. 1 had recently been performed at a Promenade Concert, on 12
September. It had been given earlier in the year and was to be played again under
Bantock in Liverpool on 18 January 1908. *Hero and Leander* was first performed on 3

December 1908 by Beecham at Hanley, *Sea Drift* being on the same programme. Now making the acquaintance of Delius's music, Brian was to become a devoted protagonist of the older composer in his native Potteries, where a fine choral tradition already had evolved.

(229)

Granville Bantock to Frederick Delius

BROAD MEADOW

KINGS NORTON

Oct 13th/07

Dear Mr Delius

I have been endeavouring to arrange to include your new work for Soprano, Baritone & Small Chorus[1] in our Birmingham Orchestral Concerts, but many difficulties exist, particularly in the way of seating accomodation, to prevent the realisation of my personal wishes on this occasion. I hope however that Mrs Wood will sing some of your Songs instead both here, as well as at Liverpool. I much desire to make myself acquainted not only with your music, which up to the present, has been limited to a perusal of your Variations for Orchestra & Chorus,[2] & of some of your Songs, but also with your personality, which is so interesting a feature in the present development of British Music. Would you be disposed to accept a hearty invitation to spend a few days here with us in the country? It would give me great pleasure to welcome you here on a visit. I would also like you to meet Mr Ernest Newman,[3] and some of the authorities, who are responsible for the management of the Birmingham Triennial Festival. This can be done so much better if you are on the spot. If you would let this be the occasion of introducing me to a further knowledge of your works, I should indeed be grateful.

I hope you will forgive the delay in my reply. Your letter has been on my desk since its arrival, but I have had several interruptions owing to the recent Festivals, and I have been hoping for some more definite news to give you. However, I shall feel I am forgiven, if you will honour us with this visit.[4]

Believe me
Sincerely yours
Granville Bantock.

Autograph letter, signed and dated, written in English on headed notepaper.

The original is in the Delius Trust Archive. It is the first of thirty-six communications (including one telegram) written by Bantock to the Deliuses between 1907 and 1911 that have been preserved.

1   *Songs of Sunset*.

2   *Appalachia*.

3   Ernest Newman (1868–1959): the doyen of English music critics, he was also a
teacher and a prolific writer, with many books and articles on music to his credit. He
wrote for a number of leading English and American newspapers, but at this period he
was best known as the critic for the *Birmingham Daily Post*.

4   'I accept the invitation with the greatest pleasure,' wrote Delius the following day.

(230)
Robin Legge to Frederick Delius

22. Oct. 07
33, OAKLEY STREET,
CHELSEA, S.W.

Dear old Frederico,

I dare not talk to you to-night before that heterogeneous mob, & I could not
write about your work.[1] Frankly I did not think the interest sustained to the
end, *because* the end was so badly played. But up to 2-3^{rds} – till after the Largo
– the poignancy of the emotion was so strong that had you gone on I must have
collapsed. I think I never was so moved by modern music as by that, in spite of
horns "cracking" etc. And for that reason, old hand as I am, I could not write.
My notice conveys nothing, I fear, though it may show one or two that I felt the
sincerity of the composition Also I felt not a little bitter at all the youths being
there & regarding themselves as your equal – But for the genuine emotion, for
the sheer loveliness of that Largo, I thank you sincerely & from the bottom of a
heart that I thought was growing stoney & cynical & hard as nails.
    À 1.15 tomorrow.

Y^{rs}
gratefully & cordially
Robin H. Legge

Autograph letter, signed and dated, written in English on headed notepaper.

The original is in the Delius Trust Archive.

1   Legge, like many of Delius's growing band of admirers in England, had attended
earlier that evening the first English performance of Delius's Piano Concerto. Theodor
Szántó was soloist, and the Queen's Hall Orchestra was conducted by Wood.

(231)
Frederick Delius to Granville Bantock

7, PEMBROKE VILLAS,
KENSINGTON, W.
Thursday – [24 October 1907]

Dear Mr Bantock.

Would it be the same to you if I left here on Tuesday evening at 6.55 . instead of Monday? I am getting up a great musical scheme, which I shall tell you all about when I meet you, and on Tuesday morning I am invited to lunch in order to meet Elgar, whom I shall also ask to join me. [1] If I do not hear from you I will leave here on Tuesday afternoon at 6.55 p m

Very sincerely yours
Frederick Delius

Autograph letter, signed and undated, written in English on headed notepaper.

The original is in the Delius Trust Archive.

1   Writing to Delius on 26 October, E. A. Baughan altered the date: 'Just a line to say that Elgar has accepted my invitation & that I have fixed the time on *Thursday* at 12.45 at Pagani's.' Delius left no record of the occasion.

(232)
Ralph Vaughan Williams to Frederick Delius

13 Cheyne Walk
S.W.

Dear Mr Delius

I hope you will not think I am making a very audacious request – I should so much like to show you some of my work. I have had it in my mind (and especially now that I have heard your beautiful concerto) that I should profit very much by your advice & if you saw my work you might be able to suggest ways in which I c^d improve myself – either by going to Paris or not. Have you ever any time to spare – and if you have would you allow me to come & see you.

I don't know if I ought to ask this on so slight an acquaintance.

Yours very truly
R. Vaughan Williams

Oct 24th [1907]

Autograph correspondence card, signed and dated, written in English.

The original is in the Delius Trust Archive. It is the first of two communications from Vaughan Williams to Delius, both dated October 1907, that have been preserved (see Letter 233).

Ralph Vaughan Williams (1872–1958): English composer. He studied at the Royal College of Music, moved on to Oxford and Cambridge and became proficient as an organist. He was musical editor of the *English Hymnal* in 1906. His interest in folk song and in the music of his French contemporaries was greatly to widen his horizons. Robin Legge first mentioned him in a letter to Delius dated 20 September 1907: 'A musician, friend of mine, R. Vaughan Williams, whose scoring is stodgy is anxious to go to Paris for a couple of months to learn something of the Frenchman's style of scoring. Can you recommend anyone who would be of use?'

(233)

Ralph Vaughan Williams to Frederick Delius

13 Cheyne Walk
S.W.
[late October 1907]

Dear Mr Delius

It is *most* kind of you and I will be with you at 3.0. I hope my two telegrams did not confuse you – your telegram arrived before your postcard – and I read "same time" as "some-time"!

Yours very truly
R. Vaughan Williams

Autograph letter, signed and undated, written in English.

The original is in the Delius Trust Archive.

Vaughan Williams has himself documented his meeting with Delius: 'I burst in on the privacy of Delius (who happened to be in London at the time) and insisted on playing through the whole of my *Sea Symphony* to him. Poor fellow! How he must have hated it! But he was very courteous, and contented himself with saying, "Vraiment, il n'est pas mesquin".' Vaughan Williams added: 'it had no direct bearing on my musical education.' And yet in the winter of 1907/1908 he went to Paris armed with an introduction to Ravel, with whom he subsequently became a great friend and from whom he learned much. It seems quite possible that at this meeting with the cosmopolitan Delius something may have been fired of the 'French fever' which Vaughan Williams later admitted as having left his 'musical metabolism on the whole healthier' (cf. Hubert Foss, *Ralph Vaughan Williams, A Study* (London: Harrap, 1950), pp. 32–6).

(234)

Max Schillings to Frederick Delius

MÜNCHEN (19) 31 Oct. 07.
Aiblingerstrasse 4. Evening.

Dear friend,

I arrived back today from Berlin,[1] – as is usually the case with me: disgusted by the Jewish music market, which holds sway there permanently; an evil, stifling atmosphere. In this market only publicity and power count, they do not deal in serious values. Thus your piano concerto appears to have been found too serious. The reception in the evening was very warm; Schmid Lindner[2] played his part excellently and with affection, I think we did justice to the work, but what I have read about it so far is sheer nonsense; someone discovered that you have now gone over to the unrestrained impressionistic manner of the new French school − − − & moreover your work is 10 years old & belongs to a "long-outmoded" movement in its melody & austere form. Priceless!

I greatly enjoyed your work. Certainly the instrumentation is rather heavy; but of course it is not really a concerto *for* piano but *with* piano.[3] I am not quite sure about the ending (from the Maestoso on); it seems to me as if it is rather too terse? Or am I wrong? I am rather ashamed that you had so colossal a success with the concerto in London, & it is a bad sign for Berlin. But there too it will probably change!

Your Mass score has just arrived; now I will see that it is secured for the Festival![4]

Best wishes

Yours
Max Schillings

Autograph letter, signed and dated, written in German on headed notepaper.

The original is in the Delius Trust Archive.

1   Schillings had conducted at the Blüthnersaal in Berlin on 29 October, and the concert had included Delius's Piano Concerto.

Schillings's anti-Semitic comments are a reminder of just how commonplace such sentiments were at this period: he was certainly not alone among Delius's friends in giving vent to them. Such friends would probably have been horrified, as the Deliuses themselves were to be, at the later rise of Hitler's Germany, so largely founded on casually anti-Jewish feelings like those expressed here.

2   August Schmid-Lindner (1870–1959): German pianist, and soloist in this first Berlin performance of Delius's concerto. A pupil of Sophie Menter, herself a pupil of Liszt, he was also a composer and teacher. He edited some of Liszt's music.

3   Reviewing the concert, E. E. Taubert's tart opinion of Delius's work was that it was 'a concerto against the piano'. In spite of the efforts of Schmid-Lindner, 'he will not have won, I am afraid, any friends for Delius's Piano Concerto' (cf. *Die Musik*, 8, No. 4, 1907/1908, Zweites Novemberheft, p. 244).

4   Schillings had for some time been pressing for a performance of *A Mass of Life* at the 1908 Tonkünstlerfest, which was to be held in Munich.

(235)
Max Chop and Céleste Chop-Groenevelt to Frederick Delius

Berlin W.50, 3 Nov. 1907
Augsburgerstr. 12.

My very dear Maestro!
My dear Madam!

I know you have reason to wonder − ; it was a long, very long period of time to wait! However, do remember that I am the editor of two musical journals and regular contributor to about twenty daily papers, specialist papers and large publishing-houses. Last week I gave a lecture in Hannover on Beethoven's C minor Symphony with illustrations at the piano, the week before that my Darling began her season with two big orchestral concerts (Tchaikovsky Evenings). That excuses me, doesn't it, and protects me from the reproach of bad faith towards you?

Thanks, and thanks once again, for sending the Piano Concerto to my dear wife. − We had heard the work here in the Blüthnersaal on Tuesday played by Prof. Schmid-Lindner under the sensitive conducting of Max Schillings. I went to the concert also as critic for the "Musikalisches Wochenblatt" and for the "Neue Zeitschrift für Musik" in Leipzig in which you will find a detailed review. It is appearing next week, I assume.

As an intimate tone-poet with a delicate, sensitive inner life you do not count on "thunderous" applause, do you? Nor was it so. But the many first-rank musicians and artists who were present received your composition with the utmost respect. Good heavens, electric light, the usual concert uproar, and − *you*, just how is all this compatible? I should like to hear the Delius in the twilight, where my gaze fixes on no contours and colours, and where with my fancy free and undistracted by anything extraneous, I can follow you into the regions of your reveries. I felt the same here as I did with "Seadrift". I was enraptured again with your harmonies, with the very individual undercurrent which flows through the concerto (Lyrical-Heroic). Of course it is not a piano concerto in the usual sense, in spite of the over-elaborated virtuoso style of parts of the work. It is a dialogue of symphonic proportions between piano and orchestra, sometimes suggestive of an improvisation, and then again like a sunset landscape veiled beneath a blue haze, or an heroically inspired will, which nonetheless requires tender impressions in order to fulfil itself. Schmid-Lindner played well, Schillings conducted masterfully, the orchestra could have provided a more discreet accompaniment; it overwhelmed many passages (admittedly I was sitting in the fourth row very uncomfortably near the platform!) − As for reviews, only one by W. Klatte in the "Lokalanzeiger" has come into my hands. I am enclosing it. There you are now the "gifted composer of Romeo and Juliet", whereas on the occasion of the first performance on the 21 February the paper had hardly a good word for you.

When you bring out your next composition, you can therefore expect to become the "gifted composer of the Piano Concerto in C minor". Meanwhile "Harmonie" Verlag have published my Delius biography. You shall have it. So this year I have had published the following larger works on you:

1. *Frederick Delius. Eine biographische Studie mit Bildbeilage.*
   (Musikalisches Wochenblatt, Leipzig. Nos. 35–37, 1907)
2. *Der Fall Delius in Berlin ("Romeo u. Julia auf dem Dorfe")*
   (Part 10 of "Kritik der Kritik" 1907, Berlin, S.Schottlaender, Schlesische Verlags-Anstalt)
3. *Frederick Delius. Biographie.*
   (In the collection "Monographien moderner Musiker", Vol. 2 1907 with portrait, C.F. Kahnt Nachf., Leipzig)
4. *Frederick Delius. Extensive single-volume biography (60 pages) with portrait and two score-facsimiles.*
   (In the collection "Moderne Musiker", Verlag "Harmonie", Berlin)
5. *Frederick Delius: "Romeo und Julia auf dem Dorfe". Uraufführung an der Berliner Komischen Oper (21. Febr. 1907)*
   (Nos. 10–13 of the "Deutsche Musikdir.-Zeitung", Hannover, Verlag Lehne & Komp.)

By the way, C. G. Sonneck of the Library of Congress, Music Division in Washington, wrote saying he was very interested in my pieces and asked why I did not say a single word about the operas "Irmelin" (1891) and "Magic Fountain" (1894) which were mentioned by Runciman in the "Musical Courier".[1] In answer I told him that both works were completely unknown to me and that I thought there must be some mistake, as I got the list of your works from you yourself. – However, you can see from this how people are now paying attention to you on the other side of the "Pond" too.

I must close! A handshake to both of you, and do not forget us. My Darling wishes to add a few lines. Many cordial greetings to your retreat in the fields of France.

Yours very sincerely
Max Chop.

Please accept many thanks for your great kindness in sending me your concerto. It is both interesting and beautiful.

Kindest regards to you and your dear wife, from

Yours sincerely
Céleste Chop-Groenevelt

Autograph letter, signed and dated, written in German. The postscript signed by Céleste Chop-Groenevelt is written in English.

The original is in the Delius Trust Archive. It is the last of twelve letters and postcards written by Chop to Delius in 1907 that have been preserved. One further letter from Chop to Delius is dated 7 January 1910.

Max Chop: see letter 200, note 1.

1   Reprinted in *A Delius Companion*, ed. Redwood, pp. 13–18.

(236)

Frederick Delius to Granville Bantock

Wednesday. [6 November 1907]
7, PEMBROKE VILLAS,
KENSINGTON, W.

Dear Bantock –

We arrived safely and on time in London.[1] I met Legge this morning only. Everything is progressing favorably Lawson the proprietor of the Daily Telegraph is very keen & interested in the scheme & will also support it financially. When you come up here on the 19th Legge wants to meet you. The scheme will not be laid before the public until January 1st & then simultaneously in the London & provincial papers. The campagne will be opened by a letter from Elgar to the Daily Telegraph in which he will propose the sckeme of a National musical league & a yearly meeting. I have placed the statutes & rules of the Tonkünstler Verein at his disposal & we are having them translated. Elgar has left for Rome & therefore the thing must be done by correspondance, which takes somewhat longer. On the 22nd inst Cassirer gives Heldenleben, 'Appalachia' & the dance of Salome here in the Queen's Hall I hope Newman will come for the Concert. We both enjoyed ourselves immensely in Broadmeadow & I should love to come again. I sent you 3 songs today & will send you some more tomorrow. Kling[2] will undertake the sale of these songs. I saw him this morning. With best love to you & M[rs] Bantock from us both.

> I remain
> Sincerely your friend
> Frederick Delius

Autograph letter, signed and undated, written in English on headed notepaper.

The original is in the Delius Trust Archive.

1   Jelka had evidently joined Delius in England, in response to a letter written about 30 October: 'It is delightful here & the Bantocks are most charming people. They at once made me telegraph for you. If you care to come do so.'

2   See Letter 223, note.

(237)

Granville Bantock to Frederick Delius

BROAD MEADOW
KINGS NORTON

Nov 7/07

Dear Delius

Thanks for your interesting letter & news. I note that the scheme is to wait announcement until Jan 1st. I presume & hope it may be 1908. The title sounds somewhat like the National Sunday League. I think National Musical Union, or British Musical League would be preferable.

I wish Cassirer had been doing some other works of yours in addition to "Appalachia". However, I am making all arrangements for coming up on the 19th, & hope to be able to stay for the 20th & 21st. Your 3 Shelley Songs arrived this morning, and I shall greedily absorb them, as well as the others, when they also arrive. I am glad to hear Kling will undertake the sale of these Songs. I have written him about "Brigg-Fair", which Ronald has agreed to conduct here in February.[1] I hope to hear that my Liverpool Committee will accept my proposal & strong recommendation to give the *first* performance!!! on Jan 18th. At least, I have offered the bait as an enticement.

Your Piano Concerto is now in the hands of 2 of our Piano Teachers at the School, & on Friday evening, I shall rehearse the orchestral parts, so as to be ready for any student. I shall do my best to play the Concerto at our Annual Town Hall Concert next June. Meanwhile the gospel shall be spread. Boughton,[2] I think, intends to do an article on your music, & I have lent him some of your work for preparation.

Let me know how things progress with you, & get those part-songs written before the 19th.[3] The Secretary at Southport has just sent me the programme & list to fill up, and I shall be consulting Walford Davies, my Colleague at the Festival, as to the works, when I come up to town on the 19th inst. Spade the flowerbeds well in London, & let me know as soon as you can all particulars of your final full rehearsals.

Kindest regards to your wife & yourself from us both.

Granville Bantock.

Autograph letter, signed and dated, written in English on headed notepaper.

The original is in the Delius Trust Archive.

1   Landon Ronald (1873–1938): English conductor, pianist and composer. He studied
at the Royal College of Music with Parry, Stanford and Parratt, and conducted widely,
both at home with the major British symphony orchestras and in Europe. He became
principal of the Guildhall School of Music in 1910, and was knighted in 1922.
Ronald was to perform *Brigg Fair* with the Hallé Orchestra in Birmingham on 19 February 1908, little more than a month after the first performance of the work had been
given by Bantock in Liverpool.

2   Rutland Boughton (1878–1960): English composer. Having studied at the Royal
College of Music, he was now a teacher at the Birmingham and Midland Institute.

3   The three unaccompanied part-songs: 'On Craig Ddu,' 'Wanderer's Song' and 'Midsummer Song'. 'On Craig Ddu' was completed in December 1907, the others early in
1908.

(238)

Frederick Delius to Granville Bantock

7, PEMBROKE VILLAS,
KENSINGTON, W.
[18? November 1907]

Dear Bantock –

I am looking forward with the greatest pleasure to your visit & shall fetch you at
3.30 P.M from 54 Great Marlboro Str.¹ We can dine here & go out afterwards or
dine in a restaurant if you prefer it. I am anxious to speak with you about the
Scheme. We have already decided that no musical critic be on the Committee –
The few names you mention – if on the committee – would cause the thing to
fail entirely.² Why! these old Johnnies who have had sufficient opportunity to
shew what they can do & have done nothing – then I should prefer Elgar, you &
myself to sign the letter & you may be sure we shall have a good following. The
others may join the Society & the more the merrier but not *lead* it, we know
where they will lead it to. All the papers must come out at the same time, that
was also decided – I have a meeting here tonight & will tell you all about it : The
rehearsal will probably be on Thursday morning – Orckestra alone. & Chorus
with small orchestra on Wednesday evening –
    With kindest regards to your wife & self from us both –

    I remain
    Very sincerely yours
    Frederick Delius

– In haste!

Autograph letter, signed and undated, written in English on headed notepaper.

The original is in the Delius Trust Archive.

1   Bantock had made an appointment with Walford Davies at 2.45 at Breitkopf & Härtel's office.

2   Bantock had written to Delius on 16 November: 'The letter that is to appear in the "Daily Telegraph" on Jan 1ˢᵗ, must in addition to Elgar's signature, be signed by all the representative musicians in the country. Richter, Wood, Hadow, Maitland, Parry, Mackenzie must all sign, if the proclamation is to have any effect. Elgar's name alone is not sufficient to carry the Provinces & as he has many enemies, this fact alone would deter many from joining the scheme.'

(239)
Granville Bantock to Frederick Delius

NORTH WESTERN HOTEL,
LIVERPOOL.
Nov 22 1907

My dear friend,

I feel you have had a gigantic success tonight.[1] It pleased me to see how enthusiastic Newman was last night over your "Sea-Drift" & "Appalachia", & when at last he said he would go up to London, (in spite of a high temperature) it gave me as much pleasure almost as if I had been able to come myself.

It was a great regret to me not to be present, but I dared not risk anything here, where the flag must be kept flying. I lent Newman the Scores, which I shall always prize, & the dear fellow will enjoy himself tonight.

Your music has struck a fibre in my being, which is beyond analysis, but which I feel is the truest and noblest chord that has yet been sounded in our art. It seems petty to offer you congratulations. You are so far beyond them. I shall be well satisfied if I can do a little to further the appreciation of your work. Meanwhile, believe me, always

Affectionately yours
Granville Bantock.

Autograph letter, signed and dated, written in English on headed notepaper.

The original is in the Delius Trust Archive.

1   *Appalachia* was given at the Queen's Hall, with the New Symphony Orchestra and the Sunday League Choir conducted by Fritz Cassirer. Both the Bantocks and Henry

Wood also had cabled their good wishes earlier the same day. Both telegrams are preserved in the Delius Trust Archive.

(240)
Cyril Scott to Frederick Delius

274 Kings Rd. Nov 23.07.

My dear Friend. I must just send you a line in appreciation of your work – although my own productions may not be over sympathetic to you – yet I hope that will not lead you to think I can not rise to the beauties of yours!! If appreciation depended on what one could do one's self, the auditorium would be distinctly empty. The sound of that pizzicato var. was simply celestial – not to talk of original. Delightful! – & so much more *you* – than the concerto which I could not help feeling was not an adequate expression of yourself.

Please do not trouble to answer this & once more bravo!

Very sincerely yours
Cyril Scott.

––––––––––––

Autograph correspondence card, signed and dated, written in English.

The original is in the Delius Trust Archive.

Another member of the 'Frankfurt gang' was also present: 'last night I realized how thoro'ly brave & spiritedly experimental a being that dear Delius is. Taking lots of risk, & not content with mere "safe" wellworn conventional pranks like that tiresome R. Strauss (how he wrote D Juan I cant fathom) Delius's stuff on the band sounds *so* poetic & full of tender & *rare* things. . . . I dont say his form is convincing or that he is an out-&-out genius but he's a most sympathetic & *instructive* talent, with a dear abstract, compassionate, poetic soul' (Percy Grainger to Karen Holten, London, 23 November 1907; original in the Grainger Museum). A few days later (on 29 November), Grainger wrote in similar vein to Nina Grieg: 'last Friday I had a jolly evening. Mother & I went and heard F. Delius's "Appalachia" performed at the Queen's Hall. I do so wish you could have heard it. I dont say it's a perfect work *at all*, or even a work of pure genius; but it did strike me as poetic, & individual & genuine, & *most corageously experimental*. The new things he tried for seemed to me really plucky & of vital interest & not the usual dull commonplace (& usually perfectly "safe") wheezes of so much so called "modern" stuff. Then such a lot of it was piano & tender-colored, & that is such a relief & refreshingness' (original in the Bergen Public Library).

(241)
Havergal Brian to Frederick Delius

Hartshill
Stoke-on-Trent

1907
Nov 24th.

Dear Mr Delius

I'm truly proud to hear so many fine things about the Concerto — and now about the Variations. English musicians are very proud of you and I offer you my heartiest congratulations on the success of the "Appalachia". A distinguished musician has written me an extraordinary letter of critical praise. I feel proud for you — We have so few men of *sincerity* in our midst — & you have won for yourself the position of greatest among them.

A few weeks ago I left a copy of your "Sea Drift" with the conductor of the principal Society here in Staffordshire. I refer to the N.S. Choral Society (Conductor — J. Whewall). I saw him yesterday morning and I now understand that "Sea Drift" will be given by them immediately after the Sheffield Festival. I also brought "Appalachia" to his notice & it will go in with the "Sea Drift".[1] You may rely upon a fine performance of "Sea Drift" by the Choir — it is a fine one. There are certain formalities to be gone through — the choir (part of it) will want a "Sol fa" translation of Sea Drift and the passing by Committee. This is only matter of a short time — after which the performances will be publicly announced. I am hoping to get a work in by Holbrooke[2] at the same concert. You must please forgive my absence from the performances of your works. I seldom go to London for I'm tied down to a business life here — my musical doings lying entirely outside it.

Please accept my heartfelt wishes for your works & yourself.

Sincerely yours
Havergal Brian

Autograph letter, signed and dated, written in English.

The original is in the Delius Trust Archive.

1   Delius was to be invited to conduct *Appalachia*; he gave it on 2 April 1908 at the Victoria Hall, Hanley. The orchestra was the Hallé, and the choir was the North Staffs District Choral Society, whose founder and conductor was James Whewall. *Sea Drift* was not given in Hanley until December 1908.

2   Joseph Charles Holbrooke (1878–1958): English composer, pianist and critic. He studied at the Royal Academy of Music, and composed prolifically, his large-scale operas for a time attracting interest. Holbrooke was no stranger to controversy, not only on

account of his music and his critical writings, but also because of his quirky character, which Delius found singularly unattractive (see Letter 254, note 1, and Letter 257).

(242)

Ernest Newman to Frederick Delius

THE WHITE HOUSE,
KINGS NORTON.
24 Nov 1907

Dear Delius,

The enclosed[1] is poor stuff, for a sick man isn't much good and it doesn't cover a tithe of the things I wanted to say, for space is limited. But if the flesh has been weak, the spirit was very willing.

I am sorry to see that the London critics have as a whole failed to rise to the height of your music. But don't worry; your quick popularity in England is, I hope, quite assured. Let me quote you a line or two from "Appalachia".

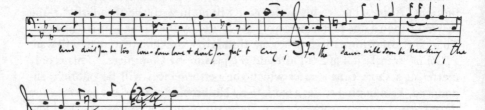

I wonder if you could spare me some time or other all your other scores, one or two at a time. I would like to make a study of them all.

With kindest regards from both of us to you both.

Always yours
Ernest Newman

Autograph letter, signed and dated, written in English on headed notepaper.

The original is in the Delius Trust Archive. It is the first of six letters and postcards written by Newman to Delius between 1907 and 1909 that have been preserved.

1   Newman's *Birmingham Daily Post* review of the London performance of *Appalachia*.

(243)
Frederick Delius to Granville Bantock

7, PEMBROKE VILLAS,
KENSINGTON, W.
[26? November 1907]

Dear friend —

Many thanks for your 2 nice letters. I was so glad to hear that our Scheme has progressed so far in your hands[1]; the provinces will turn out much more important than London. I will come on Friday with my wife & we are both looking forward with the greatest pleasure to another couple of days with you. When does the best morning train start? I should like to arrive early enough for us to see Hardings[2] in the afternoon of Friday & have Saturday before us. We must leave on Monday as we go to Paris on Tuesday morning. I have just read Newmans criticism in the Post. He is the only one that understood what I am driving at. I was very pleased with his article & if I had been called upon to explain my work in Appalachia, should have said something very similar. This in great haste —

Your affectionate
Frederick Delius

Autograph letter, signed and undated, written in English on headed notepaper.

The original is in the Delius Trust Archive.

1 In a letter dated 25 November, Bantock had recorded support from Richter, Harry Evans (conductor of the Liverpool Welsh Choral Union) and Dr Coward at Sheffield.

2 C. Copeley Harding: described by Muriel Foster in a letter to Delius as 'one of the young and rising influences on the Birmingham Festival Committee', he was approved by Delius and became Honorary Secretary to the Musical League shortly afterwards.

(244)
Frederick Delius to Ernest Newman

7, PEMBROKE VILLAS,
KENSINGTON, W.
27 November 1907

Dear Newman !

Many thanks for your sympathetic & appreciative letter which gave me the greatest pleasure.

I thought your article in the Post the best thing I have read for years, & you know what you are talking about, which the London critics dont! They say neither one thing nor the other, and dismiss the whole thing in a few hollow phrases: their praise is just as hollow. I have the full Score of "Sea-drift" with me & shall bring it down with me on Friday. My other scores I will let you have as soon as I get them.

Looking forward to the pleasure of seeing you again & having a good talk & with our united kind regards to you & Mrs Newman

I remain   Yours ever
Frederick Delius

Autograph letter, signed and dated, written in English on headed notepaper.

The original is in the Delius Trust Archive. It is the first of nineteen letters written by the Deliuses to the Newmans between 1907 and 1933 that have been preserved.

(245)
Thomas Beecham to Frederick Delius

Highfield,
Boreham Wood,
Herts.
Dec. 1st/07

Dear Delius

When I looked through 'Paris' a couple of weeks ago, I formed a rather different idea of its difficulties. I thought it was just the sort of thing my fellows would revel in. At the *Cassirer* concert, the *seven* best 1st Violins were not playing, four regular 2nd Violins, and the four principal celli too. So that you can hardly form an idea of their capacities from this particular affair. Personally I think 'Paris' is just the thing for us – I shall have my entire force in January when my own regular season – so to speak – commences.[1]

However I have inserted the 'Dance of Life' in the Programme and may do 'Paris' too – and will you now tell me where I can get hold of the Score and Parts. I shall want to try it over soon. Also I should like the material of 'Paris' and 'Brigg Fair' which I want to rehearse before Christmas as there is such short time after New Year. Also please do not forget about that Violin Suite for Marie Hall's[2] concert. If you will look in on Tuesday evening at Queen's Hall, I will show you for approval the sketch Programmes of my series –

Kind regards
Yours very sincerely,
Thomas Beecham

P.S.

Alright about 'Sapho' and 'Fereshtah'![3]

Please tell Bantock that I shall be coming on Dec. 9th by the train leaving Euston at 2.30 p.m. – arriving B'ham at 4.30 p.m. He seems to imagine that I consider the Wood Variations[4] I played the other night to be something important. Not at all! I quite agree with his judgment of them – but none the less they are better than somethings one is obliged to listen to –

Autograph letter, signed and dated, written in English on headed notepaper.

The original is in the Delius Trust Archive. It is the first of forty-eight communications written by Beecham to Delius between 1907 and 1933 that are preserved in the Archive.

Thomas Beecham (1879–1961): English conductor. He founded the New Symphony Orchestra in 1905 and swiftly came to the forefront of English musical life. Perhaps above all he was to be associated with the music of Delius, whose champion he remained for the rest of his life. Delius introduced himself to his future mentor after attending a concert of modern French and English music conducted by Beecham at the Queen's Hall in October 1907. He liked the sound of Beecham's orchestra and promptly arranged to hire it for Cassirer's *Appalachia* performance. Knighted in 1916, Beecham inherited his father's baronetcy later the same year.

1   Beecham was to give *Paris*, with his New Symphony Orchestra, at Liverpool on 11 January and at Queen's Hall on 26 February 1908.

2   Marie Hall (1884–1956): English violinist.

3   Bantock was also a favourite of Beecham's: 'when I recall the texts of *Ferishtah's Fancies* and the Sappho Songs I cannot help believing that Bantock's settings of them will remain unchallenged for some time to come' (Beecham, *A Mingled Chime*, p. 69).

4   The Symphonic Variations on *Patrick Sarsfield* by the Irish-born composer Charles Wood (1866 1926).

(246)
Thomas Beecham to Frederick Delius

Highfield,
Boreham Wood,
Herts.
Dec. 13th/07

Dear Delius

Could you let me have the scores of –
                    Life's Dance

> Norwegian Suite
> 'Legende' for Violin
> and
> The Danish songs – ?

I shall be able to do all these things before Spring. At present I have included in my London series –

> Brigg Fair
> and
> Appallachia – of which I want very much to give

another performance (and 'Paris' – provisionally).

The Liverpool concert at which I shall be doing 'Paris' is on Jan. 11th – afternoon at the 'Philharmonic Hall'. The final rehearsal for this concert will take place on the morning either of the 9th or 10th – and if possible I should like you to be there as it will be of great help to me.

I have got the 'Parts' but cannot have the score for a few days as Cassirer has lent it to someone.

I went to Birmingham last Monday and stayed the night with Bantock. We had a long chat and cleared the air a little. The situation there is bound to arrive at a crisis soon and it is fairly evident – I think – that the star of the Progressive is in the ascendant. Bantock tells me that the articles of the 'Musical League' will not be ready till February as Newman is very busy.

I am considering the question of the Committee. It is not an easy matter to find a number of responsible and energetic people among the younger men in Town. They are mostly of the mind and disposition of your host at 7 Pembroke Villas.[1] I shall find them however sooner or later. Let me have the scores soon – Kindest regards to Mrs Delius and yourself from us both[2]

> Very sincerely yours
> Thomas Beecham

Autograph letter, signed and dated, written in English on headed notepaper.

The original is in the Delius Trust Archive.

1   Balfour Gardiner. But the Deliuses were now back in Grez.

2   Beecham had married his first wife, Utica Celestia Welles, in 1903.

(247)

Frederick Delius to Granville Bantock

GREZ SUR LOING,
S. ET M.
15 Dec 1907

My dear friend!

I have just managed to finish one part song "On Craig Ddu" Arthur Symons, which I send you. If you think it is any good I can have it published.[1] The other one² I attempted does not yet please me, so I must live with it a bit longer. I find I can never do anything in a hurry, but will try to do some more of these things when the mood takes me. Kling wrote me a very nice letter & told me that Breitkopf would publish "Brigg fair" & give me 300 Marks. It is'nt much, but I think I will do it to get Breitkopfs as publishers. Harmonie is too confoundedly slow & unenterprising. Gradually I am getting into my real way of living & no doubt shall do something decent presently. Beecham is giving "Paris" in Liverpool on January 11th I shall therefore come over on the 9th or 10th & be present at your first rehearsal of "Brigg fair." When is it? The parts are now being copied. We have planted all our bulbs now & shall have a fine show of flowers in Spring. I do hope you will manage to come here for the *bal des quat'z arts* in April. Julian's ball is in February perhaps you might come for that also. It is nothing to run over here for a week if you can manage to get off from the Institute But the 4z arts is of course *the* one to go to. Let me know if there is anything new re the musical league. I suppose it will be published in the papers about the time I am over in England. Remember me kindly to Newman. With love to you & your wife

I remain affectionately yrs
Frederick Delius

Autograph letter, signed and dated, written in English on headed notepaper.

The original is in the Delius Trust Archive.

1   'On Craig Ddu', a setting of Arthur Symons's poem, was published in 1910 by Harmonie Verlag, together with the two other part-songs finished early in 1908.

2   'Wanderer's Song'.

(248)
Frederick Delius to John Coates

GREZ SUR LOING,
S. ET M.
16 Dec 1907

My dear Coates!

Many thanks for your letter which finds me again in France. I return to London at the beginning of January when I hope to see you. Kapellmeister Cassirer intended to give my drama "The Village Romeo & Juliet" in a concert (& may still do it somewhat later in the season) but the work could not have been produced quite so quickly as he thought & therefore he postponed it. I send you today a one Act music drama "Margot la Rouge" which might be something for Moody

Manners[1] — the orchestra is only a small one. Perhaps you would translate it. There is a splendid part for you in it. Look it over. My music does not sound on the piano — so I warn you! But it will be very effective when played. The village R. & J. I wrote in English.[2] I am sure you are splendid on the stage & I have also heard so in Germany.

With best greetings

I remain
Yours ever
Frederick Delius

Autograph letter, signed and dated, written in English on headed notepaper.

The original is in the collection of Albi Rosenthal Esq.

1   The Moody Manners Opera Company was founded by Charles Manners and Fanny Moody, a husband and wife singing team. As well as touring the provinces, the company played two seasons at Covent Garden. Coates had written to Delius on 7 December mentioning an 'arrangement' he had for singing with Manners.

2   Coates's letter of 7 December had shown him anxious to see a copy of *A Village Romeo and Juliet*, adding: 'if you want a translator *let me do it* — that is another thing I was born for!"

(249)
Frederick Delius to Granville Bantock

GREZ SUR LOING,
S. ET M.
21/12/07

Dear friend —

Your letter just arrived. I am so glad everything is going on so well concerning the musical League. If we only could get hold of Ernest Palmer as treasurer, it would be a splendid thing.[1] I am very eager to see Newman's Constitutions & am sure they are very cleverly drawn up, however dont bother to send it on to me, as I approve d'avance & shall see it all when I come in January. The whole thing must come out early in January & subscriptions invited. Balfour Gardiner promised me £100 if I brought the Scheme to a head. When is the rehearsal of Brigg fair? as I shall come over for it & will send you the full score as soon as I have corrected the parts, which should arrive tomorrow or day after. Between the 11th & 18th I should just love to conduct your students' orchestra to try my hand at it — I am conducting hard at "Appalachia" & really believe I shall be able to do it.[2] The reply I received from Sheffield was almost rude.[3] They said in 4 lines that the Committee refused my offer & would either play it or take it off the programme. It really seems preposterous (there never having been any question of 1st performance) they should now take up this attitude. Just fancy to require the first performance of a work 2 years before the Festival without any remuneration. Wood is of course behind it all. I feel quite sure he could easily have arranged it if he had wanted to. It is really taking my bread & butter away from me; for, all I get from the editor is a percentage on the music sold & performances. They seem to be able to afford to pay him (Wood) a big fee! However, I dont care whether they play it or not. Brian wrote me such a nice & sympathetic letter, what a nice fellow he must be. I am looking forward to a better acquaintance with him & his work. I am also so glad that the Beecham affair[4] is settled: B is timid & a proscrastinator perhaps, but entirely loyal to you & Newman & will join us with his whole heart & means when he has settled that Choral Society & will no doubt be of enormous aid. His position of course was very ticklish. I sent off one part song today. An impression — My time has been entirely taken up with these prize Scores. Gracious! what a work. This will do for me for ever, I believe, as adjudicator. One has the great desire to do no one injustice & feels oneself obliged to wade carefully, & conscienctiously thro miles & miles of dreary waste. The worst are those which try to be complicated like Strauss, without any of his mastery. There are one or two that are not so bad & where one feels talent and atmosphere, but these are badly scored — strange to say — My choice will no doubt fix on one of these. I have not received the vocal score of my "Mass" as yet & will send it or bring it with me. I asked Kling to send Newman the rough copy that K sent to Risley — has he received it? I send you today another copy of "Appalachia" which I had with me here. Kling ought to have sent you one some time ago as I had ordered one for you. Of course I shall accept Breitkopfs offer if I can get free. Unfortunately in looking over my first Contract with "Harmonie" I noticed a clause in which they have the refusal of all my works & at present I am in correspondance with them & dont quite know what to do. I have however consulted a friend of mine in Berlin who knows all about these things & may find me a way out of the mire. Parry's letter would very much interest me — the old fox![5] Between the rehearsal of Brigg fair & the performance I shall be obliged to go & visit my sister for a couple of days in Nottingham & could then come up to Birmingham for the students orchestra rehearsal & we two might travel down to Liverpool again for the concert. I am very anxious to hear how the interview with Baughan went off & what has been finally settled: When is the memorial to be published? I am getting the Score of "Appalachia" off by heart. My wife is just writing to Mrs B. We both wish you a merry Christmas & lots of mince pies!! & late suppers & a happy new year with lots of performances & lots of success & lots of happy meetings both here & in England.

Affectionately yours
Frederick Delius

Give my kindest greetings to Newman

Autograph letter, signed and dated, written in English on headed notepaper.

The original is in the Delius Trust Archive.

1   In a letter to Delius dated 17 December, Bantock had discussed Ernest Palmer, who had instituted the Patron's Fund, to promote British composers and performers, suggesting him as 'the proper man for our Hon. Treasurer'.

2   Delius had been invited to conduct the work at Hanley, with the Hallé Orchestra and the North Staffordshire District Choral Society. The performance was to take place on 2 April 1908.

3   Delius had received a letter from the Sheffield Musical Festival Association, written on 27 November, which noted 'with much disappointment' that *Sea Drift* was to be given in London the following February: 'When we undertook to perform this work at our next Festival, it was on distinct understanding that it was to be the first performance in England.' In spite of this, the work was given in Sheffield by Wood on 7 October 1908, with Frederic Austin, the Sheffield Festival Chorus and the Queen's Hall Orchestra.

4   Disagreement on Musical League policy had arisen between Bantock and Newman on the one side, and Beecham.

5   Sir Hubert Parry (1848–1918): English composer, and by the turn of the century a mainstay of the English musical establishment. He was from 1894 director of the Royal College of Music, and he was also professor of music at Oxford. It appears that originally he had taken a stand against the Musical League, but according to Bantock's letter to Delius of 19 December, 'Parry has sent me rather an apologetic letter, which I will send on to you. . . . He evidently thinks he made a mistake.'

(250)
Havergal Brian to Frederick Delius

Hartshill

1907
Dec 22nd

My dear friend

I've been going through your "Appalachia" this morning. It is an extraordinary work, its sincerity makes me weep. I dont know *when* such a surprise offered itself to me. The copy only arrived this morning – I took the sincere opinion of a learned musician as to its greatness in a letter I had after the London performance. We will have it here and you shall hear your music sung. Im *proud* to know such a genius – it is most extraordinary music. May god let you write more such music.

    Yours in all sincerity
    H Brian

Autograph letter, signed and dated, written in English.

The original is in the Delius Trust Archive.

(251)
Granville Bantock to Frederick Delius

Broad Meadow
Kings Norton   Dec 23rd/07

My dear Delius

Your part-song is splendid! How on earth do you manage such things? It is a bit late for Southport, as the programme had to be made up a few weeks ago, but I will send the M.S to Kling, and leave you to arrange with him about the publication & terms etc. Do this as quickly as possible, as I will do my best, even at this late hour to get it into the Festival programme there. I must tell them that copies will be available next month, i e. January. If I do not succeed at Southport, I will strongly recommend it for Blackpool,[1] where I know several of the Committee. It is only in the North where "On Craig Ddu" will be sung as it ought to be, with sympathy & intelligence, & beautiful tone. Write to Kling without delay.

And now to thank you for your interesting & welcome letter. As soon as Baughan sends me a few type-written copies of the Constitutions — as he promised to do — I will forward a copy to you. He practically agrees to Newman's document. There is no news yet from Palmer. Baughan is expecting a reply daily. Newman will be writing to Hadow, & McNaught. Meanwhile until after Xmas, we cannot expect to get much further. I enclose Parry's letter, which you can return in your next. This closes the Episode.

The first full rehearsal of "Brigg-Fair" (after the string rehearsal on Jan 4) will be at Liverpool on Friday evening Jan 10th at 7.30 PM. You must however let me have the score & parts before, & certainly not later than the 31st inst. If you can come direct here on Thursday Jan 9th, we can travel up together to Liverpool on the Friday morning. Beecham is giving your "Paris" at Liverpool on Saturday Jan 11th, so we can stay for the performance. You can go to Nottingham on the Monday following, & rejoin us here during the week.

The Sheffield Mystery need not worry you, although it is a miserable affair. You will get your recognition here in spite of time-servers and double-dealers. You can depend upon Brian at Hanley. He is really a good-hearted, generous, enthusiastic soul, and may be relied on. He is preaching powerfully the gospel of Delius in the Potteries, and many conversions will be made. I am hoping for definite news of "Appalachia" & "Sea-Drift" at Hanley, with the positive dates. Meanwhile Brian's the Boy. He's truer than the whole London gang put together, in spite of a bitterly hard struggle to make ends meet, and feed his family. You will meet him again at Liverpool, & I believe you will be good friends.

I am amused when I think of you struggling with the rank vegetation of the Prize Cantatas. I have started deep-breathing exercises, Müller's gymnastic system, & Albrechtsberger in order to cope with this Herculean task.

Newman has received the proof of your Mass from Kling, but, like Fafner hoards it with his other treasures in his unholy retreat, & refuses to part with it. My full score of "Appalachia" seems likely to share the same fate.

There is no meeting of the Institute Orchestra until Jan 24th, as the Vacation is now on, for which I am truly thankful. If you care to try your hand on it you are welcome. But we can arrange this when you come here on the 9th prox.

By the way, where is the Histed portrait[2] you promised us? We shall want a large size, as a frame is being specially constructed for it.

As our spouses are answering each other's letters, they will doubtless convey to each other all the messages which are dear to the feminine heart, & which I am afraid we too often forget. All the same, remember me very kindly to Madame, and be assured that I heartily reciprocate all your kind wishes & sentiments (including the mince-pies.)

Ever yours
Granville Bantock

We might go over the best Cantatas & settle on the Prize while you are staying here. Can you forward them direct to me?

Autograph letter, signed and dated, written in English.

The original is in the Delius Trust Archive.

1   'On Craig Ddu' was finally given in Blackpool in 1910.

2   A photographic portrait of Delius published by the firm of Histed.

(252)
Havergal Brian to Frederick Delius

Hartshill
1907   Stoke-on-Trent
Dec 27
My dear friend

Your letter to hand has given me the greatest possible joy. Bantock is one of the best hearted fellows living – a true son of genius like yourself – and what is more he is fearless in his actions and not a snob. I shall do *all* I can for you here as I've already done for Bantock & Elgar. I would give my life if it would push on the modern school – indeed I've parted with a little energy in this neighbour-hood. There has been too much greed and selfishness in the past – & naturally it has borne no fruit. I am with you in your league & don't think much can come from London. The atmosphere there is poisonous & if I *had* to live in it I should pine away. In London people write sonnets in your praise today & stab you in the back tomorrow. Putrid atmosphere!!

Affectionate greetings
from your friend
Havergal Brian

Autograph letter, signed and dated, written in English.

The original is in the Delius Trust Archive.

(253)
Milly Bergh to Frederick Delius

Villa "Birkely"
31 December 07.

Dear friend,

At last then I have got a portrait of you – completely by chance just as every-thing should happen in this world. I cut it out of a London paper. And now it stands on my desk. – Congratulations on your two last successes – the Piano Concerto and "Appalachia". I was particularly intrigued by this little sentence. "Certainly the voice of Mr. Delius is a new voice in music". I am proud that al-ready at the time you composed "Ja vi elsker" – in the minor key for "Folkeraa-det", I realized how beautifully you worked and sensed the individuality of your whole style – and that after all is a long time ago – Since then you have cleared up all that is vague and obscure mostly because you have put your art and your work above everything else in the world — that your feelings never ran away with you is not your fault, you see — Well good luck — and a happy new year to you and fru Jelka —

Yours
Milly Bergh

Autograph letter, signed and dated, written in Norwegian.

The original is in the Delius Trust Archive. Two other letters from Milly Bergh to Delius, one undated, the other dated 3 September 1909, have been preserved.

Milly (Emilie) Bergh, *née* Ihlen (1860–1937): Norwegian singer. Her early marriage to the artist Frits Thaulow's brother ended in 1891 in divorce, and she then married the actor Ludvig Bergh, who was in 1897 to play one of the leading roles in *Folkeraadet*. Whilst married to Thaulow, she had had a relationship with Edvard Munch, his first serious love affair. According to Schulerud (p. 314), she was acknowledged to be the greatest beauty in Christiania in her day.

1908

With the year barely a week old, Delius was back in London. He was to hear Beecham perform *Paris* in Liverpool and Arbos give *Lebenstanz* in London. He returned to Grez in late January and soon found himself involved in a time-consuming correspondence connected with the founding of the Musical League. In England again at the end of March, he journeyed to Hanley, where he conducted the Hallé Orchestra in the second English performance of *Appalachia*.

Once again a work of his was scheduled for the Tonkünstlerfest of the Allgemeine Deutsche Musikverein. This time it was to be the larger part of *A Mass of Life*, a work still awaiting its first performance. The event took place on 4 June in Munich. Bantock was unable to go, as originally hoped, but instead arrived in Grez for a short holiday in July. A summer walking tour in Norway, started at the end of July, had an added piquancy in that it was undertaken in the company of Beecham, who could never have imagined just how strenuous a feat it was to be.

Delius returned to Grez on 9 September and found that the demands of the Musical League, of which he was vice-president (and Elgar, president), had by no means abated. Then within a month he was in Sheffield for the first English performance of *Sea Drift*. A month later, on 5 November, he was in Stuttgart to hear Schillings conduct *Appalachia*. And in yet another month's time he was in England again, primarily to conduct in London the first performance of *In a Summer Garden*, in its original version. There were also more meetings to discuss the Musical League's proposed first festival.

It is now clear that within little more than a year Delius had made a mighty mark on the English musical scene, a fact that did not escape the notice of one of his German critics, who noted laconically that the composer 'from now on wants to be an Englishman and wishes therefore to be acknowledged as such by us'.*

---

* *Die Musik*, 8, No. 5, 1908/1909, Erstes Dezemberheft, p. 315.

'Wanderer's Song' and 'Midsummer Song', part-songs for unaccompanied chorus (RT IV/3 and RT IV/4).

In a Summer Garden, Rhapsody for full Orchestra (RT VI/17). Spring.

A Dance Rhapsody No. 1, for orchestra (RT VI/18).

Fennimore and Gerda, opera (RT I/8). Begun.

(254)
Norman O'Neill to Frederick Delius

17bis Bould Victor Hugo
Neuilly ^s/Seine
Jan 1. 07.
[i.e. Jan 1. 08]

My dear Delius,

Just a line to send you my very sincere thanks for the charming time you gave me at Grez.[1] I greatly enjoyed my visit.

I arrived rather late in Paris after a very stuffy journey but just in time to see my old Nurse who had come to see us ! – I expect you have noticed that Englishmen always talk about their nurses or their tubs so will not be surprised at this reference ! I am off to London on Friday.

I expect Mrs Delius is delighted with the snow – The forest must look splendid now.

With greetings from both of us to both of you and again very many thanks from

Yours ever
Norman O'Neill.

Drop me a p.c. if you want a bed on the 7th.

Autograph letter, signed and dated, written in English. O'Neill mistakenly dated his letter 1907, for 1908.

The original is in the Delius Trust Archive. It is the third of thirty-five letters and postcards written by Norman and Adine O'Neill to Delius between 20 December 1907 and 23 December 1909 that have been preserved.

Norman O'Neill (1875–1934): English composer and conductor. He studied with Somervell and at the Hoch Conservatorium in Frankfurt, and married the pianist Adine Rückert in 1899. As a composer he became best known for his incidental music for the stage (*Mary Rose*, *The Blue Bird*), and his conducting was mainly done in the theatre. He became one of Delius's closest friends.

1   Delius wrote to Bantock on 2 January that O'Neill 'spent 3 days here — He is a very nice fellow indeed'. He also mentioned other visitors — Beecham and Holbrooke, who had surprised him by turning up at Grez on 31 December: 'They had come over to Paris for a few days. Beecham to try & find a good Horn player & H. to find his "Sarruso-phones". Beecham was very welcome but I cannot say as much for H. who I do not care for & also distrust, besides he is so uncultivated & such a boor & so dirty! The[y] spent New Year's eve with us & left next day.'

(255)
Frederick Delius to Jelka Delius

7, PEMBROKE VILLAS,
KENSINGTON, W.
Thursday [9 January 1908]

Dearest Jelka —

Just a word to say that all is going well — I was at a rehearsal this morning which went very well — Beecham takes good tempi & the orchestra likes the piece[1] — I leave tomorrow for Liverpool — the rehearsal is only in the evening —

Beecham is giving — Paris — Brigg fair — Appalachia & my Legende[2] — perhaps the Danish songs if he can get the proper singer — I saw Cassirer today who is getting out a circular about the "Messe" in May.[3] The Bradford Choral Society are very enthusiastic to sing it & would do it gratis — Beecham gave me another photo of his little boy which I send you — He is an excellent fellow & even helped Cassirer to get out his circular about the "Messe". I will write again from Liverpool — On my return here on the 19th I stay here again —

Lebenstanz is given at the Albert Hall on Sunday 19th inst[4] With best love to you & Helene[5]

yr loving
Fred

Write a word —

Autograph letter, signed and undated, written in English on headed notepaper. Jelka later added '1908 Jan 9th'.

The original is in the Grainger Museum.

1   On 11 January Beecham was to give *Paris* at the Philharmonic Hall, Liverpool, with his New Symphony Orchestra. Delius had attended the London rehearsal at eleven o'clock on 9 January.

2   Mischa Elman was to be soloist in the *Légende*.

3   I have so far traced no further reference to this document.

4   Breitkopf & Härtel, in London, had taken the *Lebenstanz* initiative, as is clear from
the company's letter to Delius of 3 December 1907: 'I have seen the Directors of the
London Symphony Orchestra concerning your work "Ein Tanz des Lebens", which I
have recommended to them for performance.'

5   'Helene' appears to have been an artist living in Grez at this time.

(256)

Frederick Delius to Jelka Delius

7, PEMBROKE VILLAS,
KENSINGTON, W.
[20 January 1908]

Dearest Jelka —

I arrived here yesterday morning, having left Liverpool at 12 at night[1]

A Dance of Life was splendidly played by the Symphony Orchestra &
admirably conducted by Arbos — first class — better than Haym or Buths.[2]
Unfortunately the Albert Hall is so enormous that one could not hear anything
— It might have been played in Hyde Park. Legges notice is excellent — Brigg
fair went also splendidly and Bantock conducted very well — It was no public
success, but found enthusiastic admirers among the young lot. I was very
pleased with it — it sounds very well[3] — I shall leave tomorrow morning at 11.
and arrive in Paris at 7. and in Grez next day for dinner (Wednesday) I cannot
catch the 9 train & as I have luggage it would be impossible for me to catch the
5 train in Paris. Mrs Bantock also gave me a basket for you — I met M^rs
Woodhouse at the Albert Hall looking as pretty and artistic as ever. I will get
the commissions but not the bacon — I have no room — I conduct Appalachia
at Hanley April 2. Dec 3 they also give Sea-drift I lunched yesterday with
Wood who wants me to arrange things between him & the Genossenschaft I
must try & do so. They ask a bit too much for right of performance — I shall see
Kling presently about the contract —
    With love

    yrs ever
    Fred —

I posted the letter of Helene —

Autograph letter, signed and undated, written in English on headed notepaper.

The original is in the Grainger Museum.

1   On the subject of the Liverpool concert Delius had already written to Jelka on 12 January: 'Beecham played "Paris" very well indeed − It was not quite a finished performance & he was perhaps a bit nervous but in London no doubt they will play it better − The success was mediocre. I dont think anybody but a few musicians understood it.'

2   Buths had given the first performance of the work on 21 January 1904 in Düsseldorf, and on 24 October that same year Haym had conducted it in Elberfeld. The Spanish conductor Enrique Fernández Arbós (1863–1939), initially a violinist but also to become known as a composer, orchestrator and teacher, directed the London Symphony Orchestra's Albert Hall performance on 19 January.

3   Delius's comment reinforces the view that this performance of Bantock's was indeed the first of *Brigg Fair*. It was long believed that the première had been given earlier, by Suter in Basel.

(257)
Frederick Delius to Granville Bantock

GREZ SUR LOING,
S. ET M.
Jan 28th 1907
[i.e. Jan 28th 1908]

My dear Bantock!

After leaving you on the platform at Liverpool I had quite a comfortable journey to London, but was unfortunately turned out of my sleeping car at 8 a m. with a thick London fog. "A dance of Life" went off very well. Arbos conducted it splendidly & the orchestra played remarkably well. The day after I went to hear the "Illuminated Symphony". I dont know what Newmans impression was, but this is mine. I believe Holbrooke to be a considerable humbug and certainly no artist. Apart from the fact that the whole affair smelt of self advertisement, both on the part of Trench & Holbrooke. The Collaboration of the magic lantern & the music was an entire failure − for the one drew ones attention away from the other. So one had to choose. Now for the poem & now for the music. The music was certainly not inspired by Trench's poem. Holbrooke might never have read the poem & I am not sure that he did − in any case he has not understood it & altho' I dont believe that the theme of "immortality" will ever again inspire a poet to a work of genius: the poem is infinitely better than the music. Apart from the music having nothing whatever to do with the poem − it is vulgar & obvious. H. has attained to a certain degree of efficiency as regards technique, but his musical soul is extremely dull, non sensitive & banal & the poetical & the artistic is wanting almost entirely. He is a musical "commercial traveller".[1] I have just finished another part song for mens voices which I will shortly send you. It is lovely here & warm again – we had considerable frost since my return. My wife and her friend went into exstasies over the basket which your wife confided to my care & every item was carefully examined and produced exclamations of delight. How is the league getting on & when is it going to be made public? I suppose the Committee is now complete – if not & in case you want to approach Percy Pitt, I would do so with pleasure – I am studying hard at "Appalachia" and conducting violently an imaginary Orchestra Let me hear from you when you have time. With love to you both,

> I remain
> Yours affectionately
> Frederick Delius

Autograph letter, signed and dated, written in English on headed notepaper. Delius mistakenly dated his letter 1907, for 1908.

The original is in the Delius Trust Archive.

1   Bantock was to take up the same theme in his reply of 30 January: 'Have you heard of the exposure which Holbrooke has had? Newman & other critics spotted that his music to "Apollo & the Seaman" was botched up from an earlier work, that had never been played viz "The Masque of the *Red Death*"! in which the themes are absolutely identical. Hence it was obvious why there was no relation between the poem & the music. This will damage H's already tarnished reputation more than he thinks. He is an utter humbug, & the less we all have to do with him the better.'

(258)

Olga Wood to Frederick Delius

4, ELSWORTHY ROAD,
LONDON, N.W.
Jan. 28. 1908

My dear Mr Delius,

It is *most* kind of you to have scored "Das Veilchen" Now will you be very kind and score "Abendstimmung" and "Eine Vogelweise" and if you will kindly send me the scores I will get the parts done here as I dont want you to have any trouble over it. I shall sing these three songs at Liverpool on March 21st and at Birmingham on March 25th and hope very much to do them justice[1] – and also during the "Proms" sing them in London. Henry will return the letter in a few days, he has sent it to Speyer to read.[2]

Our united kindest greetings to you both

> Yours very sincerely
> Olga Wood

Autograph letter, signed and dated, written in English on headed notepaper.

The original is in the Delius Trust Archive. Three other letters written by Olga Wood to Delius in 1907 and 1908 are preserved in the Archive.

1   Olga Wood had written to Delius on 14 September 1907: 'Bantock is very keen I should sing something of yours with orchestra Have you anything for soprano and orchestra?' And Wood himself was to report, on 30 March: 'My wife made a great success of your Songs in Liverpool & Birmingham.'

2   Edgar Speyer: London banker who took a close interest in new music and particularly helped to promote that of his friend Richard Strauss. The letter mentioned here was from Delius to Friedrich Rösch, of the Genossenschaft Deutscher Tonsetzer, and Speyer subsequently wrote both to Strauss and to Delius in a vain attempt to resolve difficulties concerning a proposed concert performance of extracts from *Salome* at the Queen's Hall.

(259)
Frederick Delius to Ernest Newman

GREZ SUR LOING,
S. ET M.
4 Feb 1908

My dear Newman !

I have not yet received the "Sea-drift" Score − if you sent it off the day you wrote, it is taking over long to arrive. Or perhaps some artistic station master or postman is having a look at it! So they are really giving the "Ring" in english! how daring! Were you able to notice what language they were singing? When shall we have an Opera in England? Do you think it will come whilst we are still alive? I mean one indep[end]ent of the snobs & on the basis of the german Stadttheater. I must say I should like to hear my own musical dramatic works performed in the language they were written in before I disappear.

  With kindest regards to you both   I remain

  ever yours
  Frederick Delius

Autograph letter, signed and dated, written in English on headed notepaper.

The original is in the Delius Trust Archive. See plates 60−61.

(260)
Frederick Delius to Granville Bantock

7/2/08
GREZ SUR LOING,
S. ET M.

Dear Bantock

Thanks for your letter — I do not yet know the exact date of the 4 z'arts ball, but will let you know as soon as it is fixed. My wife may come over with me this time to hear Brigg fair & see me conduct Appalachia — Dont you think we ought to have Beecham on the Committee? — This as an afterthought — There are now such a lot on that one more or less does not matter — Besides anyhow we shall have to have a working Committee — It was our original intention to have him sign the memorial & he might be rather offended that he is now not asked — Talk it over with Newman & decide[1] — You say we may need part of his Orchestra for some of our Festivals & we should then get better terms than from any other orchestra — Wood's & the Symphony Orchestra are *hors de prix*, so we shall no doubt have to recruit from Beecham's — If it is not too late talk it over with Newman — When is Omar[2] in Manchester? If Richter wishes I will have the orchestra Score of my "Mass" sent to him. as one cannot judge very well from the piano Score — It would be fine if it were put in the Birmingham Festival. If Richter is only not too indolent! Perhaps he would let you conduct it! if you would undertake it. Tell Newman that Sea-drift has not arrived[3] — Has the prize Cantata been decided yet — I am afraid they will now give it to a mug. If they give it to any other than the 3 I picked out I shall protest — as there is no question of the others —

   With love to your wife & self from us both —

affectionately yours
Frederick Delius

Autograph letter, signed and dated, written in English on headed notepaper.

The original is in the Delius Trust Archive.

1   Within a few months, Delius had found himself pushed by the younger musical generation into a position of distinct influence in English musical life. He must have felt slightly bemused when he wrote to Jelka on 12 January, from Bantock's address: 'They are making me vice president of the league.'

2   Bantock's cantata *Omar Khayyam*, for voices and orchestra, had three 'first' performances. Part I was given at the Birmingham Festival in 1906, Part II at the Cardiff Festival in 1907, and Part III at the Birmingham Festival in 1909. Its first complete performances were given in London and Vienna in 1912. As a work it is a testimony to

Bantock's pervading interest in the oriental arts, and for a time it was to enjoy great public and critical esteem.

3   It arrived the following day.

(261)
Landon Ronald to Frederick Delius

118, WESTBOURNE TERRACE,
HYDE PARK.W.
20.2.08

My dear Delius,

Alas! your letter followed me all over the country & reached me only after the concert was over! I'm sorry. But I fancy you'd have been most pleased with the performance, & considering the work is scarcely of a "popular" kind, it was well received. I am too sorry neither you nor Bantock were able to be present.

   Kindest greetings

   Yours very sincerely
   Landon Ronald.

Autograph letter, signed and dated, written in English on headed notepaper.

The original is in the Delius Trust Archive. One other letter from Ronald to Delius, of 2 March 1908, is preserved in the Archive.

Landon Ronald (see Letter 237, note 1) had just performed *Brigg Fair*.

(262)
Frederick Delius to Granville Bantock

[Grez-sur-Loing, early March 1908]

Dear Bantock –

To my great astonishment I see from a paper cutting that the "Holy Pabrun" was Havergal Brian's – I am very sorry he did not get the prize – If Coleridge Taylor¹ had only mentioned the "Holy Pabrun" he would have *tied* with the other² & they would have been obliged to play them both & divide the prize. I shall be in London on the 29th inst or the 28th We shall have to put a piece of Brians in the Festival! Programme –

   Yrs ever
   Fr. Delius

Autograph letter, signed and undated, written in English.

The original is in the Delius Trust Archive.

1   Samuel Coleridge-Taylor (1875–1912): English composer, of African descent on
his father's side. He had achieved early fame with his *Hiawatha* trilogy, first performed
between 1898 and 1900. He was one of Delius's fellow adjudicators in the oratorio
competition.

2   The winner of the prize was Julius Harrison, whose setting was published in vocal
score only. The full score was subsequently destroyed by Harrison, as being immature
and overblown.

(263)
Hans Richter to Frederick Delius

10 MAR 1908
Dr. Hans Richter.
"The Firs,"
Bowdon,
Cheshire.

My dear Mr. Delius,

I am afraid that I cannot and must not accept your thanks, as your piece was not
performed in Bradford. The gentlemen did not express their wish for it to be
performed until so late that I would have had to play the piece with only one
hasty rehearsal on the afternoon before the concert. In this matter I acted mainly
in the interest of the composer in that I objected to performing a work which
would have been insufficiently rehearsed. [1]

Respectfully yours
Hans Richter

Autograph letter, signed and dated, written in German on headed notepaper.

The original is in the Delius Trust Archive. It is the only item of correspondence from
Richter to Delius that has been preserved.

Hans Richter (1843–1916): Hungarian-born conductor. He studied at the Vienna
Conservatorium, afterwards becoming associated with Wagner, and gave the first *Ring*
at Bayreuth. He conducted frequently in London from 1877; and became permanent
conductor of the Hallé Orchestra from 1899 to 1911. He was a notable champion of
Elgar.

1   A day earlier, Delius had written to Bantock from Grez: 'Brigg fair was to have been
played in Bradford on the 6th March – but Kling writes me that it did not come off. I

suppose Richter did not like it!' However, following receipt of Richter's letter, Delius wrote again to Bantock, expressing the view that Richter must have acted for the best – 'Which was very nice of him I think.'

(264)
Carl Schuricht to Frederick Delius

Goslar a/Harz, Clubgartenstr. 2.
12.3.08.

Dear Maestro,

Do you remember me? I last wrote to you in Berlin from Wiesbaden, on the occasion of the première of "A Village Romeo and Juliet", your kind wife wrote me a charming reply inviting me to Berlin – – unfortunately I was unable to accept, wrote to you shortly after the performance, but my letter was returned: you had already left for Paris. –

Fate has been busy chasing me around since then: If one has little or nothing to put down, it is hard to get a job as a conductor. Now for my wanderings – I am sure it will amuse you to know that in the meantime I have been conductor of a "Spa" orchestra, and then – conducted operettas into the bargain. You can imagine how this harmonized with my artistic beliefs. – Then last autumn chance smiled on me; the post here became vacant; Max Reger and Henri Marteau recommended me with the utmost vigour, I bade farewell to the theatre & moved here.

Goslar (only 18000 inhabitants, but residence of many cultured people, as town and its surroundings enchanting; grammar school, boarding schools etc.) gives 10 important concerts each winter, to which only top-ranking artists come; included in these are 2–3 concerts given by the *mixed chorus*. This mixed chorus is what I conduct; I have at the same time a male chorus, which assists the "mixed". (Five Symphony Concerts are conducted by the Military Band-master here, who formerly organized these concerts off his own bat; one can't take it off him, anyway he's a capable musician; however, he is *going* in a year's time, and I shall then have everything in my own hands.)

Since a lot of time has been lost this year through the change in conductors, I was unable to take on anything big (occupying a whole evening) for the Choral Concerts – our first concert consisted of: 3 Bach Cantatas, a Brahms Symphony (which I conducted of course); for the 2nd which is to take place in May, we are having Frithjof, Walpurgisnacht, Gesang der Geister über den Wassern (Schubert).

Now all this time I could not forget "Sea-drift" – whenever I thought of *that* work my heart beat faster and I often felt like writing to you about it; – but as long as I had no chorus I was ashamed to keep coming to you with words alone – and not action.

Now I *have* my chorus; and so far chorus and orchestra have got down to their task for me with such enthusiasm, that *neither* is recognisable any more to the audiences; that pleases me; for the sake of the masters whose loyal servant I intend to be. – So, when I took up the position my first thought was: "Bach, then Delius!" – However, 4-fifths of the choir are untrained singers, which is why I had to arrange my programme *thus* (as above). But as the works accepted for the performance in May are almost *ready*, I wrote to Chop (who was here and like me was mad about "Sea-drift"; he then sent me "Appalachia", Piano Concerto, songs and monograph) for the score or piano reduction of "Sea-drift"; I received the latter yesterday by return of post, and I plunged into it with the appetite of a person whose hunger is years old – – "yes, yes – , *that's* how it was!" Every note came back to me and, in full draughts, I drank in the tale that I remembered so well from the Essen performance; – I wander around as if intoxicated, what a wonderful gift the piece was and is to me.

– You promised me the material for "Sea-drift", if ever I performed the work; – but I suppose that will hardly be possible, – the publishers won't allow it. But perhaps through *your* intercession we might get the music on loan, or for a considerably lower price?

And so I ask you urgently and sincerely : write by return of post to "Harmonie" asking them to send me *immediately* (*no matter on what conditions*) 40 soprano parts, 40 altos, 30 tenors and 35 basses (in other words *only* the choral parts to be sent):

What I have in mind is to take the Choir by surprise, to finish off the Walpurgisnacht quickly and to spend the time until May rehearsing the choral passages of Sea-drift. – If the Choir gets hold of it quickly, then I can probably perform "Sea-drift" any time after May. If it only progresses slowly (one can *never* say in advance, only after a few rehearsals), then I shall spend the whole summer & autumn on it and perform the work at the first concert next winter. For the rendering must be *wonderful* and I shall give my life's blood to achieve it!

Am I presumptuous? I have so set my heart on performing the work – will you give me a little help with the material?

Forgive such a long letter with so little in it! but I am *so* happy to be getting so close to "Sea-drift".

With a thousand respectful greetings to you and your kind wife –

Your *loyally* sincere,
enthusiastic disciple
Carl Schuricht,
Conductor.

Please, please let me know soon!

Autograph letter, signed and dated, written in German.

The original is in the Delius Trust Archive.

(265)
Frederick Delius to Granville Bantock

GREZ SUR LOING,
S. ET M.
[22? March 1908]

Dear Bantock –

I shall be in London on the 27th Inst & stay 7 Pembroke Villas – Are you coming up for "Omar"? Please write me here & also tell me – if you do not intend coming to London – What Hotel to stay at at Hanley & when to come – The 1st, afternoon probably! – Have you any special reason for not putting Beecham on the Committee of the Musical League? I cannot quite understand why he is not on – He is a good man & we really half gave him to understand that he would be – Please write to him & tell him that he will be the head of the London local Committee at least – I suppose it is now too late to put him on the principle Com – I am bringing you one of my photos by Histed –
Au revoir à bientôt –

Yrs ever
Frederick Delius

Autograph letter, signed and undated, written in English on headed notepaper.

The original is in the Delius Trust Archive.

(266)
Edvard Munch to Frederick Delius

[March/April 1908]

Dear friend,

I was in Paris for a few days and would have liked to visit you but had to get away again after a short time – I shall probably make another little trip to Paris soon –

Please give me the address of the "Lynx" bureau[1] (newspaper notices), "Famous Men Maker". I should like to see what the French say about my picture "La Mort du Marat"[2] – It is, by the way, only an experiment and if it isn't well hung makes no effect at all — But I think the paintings which do not go anywhere else must be exhibited at L'Independants Tell me whether my works are well hung — and where? — in which room? —

— The decorative picture is a sketch for a whole frieze in the "Kammerspiel" — Please give me the address of Wilhelm Molard too — I have been living here in Warnemunde for a long time — a German Aasgaardstrand — away from bad memories and false Norwegian friends

With best wishes to you and your wife —

Yours   Edvard Munch

53 Am Strom
Warnemunde

Autograph letter, signed and undated, written in German.

The original is in the Delius Trust Archive.

1   A news-cutting agency in Paris.

2   *La Mort de Marat*, almost certainly the 1907 version, is a painting in which Munch expressed his feelings about the disastrous conclusion of his affair with Tulla Larsen.

(267)
Max Schillings to Frederick Delius

MÜNCHEN (19) 1.4.08.
Aiblingerstrasse 4.

Dear friend,

I would have answered your last letter at once, if I had not been on the point of leaving for Berlin for the meetings of the Musikverein. After no end of trouble (orchestra strikes and quasi-anarchy reign here), we are now hoping that we have fixed the Festival here for the *first days of June*. Programme of the 2nd (last) Concert on the 4th June:
1)   Delius: Sections of the Lebensmesse (Duration ca 1 hour)
2)   Two orchestral pieces by Bleyle and [. . .][1]
3)   Bardengesang by Rich. Strauss (Male Chorus.)

I am afraid it is impossible to perform the *whole* of your work. Ludwig Hess[2] and his choir cannot master it *all*; for that, *months* of rehearsal would be necessary, & you know yourself how enormous the difficulties are for a choir which is not composed of professional musicians. Hess suggests Part 2. Please get in touch with Ludw. Hess München, Kaulbachstr. 93) & arrange details with him (assuming you agree to a performance of parts of your work). The question of soloists is extremely important. Whom do you suggest for the baritone part? He must be a *first-class* artist.

The question of the material is also important. Provisionally Hess has borrowed the choral material at his own risk. But as you know, the A.D.M.V. cannot acquire the material for the works it performs as it has no use for it. So some agreement with your publishers would have to be reached through your intercession. Please write to Hess about that too. – I hope you agree to our plan, so that we shall have the pleasure of bringing your work to the public, to begin with in parts. I look forward to it very much. – I am afraid I cannot find your letter just now & must therefore send these lines to Grez. I hope they will be forwarded to you at once!

I congratulate you sincerely on the foundation of your Musical-League.[3] I hope we can form a cartel. But why do you exclude your committee from the programmes? Is there any sense in that? I think not! (cf. the painters' associations.)

I have a terrible amount to do. Am fairly knocked out. My nerves!
Let me hear from you soon!

Very sincerely
Yours
Max Schillings

Autograph letter, signed and dated, written in German on headed notepaper.

The original is in the Delius Trust Archive.

1   Illegible in the original letter.

2   Ludwig Hess (1877–1944): German conductor and composer. He studied in Berlin and Milan, then toured as a concert singer before succeeding Mottl as conductor at Munich. He was now to give the first performance of the larger part of *A Mass of Life*.

3   Musical-League: In English in the original letter.

(268)
Ludwig Hess to Frederick Delius

Munich, 16th April 1908.
Kaulbachstr. 93

Dear Herr Delius,

A thousand apologies for not answering your very friendly lines of 7th April until today, and then only dictating via typewriter. I have been so unbelievably overburdened with my threefold work that there is simply no other way.

Your "Messe des Lebens" is one of those works where I have the feeling that there is such power and vitality in it that for the artist who renders it, putting all his power and love into it must make it an intensely rewarding experience for him. Rest assured that the preparatory work will be pursued with as much conscientiousness as pleasure on the part of all concerned.

With reference to the choice of soloists, I was unfortunately not able to wait for the wishes expressed in your letter, as the Festival is so close at hand and the Theatre management in particular had to know as soon as possible. However, I have chosen for each of the four solo parts the person I considered to be most suitable, taking into account poetic, musical, vocal and intellectual qualities, to be precise, for the most important part the baritone Rudolph Gmür, whom I consider to be the most highly gifted interpreter of parts of real character, for the contralto part, Else Schünemann or the very talented young Olga von Welden, for the soprano Fräulein van Lammen or Frau Grumbacher de Jong.[1] I hope you agree; I chose according to the best of my conscience.

Now for two other important matters.

Firstly, please send me as soon as possible a fair copy of your score, as your manuscript is illegible from a certain distance.

Secondly, I can only perform the Tanzlied if you agree to its being performed by the two lady soloists and ten of the best female voices from my choir, in other words as a threefold quartet; because on 4th May we have a performance of Liszt's Missa Solemnis and Bruckner's 150th Psalm, and four weeks later your work has to be christened in fitting style! That is a physical impossibility, even for a Choral Society that has been in existence for 100 years. Please let me have your view on this; I can imagine the effect would be very pleasing. Finally another minor artistic scruple: I fear that the *frequent* repetition of the word La La spoils the sonorities of the Mädchentanz; could you possibly agree to a cut there? Please write to me soon.

Sincerely yours,
Ludwig Hess.

Typed letter, signed and dated, written in German.

The original is in the Delius Trust Archive. It is the first of four letters written by Hess to Delius, all dated 1908, that have been preserved.

Ludwig Hess: see Letter 267, note 2.

1   In the event, the soloists were Rudolph Gmür, Mientje van Lammen, Olga von Welden and Benno Hebert.

(269)
Frederick Delius to Granville Bantock

GREZ SUR LOING,
S. ET M.
April 23/1908

Dear Bantock.

The Bal des 4'z'arts takes place on *May the 16ᵗʰ* – as I have to order my tickets, please let me know at once if you can come[1] – I do hope you will be able to – As I am hard at work again I dont think I shall be able to come over for "Appalachia"[2] & in that case you might come right thro' to Grez & we would then go in to Paris for 48 hours or more. Elgar will be able to preside at our next Committee meeting. We must try and put off our first Festival until Whitsuntide next year – And make the year end in May – In other words the subscription for 1909 to begin after the first Festival – A festival in November in a Manchester fog would be a *fiasco* & the German lot would not be able to come either. *Do come here* – take a week off or as much as you can – If you could get a fortnight we might then go together to Munich – the festival begins 2 June – My Mass on the 4ᵗʰ – I want you to know the German lot – In haste –

affectionately
Frederick Delius

Autograph letter, signed and dated, written in English on headed notepaper.

The original is in the Delius Trust Archive.

1   Grez was seeing a great deal of coming and going, with the O'Neills paying a visit to the Deliuses about this time, and Balfour Gardiner following shortly afterwards. Beecham was to come in May.

2   Beecham's performance in London on 13 June. Delius did not attend the concert.

(270)
Rosa Newmarch to Frederick Delius

Mᴿˢ NEWMARCH.   52, CAMPDEN HILL SQUARE,
W.
April 23. 1908.

Dear Mʳ Delius,

I was very glad to get your letter. I have suggested to Mʳ Bantock that it will be wise in future for the Committee to send a kind of official statement, through the Secretary, to those who are invited to organize sectional committees. One does not quite like to act on vague and hearsay directions. I will try to start a London section, although I am afraid if it involves a great deal of correspondence it will be impossible for me to do it single-handed, because I am already busier than any human being ought to be who is beginning to descend the shady side of the hill. However, (not to make any more criticisms!) I have written to Miss Ethel Smyth[1] and asked her if she will co-operate with me in forming a London committee. Before doing anything further I will await her reply. If she consents, she may have some suggestion to make as to a third member, for she has a good many influential friends. The Easter holiday has made it practically useless to do anything the last few days. Of course what we really need is a small working fund. If we could borrow a room, I should suggest having a meeting to which those interested should be invited, and getting Ernest Newman to expound the aims and objects of the M.L. This would do much to dispel any wrong ideas as to the intentions of the movement. It would be a good thing if you took the chair, or some other influential member of the General Committee. I fancy this could be worked in connection with the Concert Goers' Club, of which I am a member of committee. We should get the advantage of having the thing organized; on the other hand, I think it would be in many respects wiser if the M.L. made its own independent appeal to Londoners. When I last saw M.[r] Lane,[2] I think I made him see that it was unusual and practically impossible to get *a royalty on song-words*. But he says he frequently gets 5 guineas for the rights of a single lyric and he could not ask the Dowsons to take a guinea a song. Of course the value of these things depends, I imagine, upon the demand and there has been rather a run upon the Dowson songs. I believe M[r] Lane is away just now. I shall be in Paris next month for a few days to hear the Russian operas, if they come off. With very kind regards,

Yours sincerely
Rosa Newmarch

Autograph letter, signed and dated, written in English on headed notepaper.

The original is in the Delius Trust Archive. It is the only item of correspondence from Mrs Newmarch to Delius that has been preserved.

Rosa Newmarch (1857–1940): English music writer, critic and translator. She was an active promoter and organizer, specializing in modern Russian music.

1 Ethel Smyth (1858–1944): English composer, conductor and author. She studied in Leipzig and Berlin. By this time her operas, such as *Fantasio*, *Der Wald* and *The Wreckers*, had been given in cities as diverse as Weimar, Karlsruhe, Dresden, London and New York. Beecham was soon to promote her work energetically and enthusiastically.

2   John Lane: Dowson's publisher. Delius was concerned with Lane over the rights to the poems used in *Song of Sunset*.

(271)
Bokken Lasson to Frederick Delius

43 Hamilton Gardens
St. John's Wood
London N. W.

Dear Mr. Delius!

I take the liberty of sending you a couple of tickets to my concert on Wednesday next. It would make me a great pleasure if you would care to make use of them.
Hoping that you have not quite forgotten me —

Yours very sincerely,
Bokken Lasson.

23rd of April 08.

Autograph letter, signed and dated, written in English.

The original is in the Delius Trust Archive. It is the only item of correspondence from Bokken Lasson to Delius that has been preserved.

Caroline ('Bokken') Lasson (1871–1970): Norwegian singer. She had a notable career in operetta and *variétés*, and founded in 1912 a celebrated Christiania cabaret, Le Chat Noir. She came from a remarkable family: her father was a cousin of the composer Halfdan Kjerulf; Per Lasson, her brother, was a composer of great promise who died tragically young; her sister Oda, herself a painter of distinction, married the painter and writer Christian Krohg and later had a lengthy affair with the dramatist Gunnar Heiberg; another sister, Alexandra, married the painter Frits Thaulow; and a third sister, Soffi, married the Danish poet Holger Drachmann. Bokken's husband, Vilhelm Dybwad, was a lawyer, like her father, and it is possible that he was the same lawyer Dybwad who in the early 1920s was to be involved in contracts relating to Delius's house in Gudbrandsdal, Norway. Johanne Dybwad, Ella in *Folkeraadet*, was his first wife. Many strands, therefore, link Delius with the Lasson family.

Bokken Lasson was now living for a period in London, in order to study under Raimond von zur Mühlen. She gave recitals there, as in Berlin, Paris and New York.

(272)
Granville Bantock to Frederick Delius

BROAD MEADOW
KINGS NORTON

May 14.08

My dear Lad.

Thanks for your letter. I'm truly sorry, I cannot spring the necessary, or the time to get over to Paris for the 'bal'. It is a great disappointment. But I am reserving myself & energies for June 4 & your Mass of Life, & I hope later on to be able to spend a few days with you at Grez. I am delighted to hear about Paris, Brigg-Fair, & the 3 Part-Songs.[1] C'est bon! It is a pity that you were not able to fix the matter up with B & H, as I have always found them most reasonable. The charge for copying seems heavy, but in England, music copying is atrocious & expensive. For the parts of Omar II, B & H paid 4^{d} per page, because I had to get some of the work done in Birmingham, & I had to arrange with the copyists here, as there was not time for the work to be done abroad, where it is cheaper & better. Let me hear all your news about the 'bal'. It will be the next best thing, since I cannot be there in the flesh.

Kindest remembrances to your dear wife from both of us.

Ever yours
Granville Bantock.

You must get over here for our next League Committee in July.

Autograph letter, signed and dated, written in English on headed notepaper.

The original is in the Delius Trust Archive.

1   On 8 May, Novello had written to Delius to confirm that they would publish the three part-songs. They were also looking at *Paris* and *Brigg Fair*.

(273)
F. Oddin Taylor to Frederick Delius

Norfolk & Norwich Triennial Musical Festival.
St Ethelbert's
Norwich,   20. May. 1908.

Dear Sir,

Prize Cantata

Referring to my letter of the 8th April you will be pleased to hear that my

Committee at their last meeting authorised the payment of £10.10.0 to Mr Havergal Brian & I have sent him a cheque to-day.

Yours faithfully,
F. Oddin Taylor
Honorary Secretary

Frederick Delius Esqre

Autograph letter, signed and dated, written in English on headed notepaper.

The original is in the Delius Trust Archive. It is the last of three letters written by Oddin Taylor to Delius in 1907 and 1908 that have been preserved.

(274)
Frederick Delius to Granville Bantock

Grez sur Loing
S & M
20/5/08

Dear friend –

What a pity you could not come for the Bal – It was grandiose Gracious! what a sight it all was, and what lovely women were there – I dare not put down on paper what all took place – but I will tell you when we meet – I am so glad you are coming to Munich – we will have a good time & you will meet important people there – I leave here on the 27th – These German festivals are always very amusing & interesting – *Do not fail to come* – Is Newman coming? try & bring him – The parts of "Brigg fair" were done in Leipzig & not in England – I wrote to Kling about it & they instantly took off £1-14-0 Excuse this scrawl I am rather rocky after the 4' z arts. Be in Munich on May 30th for the performance – of Bischoffs Tanzlegendchen You can get lodgings by applying to the Committee *very cheap* – No doubt you will have received the papers –
Au revoir! in Munich
Best love to you both from us both –

affectionately yours
Frederick Delius

Autograph letter, signed and dated, written in English.

The original is in the Delius Trust Archive.

(275)
Granville Bantock to Frederick Delius

BROAD MEADOW
KINGS NORTON

June 2*nd*/08

My dear Delius

It is damnable ill-luck on my part. Just as I had made all arrangements for coming to Munich today, I find that I shall have to stop here to conduct(ed) a Demonstration of 15000 children & 14 Massed Bands in Victoria Square on the very day of the "Mass". I cannot get out of it, because the Lord Mayor has made the request, & as he is one of the governors on the Council at the Institute, I should jeopardise my position here by refusing. This is what officialdom in music leads to. I have to simply grin & bear it, and you may consider yourself damned lucky, to be independent, & free from ties of the nature that bind me like a cobbler to his last. I can only hope, lad, that thou wilt have a real grand success, & thou hast my best wishes, as thou knowest. As soon as you return from Munich, you must run over here, & get Harding to call a meeting of the League Committee after Whitsuntide. Put up with him at his house, & you will secure an influential friend in your interest on the Birmingham Festival Committee. If you delay, it may be too late, as I hear the programme is now being arranged.

Remember us both to your wife.

Ever yours
Granville Bantock

I think I could get over to Grez for a couple of days on July 6, if you could have me then, & I could return with you if you can be here beforehand.

Autograph letter, signed and dated, written in English on headed notepaper.

The original is in the Delius Trust Archive.

(276)
Frederick Delius to Granville Bantock

Grez sur Loing
Seine & Marne
June 9th 1908

Dear Bantock –

I have just arrived again in Grez – What a pity you could not come to Munich: not only to hear the Mass but I wanted so much to introduce you to the most

PLATE 49   (a) Engelbert Humperdinck; (b) Oskar Fried;
(c) Carl Schuricht; (d) John Coates.

PLATE 50 (a) In party mood: Bruno Cassirer, Else and Max Loewenberg, Fritz Cassirer; (b) Milly Bergh in her garden with distinguished guests: Helge Rode, Knut Hamsun, Ludvig Bergh.

PLATE 51   Troldhaugen, summer 1907: Edvard Grieg, Percy Grainger,
Nina Grieg, Julius Röntgen. (*Coll. Grieg Museum, Troldhaugen.*)

PLATE 52　Arve Arvesen, by Edvard Munch. (*Coll. Munch Museum.*)

PLATE 53   (a) Norman O'Neill; (b) Balfour Gardiner
(*coll. Stephen Lloyd*); (c) Cyril Scott; (d) Percy Grainger.

PLATE 54   Frederick Delius. (Breitkopf's postcard (see p. 297) was
printed from this portrait.)

PLATE 55   Granville Bantock.

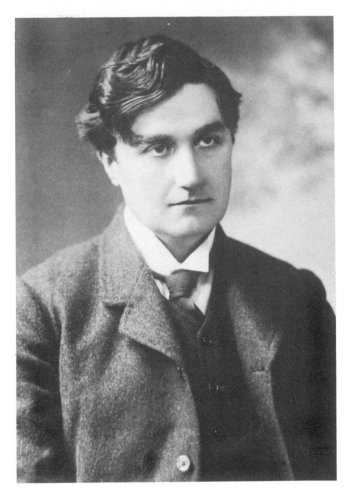

PLATE 56   Ralph Vaughan Williams.

PLATE 57 (a) Havergal Brian (*coll. Lewis Foreman*); (b) Ernest
Newman; (c) Landon Ronald; (d) Hans Richter.

PLATE 58 Thomas Beecham.

PLATE 59   (a) Richard Dehmel; (b) Otto Kling (*coll. Lewis Foreman*);
(c) Torstein Torsteinson, caricature by Fredrik Bødtker;
(d) Francesco Berger.

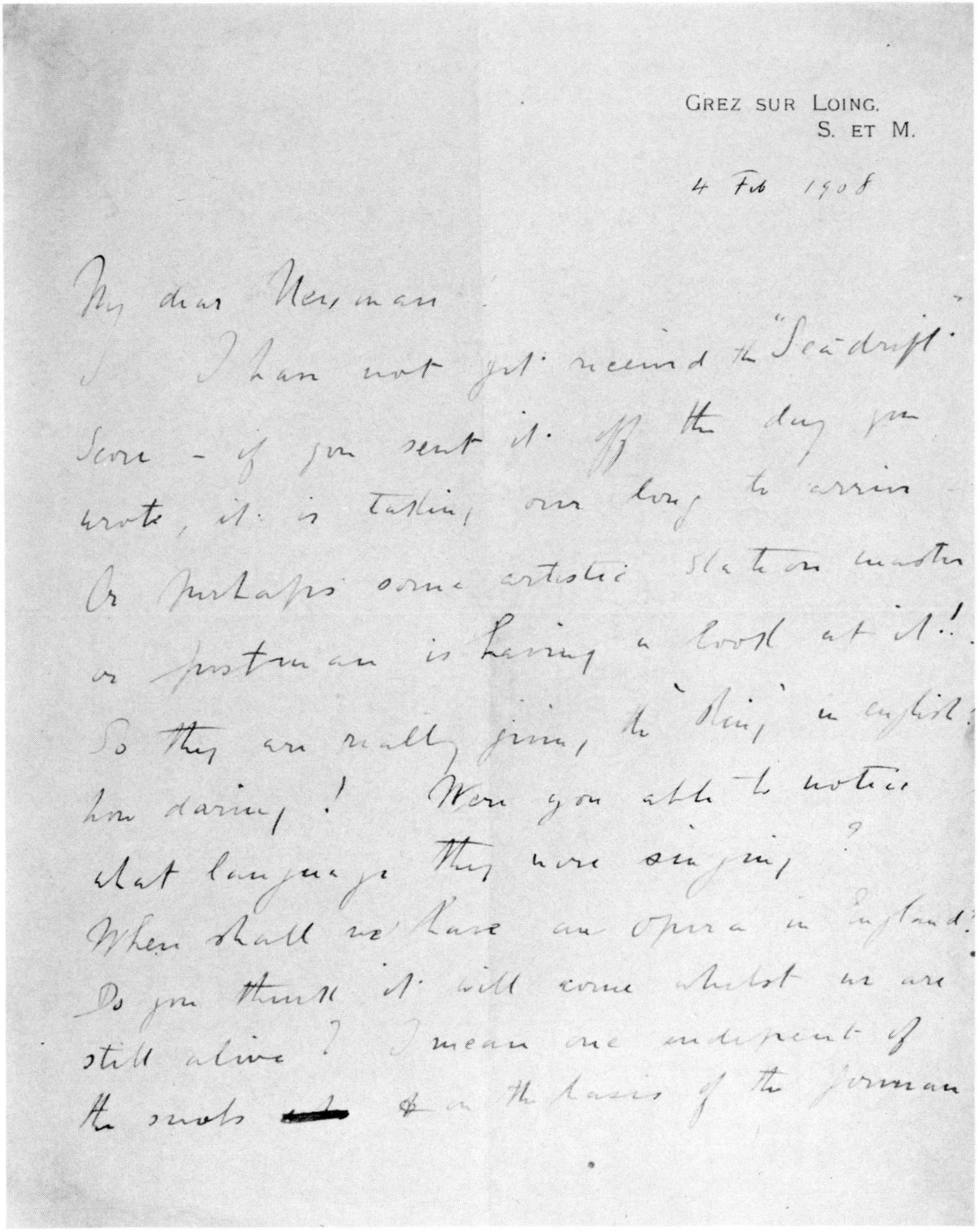

GREZ SUR LOING.
S. ET M.

4 Feb 1908

My dear Newman!

I have not yet received the "Sea drift"
Score — if you sent it off the day you
wrote, it is taking rather long to arrive —
Or perhaps some artistic station master
or postman is having a look at it!
So they are really giving the 'Ring' in english;
how daring! Were you able to notice
what language they were singing?
When shall we have an Opera in England!
Do you think it will come whilst we are
still alive? I mean one independent of
the snobs ~~and~~ & on the basis of the german

PLATES 60, 61   Letter from Delius to Ernest Newman, 4 February 1908
(see p. 335).

Stadt-theater. I must say I should
like to hear my own musical
dramatic works performed in the
language they were written in
before I disappear.

With kindest regards to you
both   Tremain

                    ever yours

            Frederick Delius

PLATE 62   Elgar and Bantock.

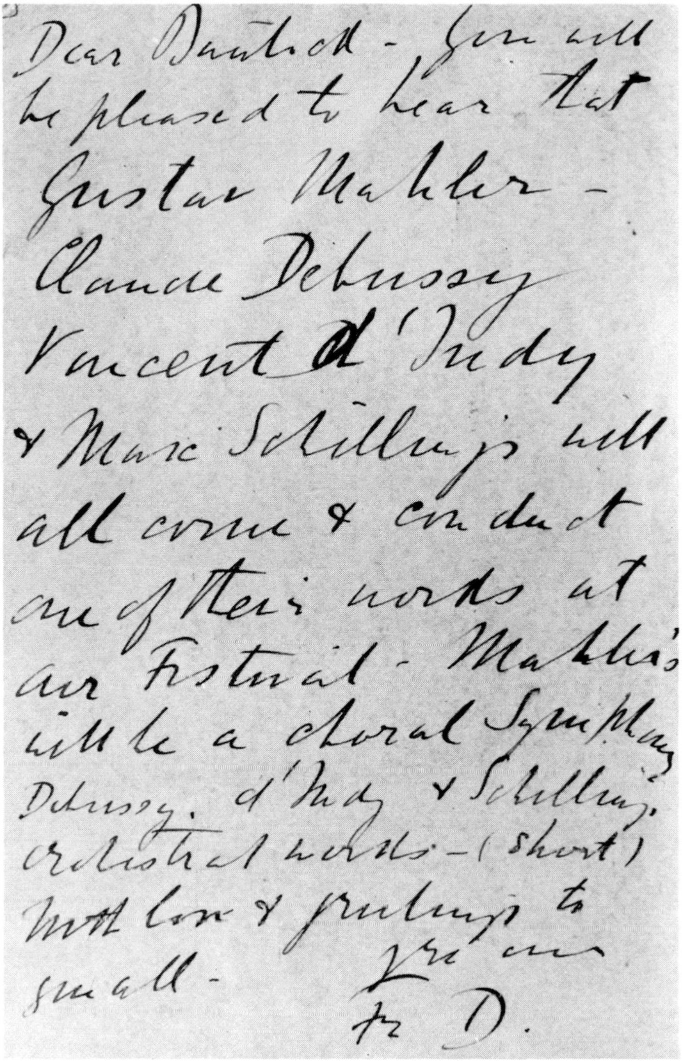

Dear Bantock — You will
be pleased to hear that
Gustav Mahler —
Claude Debussy
Vincent d'Indy
& Max Schillings will
all come & conduct
one of their works at
our Festival — Mahler's
will be a choral Symphony
Debussy. d'Indy & Schillings.
orchestral works — (short)
with love & greetings to
small — Yrs ever
Fr D.

PLATE 63   Postcard from Delius to Granville Bantock, [27 December
1908] (see p. 378).

PLATE 64 Frederick Delius in 1908.

important German composers & conductors. My "Mass" made an enormous impression −[1] In fact much more than I ever expected − the Chorus was superb & the Tanzlied went splendidly − The womans Chorus consisted of 26 picked voices, with the Solo Soprano & Alto − It is going to be performed in several towns in Germany next season − also Berlin − I am not coming over for "Appalachia"[2] as I want to keep quiet for a bit & work − Do come over here whenever you can, you know how welcome you will be & it is simply lovely here now − Nothing but Roses of all colors & other flowers − I am bathing in the river since the middle of May − Schillings made a long speech about the Musical League (in my name) & invited the German musicians to join − This was at the General Meeting − Cannot the Committee Meeting be postponed until end of September − We must on no account give a festival until next May or June − Here in Germany, the town where the festival is held *always* pays a certain amount of the Festival expenses. Otherwise the Festival would be impossible. We must absolutely get the English municipal authorities to do the same &. choose our festival towns accordingly. Mottl was there and is giving "Appalachia" & my piano Concerto in Munich this winter. When I think of Manchester in a fog & a musical Festival I shudder − In Germany the towns are so clean & well built − the Concert rooms so splendid & the whole place so suitable for music, that one might risk a Festival even in Winter, but in England, never! When will you be able to come here? Write soon − that clause about "composers on the Committee" is entirely idiotic![3] I have not met one composer who thought otherwise & in England too! We shall have of course to draw largely from Germany & France − I, myself, have realised how little there is in England − there is'nt much in Germany, but every musician can present a piece with an excellent technic. this is not the case in England, where a decent technic is an exception − With love to you both −

Yours affectionately
Frederick Delius

Come as soon as you can? If you can bring your wife − we have room for you all −

Autograph letter, signed and dated, written in English.

The original is in the Delius Trust Archive.

1   Delius had in fact already sent Bantock a postcard from Munich, on 6 June: 'I missed you very much − the "Mass" was a *great* success Chorus splendid.' The work had been given, with a number of cuts, by Ludwig Hess at the Tonkünstlerfest on 4 June.

2   A performance to be given by Beecham on 13 June.

3   Any such clause does not appear to have made its way into the printed leaflets finally given out by the League.

(277)

Torstein Torsteinson to Frederick Delius

Paris 11 June 08.

Hr Delius!

Hope you remember me from the few days at "Konnerud" summer 06. This spring, surprisingly enough, I received a grant – with it I intend to stay in Paris as long as possible.

– I would like to call on you and your wife and see your "Gaugin" whenever it is convenient.

Many greetings
Sincerely   Torsteinson.

Hotel de Seine
52 Rue de Seine

Autograph letter, signed and dated, written in Norwegian.

The original is in the Delius Trust Archive. It is the only item of correspondence written by Torsteinson to Delius that has been preserved.

Torstein Torsteinson (1876–1966): Norwegian painter. His later studies were in Paris, where he lived for most of the time from 1908 to 1925, and where the works of Matisse, Lhote and particularly Derain were greatly to influence him.

1   Delius's 'Gaugin'[*sic*] was *Nevermore* (see pp. 138–41).

(278)

Granville Bantock to Frederick Delius

BROAD MEADOW
KINGS NORTON

June 13.08

My dear Lad!

I am delighted to hear that the Mass has been such a success, & that you have many representations to look forward to this autumn.

I shall try & get over to you for a few days on July 4th, if you can put me up then, and shall look forward to seeing you in your home, as well as to making Koanga's acquaintance. I am thinking of becoming an artist, & exchanging music for painting, so I shall expect to be able to make some studies of models – from the nude of course – during my brief stay. We will then be able to discuss the future of the League, & the likelihood of the first Festival. Could you not come over for a Committee meeting on July 1, & we could return together? I am feeling a bit stiff, & shall be glad to kick my heels about a bit.

Kindest remembrances to your wife from both of us.

Ever yours.
Granville Bantock

Autograph letter, signed and dated, written in English on headed notepaper.

The original is in the Delius Trust Archive.

(279)

Balfour Gardiner to Frederick Delius

7, PEMBROKE VILLAS,
KENSINGTON, W.

14.6.08

My dear Fred,

I am just off to the house I have taken for two months (The Vicarage, Little Barrington, Burford, Oxon) so you must excuse a hasty letter. I have lots of things to say to you. First of all, hearty congratulations on the success of your Messe des Lebens: I hope that you yourself were pleased with it, & have returned full of the desire to work. I heard your Appalacchia yesterday, & enjoyed it very greatly: Beecham did it well, & the chorus, though by no means perfect was much better than at Cassirer's concert. Beecham also did my Fantasy well: it was a great event for me, & a great stimulus.

With regard to your plantation, my father expected to have the information last Tuesday, but I have not seen him since then & I suppose he will write to me in a few days about it.[1]

Please ask your wife what I am to do with her curtains, etc. This house will be shut up; & even if Mollard comes (which does not seem likely) he will be unable to get them here − On second thoughts I will send them over to the O'Neill's. I suppose you know that Norman has been terribly ill − in bed four weeks with severe neuritis. He is just beginning to recover, & ought to be out of bed in a fortnight.

Wood is doing an old Symphony of mine in the middle of August, & it is so bad that I shall have to work hard at rewriting it while I am away. After its performance I really might allow myself a holiday: would you be going to Norway so late? We are having the most beautiful summer I have ever known, & I feel quite another being.

Well, I think I have given you all the news

Ever yours
H. Balfour Gardiner

Autograph letter, signed and dated, written in English on headed notepaper.

The original is in the Delius Trust Archive.

1   Gardiner was helping to effect on Delius's behalf an enquiry into conditions at Solana Grove.

(280)
Frederick Delius to Granville Bantock

Grez sur Loing
S & M
16 June 1908

Dear Old boy –

I am so pleased you are coming here & am already looking forward to your visit. Dont make it too short! – How strange! I am also thinking of giving up Composing for painting, & am going to study *the nude seriously* this summer. We are going to have a model down from Paris so you will be able to make several serious studies whilst you are here – It is funny but only the female nude seems to inspire my artistic faculty! Bring Newman along if he can come – We can set him to writing music – as he knows so much about it! my study is at his disposal as we two will no doubt spend most of our time amongst the roses & other flowers in the garden, painting! You must get Elgar to preside at the next meeting! There is nothing important to arrange before the autumn – as a Festival this year is quite out of the question. Enclosed a balance sheet of the Allgemeiner Deutscher Musikverein. Show it to Harding – We must get people to give money to the M.L. & the towns must contribute like they do in Germany – We must get rid of the absurd English idea that everything must pay – Art never ought to pay – Art & artists ought to be paid. Now – old man – write when we may expect you – If you leave London by the first train – Charing Cross at 9. you can catch a train leaving the Gare de Lyon at 5.15 Our station is Bourron – *get a Motor taximêtre*

Yours affectionately
Fr. Delius

Autograph letter, signed and dated, written in English.

The original is in the Delius Trust Archive.

(281)
Theodor Szántó to Frederick Delius

Berlin W. 17.6.08
Neue Winterfeldstr. 49.

My dear D., Yesterday Safonoff[1] came to see me and I played him the Piano Conc. and Appalachia and I have now completely won him for you. I also showed him your photo (from the Musik. Wochenblatt) and he said he thought you seemed very nice and must be a thinker. He is now going to the Caucasus for 2 months and then back to America, where he conducts the big concerts (in New York). He is a splendid fellow. He embraced me many times and even kissed me before he left and told me that he had me locked up in his heart. I played under him once in Vienna and had not seen him since then. He told me that he is *banking* on receiving the scores of "Appalachia" and the Piano Conc. from you and studying them in the Caucasus. He told me he would get me to America with the Piano Conc. and definitely use his influence on your behalf — I have already sent the reviews to Dupuis (who proposed that I should appear in Brussels as long as 6 years ago) and to Dr Haym. The others will get them as soon as I receive further copies of reviews from Wolff. My Carmen Paraphr. is getting a performance in B. next winter. (Have just signed a contract) I am now working on the score of my Symphony, which I have of course dedicated to you. Cordial greetings to you both.

Yours
Th Szántó.

Frau Löwenbr. returns your good wishes. She went out yesterday for the first time in 4 weeks, after having sprained her foot when she was out visiting. (actually she tore a ligament)
Safonoff said he likes your music better than Debussy's because it is more profound and less sophisticated. Safonoff is getting on for 60. He was Director of the Moscow Conserv. and of the Symph. Concerts there.
Which of your compositions are already in print? "Paris" too? Are Breitkopf & Härtel already printing something of yours?
Ravel wrote yesterday to tell me that he is working on the "Versunkene Glocke" (by Hauptmann) as a fairy-tale opera.

Autograph letter, signed and dated, written in German on headed notepaper.

The original is in the Delius Trust Archive. Twenty-two letters and postcards written by Szántó to Delius between 1906 and 1909 are preserved in the Archive.

Theodor Szántó: see Letter 198, note.

1   Vasily Ilyich Safonov (1852–1918): Russian pianist and conductor. He was a pupil
of Leschetizky and at the St Petersburg Conservatory, later becoming director of the
Moscow Conservatory from 1889 to 1905. Subsequently he was particularly active as a
conductor in the United States – at this period with the New York Philharmonic.

(282)

Thomas Beecham to Frederick Delius

June 17th/08
Highfield,
Boreham Wood,
Herts.

Dear Delius

'Appalachia' has come and gone – I think it went off pretty well – the public
were quite enthusiastic, but the critics nearly all reactionary – except perhaps
the faithful R̥o̥b̥i̥n̥[1] 'who has now (and after much obvious mental struggle)
arrived at the conclusion that I am a 'musician of genuine capacity' – vide –
Daily Telegraph of next day – not a blessed word about the orchestra who blazed
away at your work like a gang of navvies. I enlarged the band, doubled the
whole Brass (in places) and Harps, and we kicked up a rare old shindy. I had the
B'ham Choir down and they sang the unaccompanied bit very nicely – better
than the Hanley crowd – with more delicacy and expression. They were hardly
strong enough for the Finale, but that was perhaps the fault of my 'doublings'.
The effect however was quite good. Where we scored was in the Funeral March
– by aid of the extra Brass, getting a big crescendo up to the *-fff-* and then
diminuendo to the *'Chorale'* – I took the whole thing rather easily, expecially
the $\frac{6}{8}$ measures which gained much thereby.

Meux[2] sang the baritone solo. I really enjoyed myself, with the work – thanks
to you – and so did the Band, who seemed quite happy and at home.

Gardiner's thing[3] turned out alright – the scoring a bit queer in parts –
imagine the effect of a Flute, Viola, and Trumpet, with Harp arpeggi for Bass!
That pretty sentimental tune in it of course pleased very much.

I have arranged with the Hanley Choir to come to London next December
(6th – 12th) to sing your *Sea-Drift*. I am going to conduct it at Hanley on Dec.
3rd and I think it is practically settled that my orchestra are to go and play. (i.e.
75 of them).

I met Nikisch a short time ago who was supposed to have given your 'Dance
of Life' at one of the concerts of the London Symphony Orchestra (it was down
on the Programme). I asked him how it went and the beggar coolly replied that
he had cut it out of the Programme. Charming people, these foreigners!

Miss Smyth's *'Wreckers'* had a great success. The stupendous Legge referred
to the occasion of it's performance at Queens Hall as a noteworthy one in the

annals of British Art. I really think it is the most idiotic and miserable rubbish I have ever heard. Fearful humbug! This is truly a damned hole![4]

Bantock's Omar Khayyam was done at Queen's Hall a little time ago and went very well. Some of it sounds quite nice.

Have you yet got the Piano copy of the Dowson cycle?[5] Please let me have one as soon as it comes out.

The Musical League has relapsed into a beautiful and touching condition of torpor. I have one or two ideas however for arousing it therefrom – about which more anon.

Armide was done at Covent Garden the other night – in German – under *Richter* – positively the most scandalous performance ever perpetrated there. These two venerable institutions (it – the 'Garden' and Richter) would seem to be in a happy condition of second childhood. There has been no novelty there this season – I wonder if this is due to Percy Pitt – he seems to be a monstrous dull dog. I am preparing already for my campaign next season – can you suggest any new works?

Let me have a line –

Kindest regards to both of you –

Ever yours
Thomas Beecham

P.S. My wife and boy both send love.

Autograph letter, signed and dated, written in English on headed notepaper. Envelope addressed: Frederick Delius Esq / Grez-sur-Loing / Seine et Marne / *France* – . Postmark: LONDON.W JU 18 08.

The original is in the Delius Trust Archive.

1   Robin Legge, music critic of *The Daily Telegraph*.

2   Thomas Meux (1869–1940): English singer, more usually of bass roles. His operatic and concert career took him to Europe and North America, and he was a teacher at the Royal Academy of Music.

3   *Fantasy*, for orchestra. This was the first performance of a work that is no longer extant.

4   Beecham was nonetheless to become a notable exponent of the works of Ethel Smyth, particularly the opera *The Wreckers*, which he was to conduct the following year at His Majesty's Theatre and whose overture remained long in his repertoire. The Queen's Hall performance referred to in this letter was a concert performance of two acts of the opera, Nikisch conducting the London Symphony Orchestra.

5   *Songs of Sunset*.

(283)
Frederick Delius to Granville Bantock

Grez sur Loing
Seine & Marne
30 June 1908

My dear old chap —

I cannot possibly come to that Committee meeting this time, I am just back
from Munich & I dont see at all why a meeting is held now — there is nothing
to settle that cannot be done without me & then Elgar is there! A Festival cannot
be held this year anyhow & all the better, as there are too many Festivals in the
autumn of this year — If the league fizzles out, then, by G., let it fizzle out   I
am not going to keep an institution that fizzles out so easily alive with my
precious breath & time! I & you have done our utmost for the affair & the others
can buck up also — Gardiner promised money *if the thing succeeded* — If it fizzles
out England is hopeless as a field for the developement of modern music — They
want another 20 years of Oratorio & religious dead music & if the league has
done nothing else it has made me make your acquaintance & given me a new &
dear friend. The whole of last year & most of this I have been rushing to & fro'
from England — I am just putting the finishing touches to my new Orchestral
work "A Summer Rhapsody"[1] & dont want to break off until you come here —,
when it will be done — Before they decide anything about a Festival they ought
to find out if the town where the Festival will be given will pay some of the
expenses — this is most important — & it is done in Germany, otherwise a M.L.
is impossible — 104 members! is not at all bad to start with, but more
propaganda must be made — Donations no doubt will come when the thing is
a success — or after the first Festival which must be held next June & lovely
weather — Write me if I may expect you on the 7th — Tell Nap[2] I wish he were
here to keep our flowers damp — it is hot & lovely — We bathe twice a day in
the river — Do come quick now —

   With our united love to you & your wife

   Yrs affectionately
   Frederick Delius

Autograph letter, signed and dated, written in English.

The original is in the Delius Trust Archive.

1   *In a Summer Garden*, in its original version.

2   The Bantocks' Aberdeen terrier, Napoleon.

(284)
Thomas Beecham to Frederick Delius

Highfield,
Boreham Wood,
Herts.
July 3rd/08

Dear Delius

We had a meeting of the M.L. today. A most doleful affair. Most of the Committee seemed chiefly bent on dissolving the whole thing. A few of us however managed to stave of[f] this disaster and it now looks as if there will be a Festival in Liverpool sometime next year. At least I think that Bantock, Evans[1] & myself ought to pull this off without much difficulty.

I should like to come to Norway very much, and if you will send me full particulars, I will arrange to meet you at Christiansand, taking the boat from London.[2]

I am trying to arrange for the 'Mass' to be done also in London next season – about which we will talk more anon. I simply love Sea-Drift – have learnt it by heart & you will be horrified to hear that I play it and sing it on the Piano to people up & down the kingdom!!! Every one likes it! But I assure you that I have learnt all the harmonies quite correctly.

With love to all,

Yours
T.B.

P.S. Can you do me a great favour? I am thinking of giving an act of "Pelleas and Melisande" at one of my concerts and I am in need of information about the rights of performance – band parts etc. etc. If I write myself to Paris I shall not get a satisfactory reply until next Spring or thereabouts. Could you inquire for me about it and let me know as soon as possible. I am getting my circular out this week. I should be so much obliged. *A. Durand* is the publisher – Also if there is any chamber music work of his besides the string quartet.

I may be coming over to Paris – first week of the New Year for a few days.
T.B.

Autograph letter, initialled and dated, written in English on headed notepaper.

The original is in the Delius Trust Archive.

1   Harry Evans (1873–1914): Welsh choral conductor, organist and teacher. He became established in Liverpool where from around the turn of the century he took on various posts, notably as conductor of the Liverpool Welsh Choral Union and as choral conductor of the Liverpool Philharmonic Society.

(285)
Robin Legge to Frederick Delius

5.7.08   33 Oakley St
Chelsea SW.

My dear Fred, Many thanks for your letters, papers etc. The Signale I found most interesting. Clearly Germany is no better off, (if so well) than this effete old country in the matter of real composers, while there seems to be nothing to choose between them in the matter of music-makers! I am afraid the Musical League is in a bad way. I attended, on invitation, the committee meeting last Friday, & the general tone was most depressing. There was a fearful amount of unprofitable talk, but hardly one definite idea promulgated. However, I hear from Baughan, that Evans, the enthusiastic young Welshman from Liverpool, & Beecham are going more or less to ignore the Committee, & acting on their own behalf, are going to "work" Liverpool, of which place, it appears both are natives, for all it is worth There is to be another meeting at the end of October, but the prospect of a festival this year has practically been abandoned. Bantock, the most wide awake of all the Committee didn't attend the meeting — I wish he had done so, as his wide & clear mind would have been of use to the chaotic rotters who were there. What struck me was the lack of genuine enthusiasm. The jewboy, Landon Ronald, damned the whole idea & was very scornful —

Things are jogging along here very much as usual. Something like an average of 6 or more concerts a day have been held during the last two months, & the opera is careering along its old sweet way: but glory be, there are signs of the concerts fizzling out now — & high time they did.

I saw Keary for a moment at the Club this afternoon. Balfour Gardiner I have heard nothing of for weeks, & have no idea if he is in town or not. Cyril Scott, too, we have not seen — his star seems to have set completely, or at least to have been eclipsed for the time being. Percy Grainger is on the point of revisiting Australia for a concert tour with Ada Crossley. He is well & hard at work, but he seems to me to be developing into a mercenary musician & a little out of the single-minded artist. Perhaps he will recover one day, but he certainly is very keen just now on being well advertised, & so is always (thro' his mother) sending me notes asking me to say so & so in the Daily Telegraph.

I will return the papers. I wish you could have the O'Neill notes of Apallachia destroyed — all the "critics" go on making the same mistake because of these notes that *A*. is a series of conventional variations & lose sight of (or never had it) the *mood* picture of the old man, represented by the theme

Byby, cordial greetings to Madame & ditto tibi

Yrs Ever
Robin H Legge

Autograph letter, signed and dated, written in English.

The original is in the Delius Trust Archive.

(286)
Norman O'Neill to Frederick Delius

THE HOSTEL,
HINDHEAD,
SURREY.
July 6 . 08.

My dear Delius,

Just a line, as I want to tell you about the M.L. committee meeting. I went up to town for it from here & very glad I was to have done so for if it had not been for Beecham, Evans, & myself, I do not think there would be any Musical League now ! –

Elgar began by finding fault with everything that had been done – He said we had not got the sympathy of the organists & bandmasters (military!) two of the most important "musical factors" in the country !!! – There are only 115 members so far – but as far as I can make out *very little* has been done by members of the committee to get members & Elgar said he would appeal to nobody for money – He is such an infernal ass that I should not think anybody would give him a penny ! –

L. Ronald threw cold water on the scheme – likewise Agnew & Harding who evidently were in favour of winding it up ! Johnson & Beecham have both offered £50 – (what about Balfour's £100? I am going to ask him about that) but *none* of the rich people round the table offered a £5 note! – Well finally after a great deal of talk we got so far as to anyhow give up the idea of having a festival this year, & Beecham & Evans are going to make enquires at *Liverpool* to see if the choir would be willing to join us in a festival there – as there seems no doubt they would be willing to do. I think that "stinking" old Manchester is fairly well knocked on the head! – Now it all comes to this – Beecham & Evans are the men who are going to start this thing if it gets started at all – McNaught may be useful & I shall do all I can. The others are no good – Bantock – Wood – Pitt – were not there – & nothing can be expected from them. We are to have another meeting in October (towards the end of the month) when Evans & Beecham will have something to say about Liverpool. It was a narrow squeak I can tell you & it was only by the skin of our teeth we managed to prevent a resolution being put & probably carried that would have done for the whole thing! – I came up here a little more than a week ago & am "quite another creature," or "feeling another man," as a warm brother might say! – We have taken a little house, charming & very old, near here for 8 weeks where we hope

to spend a happy summer ! I want to do some work very badly — both serious &
trivial — the latter for the publishers & my doctors bill! I am going up to town
next week as I have to conduct something of mine.
We go to
       Headly Mill Farm
          Standford
          HANTS
on the 18ᵗʰ July. I hope this will reach you before you go to Norway. Ask your
wife about those parcels which came for her from No. 7. Are they things that
will not spoil & will wait until you come over in the autumn ?
    With love to you both

    from
    Yours always
    Norman O'Neill.

Autograph letter, signed and dated, written in English on headed notepaper.

The original is in the Delius Trust Archive.

(287)
Francesco Berger to Frederick Delius

6 York Street
Portman Square   PHILHARMONIC SOCIETY   8 July 1908
London.

Dear Sir and honoured Master,

It will afford the Directors of this Society much pleasure if you will entrust to
them the *production* in England of some new, or hitherto unperformed Orchestral
Work. Have you such an one ready? or would you undertake to compose one &
have it ready for us during our coming season which commences in November
& ends in March next. [1]

    You are probably familiar with the history of The Philharmonic Society. That
Beethoven composed his ninth Symphony for us, — and that Cherubini, Spohr,
Mendelssohn, Weber, Berlioz, Wagner, Tschaikowsky, Grieg, Dvorak, Max
Bruch, St. Saens, Sibelius, — in fact every great Composer has in his day
contributed a Work to our Repertoire or personally appeared at our Concerts.

    Several of your compositions have recently been performed here, but we shall
feel much honoured by your favouring us with a complete novelty, only
stipulating that the Work shall not be of too great a length. Our orchestra is
admittedly the finest in England, & you are assured of a hearty welcome at the

hands of our Subscribers and Members. May I beg the favour of your early reply, and with the assurance of my profound respect remain

Yours faithfully
Francesco Berger
Hon. Sec.

Autograph letter, signed and dated, written in English on headed notepaper.

The original is in the Delius Trust Archive. It is the fifth of ten letters written by Berger to Delius between 13 July 1907 and 26 September 1908 that have been preserved.

Francesco Berger (1834–1933): English pianist, composer and teacher. He studied at Leipzig under Moscheles, and was secretary of the Philharmonic Society from 1884 to 1911.

1   Berger's following letter, dated 17 July, shows that Delius offered the Society 'A Summer Rhapsody' [*In a Summer Garden*]. The Philharmonic Society 'would wish to produce it on the 11 December under the baton of Mr. Landon Ronald'. On 29 July Berger wrote, 'We . . . are happy to agree to your conducting the first performance of your "A Summer Rhapsody".' Delius was, however, to turn down his request for programme notes: 'I do not much care for the analytical programs as they are generally done, and for modern impressionistic music they are entirely useless. Besides, I wish the audience to concentrate their attention entirely on listening to the music and not have their attention drawn away by musical examples. The title 'In a Summer Garden' puts them into the atmosphere of my work – that is really all I desire' (quoted in Robert Elkin, *Royal Philharmonic, The Annals of the Royal Philharmonic Society* (London: Rider and Company [1947]), p. 103).

(288)
Thomas Beecham to Frederick Delius

HIGHFIELD,
BOREHAM WOOD,
HERTS.
July 17th/08

Dear Delius

I have arranged to leave Hull on the 25th next, but it is possible that I may delay my going until the 27th.[1] In that case I shall get to Kristiania on Wednesday. However I shall do my best to manage the 25th. I am going to L'pool the beginning of the week and shall be seeing Evans and Johnston. I have an idea that the Choir best suited for the performance of your Mass would be that of Evans, 'The Welsh Choral Union' or whatever it is called. I am told they are very good, more pliable and sensitive than these masses of stolid British choristers. I should like to know Bantock's opinion of them as he has probably heard the choir several times.[2] I should like to know *by return*, as if he thinks they could really sing the work well, I might arrange something definite with Evans next week. I shall try to give it on a Saturday afternoon at the end of May or beginning of June. Would you also ask Bantock if he has any new orchestral work that would be likely to fit in with my scheme of things. I hope you will bring the new orchestral work you have just finished along with you to Norway − I am looking forward to seeing it immensely. I still wait patiently for the Dowson cycle and 'Romeo'. I have a meeting of a few rich people on Sunday next to discuss my operatic scheme I told you about. I hope something comes of it. I shall pull it off sooner or later, whatever eventuates *this* season. Covent Garden has been unusually thrilling this year! Armide has been the grand novelty − conducted by Richter. The whole thing sounded as if a steam-hammer were breaking a walnut-shell − the most slovenly orchestral playing imaginable. And yet all around one rise sighs and whispers of adulation − 'How perfectly beautiful! − the dear old man is quite incomparable!' − Armide − if you please! Long live the classics! The London Symphony Orchestra have announced their series of concerts next season, to be conducted by Messrs Nikisch, Richter, Safonov and Mylnarski![3] It strikes me that we are becoming more national every year! *Fagges*[4] choir are doing *Omar Khayyam* again next season − I am sorry as I should have liked to do it myself. I have resigned the *Birmingham City Choral So*ᶜ. You may tell Bantock of this but I do not wish it to be made public property for a few days.

My whole experience in Birmingham has been unfortunate and I very much regret ever having gone there. For the performance of Appalachia, as you know, I hauled the Choir up to London, who brought along with them (to boom and write them up) a doddering old idiot, Buckley by name, who has been put up as a sort of rival critic to Newman in B'ham.[5] This damned old fool wrote a column of praise on the Choir's performance and lustily trounced both myself and the orchestra, asserting that the performance of Appalachia was very mediocre and altogether wanting in mastery and finish. The same sort of thing with regard to the rest of the programme. I am sure you will not think I am overstating the case when I say that not only did the orchestra(!) not make *one technical slip*, but they played with the utmost enthusiasm, finish and splendour of tone. It was far and away the best performance we have given of a work of yours − Paris not excepted − and everyone thought the work was magnificent − Arthur Symons (Saturday Review) was most enthusiastic and would like to hear it a dozen times.

Please excuse this rambling letter − it is a dull morning − raining − and I cannot go out.

Ever yours
Thomas Beecham

Autograph letter, signed and dated, written in English on headed notepaper.

The original is in the Delius Trust Archive.

1   Delius had persuaded Beecham to join him on the Norwegian walking tour.

2   Bantock was staying with Delius at Grez, having arrived on 15 July.

3   Emil Mlynarski (1870–1935): Polish conductor, violinist and composer. He conducted widely in Europe.

4   Arthur Fagge (1864–1943): conductor of the London Choral Society.

5   Ramsden Buckley was a writer of some eccentricity. In an attempt to enlist Delius's
collaboration, he wrote to the composer on 2 October: 'I am a librettist who is doing
for word-music what Wagner and Debussy have done for the orchestra. . . . At present
I am thinking of . . . a weird idea for a short music-drama, going a long way beyond
Strauss. Weirdness, however, is not a craze with me. I am a member of the Musical
League.' An even odder epistle was to follow on 17 October.

(289)

Frederick Delius to Jelka Delius

HOTELLERNE
"UNION" OG "GEIRANGER"   *Geiranger, den* 2 August *1908*

Dearest Jelka – We have just arrived here from Grotlien where we stayed last
night[1] – I forgot to tell you that as "Memento" was steaming out of the Scheldt
early on Sunday morning the steering went wrong & just as I appeared on deck
the boat touched land – we were right up on the sand, it looked very funny –
however with great effort we managed to get off again – We arrived yesterday
morning at Grotlien – quite on the Vidder & surrounded by snow mountains
– about 12.30 the weather looked rainy & so we decided to stay over night &
also to get rid of some unpleasant french tourists with a priest! It turned out
fine in the afternoon so I took my fishing rod & went off with B. to fish. I only
got two, but we had a lovely walk on the höjfjeld – When we returned for
supper, a whole caravan of germans had arrived : there are more germans
traveling than any other nation &, I can assure you, they are most objectionable
– They have, nearly all, very bad manners – eat like swine & talk very loud:
Then they take entire possession of the sitting room & begin to play the piano
& sing in chorus german Folksongs & students songs – They are all fat & ugly:
Not one pretty girl or fine woman – When one comes into the room, he struts
in proudly & snorts around a little & then retires banging the door after him –
or he comes in, turns over all the books on the table – knocks a chair over &
then sits down at the piano Both english & french have better manners,

undoubtedly without exaggeration! Grotlien is finely situated, but from there to Merok is the finest scenery I have ever seen – fantastic – Of course you must see this – We passed one lake hemmed in by a gigantic black, blue & green Cliff of solid rock with patches of snow on the quite perpendicular side – perhaps a clear 1000 ft from the lake – The sides were reflected exactly into the entirely dark blue water & formed an extraordinary reflection –

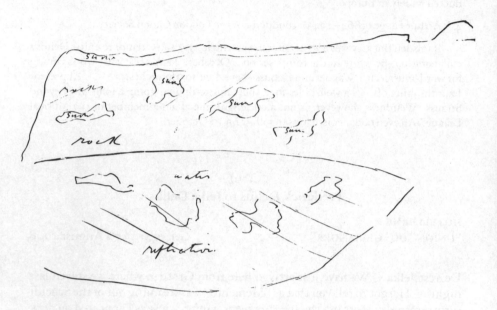

This was all purple, green, blue & white – really quite extraordinary – Then we arrived at Djupvand where there is a small Hotel – Enclosed picture – from here to Merok is worth coming to see & perhaps you ought to stay at Djupvand Hotel a bit to try & paint some of this – the view over the Geiranger fjord is quite close – I may see, however, something more suitable for you – . We are now at Merok & leave tomorrow at 7.30 for Söholt & Vestnae & Molde – shall arrive day after tomorrow. The worst of it is that wherever we arrive – people are playing the piano & never stop – I am trying to write, but really I must stop, they are hammering away at the damned instrument. The weather today has been lovely & sunny. The last 2 days were very cold – I saw Beecham once or twice looking curiously & rather enquiringly at me & he once said – Strange weather for August – but he is enjoying himself vastly – I will send off postcards every now & then & also my next address when I know it – With love

    yr affectionate
    Fred –

Autograph letter, signed and dated, written in English on headed notepaper.

The original is in the Grainger Museum.

1   The trip had started a few days earlier. Delius and Beecham had met in Christiania and then travelled north to Lillehammer and Otta. 'Beecham is enjoying himself immensely,' wrote Delius to Jelka on 29 July, 'and the more I see of him the more I like him.'

(290)
Frederick Delius to Jelka Delius

Gendeboden
18/8./08

Dearest Jelka – We arrived here yesterday evening at 6. after a glorious walk thro' Uladalen from Spiterstulen – The weather since Sunday is blazing hot & not a cloud in the sky. Gjendin looks lovely – . We left Skaare in Stryn on Wednesday, midday & walked up to Sundal Saeter We found there only a dirty little hut & nothing to eat & we had to sleep on some dry twigs with only a dirty cover – Of course we were eaten up by fleas & neither of us slept at all – next day we left at 6 a m for our big walk over the Jostedalbrae to Mysahytta – we could only get a cup of coffee & a few pieces of bread & butter but the weather was fine & sunny. It had rained the whole night – & our hut was swimming – It was a frightfully tough walk up to the glacier. 5 hours almost as steep as a house – Beecham seemed quite done up & faint & I thought we should have to turn back – he pulled together however very pluckily – I carried his knapsack & the guide carried mine – The walk over the glacier was grandiose & nothing but snow in sight & snow covered peaks – after we crossed the glacier we descended gradually to Mysahytta Saeter which was a frightful distance – We were 14 hours walking – with only a couple of sandwiches each – B could scarcely walk any more – we had to wade a stream which took me almost up to the waist. The man carried B. across. We got within 50 yards of 4 wild reindeer & a splendid stor bock.[1] At Mysahytta we found a somewhat better Saeter but just as many fleas – Our food was cheese & fladbrød only – with a few slices of fat bacon – Next day we walked to Sota Saeter where we arrived at 1 p m. & could get nothing but goats cheese & fladbrød – we then walked to Dyring Saeter & there we got a horse & haycart to carry us to Mork where we got a Stol kjaere[2] to Flekhoi in Skiaker – the road begins again at Mork – At Flekhoi we behaved like pigs over a wonderfully good supper – we had had nothing but cheese & fladbrod ever since leaving Skaare – From Flekhoi we took a Stolkjaere to Rosheim & arrived about the same time that we did on our memorable trip – We got a guide to carry the heaviest knapsack & trudged along up towards Gjuvashytten – On the way it began to pour & kept it up for an hour – just enough to wet us all thoroughly – It then stopped & we arrived at Gjuvashytten at 10.30 pm – They were all in bed, but got up & made us tea & supper – Next day sunny & glorious again & we went up Galdhøpig together with 2 other Englishmen the only other guests – The view was again splendid – In the afternoon we took it easy down to Spiterstulen where we arrived in time for supper – The other guests were 4 german women of the ugliest kind – Even the guides hanging around began to laugh as they came trudging in – Something fearful to look at – Next day, Monday, we started at 9. a m for Gjendeboden & had a most glorious trip thro' one of the wildest valleys of Jotunheimen – We got an excellent meal on our arrival with fresh trout – & clean beds – We are staying over a day here as it is so nice & clean – Today tuesday not a cloud in the sky & very warm – I went out to fish & caught one – missed a very big one as I have no landing net – At 4 I am going again with B. to help me to land the fish – We are enjoying ourselves spendidly & feel in wonderful health & spirits – Tomorrow we go to Gjendesheim & stay there a couple of days – I shall sail from Kristiansand on Friday evening 28th inst & arrive in Antwerp on Monday morning – Will you meet me there[3] – If not write me where to meet you poste restante Kristiania & also poste restante Antwerp should I not get the Kristiania letter in time – perhaps it is better for you to come to Antwerp as the trains are so good – Stay at Hotel Terminus if you have to stay the night – Otherwise leave Paris only at 1. p m. you get to Antwerp at 5. p m. The one that leaves at 7.20 p m arrives at 11. Both are excellent trains. We can stay the night at Antwerp & leave for Knocke next day – bring my Straw Hat, & my gray hat – a few thin A.K vests & a couple of nets – (We forgot to put any nets in the bag) A pair of thin underdrawers – White trousers, White ties, A box of squezers, Music paper 4 cahiers 16 lines – skratching knife, penholder, Dowson cyclus, Brown & white socks – *Black boots* – a couple more shirts – & 6 collars – *White coat*

With heaps of love – your

Fred.

I picked these flowers just under the Jostedalbrae –
Bring also whatever I have forgotten to mention –

Autograph letter, signed and dated, written in English. Envelope addressed: Fru Jelka Delius / Grez sur Loing / (Seine & Marne) / Frankrig. Postmark: ØIE 20 VIII 08.

The original is in the Grainger Museum.

From Delius's letters and postcards to Jelka we can follow the outline of the journey, which had thus far taken in Molde and Ålesund, Vatne and Saebe, and was to continue to Loen, Stryn and Hjelle. He was delighted with Beecham, writing from Saebe to Jelka, 'Beecham is an excellent travelling companion and I like him more and more – he does nothing that I do not like.'

Jelka in the meantime wrote letters from home reporting on the garden, on her painting and on events of the day: 'I suppose you also read about the Zeppelin, flying so beautifully all thro' southern Germany and then exploding into smithereens in a storm.' On 13 August she related, 'Harold Bauer I heard playing Brahmsy Music at Mrs Blackburns when I was on the bridge the other night.'

1   Large buck deer.

2   Seated cart.

3   Immersed in her painting at Grez, Jelka decided against the earlier-agreed trip to Knokke, and wrote a few days later to suggest that Delius return to Grez instead.

(291)
Frederick Delius to Granville Bantock

Grez sur Loing
(Seine & Marne)
11 Sept 1908

Dear friend —

Here I am again back in Grez — arrived day before yesterday — We had a lovely time up in Norway & splendid weather — Sunny & no wind & warm — Beecham made an excellent travelling companion & we went over some of the roughest & finest mountainous country in the world — The Philharmonic Society accepted my conditions to conduct my new work on the 11th December — £25 — so in spite of your severe criticism on my conducting — I shall try again — We must all meet at the beginning of October in order to form a plan of action for the Committee Meeting — Please arrange it in some way — Have you asked Harding to call the meeting for the 10th or 11th Oct? or any time in the week following the 7th. Beecham has excellent ideas & I believe his plan of action is the most practical — We must get the sympathy of the people who at least are trying to go ahead & who are in sympathy with the Modern movement but who at the same time represent some thing or some power in the musical world — or have some following — We must widen the Committee — We must also make a clause to exclude members of the *Com* who miss 3 meetings — What is the good of Brodsky Pitt, Wood — & Agnew & Harding if they dont give money. Well! we must settle the fate of the League at the next meeting — Get Newman to attend also — Beecham is going to found a musical paper to appear weekly & he wants Newman as a regular correspondent. Everything in the world must be done to prevent Newman from going to America — Write me what you have been doing since you left Grez — Is your cough better now? & how are you all at home — Did you spend a pleasant summer — Have you been working —
    With love to you both

    Yrs affectionately
    Frederick Delius

Autograph letter, signed and dated, written in English.

The original is in the Delius Trust Archive.

(292)
Frederick Delius to Theodor Szántó

Grez sur Loing
Seine & Marne
28 Sept 08

Dear Szántó

I received your card this afternoon & have returned the Concerto score to you
accordingly It must first be played before it goes to press. The alterations[1] seem
to me to have been made quite well although there are a lot of rather unnecessary
minor changes. In a few places the harmony will be too weak − . I have sketched
in a few notes in haste. I would like to have the score back after the performance
& also hear how you felt it sounded. For example right at the beginning I had a
trumpet [playing] the triplet   Now there is a horn
below it too, that always sounds bad − horn & trumpet − rather 2 trumpets in
that case! There are many such details in the colouring which I would not have
done − Then you have at the place where the 1st horn & celli play a counter-
theme together in the slow movement − 2 horns playing it. It never sounds so
good & then you have 1st & 2nd horn. 2nd horn is low & will not be able to play
the high D flat or will split. The good alterations are those where the orchestra
is rather toned down so that the piano comes through better. The violin solo
that you wanted extended will sound weak & it sounded fine as it was, after all.
& the place   at the end & all
these tutti places have become very feeble. As I said, I must have the score back
before it goes to press − I thank you & Herr Glenck[2] for the trouble which you
have taken & a lot of what you have done I find quite splendid, it is only that I
see a few things which will make the thing better still. With kind regards &
wishing you much success

Yours
Frederick Delius

I am afraid I have no score of the Concerto & you have pasted a lot over. Now
that I am conducting I will try to conduct the Concerto myself & to have you
engaged as soloist − We are sure to have a success with it −

Autograph letter, signed and dated, written in German.

The original is in the Library of Congress.

1   With Delius's permission, Szántó had been at work on the Piano Concerto with a view to providing the soloist with rather more of a virtuoso role.

2   Hermann von Glenck (1883–?): Zurich-born composer and conductor. He studied in Berlin and conducted opera at Weimar, Metz and – from 1908 to 1911 – Stuttgart. His compositions included a concerto for piano and orchestra. Szántó described him, in a letter to Delius on 21 September, as 'a young and *very* gifted conductor and composer'. Glenck was now collaborating with Szántó on the rearrangement of Delius's concerto, which Szántó was to play in Leipzig on 19 October.

(293)
Frederick Delius to Jelka Delius

Kings Head Hotel
Sheffield
[8 October 1908]

Dearest, Just a word to say the performance[1] went of[f] very well – It was a huge success – altho' I dont believe anyone really understood it – Austin sang wonderfully – The Chorus was wonderfull – but too loud – Woods Orchestra knew it perfectly, but he did not always take the right Tempi – Sometimes too slow & then too fast – However, it went quite well – I will keep some notices for you – Newman's & some others are awfully good – I have only read one at present – but Austin read some more – A kiss to you & the baby & kindest regards to Helene – I shall have to have my tooth out in Paris, so shall stay over one night. More presently –

yrs loving
Fred

– Got your letter –

Autograph letter, signed and undated, written in English. The notepaper bears the printed heading 29, TAVISTOCK SQUARE. W.C., which was crossed out by Delius. Jelka later added '1908'.

The original is in the Grainger Museum.

1   Leaving for London on 4 October, Delius had travelled to Sheffield on 6 October in order to attend a rehearsal of *Sea Drift* that day. The concert took place on the following day as part of the Sheffield Festival; Wood conducted the Sheffield Festival Chorus and the Queen's Hall Orchestra, and Frederic Austin was the soloist.

Bantock had written admiringly on 3 October: 'The orchestra sounded glorious when your work was rehearsed in London. Thou canst score, lad! How dost thou do't?'

(294)
Harmonie Verlag to Frederick Delius

BERLIN, 15.10.1908.

Herrn
  Fredrik Delius
    Grez sur Loing
  Seine et Marne

Dear Sir,

We send you by the same post a copy of the newly printed piano score of "Sea Drift" and hope you will like the new make-up.

We also wish to inform you that Herr Scheffler,[1] the orchestra conductor, has written to us from Hamburg that he cannot organize the Delius Evening this year, as the financial risk for him would be too great. He is extremely likely to perform "Appalachia" and "Sea Drift" next year.

In addition, we again ask you to let us know what you think of the new version of the Piano Concerto. You will now see many things somewhat differently and will be obliged to admit that we foresaw the difficulties only too clearly. E.g. what is to happen if the opera is to be altered in the same sort of way? One thing of which we are quite sure is that there is a great deal you will change in the event of a new production. We should presumably have the pleasure of printing everything again. As soon as we have succeeded in getting a performance, which is not a simple achievement under these circumstances, as only the foremost theatres can be considered, we shall get down to printing.

  Yours faithfully
  KF[?]
  "Harmonie"

Your observations about Herr Szanto's alterations to your masterpiece are completely unfair. In our opinion you should be grateful to the gentleman for taking the trouble without any recompense to make an otherwise impossible work for piano fit for performance. He continues to publicize the work as widely as possible and is at present playing it in 2 Philharmonic Concerts and in reward and thanks for this, you reproach both him and us!

Typed letter, initialled 'KF'[?] [Kurt Fliegel], and dated, written in German on the headed notepaper of Harmonie Verlag. The postscript is in longhand.

The original is in the Delius Trust Archive.

1   John Julia Scheffler (1867–1942): German conductor and composer. He studied in Hamburg and conducted at a number of German theatres before becoming choral conductor in Hamburg, where he remained active for the rest of his life, gaining renown for his work with male voice choirs.

(295)
Frederick Delius to Harmonie Verlag

17.10.08

Dear Sir,

I hereby inform you that all the alterations in my Piano Concerto have been made without my permission. My Concerto is no piano showpiece with orchestral accompaniment, where the orchestra plays a subordinate role, as Herr Szanto seems to have conceived it.

As Herr Mottl in Munich is performing the Piano Concerto in January, I will attend the performance. As I was very satisfied with the effect of my score in London, I do not feel that there is anything at all to be altered.

I permit Herr Szanto only the two performances in his version, Leipzig [19.]10.08 and Halle 20.10.08 and will take legal action in respect of all further performances.

Yours faithfully,

Frederick Delius

PS   Until now nothing at all in my works has subsequently been altered and I reject the rest of your remarks as a thoroughly unworthy reply.

From a transcript written in German preserved in the Delius Trust Archive.

(296)
Frederick Delius to Theodor Szántó

GREZ SUR LOING,
S. ET M.
17 Oct 1908

Dear Szántó

Last year the Concerto made a perfectly correct impression on us in London Fried did not say a thing to me about too heavy orchestration either – The piece is *not* to become a piano showpiece with a faint orchestral accompaniment as you seem to wish − & even if the Leipzig critics *find it delightful* − the piece is orchestra & piano − I admit that I have only been able − as I wrote to you − to take a cursory look at your altered score & as I wrote to you it is all quite nicely & cleverly done but the whole character has gone & the whole thing has become superficial. Particularly e.g. in the big climax where the brass has been completely cut out, it has become awfully banal, loses character & accent completely − Mottl is giving it in Munich in January & I shall be present − I received an insolent letter from "Harmonie" in which I learn that without your alterations the Concerto is quite impossible − You alone can have said that − If you find this true then you must not play it, for I have written to tell "Harmonie" that I just give my permission for the performances of your modified version in Leipzig & Halle[1] only − & I only do this for your sake as I believe that you meant perfectly well − in respect of all further performances of a score which I neither recognize nor sanction I shall take legal action − There are already enough superficial piano concertos around without my enriching the world with yet another − & as you know, I would not take *one* step out of my way in order to attain a popular success − Why e.g. did you not at least ask before − Shall we undertake this work? −

With best wishes

Yours
Frederick Delius

Autograph letter, signed and dated, written in German on headed notepaper.

The original is in the Library of Congress.

1   A review by Martin Frey of the Halle performance commented that the piano part was 'technisch zu sehr überladen', − going some way towards justifying Delius's criticism (*Die Musik*, Berlin, 8, No. 4, 1908/1909. Zweites Novemberheft, p. 251).

(297)
Frederick Delius to Granville Bantock

GREZ SUR LOING,
S. ET M.
21/11/08

Dear friend −

Your letter just arrived − Firstly let me congratulate you on your appointment to the post of Professor at Birmingham − I was awfully glad to hear it − Bravo! Schillings would be willing to come over & conduct one of his works at our Festival[1] − I think I could also get Gustav Mahler − the finest conductor in the

world – to come & conduct one of his Symphonies – or Choral Symphonies –
Ravel I can get at any time – If we give a chamber music concert – Bax has
written a fine quintette[2] – We must bring off a fine & interesting Festival – I
shall do my utmost to come to Hanley[3] & then to Birmingham as we must speak
it all over – We must get reduced prices in the Hotels & someone must give a
spread of cold meat & beer one evening to get all the members together & make
a few speeches – wish the foreign members welcome They will all join when
they see one or two of their musicians on the program – If Mahler & Schillings
come over it would be a splendid set off. I went to Stuttgart for Appalachia[4] &
they gave a splendid performance of it – The Queen was there – I am conducting
like blazes & beat a better 6/8 now – Au revoir, Herr Professor & à bientôt

    Yrs ever
    Frederick Delius

If that influential fellow in Hanley would put me up, I could, I believe, get
some money out of him for the Festival!

        ———

I have to be in London on the 5th of Dec. so get the meeting for the 4th
afternoon –

Autograph letter, signed and dated, written in English on headed notepaper.

The original is in the Delius Trust Archive.

1   The committee of the Musical League had at last decided to organize a festival in
Liverpool the following year 'for about May 8th', as O'Neill wrote to inform Delius on
11 November.

2   Arnold Bax (1883–1953): English composer. He studied at the Royal Academy of
Music. The young composer's output had so far consisted largely of piano pieces and
songs, but he was to reach fulfilment in orchestral works of symphonic scale. He was
knighted in 1937 and was later to become Master of the King's Musick.
    In his letter of 11 November, O'Neill had been the first to alert Delius to the qualities
of Bax's work: 'I heard two quite remarkable string quintet movements by young Bax
last night – we ought to do something by him I think.' Gardiner, in a letter written
two days later, echoed O'Neill's praise: 'most imaginative music, & beautifully written.'
(See Foreman, *Bax*, pp. 52–4.)

3   *Sea Drift* was to be given under Beecham in Hanley on 3 December and subsequently
in Manchester.

4   Schillings had given the work on 5 November.

(298)
Frederick Delius to Jelka Delius

7, PEMBROKE VILLAS,
KENSINGTON, W.
[12 December 1908]

Dearest Jelka –

Just a word in haste to tell you about the Concert – I was quite cool when I found myself on the conducting stand & made no mistake[1] – The Orchestra played *most* beautifully – & it sounded beautifully for me – I dont believe many people understood the piece but they received it very favourably & called me 3 times – Busoni wants me to conduct it on the 2nd January in Berlin, but I have not decided yet – What shall I do? I hate travelling about when I want to work – I travel back tomorrow 13th with Busonis & shall stay the night in Paris – as no doubt the passage will be rough – it is blowing hard here – Shall come out by the 5 train on Monday – I got the mincing machine, sponge bag, nail brush – but am afraid I shall not be able to get the stuff. Just received a cheque for £25 from the directors – [2]

With love
your Fred

Autograph letter, signed and undated, written in English on headed notepaper. Jelka later added '1908 12.12'.

The original is in the Grainger Museum.

1 On 10 December, following a rehearsal, Delius had written to Jelka, 'I seem to have more control over myself than at Hanley. . . . I beat once or twice 3 in a 4 bar – absentmindedness! – perhaps tomorrow I shall be quite master of myself.'

2 Delius's fee for the performance. He had just conducted *In a Summer Garden* at the Philharmonic Society's concert on 11 December.

(299)
Frederick Delius to Granville Bantock

GREZ SUR LOING,
S. ET M.
17th Dec 1908

My dear friend!

Here I am back again in Grez – Many thanks for your wire which I got in time & early enough to screw up my failing courage – I conducted without a catastrophe & that is about all — I dont think I shall try any more — Cassirer told me that you were annoyed that Beecham had accepted to conduct the Halford Band — *This is not correct* He has entirely refused to conduct this Band, — or any other in Birmingham — He is forming another Orchestra in London as the New Symphony Orchestra was too badly managed & began the deputy business again — Some of the best players did not come to Hanley & Manchester & he gave them an Ultimatum on his return to London — which they refused[1] — If you have anything to say in the matter, please do not recommend the New Symphony Orchestra for Birmingham or Hanley — Beecham's will probably be called the Metropolitan Orchestra — He has formed a Syndicate — of Ten Members at £250 each — He being one & is running the Orchestra entirely — This deputy System must be crushed at any price — The New Symphony Orchestra is getting engagements in the Provinces & sending deputies — Just like the Hallé Band & Wood's old Band — I missed you in London very much — would like you to have heard my "Summer Garden" No one understood it, I believe, except a few — I had not given them any analytical notes, so the critics had nothing to catch hold of — They want something which sounds like something they have heard before — As Runciman would say — they like an old friend to come smiling towards them — I heard Elgar's Symphony[2] in London — It starts off with a theme out of the Parcival Prelude — a little altered — The slow movement is a theme out of Verdi's Requiem — a little altered — The rest is Mendelsohn & Brahms — thick & without the slightest Orchestral charm — gray — and they all shout "Masterwork"! — The only thing to be said in its favor is that it is better manufactured than the rest of the English composers' compositions — But it is a work *dead born* — I am now at work on my new Dramatic Work "Niels Lyhne"[3] Let me hear from you soon — We both send our love to you & your wife —

Yrs affectionately
Frederick Delius

P.S
    My wife is going to write —

Autograph letter, signed and dated, written in English on headed notepaper. Envelope addressed: Granville Bantock Esq[re] / Broadmeadow / Kings-Norton / nr Birmingham / Angleterre.

The original is in the Delius Trust Archive.

1   'Beecham sacked his orchestra,' reported O'Neill on 31 December, '& "got another in a week" he say's!'

2   Elgar's First Symphony had first been performed under Richter in Manchester on 3 December and repeated in London on 7 December.

3   The opera *Fennimore and Gerda*.

(300)

Frederick Delius to Granville Bantock

[Grez, 27 December 1908]

Dear Bantock – You will be pleased to hear that Gustav Mahler – Claude Debussy Vincent d'Indy & Max Schillings will all come & conduct one of their works at our Festival – Mahler's will be a choral Symphony Debussy, d'Indy & Schillings orchestral works – (short)[1]
With love & greetings to you all – Yrs ever

Fr D.

Autograph postcard, initialled 'Fr D.', and undated, written in English. Addressed: Granville Bantock Esq[re] / Broadmeadow / Kings Norton / nr Birmingham / Angleterre. Postmark: GREZ 27 [?] 12 08.

The original is in the Delius Trust Archive. See plate 63.

1   The League was duly impressed: 'I congratulate you upon your extraordinarily effective diplomacy,' wrote William McNaught, its secretary, on 28 December. 'Very glad to hear about Mahler,' wrote O'Neill three days later,' – but he must not be allowed to take up even half a programme!' Nonetheless, the first festival of the Musical League now seemed set to become a major international event.

Delius: Memories of Childhood (i)

I remember as a very little boy playing cricket on the waste land at the bottom of Claremont with a big stone for the wickets, and how I hated having to go in on summer evenings at about half-past eight before it was dark.

I scarcely ever missed a cricket match at the Bowling Green cricket club on Saturday afternoons and always enjoyed the bottle of ginger-pop that I used to buy for 2^d.

With what excitement we small boys of the district learned that the South Sea Islanders were coming to play the Bradford C.C. – and how the word "cannibal" was whispered around! When they came, of course, I was there.

I see one of them coming out of the visitors' tent to bat wearing a sort of scarf round his head. On another occasion I saw a match in which "W.G" and E.M. Grace played against 18 of the Bradford team. George Ulliot, Bradford's professional, bowled "W.G" middle-stump and so was given a sovereign by Mr. Priestman who was playing for Bradford. I often attended county matches in the district and shall never forget the old fellow who went round the field selling score-cards and calling out,

"Anyone say a card 'ere?
They're numbered on the card in the order of going in!"

We always spent six weeks at Filey, so I used to go over to Scarborough to see the Cricket Festival. How we looked forward to the day when we started from the Midland Station in a special saloon carriage for the sea-side!

When I was a little older I was fond of making walking tours in the Dales. What good fare we got at the cottages we stayed at! Thick Yorkshire ham and eggs and new home-made bread and butter.

Just before Christmas the waits used to come round in the early hours of the morning and play their strange tune – I still remember the melody – and early on Christmas mornings the choral singers would sing "Christians awake!" in the garden outside our house.

As a child I had only heard music of Handel, Bach, Haydn, Mozart and Beethoven, and shall never forget the thrill I got when I first heard someone play the posthumous waltz of Chopin, which seemed as if an entirely new world had opened to me. My attempts to play it by ear must have been curious to listeners, but still I managed to do it.

The next great thrill I got was when I heard Wagner's music. It was the Walküren Ritt played by the Hallé orchestra. I must then have been seven or eight.

———————

[MS in the Grainger Museum, dictated to Percy Grainger]

Delius: Memories of Childhood (ii)

My father loved music intensely and used to tinker on the piano when he knew he was alone. He was a great concert-goer and he often had chamber-music in his house. My mother was not musical at all, but she had great imagination, and was rather fantastically inclined. She was very romantic, and out of the smallest episode would invent a wonderful story, which she then came thoroughly to believe. My brother, Max, and I used to buy 'penny-dreadfuls', such as *Dick Turpin*, *Sixteen-string Jack*, and *Sweeny Todd, the Barber of Fleet Street* – in this tale the barber's customers used to disappear through a trap-door, and were taken away to be converted into pork-pies! We used to read these books in bed when we were supposed to be asleep, and we had a contrivance to turn the gas up or down by means of a string. Once, my mother caught us in the act and confiscated a whole pile of these penny-dreadfuls. A few days later we surprised her, with a very red and excited face, poring over them herself. We lived in a house called Claremont, Horton Lane, which was, at that time, out of the town and on the edge of the moors, on the road that leads towards Bingley. We children had two ponies and I loved riding over the moors to Ilkley – then only a tiny village – where we often spent the summer. Once, my brother Max, who was two years younger than myself, and I, after reading some extraordinary story, ran away from home so as to have an adventure. I was then about eight years old. We actually got up one morning at four o'clock, having previously laid in a store of necessary provisions, which consisted chiefly of sweets, and made our way on foot across the moors to Ilkley. We arrived there late in the afternoon; it was beginning to rain, and our prospects looked very miserable, when we were suddenly confronted by a friend of the family, who knew us very well and wondered what we were doing there. Our confused answers must have made him suspicious, for he took us to the railway station, telegraphed to our parents and handed us over to the guard of the Bradford train.

As a little boy, I used to take sudden and violent dislikes to people, and developed a strange habit of going to visit quite unknown people, to whom I had taken a fancy. One of my great likes was a sailor-lad who sometimes came to Bradford. He belonged to a big merchant-vessel and I loved to hear him talk about his travels in strange lands and seas. His departure on a fresh voyage always filled me with envious sadness.

I cannot remember the first time when I began to play the piano: it must
have been very early in my life. I played by ear, and I used to be brought down
in a little velvet suit after dinner to play for the company. My mother would
say: 'Now make up something', and then I improvised. When I was six or
seven, I began taking violin lessons from Mr. Bauerkeller, of the Hallé orchestra,
who came over from Manchester especially to teach me. Later on, I had another
teacher, Mr. Haddock from Leeds. My first great musical impression was
hearing the posthumous Valse of Chopin which a friend of my father's played
for me when I was ten years old. It made a most extraordinary impression on
me. Until then, I had heard only Haydn, Mozart and Beethoven, and it was as
if an entirely new world had been opened up to me. I remember that after
hearing it twice I could play the whole piece through from memory.

———————

[From Philip Heseltine, *Frederick Delius* (London: John Lane, The Bodley Head, 1923),
pp. 3–5]

Delius: Summer Diary 1887[1]

*Juli 15*th. Left Hamburg per steamer Lofoten, small boat. First 10 hours quiet. Towards night a storm sets in & knocked most passengers off their legs & I amongst them. Rough night. A young Norwegian, my cabin mate, also very bad. Got on deck again next morning about 10 a.m. Arrived at Christian-sand at 12 a.m.

*July 17*th. Changed to steamer Fin(ne)marken & left at 2 p.m. for Stavanger. After another rough time of it arrived at 6 a.m. at Stavanger and looked at the old church, which is 900 years old & very antique looking. After buying a few necessaries I had breakfast in a little restaurant & left for *Sandeid* at 12 a.m. Weather was beautiful.

*Monday 18*th *July*. During the day passed beautiful scenery & charming little farms hidden here & there in little bays. Arrived at Nedstrand at about 6 p.m., a beautiful little place, where citizens of Hardanger go in the summer, then went down the Vindefjord, the hills now becoming larger & more romantic, then the Yrkjefjord, a most lovely place, Yrkje at the top of it lying beautifully, then up the Vatsfjord to Stokka, & then back & up the Sandeidfjord to Vikedal & Sandeid. Vikedal lies beautifully in a little valley between two immense rocks, a few scattered houses running down to the fjord. Sandeid lies at the top of the fjord, also beautifully situated. Here I disembarked. A Norwegian schoolmaster, who spoke a little German & who was evidently very intelligent, had in the meantime invited me to his wedding on the morrow at Ølen. His bride met him at Sandeid, so we all 3 got in a skyds[2] & drove on towards his parents' Hof[3] near Ølen, his bride sitting on his knee. Now 11.30 p.m. & raining a little. Scenery very rocky & mountainous. Arrived at the Hof, where

---

1   'There is also a little diary of Fred's, some of which might be decipherable under a microscope: it seems to have been kept during one of his first visits to Norway' (Balfour Gardiner to Percy Grainger, 24 July 1938). The diary had been found among Delius's effects at Grez, and Grainger accepted Gardiner's offer of this and various bundles of letters as a contribution to the newly founded Grainger Museum in Melbourne.

2   Small carriage, post-chaise.

3   Farm, estate.

we had some supper, consisting of kake, vafil kake & kling,[4] 3 kinds of Norwegian regular dishes, with good coffee & butter. The Hof is very clean & everybody very friendly. I am the first Englishman his parents have yet seen, so cause much interest. His parents are intelligent & kind people, & it really does one's heart good to meet such honest, unaffected & unspoiled people. I slept in the large room with the son. 3 large beds stand in the room with the names of the ancestors painted on in white letters. One has Larsdattir Heggeboe. There are 9 in the family altogether, 5 girls & 4 boys, all nice-looking & very clean-looking also.

Today, *July 19*ᵗʰ, the wedding comes off. On the Hof they have 1 horse, 6 cows & 40 sheep, besides much good land. The old Hof belongs to the brother of Heggebo, who as the oldest son got the old Hof. The younger son then had to build a new one, although he got half the land. The law of primogeniture is throughout Norway, i.e. the old Hof goes to the eldest son. Wedding guests began to arrive at 11 a.m. & at once set to, to eat cake & coffee. Piles of cakes all over the long tables in the big room. Honest, straightforward folk, these Norwegian peasants. They come in, shake hands & ask all sorts of questions. A batch of 6 or 7 arrive at a time & after shaking hands all round they sit down at a table & look very solemn, no-one speaks a word, it might just as well be a funeral. Then coffee & cake is brought & they set to. After they have finished they shake hands again & say Tak Tak. Then another batch comes in, until all the guests have arrived. 55 persons attended this Brüllop/wedding, & I shook hands at least 300 times. After all guests arrived, went in to the big room & had coffee, kake, kling, vafil kake, butter & cheese. Everybody sitting round the table looking very solemn, not saying a word. The best man now made a speech & read a prayer, sang a hymn all alone & at length (for he seemed to deliberate long & often) he gave the sign to set to, whereupon all commenced to eat. After they are done, the same man says a few more words, another long prayer & another hymn, & we go out. Then Best man reads out the couples who go together to church, 1ˢᵗ a young man, then a young woman. I had the prettiest little girl allotted to me, Ingeborg Boknas,[5] 17 years old & really a beautiful little thing. The bride in a golden crown goes first, then we all follow. When we get to the bottom of the *Gaard*,[6] Skyds & cariols[7] are waiting there & we all drive 2 & 3 in a skyds to the church at Ølen. Another couple is also there, from a Gaard at the other end of valley. The Priest then comes, says a long prayer. The choir consisting of one man (the best man at our wedding) sings all by

---

4   Cake, waffles and flatbread.
5   Apparently a misspelling for Bjørkjenes: the girl's name and address is jotted down later in Delius's notebook.
6   Farmstead, estate.
7   Small cart, trap.

himself a hymn, responds all alone. Really very funny to a stranger, but not a smile is to be seen. The Priest then blesses, & we all go out & drive back to Heggebo's Hof at Ølen. Then we eat again. Lamb & what they call *Plommer*, a sort of soup made of prunes. After this, & also before, the best man makes speeches & prays for at least 15 minutes, & dead silence reigns. No-one speaks much. Whenever I talk, dead silence reigns & they all listen in wonder, now & then giving vent to exclamations of approbation whenever the son, Olaf Heggebo, answers me in German. After this we go out & walk about the Hof, then eat again. The best man assigns the places at table, quietly taking girls & men by the arm & leading them to their place. We ate 8 times that day. The last time at 2 a.m. A sort of loving cup was always being handed round, everybody drinking as much as possible. Beer (peculiar) was the drink. My little partner Ingeborg seemed to be very intelligent & somewhat better than the rest. I learned afterwards that her father had the biggest & richest gaard in Ølen. They were all very kind to me & asked me to write & come back again. At length the guests begin to go. The bride & bridegroom are escorted to their bedroom. I sleep in the loft tonight in a little box bed with straw & a blanket. I dont undress, but am fearfully tired. 2 other young men sleep in a bed close to mine.

20th. In the morning I wash in the room where the bride & bridegroom are in bed. Everything is very primitive, but nothing *ever indecent*, always childlike & simple. After answering numerous questions I prepare to go & am accompanied part of the way by the bride, bridegroom & best man. After a hearty handshaking & Tak for alt & Tak for igor,[8] I go on to Eide gaard & say goodbye there to Eide & kone[9] & then trudge on to Etne. A few miles from Etne, I come across another wedding party, also married yesterday at Ølen. As it is raining, I go in to the gaard for shelter & am at once surrounded by the wedding guests, who ask me all sorts of questions – where I am from, where I am going to, if I am English & if married, & when I answer rather surprised, No, not yet, *loud applause & laughter*. They press some refreshments on me. I continue my way to Etne, where I arrive at 2 p.m. Etne is beautifully situated at the head of a fjord, a few Hofs & a landhandler[10] constitute the village. I take some lunch at the landhandler & then go on at 4.30 towards Skånevik. Weather now very cloudy & the high mountains all hidden by mist. I have to cross the Ulvenaase, more than 3300 ft high, & prepare for rather a wet time. Excessively steep, & after the last gaard is passed, scenery becomes more weird & rough. The view down towards Etne is magnificent. The sun for a moment flashes a few rays over the long valley. I, from amongst the clouds, look now on almost a fairylike scene – the light & shade effects I never saw before, but only for a few minutes, & then

8   Thank you for everything, and thank you for yesterday.
9   Wife.
10 Local store, country store.

all is again bleak & misty, & I am getting wet through, with a cold wind sweeping down the mountain. At last I am at the top. Oh! how cold & bleak. A sheep now & again runs away, frightened. Now I descend, dripping wet & in a short time come, so to speak, out of the clouds, & have a magnificent view of Skånevik fjord, all coloured deep blue, for the sun is shining there. In a few moments I have come from winter to summer – the contrast is admirable. I pass a lovely little foss,[11] & then a gaard or 2, & at length Skånevik begins. Lovely little place, on the slope towards the fjord, beautifully cultivated gaards in number, & here & there a Saeter[12] in sight – high up amongst the hills to the right. Put up at the landhandler, where I get a good meal & my things dried, & have of course to go to bed, as I have only one suit. Get a good bed tonight.

July 21. Take a bath in the fjord, which is very enjoyable, & then stroll about Skånevik. At 12.30, dinner & a chat with the landhandler, a very nice & well informed man. He read some of the Fritiofs Saga for me & explained it. Then walked with me over to Nes, about ½ hour, where I got a boat to take me to Fjaera. The Åkrafjord is the most romantic I have seen as yet, gigantic cliffs & mountains hemming in the fjord. The wind behind us, so we go at a good speed, passing the most lovely scenery, little gaards here & there on the cliff sides, & now & again a waterfall rushing down 2 or 3000 ft. After 4 hrs we arrived at Fjaera & I observe another boat just landing, on which are 2 ladies & a child who travelled on the *Lofoten* from Hamburg, Swarting by name. We had tea together, then they went off in the *stolkjaerre*[13] to Odda. Fjaera a lovely little place, quite hemmed in by gigantic rocks 3000 ft high. The place consists of 3 or 4 houses.

July 22nd. Got up at 6, left at 7 for Odda, via Jøsendal. Scenery very fine. Not quite as wild as Åkra, but very beautiful. At Jøsendal had some goat's meat & cheese at a small gaard. Had to wait 1½ h. for a skyds & met the German people again. Left at 1.30 p.m. in a stolkjaerre for Odda, & passed some magnificent scenery. Got a fine view of the Folgefonn, & passed also the Låtefoss, Hildalfoss, a fine waterfall, large volumes of water. Then along the beautiful Sandvinfjord until Odda came in sight, away down the valley at the head of the Sørfjord. The scenery from Jøsendal is really grand, enormous precipices & rocks hemming in both sides of the valley. At Odda went to Hardanger Hotel, of course crammed with English people. Went along the fjord & had a bathe. There a chat with an Englishman – began to rain.

July 23rd. Rose at 6, & left by boat for Eide, where I went to Jaunsen's Hotel & met the young Norwegian, my berthmate on the Lofoten. His family stay here for 6 weeks in the summer. We took a fine walk up the mountains together.

---

11   Cataract, waterfall.
12   Outfarm, summer farm.
13   Seated cart.

In the afternoon went along the side of the fjord to have a bathe – Granvinfjord – raining every 15 minutes. At last we found a nice place in a little cove. I went in for 5 minutes. The peculiarity of these fjords is that there is deep water right up to the shore. It sinks suddenly from the rocks, is very dangerous for non swimmers. Had good supper at 6.30, & left by SS Vikingen at 8 p.m. for Vik, where I arrived at 10 & put up at Naesheims Hotel. Hotel full, so had to go over to a little house nearby. Primitive room. The scenery up the Eidfjord is wild & romantic. It rained much, but as we approached Vik the rain stopped, but the whole mass of mountains looked bluish black, the tops made invisible by the clouds. The sight was the weirdest I have yet seen here. Vik lies hemmed in on all sides by gigantic mountains 3–4000 ft high. *Weather wet.*

July 24ᵗʰ. Rose at 6.30 & left for Vøringfoss. Missed the way & got on the new road, which is unfinished, so had to turn back. Hired a boat & guide, rowed across Eidfjord, & then walked thro' rough, wild scenery to Vøringfoss. Raining most of time. Had some bread & butter at a house near the falls, & then went to see the greatest fall in Norway. Magnificent sight. An enormous volume of water, dropping 700 ft. After, we went up the mountain & saw the fall from above. From here we went across the Hardanger Vidde, the bleakest, wildest place I here saw, not a living thing to be seen, to a Hof called Garen, where a new little house is. This is 2 Norsk mil[14] from Vik. We rested here a few minutes & then set out across the wild hills for a Saeter 8 English miles away. After trudging knee deep thro' swamps & bogs, climbing over rocks & hills, we reached the Saeter after 3½ hrs tramp. I was very tired & could not have gone very much further. I walked 36 Kils that day. The Saeter was a hut built of stone, 2 Saeter jentere[15] lived there & minded 60 cows. A Norwegian lieutenant named Bentzon had come up here from the Garen 3 days ago. Very nice man, speaking English & French fluently. We had a rough & tumble time of it. I was wet to the skin, water oozing out of my boots. We had a big fire, the smoke driving us out every now & then. Made some tea – how glorious it tasted. Luckily there was a little cold mutton to eat. After sitting & chatting in front of the fire we went to bed, the Lieut. & I in one bed & the 2 girls in the other. The bed was fearful. I lay up against the storm wall, huge stones sticking out into the bed. The Lieut. at my side, dried twigs were our mattress. We had rather a bad night. The cold intense. The hut lies 3500 ft high. In the night several Norwegian peasants came into the hut & boiled some coffee. They had come a long way also.

25ᵗʰ. Got up at 8, & made tea again. Dried our things & started again for Garen. Got wet again & arrived at 3.30 at the Hof where we got our dry things & had some dinner.

---

14   Fourteen English miles.
15   Girls.

July 26th. Rose at 8. Had an excellent breakfast. Weather very cold, 9° in room, raining. Took a little walk in the moors. Had dinner at 3. Weather now very fine. After dinner went to fish with Bentzon & Blorn, who had come in the meantime back from the Saeter, crossing us on the way yesterday. No luck, too cold. Magnificent sunset, all the hills bathed in a purple light & the snow dyed red. Enjoyed the sight for some time & then went in & had tea at 8.30, a chat, & then bed.

July 27th. Fearful storm blowing rain. Evidently bottled up here for the day! The owner of this Hof, Ole Larsen Garen, is the best guide in the Hardanger & has gone over to Hallingdal in 5 hrs on snow shoes – it takes 3 days ordinarily. He has also a herd of 250 reindeer up in the mountains. Had a fish in the afternoon & a chat at night.

28th. Rose at 7, had breakfast at 8.30, & then went towards Vik accompanied by B & B, who took me a little of the way, then gave me 3 cheers, a hearty farewell, & then we parted. A beautiful walk of 5 hrs to Eidfjord, a bath in the fjord & a little music. Had lunch on the way, by the side of a foss. Took some sandwiches with me from Garen. Vik, Måbo, Høl, Garen, Maurset, Storlii, Krossdalen were the places I visited on this little trip up the Hardanger Vidda. Met at Naesheims Hotel 3 Manchester men, had dinner, & had to rush for boat – it had already started, but waited for us whilst we rowed out to her in a boat. Arrived at Ulvik at 8.30. Put up at Vestr[h]eims Hotel, very full.

29th. Rose at 7 a.m. Had a bath in the fjord with the 3 Englishmen, & then started for Eide over the mountains. Very steep, but magnificent view over the Ulvikfjord. Day lovely, but extremely hot. Arrived at Granvin at 1.30 & at Seim at 2. Had dinner & took a stolkjaerre to Vossevangen. Road rises for 5 or 6 miles, magnificent scenery, perpendicular black rocks rising at least 4000 ft. Past a lovely fall, the *Skjervefoss*. From the top of the hill, 3000 ft high, we had an exquisite view down the valley. Arrived at Vossevangen at 6.30 p.m. Very full, all 4 of us in a large room. Excellent tea, a little walk, had my boots repaired, a little music, & then bed.

July 30th. Rose at 5.30. Englishmen left for Bergen, I for Gudvangen. Fine walk, passing Tvinde, with a lovely foss. Some rain, but cleared off again. Arrived after 4 hours at Vinje, where I had lunch & hired a carriole to take me to Gudvangen. Walked 22 kil^tres, drove 26. Gudvangen lies hemmed in by enormous rocks 4–5000 ft high, going perpendicularly out of the Sognefjord & Naerøydal. The Naerøydal is the finest I have seen yet. It goes from Stalheim to Gudvangen, the road winding at the bottom of the valley, numerous waterfalls falling from the highest rocks into the valley, almost all falling in spray. Had tea at Gudvangen & left for Laerdalsøyri at 7 p.m. by boat Laurvig. The Sognefjord here is grand & the effects of the setting sun quite exquisite. Rocks 5,500 ft high. Lots of English. Arrived at 12.30 at Laerdalsøyri. Put up at Hotel Laerdals^en.

Rose at 8.30, *July 31ˢᵗ*. Lovely day, extremely warm. Had a bath in the fjord. Started with 2 Americans from Philadelphia. Had dinner, chat, & a stroll about. Tea. Met 2 English musicians, Mʳ Kearne & Mʳ Blut, Royal College of Music. Kearne is from Riverside, Los Angeles, Cal., knew von Weller well. Left by the Hornelen at 3 a.m.

Aug 1ˢᵗ. Boat very full. Quite rough, felt a little seedy. Weather hazy, but cleared up about noon. Passed some very romantic scenery. Arrived at Vadheim 1.30, had a poor dinner, & then left in a stolkjaerre for Sveen, via Sande. After a cold drive arrived at 7.45. Delightful little place, so quiet & serene looking. Stayed at a private house on the fjord, a large house with a beautiful fruit & flower garden to it. A motherly old lady lived there, was very kind indeed. Excellent tea, & bedroom. Slept like a top & rose at 7 a.m.

Aug 2ⁿᵈ. Found the old lady knitting in the dining room & waiting for me. Left after a hearty breakfast at 8 a.m. down the Dalsfjord in a boat for Dale. Raining hard, soon stopped, but a cold wind blowing. Scenery very fine. Hills not too high, but more wild. Arrived at 11.15 and went to a house where they keep travellers. Everything very nice & clean. Had a good dinner. Afterwards went to see Olsen. Found him at the house of a friend of his, together with Robert Hickmüller, who is staying here with him. Quite pleasant. Went a little walk & they had supper at my house.

Aug 3ʳᵈ. Rose at 8. Lovely morning. Everything warm & genial. Birds singing. Olsen & Hickmüller came down at 9.30 & we went a little run to a cliff nearby. From there we climbed the rocks & had a lovely view of the fjord. Really a charming place, *Dale*, & looks so beautiful in the sunshine. Went & had a bath in the little cove where the boat was. Very cold, dried in the sun. Returned home & had dinner. At 2.30 went up to Steia to see Olsen. Had coffee, then played 4 händig with Olsen & went up to Mrs Nitter, where we had refreshment. 2 daughters, very nice. Olsen engaged to the S's eldest. Had supper with Olsen at the boarding school Nikka Vonen,[16] 8 girls were there, the others home for holidays. Left Dale at 10.30. Night glorious   full moon. To the left the glowing of the already set sun, to the right the black rocks of the fjord casting immense shadows. The whole scene never to be forgotten. I never remember a scene so beautiful in light & shade. This is what I came to see in Norway. Stayed on deck until 12.45. Had a nap in the ladies' cabin on deck. Arrived at Florø at 3.15. Florø, a little town, 400 people, lies beautifully at the head of a fjord approached thro' endless skaergaard.[17] The sun just rising. The sky is green & saffron, & the first rays color the whole area with rose tint. Really exquisite. We wend our way (I with a Miss Vonen & Miss Nitter on their way to Trondheim) up the road by the side of the fjord towards a little house where they take lodgers. Went to bed for 4 hrs.

---

16   Nikka Vonen's girls' school: an educational centre of repute.
17   Skerries, archipelago.

Aug 4th. Rose at 8.45. Weather beautiful, seagulls filling the air with their cries. Hearty breakfast. Walk out with the two ladies & go over the hill to the left of the fjord. Presently come to a hill overlooking the fjord on the other side. Such an expansive & exquisite view I never saw before. We sat on a hill almost like in a panorama – all round us the lovely scenery extended for 100^s of miles, the sun shining, the fjord dyed a deep blue, & only a few fleecy clouds hanging afar off over the tops of the highest peaks. Decidedly the most beautiful place in Norway in my estimation. And whilst the ladies are knitting & doing needlework sitting on the heather, I went down into a cove & enjoyed a delicious bathe. Could dive right off the rock into 50 ft of water. Dried in the sun, – Oh, how delightful! Then basked in the sun & looked silently on the lovely scene. Had dinner at 2, & returned to this spot on the hill at 4 p.m., took a bad sketch of it, & chatted. Then a walk to a hill a few hundred yards towards the sea. Another lovely view from there. Returned to our house & had supper at 8. After supper, the two ladies & Mr Hauglund, a young student, & myself walked up past the Church to a hill. About ½ distance on the way a young Norwegian lady joined us dressed in National Tracht[18] – very beautiful – spoke English very well. Had a magnificent view from the top of the hill. The sun just setting, but a little cloudy now.

Aug 5th Friday. Rose at 7. Steamer Norstjerne arrived, so had to go on board quick. Had breakfast with the two ladies. Weather lovely, sun shining gaily. I wrote 2 Canons & a song[19] on deck. Had a little rolling as we passed from Melshorn to Ålesund, but it affected no-one. Had dinner at 2. Some pleasant English people our vis-a-vis – wife & husband. Passed Hornelen, a wonderful rock rising 3000 ft sheer out of the water. Arrived at Ålesund at 4.30. The 2 English people, myself & the two ladies went on ashore with a boat & took a walk up the mountain close to the town & rather overhanging the town. The view we got from the top I never shall forget. Certainly the most magnificent I ever saw, or ever shall see. Similar to Florø, but grander. We saw over the Romsdalsfjord & several other fjords, also miles out to sea, the whole forming a magnificent panorama. We lay down on the heather for ½ an hour & basked in the sunshine & lovely view, then returned to the ship. Left Ålesund at 8. Å.^{d} is a clean, flourishing little town & struck me very favourably. Had tea & then sat on deck, watching the setting sun. The sun sets so beautifully behind these black skaergaarden. Every now & then we caught a glimpse of the open sea as we threaded our way thro' the little islands along the coast. The moon now rose & shed its light over the weird scenery. Arrived at Molde at 11.30. Goodbye to my two Norwegian friends, with whom I had spent such a pleasant 3 days, & I stepped into the boat & made for shore, the steamer standing out in the fjord

---

18   *Tracht* (German)–Norwegian *drakt*: dress, costume.
19   RT X(ii) 3. The song was an earlier setting of Ibsen's 'Little Håkon'.

with the moon shining behind it. How black it looks, like some great monster. Went to Hotel Molde, a nice little hotel, & slept well.

Aug 6. Had a good breakfast, then went to the post & received a letter which I was expecting from Camilla. Then took a walk along the promenade, & also a bath in the fjord. How delicious it tasted. A comfortable little bath house here. After dinner, took a walk up the mountain & had a good view of the fjord, then had a look over the Grand Hotel.

Aug 7*th*. Rose at 6.30, had a bath in fjord & left at 12.30 by steamer "Robert" down the Romsdal & Molde fjord to [Åndals]nes, where we arrived at 5.30. The scenery really grand. Not quite as fine as the Ålesund & Florø, but in its way very fine − bolder & higher. Met 3 Englishmen. Stayed at Hotel Bellevue. After supper, had a row on the lake, then a chat & bed.

Aug 8*th*. Rose at 6, & left at 7. Walked 7 kilos. Then began to rain heavily, so took a carriole up to Flatmark, followed by the 3 Englishmen in 3 carrioles. Raining & blowing big guns. Passed the Hornelen[= Romsdalshorn] & Troll-tinder, enormous rocks. From Flatmark to Ormheim 11 K^{ls} I walked, & came there in time to catch up the 3 Engl. at dinner. Left in Carriole for Stuguflåten. Weather very lovely, warm & sunny. View grand down the Romsdal. Passed a lovely foss, the Slettafoss, rushing down a narrow gully at an enormous rate. Then at Ormheim we had a good view of the Vermafoss. Very hilly up to Stuguflåten, 2000 ft high. Very old Gaard as station, but everything very comfortable. Had a little walk up the hill, & then tea at 7. Very good.

Aug 9*th*. Rose at 6.30, & left at 7.15 in Carriole. Very cold. A little rain at Mølmen. Changed horses & went on to Lesjaverk. Arrived at 10.30 & walked from here to the Hoset, 10 kilometres. Had an excellent lunch for 25 øre, splendid walk, & then drove in Carriole to Holaker, where I met 2 Norwegians who I had seen at Stuguflåten. They were going to walk to Dombås, so we all set out, after an excellent dinner, at 4.30, and arrived at Dombås at 7 p.m. The way was lovely, thro woods, winding along the side of the hills hemming in the Gudbrandsdal, the most fertile valley in Norway. Large farms with large Hofs all along the road & running down towards the river. The hills in the distance looked beautiful & cast shadows in dark blue & black, which I never saw before. The effects of the sun were really fairylike. Rested for 15 minutes on the heather. At Dombås got an excellent meal & looked around a little. Went to bed at 10 p.m.

Aug 10*th*. Rose at 8, had breakfast, & left with my two Norwegians − Mr Borg & Mr Lindemann − for Fokstua, 11 kil. all uphill over the Dovrefjeld. Magnificent view of the Gudbrandsdal on one side & the great Dovre mountains with Snøhetta 7500 ft also, on the other. Passed many Saeters on the way. Fokstua lies 3150 ft high, & is a nice little gaard, nice people. Left here at 1.30 & walked over the Dovre to the Hjerkin, the way very barren & öde. [20] We rested

---

20   Desolate.

every hour & had a little Portwine which one of the Norwegians had. Arrived at 6.30 at Hjerkin, a very large Gaard. Got a good room & had supper at 8. After supper, all went into the large old kitchen, where an enormous log fire was blazing. Several ladies from Christiania were there, also 4 men from Christiania, Lt Col [. . . . . .] Oates & wife also. We then watched them dance the national dances, such as spring dance & Halling. The only music we had was the singing of the girls. It was very picturesque, & the great fire covered everything with a strange glow. The thermometer only 5° Réaumur. Hjerkin lies 3100 ft high. After much amusement went to bed at 10.30.

Aug 11th. Rose at 8. Had breakfast. Paid bill, 2.50 & 50 trinkgeld,[21] for supper, lodging & breakfast, & we all then started for Krokhaug. After walking 1 hour, stopped at a Saeter & had Rommer Øl[22] & sweet milk, a great bowl full, & as much milk as we could drink for 50*øre*, *3 of us*. Then had a fine view of the Skrediho[?] Arrived at Dalen at 3, *17 kils*. Had an excellent dinner of reindeer steak & salmon, all for 80 øre. Then Borg & I started on foot for Krokhaug, Lindemann driving in Carriole as his foot was bad. After a charming walk of 3 hours, 17 kilometres, we arrived at the Station Krokhaug & had a good tea. On the way passed fields quite white with big daisies. A lovely sunset, red & yellow mixed up beautifully with steel-grey clouds.

Aug 12. Left at 9 for Lilleelvedal [= Alvdal]. Walked 17 kils in 2 plus & had dinner at the station. Then Lindemann took Carriole & Borg & I went in a Skyds. Pouring with rain all the way. Drove 32 kilos. Arrived at 6.15 & had tea at 7.30. Very cold, only 4° Réaumur.

Next morning, *13th*, very fine, but cold. Left at 7.5 for Hamar. Arrived at 2 & had excellent dinner. Passed Lake Mjøsa, the largest lake in Norway. Beautiful fir forest on the way to Christiania. Passed Eidsvold & had 10 minutes for coffee – a little watering place. Arrived at Chr.iania at 7.20 & Lindemann & Borg took me to Anne Kure's private Hotel. Very comfortable. Had some trousers made at Martinius Hagen & got them next day Sunday.

14th. Went out with Borg & had dinner at Lindemann's at Ljan. Very nice, & beautiful fjord view. Lindemann rowed me over to Jacobsens on Malmøya, where I made the acquaintance of Camilla's family here & in their summer residence on Malmøya. Very beautiful. Also made acquaintance of Borhavn, who married Camilla's sister. Left for Chr.iania at 11 p.m. after a pleasant evening.

Aug 15th. Dined with Borhavn at Gravesens & saw Viking ship after dinner. At night went out to B's house & had a pleasant evening. He took me home again.

Aug 16th. Went out & spent the whole day at Jacobsens & had a fine sail all the afternoon in their sailboat.

---

21   *Trinkgeld* (German): tip.
22   Beer.

Aug 17th. Went out again a long walk over the Island[?] to *Verdens End*, lovely view.

Aug 18th. Fine bath. Spent nearly all the time at Malmøya, going down there at 1.30 by steamer & staying until 10 p.m.

On *Saturday 20th*, Borhavn got a yacht. I & Jacob & Borhavn went out fish spearing at night. Very fine, but little success. B & I slept on board the yacht.

Next morning fine bath.

26th. We all went to the regatta in a boat, Gerda Fideln[?], the Askerhaus[?], B & Jacob. Very good racing. Then dinner, & in the afternoon we all rowed across to the boat house at Ormsund & saw an amateur performance. Then had a fine walk round Malmøya, & tea at 8. Then we rowed across for the dancing at night. Cam & I took a walk round Ormsund & returned to Malmøya at 11.30. I & B slept on the yacht again.

In the morning a delightful bathe.

On Tuesday night the *30th* I left per steamer Excellencen for Christiansand. Borhavn, Jacob & Hans saw me off. Beautiful moonlight night, but somewhat rough

31st. Lay down in my Cabin all day, but not sick. Came on deck now & again to look at the fjords & coast. We stopped at Moss, Larvik, Kragerø, Lillesand, & at last arrived at Christiansand at 6.30 p.m. Went to the Hotel, &

Sept 1st, left on steamer Norstjernen for Hamburg. Very rough indeed. 24 hours late.

———————

[Autograph MS in the Grainger Museum]

Delius: Recollections of Grieg

I first met Edvard Grieg whilst I was studying at Leipzig in the autumn of 1887. I had just returned from Norway where I had spent my summer holidays on a walking tour in the mountains. During my stay in Leipzig I had become great friends with Christian Sinding, the Norwegian composer, and we always took our midday meal together at the Panorama Restaurant. One day on our way thither suddenly Sinding said to me: "There's Mr and Mrs Grieg", and I saw coming towards us two quite small people. Sinding knew the Griegs – already introduced.

I saw a little man with a broad-brimmed hat and long hair and on his arm a little woman with hair cut quite short. I was speedily introduced. We all four then made our way to the Panorama Restaurant to have dinner. I was very proud at having made his acquaintance, for since I was a little boy I had loved his music. I had as a child always been accustomed to Mozart and Beethoven and when I first heard Grieg it was as if a breath of fresh mountain air had come to me.

Grieg, learning how well I knew Norway and hearing that I had just returned from a mountain-tour, naturally took great interest in me and we soon found ourselves comparing notes of mountain trips in Jotunheimen and the Hardanger Vidder.

After dinner, we all took a walk round the Promenade, Mrs Grieg going home, and every day for many months we dined together, played a rubber of whist and then took a walk round the Promenade. Sometimes varying by going through the Rosental, a beautiful park. Then we all returned to our separate abodes to work. I lived at 9 Harkort Str. and Grieg at 8 Hertel Str. He had then just finished his C Minor Violin Sonata, which had its first performance during the winter season at the Gewandhaus chamber concerts, Adolf Brodsky playing the violin and Grieg the piano. It was a beautiful performance and I was very enthusiastic, and after the concert I wrote Grieg an enthusiastic letter with my impressions, enclosing in the letter a sprig of heather which I had gathered on the Hardanger Vidder. Next day I was very much moved to see what a deep impression this had made upon him.

We also very often went to the Opera together, for "Nibelungen", "Tristan" and "Meistersinger" were constantly given and of course we never missed a performance. I was 23 then and he was a little over 40. After the opera, or wherever we had been, Grieg always took Sinding and me to a wine restaurant and gave us a nice supper and claret (Bordeaux – his favourite wine), talking a great deal and staying very late. Sometimes Johan Halvorsen, the Norwegian musician, would be of the party.

[Christmas in Leipzig: On Christmas Eve, 1887, Grieg invited me, Sinding and Halvorsen to spend Christmas Eve at his rooms, and a very delightful evening it was. After a hearty supper and a good deal of wine, we had music: Mrs Grieg singing all Grieg's Vinje songs most beautifully, Halvorsen playing the C minor Violin Sonata, Sinding accompanying Mrs Grieg to several of his own songs, and I playing a piano piece I had just composed – a Norwegian Sleigh-Ride. We had all had rather more than was good for us to drink, and left in the early hours of the morning. As a Christmas present, Grieg gave me his Piano Concerto with a dedication.]

I was working at the time with Hans Sitt at orchestration and was working at an orchestral suite, which I called "Florida", and it was arranged that it should be played at a rehearsal of a military orchestra in the coming spring. Sitt had arranged for an orchestra of about 60 to give me a 2 hour rehearsal in the Rosental Restaurant and all it would cost me would be a barrel of beer for the orchestra. This accordingly took place one spring morning, the audience being Grieg and Mrs Grieg, Sinding and myself, Sitt conducting. In the Suite was a very noisy nigger dance where I had used the trombones very noisily and *ff*, and Grieg after the performance said to me that he found it "scheusslich interessant".

During that winter season, Tchaikovsky came to Leipzig, and also Brahms, but I never met them. My friendship with Grieg lasted till his death in 1907, although the last 10 years of his life I saw very little of him. The spring of '88 Grieg was engaged to play at the St James's Hall, London (his first appearance in England), and as I was going home also, I arranged to be present at the concert, which was a great success. My parents were in London at the time and we all had dinner together at the Hotel Metropole and Grieg persuaded my father to let me continue my musical studies.

I then went to Paris to stay with my uncle, Theodor Delius, and the summer of '88 I spent in Brittany, first at Perros-Guirec and afterwards at St Malo, where I did a good deal of work, only returning to Paris at the end of September. As I found living with my uncle (his luxurious life) hindered me considerably in my work, I went out to Ville d'Avray and hired a small chalet on the lake and spent the winter there doing a great deal of work. In the spring 1889 – March – I left for home in Bradford to spend a few weeks with my family, spending a fortnight at Ilkley at the Wells House, a hydropathic establishment. As Grieg was playing again at the Free Trade Hall, Manchester, I went over there to meet him again and be present at the concert, going back to Paris in April, where I stayed with my uncle again, and leaving for Norway on June 20th, having been invited to spend the summer to stay with Grieg at Troldhaugen, near Bergen, and to take a walking tour with him and Sinding in the mountains of Jotunheimen. I left for Norway via Havre to Christiania, and having stayed with a relation of Sindings for a few days at Nesodden, we both left for Bergen by boat round the coast. On arriving at Bergen we were met by Grieg, who conducted us to his home near Bergen at Hop Station. He lived in a very comfortable little wooden house called Troldhaugen, situated rather high up on a promontory jutting out into the fjord. Here we spent a very agreeable week fishing and walking, Grieg playing some of his latest compositions to us, and making excursions to Bergen to buy the necessary knapsacks and provisions for our projected walking tour in Jotunheimen. A friend of Grieg's, Prof. Nicolaysen, had lent Grieg his hut on Gjendin and it was thither we were bound. When we had completed our arrangements, we left for Voss in Hardanger and thence via Gudvangen and the Sognefjord to Laerdalsøyri. From there we drove to Nystova, which is at the opening of the Jotunfjeld, and walked to Framnaes on Lake Tyin. From Framnaes we rode to Tvindehaugen and then made the ascent of Skineggi and had a wonderful view of the range of the Bygdin mountains. At Nystova we had made the ascent of Stugunøsi, creeping along its back to the top, and got a wonderful view of the Jotun mountains. Grieg and Sinding went down the proper way, but I went down a more direct and very much steeper way and almost came to grief. When I arrived at Nystova they were just on the point of sending out after me. From Skineggi we descended on the other side to Eidsbugaren on Lake Bygdin and from there we walked over Høistakka to Lake Gjendin, lying in the midst of mighty mountain peaks; it was a very beautiful walk. At Gjendeboden we were met by our guide, Viste Kleiven, who rowed us to our hut, Leirungshytte, a row of several hours. The hut was situated at the border of the lake and at the foot of a waterfall, and opposite was Besseggen and Besshø.

Here we spent a very pleasant time, fishing, boating, walking. Our principal food was trout from the lake, wonderful trout. Milk and cream we got from a saeter at Memurudalen on the other side of the lake a few miles away. We ate flatbrød, the flat Norwegian oatcakes, and every evening we had hot whisky toddy and played cards.

At last Grieg returned to Bergen via Laerdalsøyri. We went together to Nystova, where we had a nice supper together with a bottle of port wine and we drank many skaals for the last time. Next day Sinding and I returned by slow stages to Christiania via Valdres. I went from there to Fredriksvaern for a week's sea-bathing and fishing with Musikdirektor Iver Holter. Then I returned to Havre on the Kong Dag and thence to Paris.

———

[MS in the Grainger Museum, dictated to Percy Grainger]

Delius: Summer Diaries 1888–1891

Bretagne [1888]

Left Paris Wednesday night the 21st July from Montparnasse at 8.2. Had two bad-smelling peasants with a baby in the same compartment. Arrived at Lannion at 8.30 a.m. (22), got in to the bus of the Hôtel de la Plage Trestraou, Perros-Guirec, & arrived there after about 1½ drive. Perros-Guirec is a small village, overlooking the bay of Perros on one side & Trestraou on the other, a most beautiful view reminding me somewhat of Norway. The Hotel belonging to a Monsieur le Bekau [?], quite comfortable & [. . .]. Spent a week there together with Max.¹ Had a most delightful time, fishing & bathing. The last 2 days, 2 young Englishmen came, Parker & Lindley. Left together on Thursday morning at 6.30 (26th). Had a beautiful bathe at 5.30 a.m. Left Lannion at 12.55. After a tedious journey & changing several times, arrived at St. Malo at 11 p.m. Went to the Hôtel de l'Union. The 27th bathed, went a good walk up to Paramé, went into the Casino, had dinner at 7 p.m. Max preparing to leave for England by the Southampton boat; blowing quite hard. Saw him on to the steamer at 8.30, boat left at 9 p.m. On Monday 30th went to my new lodgings, M^{dme}· Chapalan, on the Sillon. Very pleasant.

Aug. 14th. Went on board a Norwegian ship 'Wikingen' & had a chat with the captain, who came from Tønsberg. Went a walk to St. Servan, after drinking a glass of whisky in his cabin.

Norvège [1889]

June 20th. Left Paris 1 p.m. Travelled with a delightful little French Demi-Mondaine. Arrived Havre 5.30 & went at once on board 'Kong Dag', which left at 6.15. Rather rough. Managed dinner & felt better.

Frid.21. Fog all day. Raining[. . .]. Passed several vessels very close. All well.

Saturday. Clear but rough.

---

1   Delius's brother.

Sunday. Delightfully calm & warm. Land in sight. Arrived at Arendal at 12.2 p.m. – Made the acquaintance of a young Russian, Brologeski. Went ashore – it looks over to the Christiania fjord, one of the finest panoramas I ever saw. The setting sun glaring, sending its last rays over the scenery, the fiery glow now leaving[?] the sky.

Arrived at 2 a.m. and was met by Arvesen & his father.[2] Met Wisdal.[3] Slept at the Britannia Hotel. Met Halvorsen. Played Grieg sonata at Warmuth's with Arvesen, then dined at Gravesens with Holter, Soot, Wisdal, Arvesen & Halvorsen. At 5 p.m. left for Nesodden with advokat Mejdell. Beautiful walk to his home, a cottage delightfully situated between two fjords. Met Christian Sinding again, had a delightful evening & chat in a delightful corner of the pavillion[?] & then went to bed.

Tuesday. Bath, breakfast at 10, chat, bath in fjord, & then dinner. Coffee & bathed a little [. . .] little [. . .], then a long walk into the country after tea. Went up onto a hill, & sat for 2 hours admiring the scenery and Christiania.

Wednesday. Fished all day, bathed.

Thursd. Worked all day.

Frid. Got up at 6, & walked over to Drøbak with Sinding. Most delightful walk thro pine forest [. . .] kilometres, arrived at 10 [. . .] at the Gades. Had a bathe, a sail – then dinner, a sleep, another bathe, a walk on the hills above the town, then supper. On my way to the Hotel, got into conversation with a Mr Parr, large in shipping. Hotel good.

Saturday. Rose at 7.15, took a sea-bath, then got aboard the 'Kong Sverre' & arrived at Christiania at 9.30. Found my luggage had been forgotten in Blylaget. Had to return. Took a bath, then work a little.

Sunday. Bath. Left Blylaget for Christiania. Had dinner at Hotel Royal. Left by the 1.50 p.m. train for Hamar. Arrived 5.20. Arvesen met us. Walked up to Sagatun, met Arvesen's family, had a fine cool tub. Sagatun is a fine built house, overlooking Mjøsa. Charming place.

Monday. Walked about a little. Played croquet.

Tuesday. Took a walk with Sinding to Soehlie's gaard, a magnificent farm, 3 kilometres from Hamar, overlooking the lake Mjøsa. Met the young Miss Soehlie & the mother.

Wednesday. Spent the day at Soehlies. Delightful people & beautiful house, with all modern comforts.

Thursday. Walked.

---

2   Olaus Arvesen (1830–1917): leading pedagogue and educational reformer. He founded the first folk high school in Norway, *Sagatun* at Hamar. He was also a politician and a newspaper editor.

3   Possibly Jo Visdal (1861–1923): Norwegian sculptor. He studied in Paris and was to become one of the most skilful of Norwegian portrait sculptors.

Friday. Young Hills [?] fetched us in a carriage at 12. Spent the day at Soehlie's. Ingeborg's birthday. About 20 friends assembled to celebrate the day. Returned at 11.30.

Saturday. Read & walked a little. *Rain* for the 1st time since 5 weeks.

Sunday. Concert, Arvesen. Ragnhild Soehlie got diptherie.

Monday. Left by 9 a.m. train for Christiania. Arrived at 12. Met by Sinding, lunched, left at night by steamer 'Kong Sverre' for Fredricksvaern.

Arrived next morning at 7.30. Met by Holter.

Wednesday. Sinding arrived. Sail to Sauvika & back. Bathe in the afternoon off the rocks.

Thursday. Sail & fish all day. Bath.

Fri. The same.

Saturday. Left for Larvik by carriage at 9 p.m. Got on board the 'Jupiter', bound for Bergen. A delightful ship & very calm passage. Passed the well known coast.

Sunday. Arrived at Christiansand at 11 a.m. Went ashore & had a bath from a boat. Left at 1 p.m. Arrived at Egersund at 9 p.m. Delightful evening.

Monday 15th. Arrived at Bergen at 2.30 p.m. Met by Grieg on the pier, went at once to Troldhaugen, delightfully situated on a fjord.

Tues. Bathed, walked & fished.

Wed. Bathed. Went to Bergen to do some shopping. Met a Miss Anna Mohn, who I had met in Eide 2 years before. Very nice.

Thurs. Went to Mohns to dinner. Went over their stores. [. . .}

Friday. Bathed, fished. In the evening Franz Beyer & wife came to supper.

Sat. Went to Beyers to supper.

Sund. Bathed & fished.

Mond. Did some shopping.

Tues. Left in the afternoon by Voss Banen for Vossevangen. Train crowded with English.

Wed. Left at 7 a.m. in carriage for Gudvangen & Laerdalsøyri. Delightful day. Dinner at Gudvangen. Laerdalsøyri at 7.30. Nice hotel. Drank Toddy on the balkony.

Thurs. Left in carriage at 8 a.m. for Nystova via Maristova. Delightful scenery. Stopped for dinner at *Borgund* (a very interesting church). Arrived at Nystova at 8 p.m. after a magnificent drive over a Vidde. Slept on the floor in the drawing room.

Frid. Made the ascent of Stugunøsi & had a great panorama of Jotunheim.

Sat. Left for Framnaes (Lake Tyin). Stayed the night & left early next morning by boat for Tvindehaugen. Left at once for Eidsbugaren via Skineggi. Grand view of Bygdin & mountains from the top. Arrived at Eidsbugaren at 4½ p.m. Dinner, Prof. Sars [?] & Dutch lady, Miss Jilsine. Slept with 8 others in same room.

Left at 12 next day, *Mond.*, for Gjendin. Grand march on a vidder. Arrived at Gjendeboden 6 p.m. Dinner 7.30. Quiet chat with Grieg & Sinding. Slept with Grieg.

Bathe in the morning. Met by our guide, Vistikleivin, & left in a boat for the hut of Dr Nicolaysen. After delightful row, arrived at 2.30. Dinner I cooked.

Wed. Went on long walk. Fished in the foss nearby. Splendid trout (Had a dangerous walk with Sinding).

Thurs. 1st Aug. Went to Gjende's house in boat. Had dinner, received letters, rowed back.

Frid. Fine, lovely day. Long walk on the hills. Rain in afternoon.

Sat. Rowed with Vistikleivin to a Saeter across the lake to fetch eggs & milk. Got back at 3.30. Dinner. Delightful day again (Leirungs Hütte).

Sund. Quiet day. Not a cloud. Caught fish.

Mond. Rain all day.

Tues. Rain all day. Took a walk at night in the hills. Got very wet.

Weds. Rain & sunshine. Took a walk with Grieg & Sinding. Delightful view.

Thurs. 8th. Started at 11 a.m. for Gjendeboden with Visticleivin. Rowed half way. Arrived at 2 p.m., got letters, started with knapsack over the Vidder. Grand view & weather. Descended Høistakka at 7. Met by a boat. Arrived at Eidsbugaren at 8. Met 2 Frenchmen. Good beds.

9. Started early for Tvindehaugen. Arrived at 11, took leave of Visticleivin. Rowed with 2 men to Framnaes. Dinner. Walked to Nystova, arrived at 7. Last night with Grieg, he going next day back to Laerdalsøyri. We (S & I) to Valdres. Cards & portwine, for last time.

Sat. 10th. Left at 9 a.m. in skyds for Skogstad. Grieg the other way, after a hearty farvel!⁴ Delightful driving thro' a delightful valley. Øylo struck me as being the most beautiful place as yet. *Fagernes* also delightful. Stayed the night.

Sun. Started at 11 in a carriage for Odnes. Delightful scenery. Arrived after delightful drive at 8 p.m. Met the Queen of Sweden on the road.

Mon. Left per S. boat at 7.30 down the Randsfjord for Randesfjord. Arrived at 12.30. Dinner. Train to Hønefoss, skyds to Sundvollen. Very hot, delightful. Bathe in Tyrifjord. Lovely scenery. Went up to Dronningens Udsigt. Magnificent supper at 8.30. Bed.

Next day, carriole to Sandvika & train to Christiania. Left Sinding & left by 'Kong Haakon' for Fredricksvaern.

Arrived *Wed.* at 7.30 a.m. Met Holter. Delightful. Went bathing & sailing. Two or 3 dangerous sails.

Splendid picnic to Navunfjord [?] the last day, *Tues. 20th.*

Wed. 21st. Left per 'Skien' for Christiania. Met two girls, Miss Hagen from Larvik. Went to Britannia Hotel.

---

4   Farewell.

Thursd. Sinding came. Turkish bath. Embarked at 1 p.m., 'Kong Dag'.

Jersey [1890]

Left Paris for Granville 8.30 a.m., Wednesday. Arrived Granville 3.20 p.m. Went to Hôtel du Nord et des 3 Etoiles. Stayed one night. *Thursday*. Went to Avranches. Very wet weather. Took a walk on the beach. Had lunch at the Hôtel de la Gare. Very good. Left for Granville at 2.30 p.m. Left Granville for Jersey at 5.30 p.m. Fine passage. Arrived at 7.30. Went to Hotel de l'Univers (Meunier). Stayed one day. Found room in Havre de Pas, Ceylon Villa, Mrs Fletcher. Very comfortable. Walked & bathed twice daily. Stayed 3 weeks, leaving for Granville on July the 26, Saturday, arrived at Paris at 11 p.m.

Norway 1891

Left Paris for Antwerp 8.15 a.m. on *Wednesday the 24th*. Arrived Antwerp at 3 p.m. Went to the Zoological Gardens & spent the evening at the Taverne Royal – Slept on board the 'Prospero'.

Thurs 25. Went to the Cathedral & the Museum with a guide – Left Antwerp at 6 p.m. Arrived in the open sea at 10 p.m.

Fine journey. A little fog.

Arrived Christiania at 9 p.m., *Sunday the 28th*, after a beautiful view of Christiania fjord at sunset.

Left Christiania for Gjøvik, *Friday the 3rd July*. Met Bjørnsens & Frk. Oselio[5] at the Hotel.

July 4. Went a drive. Concert in the evening: Arvesen, Oselio.

Left Gjøvik for Aulestad at 4 p.m. *Arr.* Lillehammer at 7. Splendid view from the top of the Victoria Hotel. *Arrived* Bjørnsen's at 10.30 p.m.

Mon. 6th. Went round the Gaard, & a long walk.

7th. Went a long walk. Splendid bath with Bjørnsen. Music & a long walk. Bjørnsen read his Fred Oratorium[6] for us.

8th. Long walk – Photographed in the fields with Dagny & others. Splendid bath with Bjørnsen. Walk with Dagny & four young ladies.

9th. Early drive to a Foss, an hour's drive.

10th. Long walk, bath, etc.

---

5   Gina Oselio (1858–1937): *née* Ingeborg Aas, she was to marry Bjørn Bjørnson, son of the poet, in 1893. An operatic soprano, she studied in Stockholm under Fritz Arlberg (father of Ida Ericson Molard's daughter Judith), and in Paris under Marchesi. She sang in many of Europe's concert halls and opera houses, and her best-known roles were Carmen, Marguerite in *Faust*, and Azucena in *Il Trovatore*. Her marriage was to be dissolved in 1908, and she spent much of the latter part of her life in Paris.
6   *Peace Oratorio.*

11th. Left Aulestad at 5.30 p.m. for Lillehammer. Fine evening in the top of the Hotel with Ström,[7] Molnaes, Julie Nilsen, Bergliot Bjørnsen.

12. Left Lillehammer at 8.30 per steamer for Eidsvold. Arrived Christiania 7 p.m. Met Miss Bötger[8] of Christiansand. Passed pleasant night with her. Went to Fredriksborg & walked home to Naalens Hotel.

13th. Dined with Miss Bötger at Grand Hotel & left for Drøbak by steamer at 5 p.m. Met Sinding. Round to Gades, where I stayed until

Wednesday 15th. Had a fine trip on a private steamboat. Luncheon & put in to Falkenstein, where we had coffee. Drove to Horten, where I took the train for Larvik & carrioled from there to Fredriksvaern. In the night at 12, fire alarm. The whole town rushed out to see the Bathing House burned down.

16th, 17th, 18th. Stayed in Fredriksvaern. Spent most of my time with Hjalmar Johnsen & the Backers.[9]

Left on *Sunday the 19th* per Motala for Bergen – Met Holter at Christiansand. Rather rough passage to Egersund, where we took the train over Joedom [?] to Stavanger. Good dinner at the Club. Left Stavanger per Motala at 7.

Arrived at Bergen next morning. Met by Grieg & went out to Hop & Troldhaugen.

Spent a delightful week sea-bathing, fishing & taking walks. Then all of us – Griegs, Holter [?] & I, left for Hardanger – Lofthus on the Sørfjord – where we stayed a few days. We all left for Odda, where we stayed the night, leaving by carriage next morning for Haukeli via Røldal – a lovely spot, where we stayed the night, visiting an old church down in the valley. Next day a heavenly drive in the sunshine to Haukeli Saeter, where we had a good dinner & a good bottle of Burgundy. Next morning, Grieg being rather unwell, I took a walk with Mrs Grieg on the Vidder – picking lovely blue & brown gentian flowers. Again a lovely day. Next day said farvel to the Griegs & left in the pouring rain for Grungedal, Botn, Vinje, Dale.

[Autograph MS in the Grainger Museum]

------

7   Perhaps Halfdan Strøm (1863–1949): Norwegian painter.
8   Presumably Charlotte Bødtker.
9   Perhaps Harriet Backer (1845–1932): Norwegian painter.

A note on the editing of Delius's diaries

Although I have tried to preserve the shape, as well as something of the immediacy, of these summer diaries, it has proved necessary to edit them, at least to a modest extent. They are nonetheless reproduced in full.

Delius's spelling of Norwegian place names was often inaccurate. This, together with the fact that Norwegian orthography has undergone a major revision since Delius wrote these accounts of his travels, has led me to prefer the modern spelling of such place names. I hope this may make it rather easier for the reader who is armed with maps of an appropriate scale to retrace the composer's footsteps in the course of these three early trips to Norway.

Where personal names are concerned, no editing has been undertaken. Although this may seem slightly inconsistent, many of the people mentioned by Delius were no more than passing acquaintances, and it is all too often impossible to confirm whether he recorded their names correctly. The reader is therefore referred to the index for the correct forms where they are known: for example, Bjørnson (for Delius's perpetual Bjørnsen), Frants (for Franz) Beyer, Bødtker (for Bötger), etc.

Delius's punctuation was irregular and occasionally misleading. I have therefore repunctuated the entire text and capitalized words where necessary, as distinct from my general practice in the letters.

These diaries, written as they are in a slim notebook and in Delius's smallest hand, have proved exceptionally difficult to transcribe, and there have been times when it has proved necessary finally to accept a word or words as being undecipherable. Such words are recorded as ellipses within square brackets. A question mark in square brackets indicates that the preceding word is only semi-legible in the original.

I am grateful to Andrew Boyle for his much valued co-operation in jointly working through and checking with me these diary transcripts.

Delius: Recollections of Strindberg

I met Strindberg in Paris in the early nineties at the studio of Ida Ericson, a Swedish sculptress married to William Molard, a French-Norwegian composer. Later on I met him quite frequently at the 'Crémerie' of the Mère Charlotte, Rue de la Grande Chaumière (Montparnasse), where artists received unlimited credit. It was a little place of the utmost simplicity, where hardly ten people could sit down at a time and where one's meal generally cost one a franc, or a franc-fifty including coffee.

Strindberg lived in a *pension de famille* just opposite, at No. 12. Among the *habitués* of the Mère Charlotte at that time were Strindberg; a Polish painter named Slewinsky; Mucha, a Czech designer of decorations and *affiches*; Paul Gauguin, the great painter; Leclercq, a poet; the *maître de ballet* of the Folies Bergère, also a Czech; and myself. I lived at that time at Montrouge, Rue Ducouëdic, and generally took my meals at home, but I occasionally lunched or dined at Madame Charlotte's to meet Gauguin and Strindberg. Or I would sometimes fetch Strindberg for a walk in the afternoon and we would go through the Luxembourg Gardens and around the Panthéon, again up the Boulevard Raspail, and down the Boulevard St. Michel, turning down the Boulevard St. Germain towards St. Germain des Prés, then up again through Rue de Tournon, the Galeries de l'Odéon and back, through the Luxembourg Gardens.

Another favourite walk of ours was to the Jardin des Plantes. Strindberg seemed extremely interested in monkeys at that time. He had a theory that the gorilla was descended from a shipwrecked sailor and an ordinary female monkey. One of his great proofs of this was the similarity between the inside of the paw of the gorilla and the palm of the hand of an old sailor. He showed me photos of both, and indeed there was a great resemblance.

Strindberg was then also greatly occupied with alchemy, and claimed to have extracted gold from earth which he had collected in the Cimetière Montparnasse, and he showed me pebbles entirely coated with the precious metal. He asked me once to have one of these samples analyzed by an eminent chemist of my acquaintance. My friend examined it and found it be covered with pure gold. He was hugely interested and expressed the desire to make Strindberg's acquaintance. So I arranged a meeting in my rooms for a certain Wednesday afternoon at three o'clock. My friend arrived quite punctually, but we waited an hour in vain for Strindberg. At a quarter past four a telegram arrived with these words: 'I feel that the time has not yet come for me to disclose my discovery. – Strindberg.' The scientist went away very disappointed, saying to me: 'Je crains que votre ami est un farceur.'

Strindberg also professed to have extracted pure carbon out of sulphur, and in fact I found him sometimes in his room stooping over an open coal fire stirring something in a retort. At the time he did not tell me what he was doing, but afterwards it dawned on me that the carbon probably came from the coal smoke of the open chimney.

Another day he told me that he had discovered a way of making iodine at half the usual cost, and that he had inspired an article in the *Temps* about this new method. The article created an immense sensation, especially in Hamburg, where iodine seemed to be monopolised; for in one day iodine dropped forty per cent on the Hamburg Exchange. Unfortunately, nothing further was ever heard of this affair.

He was very much interested in spiritism at that time. Paul Verlaine had just died and Strindberg had in his possession a rather large photo of the poet on his death-bed. He handed me the photo one day and asked me what I saw on it. I described it candidly, namely, Verlaine lying on his back covered with rather a thick eiderdown, only his head and beard visible; a pillow had dropped on the floor and lay there rather crunched up. Strindberg asked me did I not see the huge animal lying on Verlaine's stomach and the imp crouching on the floor? At the time I could never really make out whether he was quite sincere or trying to mystify me. However, I may say I believed implicitly in his chemical discoveries then. He had such a convincing way of explaining them and certainly was very ambitious to be an inventor. For instance, Röntgen rays had just been discovered, and he confided to me one afternoon over an absinthe at the Café Closerie des Lilas, that he himself had discovered them ten years ago.

His interest in spirits caused Leclercq and me to play off a joke on him. I asked them both to my rooms one evening, and after dinner we had a spiritistic séance in the form of table-rapping. The lights were turned down and we joined hands round a small table. After ten minutes' ominous silence the table began to rap and Leclercq asked it what message the spirits had for us. The first letter rapped out was 'M', and with each letter Strindberg's interest and excitement seemed to increase, and slowly came the momentous letters 'M E R D E'. I do not think he ever quite forgave us for this.

It was at that time Strindberg wrote his pamphlet 'Sylva Sylvarum'. He certainly was extraordinarily superstitious, for often on our walks he would suddenly refuse to go up a certain street on the pretext that some accident or misfortune was awaiting him there.

Edward Munch, the Norwegian painter, had just arrived in Paris and came to see me in my rooms in the Rue Ducouëdic, and I asked him to accompany me to see Strindberg, whom he had already met before, and who had now

removed to the Hôtel Orfila in the Rue d'Assas. We found him poring over his
retorts, stirring strange and evil-smelling liquids, and after chattering for five
or ten minutes we left in a most friendly manner. On fetching Munch next day
to go to lunch he showed me a postcard just received from Strindberg, worded
something in this wise, as far as I can remember: 'Your attempt to assassinate
me through the Müller-Schmidt method (I forget the real names) has failed.
Tak for sidst.'[1] It appears the method to which he alluded consisted in turning
on the gas from the outside, so as to suffocate the person within, or some such
proceeding. And this was not the only time he suspected that an attempt had
been made to assassinate him. Some time before, when Przybyszewski and his
wife, old friends of his, arrived in Paris, he confided to me that they had only
come to kill him.

He was extremely touchy and often imagined he had been slighted without
any cause whatever, as the following incident will show:

---

1   Strindberg's letters document this episode with exemplary clarity, and the postcard
he sent to Munch has survived. It is postmarked 19 July 1896, and although differing
in detail from Delius's sketchy recollection of its content, it serves to confirm in large
lines the events of the evening:

  The gas-apparatus seems to be based on Pettenkofer's experiment: blow out a light
  through a wall.
  But it works badly.
  Last time I saw you I thought you looked like a murderer − or at least his
  accomplice.

Strindberg makes no mention of Delius in his letters, and on this occasion this is
hardly surprising, as Delius could simply not have been there. He had been settled in
Norway since early June. The evidence is perfectly clear, supplied by a number of letters
from the composer to Jelka Rosen, Jutta Bell and Randi Blehr, and from Grieg to
Delius − all of which were written at different times between mid-June and mid-
August. Delius stayed for most of the summer on a farm at Søndre Aurdal in the Valders
(or Valdres) region, less than 150 kilometres north-west of Christiania. He could not
have been in Paris on 19 July.

The most likely explanation is that Delius did indeed visit Strindberg in the company
of Munch some time in May shortly before leaving for Norway. After all, we know that
he was accustomed to seeing a great deal of the Swede during Strindberg's stay in Paris.
In the event, Munch and he found a preoccupied Strindberg in the midst of his chemical
experiments, and the short visit probably passed amicably. Delius may indeed have
fetched Munch for lunch the next day, but whatever passed between them was not a
discussion of the tenor of the celebrated postcard, for Munch's fateful visit to Strindberg
was not to take place until several weeks later. Much more likely it was on a still later
occasion, after Delius's return from Norway and well after Strindberg's hasty escape
from Paris, that Munch showed the postcard to Delius: a time sequence that had become
blurred when Delius, nearly a quarter of a century later, published in Philip Heseltine's
journal, The Sackbut, these memories of Strindberg.

We would often gather at night at the studio of one of our mutual friends (Molard), a very amusing and Bohemian interior. When we left, our hosts would use the occasion to accompany us downstairs into the yard in order to empty their 'boîte à ordures' and to give Bob, their little bastard dog, a chance of getting a little fresh air. Strindberg had been great friends with this couple and had been taking his meals with them for a couple of months at least. It appears Strindberg was there alone one night and it was getting late and they were evidently very tired, when the hostess suggested 'si nous descendions la boîte à ordures,' a ceremony which had become quite a known institution. Strindberg went down with them and said 'good night' in the wonted friendly way, but never entered their house again, taking the allusion to the 'boîte à ordures' as a personal insult to himself.

Shortly after Munch's supposed attempt to assassinate Strindberg I left for Norway, and on returning heard that he had left for Sweden. I never saw him again.

[From *The Sackbut*, 1, No. 8 (December 1920), pp. 353–4]

Jelka Delius: Memories of Frederick Delius

It is with great difficulty that I have made up my mind to write down my souvenirs of my happy life with Frederick Delius who died last summer. I feel I cannot write objectively, I must tell as truthfully as I can what I remember – but it will be always in connection with myself. That is, I suppose, because I am a woman.

I first met Delius in January 1896 in Paris at the house of a Swedish sculpt(o)ress, Mme Benedix-Bruce; her husband was a Canadian painter. Knowing how much I loved the songs of Grieg which I sang so often, she always said: 'You must know a young Englishman, a friend of ours. He also loves Grieg and composes music himself, and he lives in a funny old house up in Montrouge where there is no concierge'. I really did not care for Mrs. Bruce whom I had met the summer before in Grez-sur-Loing where I was painting. She was so masculine, ugly and autocratic and prude. I always pitied her husband when every Sunday in a boat on the river with her two goats and her dogs she read him long sermons in Swedish. In her studio she had the lifesize nude statue of the baker in Grez which she had done for the 'Salon'. This nasty statue stood in her sittingroom in a corner with its back to the public, so as not to show his sex, altho she had modelled this part in great detail. This seems to me symbolic of the hypocrisy of the woman and many others like her. I did not wish to see this young man she always spoke of. But once when I dined there with my mother who was living with me in Paris, he was there too; an aristocratic looking, rather tall, thin man with curly dark hair with a tinge of auburn and an auburn moustache which he was always twisting upwards. He had a red tie, a remnant of his association with Russian 'Reds'.

At that time I was full of enthusiasm for Nietzsche's Zarathustra which I was reading, and I was greatly surprised when this young Englishman said he knew and loved Zarathustra. It was out of my copy of Zarathustra that he later composed the 'Mass of Life'.

I was at that time surrounded by a lot of young painters and art students who had never read anything and were absolutely uninteresting. After dinner Mrs. Bruce asked me to sing something – as was then the fashion before there were radios or gramophones. I sang the 'Swan' and 'Solveig's Song' of Grieg – with a naïveté I have often marvelled at later on, for I had but a small soprano voice and had only had just a few singing and breathing lessons. But I loved singing, and I had that one quality, that I always knew instinctively how to sing a song. Anyhow Delius seemed to like my singing, for he told me he would come to my studio and bring me a book of his own songs.

He walked home with us and now began a happy, wonderful time. He often came to my studio. The first time I was not there and he told my concierge peremptorily to see to it that I was there next day when he would return. I was at the time painting a big picture for the 'Salon' (the then new one). It was to be called 'Le dernier Accord', and it represented a nude woman sitting in a landscape enveloped in the last golden red evening sun and striking this chord on a harp. Beside her and behind the tree stems etc. all was golden and the shadow just creeping up to her feet. Having up to then only known all these silly men who either fawned on me or were obviously bitter and jealous of my painting, it was lovely to have a friend who took me seriously and who was always sincere. This sincerity Frederick kept thro' his whole life, and it was a wonderful quality which carried him safely thro' the most difficult situations where I would not have dared to be so truthful.

He brought me the promised book of songs. They were the Seven Songs published by Augener, and the Five Songs, also Augener's, which he brought me after I had sung the first ones to him. Later he bought the Seven Songs back from Augener who still has the book of Five Songs. Oh, what a glorious revelation these songs were to me! The harmonies, the 'Stimmung' were so delightful, more so than anything I had known before in music: the 'Cradle Song', 'Auf der Reise zur Heimat', 'Venevil', and 'Twilight Fancies'. The latter seemed to express my own feelings so wonderfully:

> 'Da weint sie hinaus in den sinkenden Tag:
> Wie weh mir im Herzen,
> Steh, Herrgott, mir bei!
> Und die Sonne sank.'

Even now when this song is so popular and hackneyed, I cannot think of it without a pang of the old passionate longing. For it symbolized my fear that such a poet as Delius could not find anything in me; that his evident interest and friendship would soon be over and that the world would then be a blank — the sun gone down for ever. The young ladies and gentlemen who murder this song so often on the radio do not seem to be aware of its depth.

What was so glorious at this time was that Delius liked to go for long afternoon walks with me. We took [the] train to get outside Paris and then went for a long ramble, talking or silent, enjoying the beginning and progress of spring. On our return we went to his dear little flat in rue Ducouëdic on Montrouge. It was a small old house. But he had persuaded the old propriétaire to knock two small rooms into one, and that made a delightful two-windowed sitting room with a grand piano, a red carpet and square table. Next to it a

small bedroom with a very big bed, and a tiny kitchen. He then rushed out and
got a nice beefsteak, some eggs and a big bunch of watercress. He put the kettle
on the sitting room open fire, and we lit a little charcoal fire in the kitchen, on
which he did the cooking. And he always did it extremely well. He said he had
learnt all that in Florida on his orange grove. Sometimes he used to play for me
parts of his opera 'Irmelin', on which he was then working. I remember a
beautiful bit about the sun rising on a stream. Then he would do the beefsteak
and fry the eggs and lay them on top, pouring the gravy carefully over them. It
seemed to me that nothing in the world could ever taste better (and nothing
ever did). Then he would clear away and leave the washing up to his faithful
femme de ménage, Mme Figeac, next day. I felt I had better rush away at once
then, as he seemed to want to get to work. It was my salvation, I think, that I
understood this, because it always enraged him when people did not leave him
to work. He could not compose in the daytime as there was too much noise,
especially exasperating was a man making and repairing copper utensils with
constant hammering. But in the evening all was peaceful. The words of the
Verlaine song:

> 'Le ciel est, par-dessus le toit, si bleu, si calme!
> Un arbre, par-dessus le toit, berce sa palme . . .'

are in my mind for ever linked to the view from his windows.

From these paradisiacal afternoons I used to come home to my mother's with
arms full of wild cherry blossoms etc. and there were fearful rows, particularly
once when my youngest brother was in Paris and I had really promised him to
go and visit the Catacombs with him. My mother thought it inconceivable that
I preferred going out with a stranger, when I could have been in those Catacombs
with my own brother!! Of course when Frederick fetched me to go out all else
was forgotten.

From this time the picture of Delius coming along the Avenue du Maine,
where I had my studio, stands out most vividly; an old grey hat, his blue
vivacious eyes, pale face and red tie, accentuating the pallor. He wore a
McFarlane coat (of greyish tweed, a cherished garment that lasted here in Grez
for many winters). The flaps of the McFarlane he used always to throw back
over his shoulders. So I see him against the grey and rather shabby Avenue du
Maine; and I remember the pang of anxiety his pallor gave me. He worked half
the night, smoking and drinking red wine, and then stayed in bed late, but
disturbed by all the noises in that populous courtyard. At last I packed off my
picture to the 'Salon' and went for a few days to Grez-sur-Loing. When I told
him I was going there, he arranged to go to Bourron at the same time, as his
friend C.F. Keary, an English author, was there who was writing the libretto
for Fred's opera 'Koanga'. The words were taken from Cable's story, and Delius
had made the scenario himself, but always found the actual wording very
difficult. However he was not enthusiastic about Keary's words either. They

were 'ungeschickt' 'mal habile' in the extreme and in the more lyrical parts
rather highflown, and the two kinds of words never fitting together. However
Fred was not very critical as he was so eager to get to work. He destroyed the
worst of the stilted words and got Keary who was a charming man and friend,
to make some more. After one of these discussions I went with Fred to walk in
the forest just above Bourron. We passed a dead tree-trunk, all worm-eaten and
hollow, and I was quite astonished when Fred started to dig into this worm-
eaten wood with the greatest energy and reduced it all to pulp. Did he thus
vent his feelings about the libretto? On our return I lunched with them, and
Fred had his violin and played negro melodies on it for us. He played it rather
like the Norwegian peasants play the Hardanger-Fele (fiddle) as much as
possible with the harmonies. All this was again a new world for me. When Fred
came to see me at Grez, we rowed on the river, then running extremely high.
We managed to get thro' under the old stone bridge of Grez with great difficulty
and struggled on until we got to the landing place of an old deserted but lovely
garden belonging to the Marquis de Carzeaux, with an old rambling, but very
cosy looking house at the top, facing the street. I had had permission for several
summers to go and paint in this glorious garden. I used to take my nude models
there and work undisturbed, except when the 'Curé', who lived next door in the
Presbytère, mounted on a little terrace high up on the ancient church (attributed
to Charlemagne). Sometimes he had some other priests to lunch and they would
all go up there and enjoy our goings on, especially the sight of my lovely model
Marcelle. Delius was enchanted on this spring day with blue sky and fleeting
clouds and against it the grey pile of the big solid old church and on the other
side the ruin of an early medieval castle, 'la Tour de Gal', which also had that
beautiful grey tone, with its hollow window holes, standing rather high, and
the peaceful village houses built up around it. The garden had run quite wild.
There were beautiful old trees near the river, and little wild primroses and
violets were already in bloom. We picked some and pressed them in Nietzsche's
'Fröhliche Wissenschaft', and Fred said: 'A place like that one could work in, it
is so beautiful and quiet and unspoilt'. These words proved to be prophetic –
but neither of us thought of that at all at that time. What made the garden so
lovely was that it ran right down to the river, there being no path or public
right of way. On the opposite side there was a meadow bordered by French
poplars; no houses could be built there as it was so often flooded in spring

That early summer Fred brought me two Verlaine songs and a German song
published by a French firm, but which he later also bought back, I ignore why.
The two Verlaine songs are still beautiful: 'Il pleure dans mon coeur' and 'Le
ciel est, par-dessus le toit'. It was with the greatest delight that I studied these.

In the summer 1896 Frederick went to Norway; he stayed most of the time
in Valdres on a farm called Haugen, and in some charming letters he wrote me
from there, he describes his life there and the death of the old grandmother on
the farm. The funeral was done according to the old tradition, and in order to

do all the baking, killing and cooking for the mass of guests from everywhere around, the dead woman had to be kept fresh in the cellar for a whole week.

On this trip Fred also made a concert tour together with his friend Jebe and with Knut Hamsun. The latter is the well-known Norwegian author. He had quite an imposing appearance and always went about with a grey top-hat and frock coat altho' the tour took place in all sorts of mountain resorts. Jebe played the violin very well. He had studied in Leipsic and had now been playing in the Colonne orchestra in Paris for several years. Fred himself of course accompanied Jebe, but also gave a number of solos, I think mostly by Chopin. He always had a rather peculiar smile when mention was made of these performances as he was never a great pianist. Hamsun and Jebe on the other hand were apt to get rather drunk. On one occasion Hamsun entered an hotel where they were to perform rather pompously as was his wont. Suddenly he fell down full length on the steps of the veranda where all the guests were assembled, shouting: 'Jeg traenger Luften!' (I need air).

At about Christmas I went to sup with Fred at rue Ducouëdic. His Norwegian friend, the violinist Halfdan Jebe was there too, and they intended to go back to the orange grove in Florida for some months. Fred wanted to see the place as the negro in charge pocketed all the gains. I was miserable about Fred's going so far away, and the terrible fear – a kind of obsession – clutched at my heart that all would [be] over, that he would have forgotten our friendship on his return. He was so fascinating and had so many women friends, lovely Scandinavians, English and French. I was only too conscious how awful I looked with my lovely light blonde hair tightly twisted and pulled into an 8 on the top of my head, with a fashion of clothes, tight waists and Gigot sleeves, most unbecoming to me, and my clothes being mostly ordered by my mother and made by bad dressmakers. I never had had leisure to think of and get clothes, for all the time in Paris I had worked 10 hours a day in the studio and then still I had to keep my mother amused, go to concerts with her or dine with her old Russian friend Mme Damke. Mons. Damke had been a composer and had written awful, unoriginal songs which I had to sing after dinner. When I got to know the Delius songs I insisted on singing those instead, and the old lady became suspicious at once that something had changed me; especially as she knew Delius's uncle in Paris who had often spoken to her of his gifted nephew. She called the songs 'Vos mélodies Deliucieuses' and said to my mother: 'Ah, méfiez-vous, Madame, la musique a perdu tant de filles'.

Well, I struggled thro' this winter of 1896–7, feeling very unsettled, uncertain and unhappy. The Paris life with all my admirers, whom I hated more and more, did not give me any real satisfaction, and my longing and constant thought of Delius governed all my thoughts. In the spring I was informed that the Marquis de Carzeaux was trying to sell his property in Grez as he was in great need of ready money, having lent a million francs to the then notorious Mme Humbert with her celebrated 'Coffre fort'. She seemed a marvellously clever woman who convinced everybody that her Coffre fort contained untold riches of which those who lent her money now, whilst it could not yet be opened, would partake. How intelligent people could believe all this is a mystery. The Marquis had borrowed from usurers so as to lend her the money and was therefore hard pressed.

The proposed sale of the property was a terrible blow for me. Where was I to paint if I was deprived of the garden? And now more than ever I felt that I ought to live more in Grez and less in Paris. The property would surely be sold at once, as it was offered rather cheaply, yet for a sum that seemed crushingly formidable to me: 35,000 francs (about 1400£). I suddenly *knew* that I must absolutely buy the place. I had a little money from my father and could scratch together enough to pay half that sum, and my mother *must* be convinced and persuaded to lend me the other half. The struggles, anxieties, discussions, setbacks, hopes and fears of this time are beyond description. And all through it I knew I *must* have the place, live in the house, forget Paris, start living my own life and no longer sit and wait for Fred who surely did not care for me at all. I had a great friend, Ida Gerhardi, a very gifted portrait painter, German, whom I knew from childhood, altho' she was a good bit older than I was. She lived in Grez with me that spring and was a most wonderful, indefatigable help to me in all this. At last we had got my poor mother to acquiesce, and she arrived in Grez with the money, for it was the one condition of the Marquis that it had to be paid and laid on his table at once. My mother could not sleep a wink, terribly afraid as she was that she would be murdered with all that money on her. When at last we were on our way to the Château of the Marquis in a little pony-cart, we found that from sheer exhaustion of fear and excitement she had forgotten the money under her pillows!!

Delius was still in Florida and knew nothing of all this. I took possession of the place on May 17th 1897. For furniture I had only the few things from my studio which I gave up. The first night I slept quite alone in this glorious place. The Gloire de Dijon roses had grown up to the first floor and scented my bedroom; the moonlight, a great owl flying at dusk from the church to the ruin, the wild garden now so overgrown that for nettles one could not see the flagstones in the yard. Then Ida came, bringing with her a few more necessary pieces of furniture which she had persuaded her friend Röderstein to give her.

It must have been about the end of June – and I was painting the walls of a tiny room on the street that had formerly been a tobacconist's shop and which we wanted to use as a little dining room – that the postman dropped thro' the window that fateful postcard that almost made my heart cease beating: it was from Fred and said that he was back from Florida and coming to see me the next day, having heard that I was living in Grez. Oh, was all the old anxiety to begin again – and yet, how heavenly it was! And then he came, as simply and naturally as was his wont, with a little suitcase and said: 'I suppose you can put me up.' The idea that I, a young girl, should have this man staying at the house simply staggered me — so unsophisticated and old-fashioned was I. Happily in my quick-working brain this thought was at once superseded by a more practical one: we had nothing to furnish a room with for him. So I answered that we could get him a room in the house opposite and he could be with us all day and have his meals with us. He stayed over the weekend and then only went back to Paris to fetch his music and a few clothes. I had hired an upright piano and that I put into an empty room with a chair and a table and there he was to work. I had no servant, but a great store of energy and the constant help of Ida, who threw herself heart and soul into all this and was like my second self.

So simply it was that my happy life at Grez began. From the outset Fred worked there most contentedly. In the afternoon we had beautiful walks. We painted in the garden and had our evening meal in the yard with the gorgeous summer-evening sun glowing on the big trees near the river that made the background of our vista. Talking of all those inexhaustible subjects until the sun faded and the moon rose over the river and came up to shine on the simple, white old house and the purplish-brown roofs and grey walls.

Ida and I shared a room and often heard Fred until late into the night at work or improvising, as he was still in the habit of working at night. Only gradually could I wean him from this and get him to use the fresh mornings after a good night's rest.

One day a delightful looking Bretonne of about 48, the former servant of an American-Swedish artist family living in Grez, came back on a visit. I was able to secure her as a factotum, and a splendid woman she was, really doing everything and yet finding time to help in the garden. She could not read or write, but she understood everything and never let herself be cheated. She soon decided that it was sinful waste to let 'Monsieur', as she called him from the first, hire a room in the village when we had a whole house. So we managed to get a bed etc. and fitted up two adjoining rooms for Fred, both with the view to the garden. The piano was taken up there until I bought a new upright, as the hired one never stayed in tune.

I remember an evening while Fred was still working in his empty room downstairs, when he called me and Ida to hear a song he had written to words of Nietzsche. It was the 'Mitternachtslied' from Zarathustra: 'O Mensch! gib Acht!' etc. and formed the nucleus of the great 'Mass of Life'. It was quite wonderful. We sat on cushions on the floor, and Fred at the piano with a flickering candle played to us that solemn and intense song, '. . Doch alle Lust will Ewigkeit . .'; the greatest yearning of humanity was expressed so beautifully, and I was overcome with the wonder of it all, that in my house this had been created, that Fred was so gifted and had all his life before him to create such beautiful things. I resolved to give him all help and assistance in my power.

At this time Fred composed several songs with Danish words by J. P. Jacobsen. A Norwegian writer of great talent, Gunnar Heiberg, was staying at Grez that summer and he taught me my first Norwegian lessons in translating the words of these songs for me; he had written a drama 'Folkeraadet', a clever satire of misguided patriotism and its inefficacy, for the battle in this drama is won by a simple waiter who was quite unaware of the great patriotic issues and simply saved the situation. Heiberg asked Fred to write him some incidental music for the play. He did so and went to Norway in the autumn for the first performance.

All this is described so well in Philip Heseltine's Delius Biography that I will not say more about it. On rereading the book, I find that that period which formed the apogee of my life, *Delius's coming to Grez*, is not mentioned at all, altho' it is of the greatest importance also to him, as all the works that have survived and been published were written beginning with his coming to Grez.

There was the Piano Concerto already nearly finished in its first version. He wanted very much to give an audition of it, and a lady of the French aristocracy and friend of his offered to have it played on two pianos at her house. I knew a German-French pianist, Henri Falke, a 'Premier Prix du Conservatoire', and I got him to study and play the piano part. It was a sort of musical 'at home', and I must say Falke played very drily and without much understanding. Fred himself played the orchestral part on a second piano. The audience could not make much of it, but I who knew the music, felt it to be a great and poetic work. Now, nearly forty years later, it is played continuously, but Fred himself had got tired of it and did not care to hear it anymore. There was also the Negro-opera 'Koanga', two acts of which were written, the first version of 'Appalachia'; he was not quite pleased with its form, and all this he began to work on in Grez. On his way back from Norway he went to Germany, and thanks to the enthusiastic pleading of Ida Gerhardi, Musikdirektor Dr. Haym did 'Over the hills and far away', an orchestral work, the first to be performed in Germany. It was in M.S. of course and has never been published. This was a great event, for Dr. Haym took great pains and loved this music, and from then on brought out a number of Fred's works in spite of the great difficulties in which he got with his Konzert Gesellschaft. It is difficult to imagine nowadays into what fury people got at that time about music that had any fresh personality and unaccustomed harmonies. It was universally condemned by all, except a few enthusiasts who instinctively understood and felt its beauties. Professor Julius Buths, Musikdirektor in Düsseldorf and a great friend of Dr. Haym's in Elberfeld, came over for this concert, and altho' he was rather forbidding and critical, one could notice that he was very interested. A year or so later, Fred sent him the score of his 'Midnight Song from Zarathustra.' Buths went to great pains studying it, and to this end copied out the whole orchestral score. In the end he wrote to Fred that he could not in all conscience perform it.

[From a typescript in the Gerhardi/Steinweg collection]

The Journalist

by C. F. Keary (see pp. 125–6)

Keary's book is very good. He has taken an awful lot of sayings out of my mouth for Johnson, but the characters are alive and artistic on the whole.
—————Fritz Delius to Jelka Rosen, 28 November 1898.

Sophus Jonsen (Keary's actual spelling) is an Anglo-Danish playwright in his late thirties. A man of many talents, he has studied art and painted in Paris. Widely read, too, he is able to discourse on contemporary literature with the same practised ease as he discourses on art, music and the theatre in modern Europe. He dabbles in alchemy, and is a disciple of Nietzsche. He is equally at home in England, France or Germany – where he presently lives in Munich – as he is in the land of his birth, Denmark. His character is strong, his mind his own, and his views are stubborn and unshakable. His ingrained cynicism is usually turned to the mockery of the bourgeoisie and of philistinism in general – especially when manifested in England. He is recognizably an outsider.

Although it is almost impossible to guess that he is not an Englishman, there is something in his accent that gives him away, 'something trailing . . . along with the suspicion of a burr, as in the Northumbrian dialect'. His cynicism has a physical manifestation: we are told that his smile can be good-natured; but more often than not there is a half-sneer about his lips, and his voice has a sarcastic ring to it. There is 'something uncanny' about him, and the general impression that he gives is faintly sinister. Dick Vaux, the vacillating hero of Keary's novel, discerns something of an *alter ego* for himself in the man, who, he feels, 'belonged to a different world from this London one. And a devilish bad world too! And yet a world of freedom, of inspiration, such as London did not know'. In his eyes, Jonsen is a 'tremendously combative' person, who 'doesn't seem to have anything to do with our moral laws', but seems rather 'to come out of another world, somehow. He might be a Martian or an inhabitant of Jupiter'.

Jonsen's morals are free indeed for his time. When he first went to Munich, he had expected to find German girls particularly modest: 'I precious soon found out my mistake, I can tell you.' He asks Vaux to join him in the city, where there are 'special pleasures and amusements which belonged to this winter time, such as the tourist did not know of'. His *je m'en fichiste* hedonism comes naturally, as when he is cordially asked if he has been prospering: 'I don't know about that — prospering. I dare say I've enjoyed myself as well as another, if that's what you mean by prospering.' Discussion of marriage amuses him, and he condones the attitude of the man who might 'want to please some other woman if he was married'.

Jonsen has, too, a perhaps unexpected taste for the more worldly things of life: he enjoyed seeing some 'rattling good' bicycle races at the Hippodrome when he passed through France recently.

'Not less noticeable was his appreciation of his own work'

Jonsen's latest play — he goes to London to see it performed in his own English version — is heavily laced with Symbolism. It is the talk of the day, and through it float odd figures and ideas that occur from time to time in Delius's *A Village Romeo and Juliet*. (Keary had started work on his own first version of a libretto for the composer in the earlier part of 1897.) The society depicted in the play is 'absolutely *bourgeois*', although the action takes place 'in a most beautiful legendary country', and a piece of borderland between two countries plays its part in the story. The Wanderer in the play hints at the Dark Fiddler of *A Village Romeo*, and there is a child who 'is meant to be the Uebermensch'. In his play Jonsen is felt to have had 'a way of imparting . . . a touch of sensuality, and of confounding the passions'.

'That Hauch was an extraordinary man'

It is quite possible that Keary knew Halfdan Jebe: there is in the novel a vignette of one of Jonsen's closest friends, Hauch, a violinist, philosopher and womanizer, who seems to bear much the same relationship to Jonsen as Jebe bore to Delius. Hauch has had many *amours*, some of them not particularly tasteful, some 'not so squalid'. Vaux, the journalist, joins him and Jonsen on a walking tour in the Bavarian highlands: 'That Hauch was an extraordinary man! Where had he not wandered and on foot, paying his way mostly by playing on his violin, a little fiddle which he kept specially for such journeys, and carried in its case strapped on his back?' This curious figure made a profound impression on Vaux that was to last long after the tour: 'The memory of Hauch haunted him most, Hauch with his enchanted fiddle and his squalid loves.'

'This faculty both of provoking and facing strong dissent was one of the things which made the Dane enigmatic and impressive'

On morals and morality

'Think of all the time you waste over your English fetishes, your social observances, your moralities — '

'I never pretend to have any of what you call morals . . . because here one must *pretend* to have them, even if you haven't, mustn't you?'

'You know when you've come back to Old England: I'm damned if you don't.'

'As if they had any morals to be corrupted in the first place! . . . The bourgeoisie as much as anyone else — all the crowd.'

'Why, my dear fellow, you don't suppose that mankind is always going on for ever to be hedged in by the blinkers and the reins, and to go on in this jog-trot way for ever, till the end of time, and be bound by all the rotten conventional laws, and the traditional moralities.'

On the bourgeoisie
'Les gens chic je m'en. . . .'

On the Uebermensch
'He ought to win. He's the man who knows his own mind and what he wants.'

'People have got to fight it out. They've got to be original, and that means each man for himself.'

'Unscrupulous! That's another of your traditional ideas. A man must be so afraid of treading on other people's corns that he never makes a step forward. I tell you, my dear fellow, that's the most important thing of all that we've got to get rid of, that idea that you must be always afraid of hurting somebody. You've got to hurt a lot of people – you've got to hurt all the damned *bourgeoisie* as much as you can – if this world is to step a bit forward. It's your infernal English notion of comfort that comes in there. . . . And of course your hypocrisy . . . that's always part. What you call consideration for others is only cowardice; it's being afraid that other people will pay you back.'

'You've got to be a man and not an echo – like those.'

On the artist and his public
'The public! Well, tell me what the public ever understand.'

'Understand! Of course they won't understand! An artist must suffice to himself!'

On literature
'I tell you literature never is decent.'

'It's like the English people, they always want everything to *mean* something. A theme is the only sort of writing they have any idea of – an essay. I don't say the only literature, because literature it is *not*. That's why the most popular English writer was Macaulay. . . . A Lord, too! It's all of a piece. And their idea of love is just of the same character.' [Here Jonsen is accused of dragging in morality or immorality] 'Because, my dear fellow, you can't get rid of that. It stands at the root of everything. What you want, my dear fellow . . . is to be *naïf*. I tell you you'll never do anything – I don't mean you particularly, but any of those over there . . . as long as you're held down by all those conventional ideas.'

'One gets sick of hearing anything eternally *discussed*. That, I say, is what you do in England. You always want to be writing essays – essays to show that a man should take beef rather than mutton, by some one who likes beef the best.'

On English music

'That's just it, my dear fellow. . . . What is it? I never saw it.'

'If there had been any music produced in England I should have heard it fast enough.'

* * *

Voices from the tramway of the skies

It will be clear from these particularly characteristic examples that Keary has indeed 'taken an awful lot of sayings' out of his friend Delius's mouth. And it must be admitted that virtually all the interest in *The Journalist* today lies in just this unusual fact. How Delius was able to describe the characters in the novel as 'alive and artistic' is something of a mystery, for the book has not worn well. Jonsen is the clearest cut personality, but a host of other characters wander inconsequentially and rather pallidly through more than 300 laboured pages. The writing is undistinguished and often surprisingly clumsy. Keary may have been a scholar, but he was certainly not a stylist. It is strange indeed that Delius persisted with him as a librettist after *Koanga*. On reading *The Journalist*, however, one finds it not at all surprising that Delius was to abandon Keary's *Village Romeo* text in favour of his own.

If plot and characters have sunk with scarcely a trace, what is left of this odd, squarely Victorian *roman de mœurs*? Here and there a rivetting moment of recognition, as Delius's own voice sounds eerily but unmistakably out of a lost century. And just occasionally, too, a passage of almost equally deathless prose – Keary's own voice, faintly, quaintly staking its modest claim to immortality:

He set out for a great walk towards the north, marching along long roads with vistas of houses which seemed to stretch to infinity, whereby rushed in steady course one after another the tram cars. This eternal succession of houses, these unceasing trams were to him symbols not of monotony or ugliness but of beauty. The last might typify in mystic fashion the passage of the planets along the tramway of the skies; those houses white in the sunlight might stand for the Watling Street of heaven, the Milky Way.

Bibliography

The following limited list is based on a range of works consulted for background purposes or suggested for further reading, covering Delius's life until 1908. It includes all the books written on Delius, together with a considerable number of essays devoted to his life, rather than to his music. Although some more specifically musicological articles are cited, for the most part they contain biographical detail of interest or refer to and quote from letters between Delius and others. For a basic bibliographical guide to essays on Delius's music, the reader is advised to turn to the current edition of *The New Grove Dictionary of Music and Musicians* or to my earlier bibliography published in 1972 as an appendix to Alan Jefferson's *Delius*.

Abraham, Gerald. 'Delius and His Literary Sources'. *Music and Letters* (April 1929), pp. 182–8. Reprinted in his *Slavonic and Romantic Music: Essays and Studies*. London: Faber, 1968, pp. 332–8.

————. 'Delius and the Ethos of *Art Nouveau*'. *Art Nouveau Jugendstil und Musik*. Beiträge . . . Herausgegeben aus Anlass des 80. Geburtstages von Willi Schuh, von Jürg Stenzl. Zurich: Atlantis Musikbuch-Verlag, 1980, pp. 187–92.

Almqvist, Gisela. 'Ida Ericson – en bortglömd skulptris: Hennes tid och miljö'. Dissertation, Stockholm, 1966.

Amundsen, Leiv, gen. ed. *Gyldendals Ett-Binds Leksikon*. Oslo: Gyldendal Norsk Forlag, 1958.

Arbo, Jens. 'Arve Arvesen 60 år'. *Tonekunst*, 18 (Årg. 1929), pp. 246–7.

Bänfer, Carl, ed. *Ida Gerhardi 1862/1962*. Exhibition catalogue. Münster, Detmold, Hamm, Lüdenscheid, n.d. [1962].

Bantock, Myrrha. *Granville Bantock: A Personal Portrait*. London: Dent, 1972.

Barbour, George M. *Florida for Tourists, Invalids, and Settlers: containing practical information regarding climate, soil, and productions; cities, towns, and people;*

the culture of the orange and other tropical fruits; farming and gardening; scenery and resorts; sport; routes of travel, etc., etc. New York: Appleton, 1882.

Bauer, Harold. *Harold Bauer: His Book.* New York: Norton, 1948.

Baum, Marie-Luise. 'Hans Haym, 1860–1921: Dr., Königlicher Musikdirektor, Professor' (Wuppertaler Biographien, 9. Folge). *Beiträge zur Geschichte und Heimatkunde des Wuppertals,* 17. Wuppertal: Born-Verlag, 1970, pp. 37–48.

———. 'Hans Haym'. *Rheinische Musiker,* 7 (1972), pp. 42–3.

Beecham, Sir Thomas, Bt. *A Mingled Chime: Leaves from an Autobiography.* London: Hutchinson, 1944.

———. *Frederick Delius.* London: Hutchinson, 1959. Reprinted, with a discography by Malcolm Walker and an introduction by Felix Aprahamian. London: Severn House, 1975.

Benestad, Finn, and Schjelderup-Ebbe, Dag. *Edvard Grieg: mennesket og kunstneren.* Oslo: Aschehoug, 1980.

Bird, John. *Percy Grainger.* London: Elek, 1976. Paperback ed., with new illustrations, London, 1982.

Bjørnson, Bjørnstjerne. *Aulestad-breve til Bergliot Ibsen.* Ed. Bergliot Ibsen. Kristiania and Copenhagen: Gyldendalske Boghandel, 1911.

Bottomley, Alan, ed. *Frederick Delius 1862–1962: Centenary Festival, Bradford, March 29–April 7 1962.* Programme book with essays. Bradford, 1962.

Boyle, Andrew J. 'The Song of the High Hills'. *Studia Musicologica Norvegica.* Oslo, 1982.

Brandt, Frithiof; Shetelig, Haakon; and Nyman, Alf, eds. *Vor Tids Kunst og Digtning i Skandinavien.* Copenhagen: Martins Forlag, 1948.

Bray, Trevor. *Bantock; Music in the Midlands before the First World War.* London: Triad Press, 1973.

Brian, Havergal. 'The Art of Delius'. *Musical Opinion,* 47, Nos. 558–64; 48, No. 565 (March–October 1924).

Brunet-Moret, Jean, and Jamin, Armand. *Ville d'Avray et son histoire.* La Municipalité, Ville d'Avray, 1970.

Busoni, Ferruccio. *Letters to His Wife.* Trans. Rosamond Ley. London: Edward Arnold, 1938.

Cable, George Washington. *The Grandissimes.* New York: Scribner, 1880; London: Hodder and Stoughton, 1899.

Calvé, Emma. *My Life*. Trans. Rosamond Gilder. New York and London: Appleton, 1922.

Cardus, Neville. 'Delius'. Chapter 9 of his *Ten Composers*. London: Cape, 1945, pp. 139–52. Revised as Chapter 10 of his *A Composers Eleven*. London: Cape, 1958, pp. 215–35.

Carley, Lionel. 'Carl Larsson and Grez-sur-Loing in the 1880s'. *The Delius Society Journal*, 45 (October 1974), pp. 8–25.

————. 'Delius's "Norwegian Suite" '. *Anglo-Norse Review* (London) (December 1978), pp. 12–14.

————. *Delius: The Paris years*. London: Triad Press, 1975.

————. 'An English-American Hardangervidde-man'. In *Frederick Delius og Edvard Munch*. Ed. Eggum and Biørnstad, q.v., pp. 29–33.

————. 'Hans Haym: Delius's Prophet and Pioneer'. *Music and Letters*, 54, No. 1 (January 1973), pp. 1–24. Reprinted in *A Delius Companion*. Ed. Redwood, q.v., pp. 187–215.

————. 'Impulsive Friend: Grainger and Delius'. Chapter 4 of *The Percy Grainger Companion*. Ed. Foreman, q.v., pp. 31–50.

————. 'Jelka Rosen Delius: Artist, Admirer and Friend of Rodin. The Correspondence 1900–1914'. *Nottingham French Studies*, 9, No. 1 (May 1970), pp. 16–30; 9, No. 2 (October 1970), pp. 81–102.

————. '*A Village Romeo and Juliet* (1899–1901): A Brief Account of Delius's Operatic Masterpiece from Its Inception to Its First Performance'. *The Delius Society Journal*, 73 (October 1981), pp. 11–16.

————. *Young Delius: Catalogue: An Exhibition Held at the Royal Festival Hall, London, 1 November–14 December 1977*. Duplicated catalogue. London: The Delius Trust, 1978.

————, and Threlfall, Robert. *Delius: A Life in Pictures*. London: Oxford University Press, 1977.

————, and Threlfall, Robert. *Delius and America*. Exhibition catalogue. Camden Festival, London, 1–20 May 1972.

Catinat, Jacques. *C'est arrivé à Croissy S/S*. Paris: Éditions S.O.S.P., 1970.

Chamier, J. Daniel. *Percy Pitt of Covent Garden and the B.B.C.* London: Arnold, 1938.

Chop, Max. *Frederick Delius*. Berlin: Harmonie, 1907.

————. 'Frederick Delius'. *Monographien Moderner Musiker*, 2. Leipzig: C. F. Kahnt Nachfolger, 1907, pp. 84–97.

Danielsson, Bengt. *Gauguin in the South Seas*. Trans. Reginald Spink. London: Allen and Unwin, 1965.

Delius Centenary Festival: Frederick Delius 1862–1934. Exhibition catalogue. Bradford City Art Gallery and Museums, 30 March–13 May 1962.

Delius, Clare. *Frederick Delius: Memories of My Brother*. London: Ivor Nicholson and Watson, 1935.

Delius Exhibition, January 29–February 3, 1963. Exhibition catalogue. Cummer Gallery of Art, Jacksonville, Florida, 1963.

Delius, Frederick. 'Recollections of Strindberg'. *The Sackbut* (London), 1, No. 8 (December 1920), pp. 353–4. Reprinted in Heseltine, *Frederick Delius*, q.v., pp. 49–52.

———, and Papus (Dr Gérard Encausse). *Anatomie et Physiologie de l'Orchestre*. Paris: Chamuel, 1894.

Delius Society Newsletter (later *Journal*). London, 1962– .

Del Mar, Norman. *Richard Strauss: A Critical Commentary on His Life and Works*. 3 vols. New ed. London: Barrie and Jenkins, 1978.

Dent, Edward J. *Ferruccio Busoni: A Biography*. London: Oxford University Press, 1933; London: Eulenberg, 1974.

Eaglefield-Hull, A., gen. ed. *A Dictionary of Modern Music and Musicians*. London: Dent, 1924.

Eastaugh, Kenneth. *Havergal Brian: The Making of a Composer*. London: Harrap, 1976.

Edvard Munch: Symbols & Images. Introd. Robert Rosenblum. Essays by Arne Eggum, Reinhold Heller, Trygve Nergaard, Ragna Stang, Bente Torjusen and Gerd Woll. [With a Checklist of the Exhibition]. National Gallery of Art, Washington, D.C., 1978.

Egan, Richard Whittington, and Smerdon, Geoffrey. *The Quest of the Golden Boy: The Life and Letters of Richard Le Gallienne*. London: Unicorn Press, 1960.

Eggum, Arne, and Biørnstad, Sissel, eds. *Frederick Delius og Edvard Munch*. Exhibition catalogue. Munch Museum, Oslo, 2 April–13 May 1979.

Encausse, Philippe. *Papus, Dr. Gérard Encausse, sa vie, son oeuvre*. Paris, 1932.

Fenby, Eric. *Delius*. London: Faber, 1971.

———. *Delius as I Knew Him*. London: Bell, 1936; London: Quality Press, 1947. Revised and edited by the author, with an Introduction by Sir

Malcolm Sargent, London: Icon, 1966. New and rev. ed., with additional material, London: Faber, 1981.

Ferroud, P. O. *Autour de Florent Schmitt*. Paris: Durand, 1927.

Fieldhouse, Joseph. *Bradford*. London: Longman, 1972.

Foreman, Lewis. *Bax: A Composer and His Times*. Foreword by Felix Aprahamian. London and Berkeley: Scolar Press, 1983.

————. *Havergal Brian and the Performance of His Orchestral Music: A History and Sourcebook*. London: Thames Publishing, 1976.

————, ed. *The Percy Grainger Companion*. London: Thames Publishing, 1981.

Frederick Delius: Centenary Festival Exhibition. Exhibition catalogue. The Royal Festival Hall, London, 1–21 June 1962. [An amended version of the Bradford centenary catalogue]

Gauguin, Paul. *Lettres de Gauguin à Daniel de Monfreid*. Ed. Annie Joly-Segalen. Paris: Falaize, 1950.

————. *Lettres de Gauguin à sa femme et à ses amis*. Ed. Maurice Malingue. Paris: Grasset, 1946.

Gauguin, Pola Rollin. *Christian Krohg*. Oslo: Gyldendal Norsk Forlag, 1932.

Gérard-Arlberg, Gilles. 'Nr 6, rue Vercingétorix'. *Konstrevy* (Stockholm), 35, No. 2 (1958), pp.64–8.

Goldscheider, Cécile. *Rodin*. Paris: Les Productions de Paris, 1962.

Grainger, Percy Aldridge. 'About Delius'. In Heseltine, *Frederick Delius*, 2nd ed., q.v., pp. 170–80.

————. 'The Personality of Frederick Delius'. *The Australian Musical News* (Melbourne), 1 July 1934. Reprinted in *A Delius Companion*. Ed. Redwood, q.v., pp. 117–29.

Gregor, Hans. *Die Welt der Oper – Die Oper der Welt. Bekenntnisse*. Berlin: Bote & Bock, 1931.

Grieg, Edvard. *Breve fra Edvard Grieg til Frants Beyer, 1872–1907*. Ed. Marie Beyer. Kristiania, 1923.

————. *Breve fra Grieg. Et Udvalg*. Ed. G. Hauch. Copenhagen, 1922.

————. *Briefe an die Verleger der Edition Peters, 1866–1907*. Ed. Elsa v. Zschinsky-Troxler. Leipzig: C. F. Peters, 1932.

Haym, Hans. *Delius. Eine Messe des Lebens. Thematische Analyse*. Universal-Edition No. 3913. Leipzig and Vienna, n.d. Translated as *Delius. A Mass of Life. Introduction to the Words and Music*. Universal Edition No. 8256. Vienna and New York, n.d.

Haym, Rudolf. Lecture to the Delius Society, London, 4 November 1971. Duplicated text distributed to members of The Delius Society, London, 1971.

Heiberg, Gunnar. *Folkeraadet: Komedie i Fem Akter*. Copenhagen: Gyldendal, 1897.

————. *People's Parliament: Comedy in Five Acts*. Duplicated text, trans. from the Norwegian by Lionel Carley, London, 1981, for performance at The Fourth Delius Festival, Keele, Staffordshire, 1982.

Hemmings, F. W. J. *Culture and Society in France 1848–1898. Dissidents and Philistines*. London: Batsford, 1971.

Heseltine, Philip. *Frederick Delius*. London: John Lane, The Bodley Head, 1923. Reprinted with additions, annotations and comments by Hubert Foss, London: The Bodley Head, 1952.

Hoare, Geoffrey G. 'Delius Slept Here?' *Cotswold Life* (Cheltenham), 89 (March 1976), pp. 26–8. Reprinted in *The Delius Society Journal*, 54 (January 1977), pp. 5–9.

Holbrooke, Joseph. *Contemporary British Composers*. London: Cecil Palmer, 1925.

Holland, Arthur Keith. *The Songs of Delius*. London: Oxford University Press, 1951.

Hollander, Hans. *Die Musik in der Kulturgeschichte des 19. und 20. Jahrhunderts*. Cologne, 1967.

Howes, Frank. *The English Musical Renaissance*. London: Secker and Warburg, 1966.

Hucher, Yves. *Florent Schmitt. L'homme et l'artiste. Son époque et son œuvre*. Paris, 1953.

Hudson, Derek. *Norman O'Neill – A Life of Music*. London: Quality Press, 1945.

Hull, Robert H. *Delius*. Vol. XII of *The Hogarth Essays*, Second Series. London: Hogarth, 1928.

Hutchings, Arthur. *Delius*. London: Macmillan, 1948.

Ibsen, Bergliot. *The Three Ibsens: Memories of Henrik Ibsen, Suzannah Ibsen and Sigurd Ibsen*. Trans. from the Norwegian by Gerik Schjelderup. London: Hutchinson, 1951.

Jahoda, Gloria. 'The Music-Maker of Solano Grove'. Chapter 13 of her *The Other Florida*. New York: Scribner, 1967, pp. 246–69.

———. *The Road to Samarkand: Frederick Delius and His Music*. New York: Scribner, 1969.

James, John. *Continuation & Additions to the History of Bradford and Its Parish*. Bradford, 1866. Reprinted by E. J. Morten, Manchester, 1973.

Jaworska, Wladyslawa. *Gauguin and the Pont-Aven School*. Trans. Patrick Evans. London: Thames and Hudson, 1972.

Jefferson, Alan. *Delius*. London: Dent, 1972.

Jones, Philip. 'The Delius Birthplace'. *The Musical Times*, 120, No. 1642 (December 1979), pp. 990–2.

Keary, C. F. *The Journalist*. London: Methuen, 1898.

Keller, Gottfried. *Romeo und Julia auf dem Dorfe*. Ed. [with an Introduction] Margaret A. McHaffie. London: Nelson, 1956.

Kennedy, Michael. *Portrait of Elgar*. London: Oxford University Press, 1968.

———. 'The English Musical Renaissance 1880–1920'. *Gramophone*, 60, No. 711 (August 1982), pp. 211–22.

Kjellberg, Gerda. *Hänt och sant*. Stockholm: Norstedts, 1951.

Lagercrantz, Olof. *August Strindberg*. Stockholm: Wahlström & Widstrand, 1979.

Langaard, Johan H., and Revold, Reidar. *Edvard Munch fra År til År / A year by Year Record of Edvard Munch's Life*. Oslo: Aschehoug, 1961.

Lara, Isidore de. *Many Tales of Many Cities*. London: Hutchinson, n.d. [1928]

Larsson, Carl. *Jag*. Stockholm: Bonniers, 1931.

Lavery, Sir John. *The Life of a Painter*. London: Cassell, 1940.

Lloyd, Stephen. *Balfour Gardiner*. Cambridge University Press [in preparation].

———. 'Delius as Conductor'. *The Delius Society Journal*, 46 (January 1975), pp. 4–20.

———. *H. Balfour Gardiner 1877–1950: Composer – Patron – Forester*. Programme for Centenary Concert. St John's, Smith Square, London, 6 November 1977.

———. 'A Partnership of Genius'. *The Delius Society Journal*, 63 (April 1979), pp. 5–15.

Loize, Jean. *De Maillol et Codet à Segalen — Les Amitiés du peintre Georges-Daniel de Monfreid et ses reliques de Gauguin*. chez Jean Loize, 1951.

Low, Will H. *A Chronicle of Friendships. 1873–1900*. New York: Scribner, 1908.

Lowe, Rachel. 'Delius's First Performance'. *The Musical Times*, 106, No. 1465 (March 1965), pp. 190–2.

———. 'The Delius Trust Manuscripts'. *Brio*, 5, No. 1 (Spring 1968), pp. 5–9. Corrigenda in *Brio*, 5, No. 2 (Autumn 1968), p. 10.

———. *A Descriptive Catalogue with Checklists of the Letters and Related Documents in the Delius Collection of the Grainger Museum, University of Melbourne, Australia*. London: The Delius Trust, 1981.

———. *Frederick Delius 1862–1934: A Catalogue of the Music Archive of the Delius Trust, London*. London: The Delius Trust, 1974.

———. 'The Music Archive of the Delius Trust'. *The Music Review*, 34, Nos. 3/4 (August–November 1973), pp. 294–306.

Malmberg, Ernst. 'Svenskar i Grèz'. *Vintergatan* (Stockholm) (1940), pp. 81–92.

Maszkowski, Karol. 'U Madame Charlotte (1894 r.)'. *Sztuki Piekne* (Warsaw), 2 (1925–6), pp. 24–6.

Meyer, Michael. *Henrik Ibsen*. 3 vols. London: Hart-Davis, 1967–71.

Michon, Jacques. *La Musique Anglaise*. Paris: Librairie Armond, 1970, pp. 266–9.

Molard, William. A number of MS. letters. Papiers Jean Rictus, Bibl. Nat. MS. Nouvelles Acquisitions françaises 22. Correspondance de Molard.

Monfreid, Georges-Daniel de Monfreid. Carnets. MS. notebooks and diaries in the possession of Mme Annie Joly-Segalen, Bourg-la-Reine, Paris.

Mucha, Jiri. *Alphonse Mucha: His Life and Art*. London: Heinemann, 1966.

Munch, Edvard. *Edvard Munchs Brev. Familien. Et udvalg*. Ed. Inger Munch. Oslo: Munch-museet, 1949.

Nectoux, Jean-Michel. *Fauré*. Paris: Éditions du Seuil, 1972.

Nettel, Reginald. *Havergal Brian and His Music*. London: Dennis Dobson, 1976. An expanded edition of *Ordeal by Music: The Strange Experience of Havergal Brian*. London: Oxford University Press, 1945, 1947.

———. 'In League for the Sake of Music'. *The Delius Society Journal*, 60 (July 1978), pp. 5–17.

————. *Music in the Five Towns 1840–1914: A Study of the Social Influence of Music in an Industrial District.* London: Oxford University Press, 1944.

————. *North Staffordshire Music: A Social Experiment.* Rickmansworth: Triad Press, 1977.

Orenstein, Arbie. *Ravel: Man and Musician.* New York and London: Columbia University Press, 1975.

Orr, C. W. 'Debussy and Delius: A Comparison'. *The Daily Telegraph*, 12 October 1929.

Oyler, Philip. 'Delius at Grèz'. *The Musical Times*, 113, No. 1151 (May 1972), pp. 444–7.

————. 'Some Memories of Delius'. Chapter 4 of his *Sons of the Generous Earth.* London: Hodder and Stoughton, 1963, pp. 41–54.

Palmer, Christopher. *Delius: Portrait of a Cosmopolitan.* London: Duckworth, 1976.

————. *Impressionism in Music.* London: Hutchinson, 1973.

Popperwell, Ronald G. *Norway.* London: Benn, 1972.

Randel, William. 'Frederick Delius in America'. *The Virginia Magazine of History and Biography*, 79, No. 3 (July 1971), pp. 349–66. Reprinted as 'Delius in America' in *A Delius Companion.* Ed. Redwood, q.v., pp. 147–66.

————. ' "Koanga" and Its Libretto'. *Music and Letters*, 52, No. 2 (April 1971), pp. 141–58.

Redwood, Christopher, ed. *A Delius Companion.* London: John Calder, 1976, 1980.

Reich, Dietbert, ed. *Romeo und Julia auf dem Dorfe.* Schweizerische Erstaufführung 20.12.1980, hg. v. Opernhaus Zürich. Programme book. Zurich, 1980.

Röntgen, Julius. *Edvard Grieg. (Herinnerungen en brieven).* Beroemde Musici, 19. 2nd ed. Den Haag: Kruseman, 1954.

Rothenstein, William. *Men and Memories.* Vol. 1. London: Faber, 1931.

Rubin, Louis D., Jr. *George W. Cable: The Life and Times of a Southern Heretic.* New York: Pegasus, 1969.

Rugstad, Gunnar. *Christian Sinding, 1856–1941: En biografisk og stilistik studie.* Oslo: Cappelen, 1979.

Sadler, Fernande. *Grès-sur-Loing: Notice historique.* Fontainebleau: M. Bourges, 1906.

Schmidt, Torsten Måtte. 'Madame Charlotte, Strindbergs okända väninna'. *Horisont* (Vasa), 22, No. 5 (1975), pp. 32–40.

Schulerud, Menz. *Norsk Kunstnerliv.* Utgitt til Kunstnerforeningens 100 Års Jubileum. Oslo: Cappelen, 1960.

Skavlan, Einar. *Gunnar Heiberg.* Oslo: Aschehoug, 1950.

Smith, John Boulton. 'Frederick Delius and Edvard Munch'. In *Frederick Delius og Edvard Munch.* Ed. Eggum and Biørnstad, q.v., pp. 9–27.

————. *Frederick Delius and Edvard Munch. Their Friendship and Their Correspondence.* Rickmansworth: Triad Press, 1983.

————. *Munch.* London: Phaidon, 1977.

————. 'Portrait of a Friendship: Edvard Munch and Frederick Delius'. *Apollo* (January 1966), pp. 38–47.

Söderström, Göran. *Strindberg och bildkonsten.* Forum, Sweden: 1972.

Stang, Ragna. *Edvard Munch: The Man and the Artist.* Ed. John Boulton Smith. London: Gordon Fraser, 1979.

Stefan, Paul. *Oskar Fried: Das Werden eines Künstlers.* Berlin: Erich Reiss Verlag, 1911.

Stenersen, Rolf. *Edvard Munch: Naerbilde av et geni.* Oslo: Gyldendal Norsk Forlag, 1946.

Stockbridge, Frank Parker, and Perry, John Holliday. *Florida in the Making.* New York, Jacksonville, and Kingsport, Tenn.: de Bower, 1926.

Streatfeild, R. A. 'Frédéric Delius'. In his *Musiciens Anglais Contemporains.* Trans. Louis Pennequin. Paris: Éditions du Temps Présent, 1913, pp. 49–68.

Strindberg, August. *August Strindbergs brev.* Vols. I– . Ed. Torsten Eklund. Stockholm: Bonniers, 1948– .

————. *Bland Franska Bönder: Subjektiva Reseskildringar.* Stockholm: Bonniers, 1889.

————. *Inferno, Alone and Other Writings.* New translations ed. and introd. Evert Sprinchorn. New York: Doubleday, 1968.

Sutton, Denys. *Triumphant Satyr: The World of Auguste Rodin.* London: Country Life, 1966.

Tell, Wilhelm. *Ida Gerhardi 1862–1927.* Lüdenscheider Beiträge, 8. Volkshochschule Lüdenscheid, 1960.

————. *Ida Gerhardi, Ihr Leben und Werk. Zur 50. Wiederkehr ihres Todestages am 29.6.1977*. Exhibition catalogue. Kunstgemeinde Lüdenscheid, 1977.

Temperley, Nicholas. *The Romantic Age 1800–1914*. Vol. 5 of The Athlone History of Music in Britain. London: Athlone, 1982.

Tempo, 'Delius Number', No. 26 (Winter 1952–3). [Includes essays by various contributors, together with a description of the Delius Trust and its responsibilities]

Threlfall, Robert. *A Catalogue of the Compositions of Frederick Delius. Sources and References*. London: The Delius Trust, 1977.

————. 'Delian Studies: Notes for an Iconography'. *Delius Society Newsletter*, 26 (Winter 1970), pp. 3–7. *See also* 'Amendments to the Iconography'. *Delius Society Newsletter*, 28 (Summer 1970), pp. 12–13.

————. 'Delius Music Manuscripts in Australia'. *Studies in Music* (Perth, W.A.), 7 (1973), pp. 69–76.

————. 'Delius's Piano Concerto – A Postscript'. *Musical Opinion*, 95, No. 1129 (October 1971), pp. 14–15. See also *A Delius Companion*. Ed. Redwood, q.v., pp. 239–47.

————. 'Delius's Unknown Opera: *The Magic Fountain*'. *Studies in Music* (Perth, W.A.), 11 (1977), pp. 60–73.

————. 'The Early Versions of Delius's Piano Concerto'. *Musical Opinion*, 93, No. 1115 (August 1970), pp. 579–81. See also *A Delius Companion*. Ed. Redwood, q.v., pp. 239–47.

————, and Carley, Lionel. 'Dating a Delius Song'. *The Delius Society Journal*, 51 (April 1976), pp. 11–14.

Thue, Oscar. *Christian Krohgs Portretter*. Oslo: Gyldendal Norsk Forlag, 1971.

Torsteinson, Sigmund. *Troldhaugen: Nina og Edvard Griegs Hjem*. Oslo: Gyldendal Norsk Forlag, 1959.

Upton, Stuart, and Walker, Malcolm. *Frederick Delius: A Discography*. London: The Delius Society, 1969.

Vaughan Williams, Ursula. *R. V. W.: A Biography of Ralph Vaughan Williams*. London: Oxford University Press, 1964.

Walker, Malcolm. *Delius on Record – An Annotated Discography*. London: Westport Publications [in preparation].

Warlock, Peter. Pseudonym for Heseltine, Philip, q.v.

Weissenberg, Esteri. ' "Donnons nous encore une fois la main". Strindberg-minnen'. *Ord och Bild* (Stockholm) (1949).

Wood, Henry J. *My Life of Music*. London: Gollancz, 1938.

Wyndham, H. Saxe. *August Manns and the Saturday Concerts*. London: Walter Scott Publishing Co., 1909.

————, and L'Epine Geoffrey, eds. *Who's Who in Music, A Biographical Record of Contemporary Musicians*. London: Pitman, 1915.

Young, Percy M. *A History of British Music*. London: Benn, 1967.

Index of Correspondents

(by letter number)

INDEX

Variant spellings found in the correspondence and in the appendices are given in parentheses following the main entry in this index, which covers pp. 1–419. Numbers in bold type indicate the principal reference.